DISNEY | SQUARE ENIX

KINGDOM HEARTS
CHAIN OF MEMORIES

2

Adapted by
Shiro Amano

TOKYOPOP®

HAMBURG // LONDON // LOS ANGELES // TOKYO

Kingdom Hearts Chain of Memories Volume 2
Created by Shiro Amano

Associate Editor - Peter Ahlstrom
Retouch and Lettering - Kimie Kim
Cover Layout - James Lee

Editor - Bryce P. Coleman
Digital Imaging Manager - Chris Buford
Pre-Production Supervisor - Erika Terriquez
Art Director - Anne Marie Horne
Production Manager - Elisabeth Brizzi
Managing Editor - Vy Nguyen
VP of Production - Ron Klamert
Editor-in-Chief - Rob Tokar
Publisher - Mike Kiley
President and C.O.O. - John Parker
C.E.O. and Chief Creative Officer - Stuart Levy

A  Manga

TOKYOPOP and ◌ are trademarks or registered trademarks of TOKYOPOP Inc.

TOKYOPOP Inc.
5900 Wilshire Blvd. Suite 2000
Los Angeles, CA 90036

E-mail: info@TOKYOPOP.com
Come visit us online at www.TOKYOPOP.com

ISBN: 978-1-59816-638-5

First TOKYOPOP printing: February 2007
10 9 8 7 6 5 4 3 2 1
Printed in the USA

KINGDOM HEARTS
CHAIN OF MEMORIES

Disney SQUARE ENIX

KINGDOM HEARTS CHAIN OF MEMORIES

2

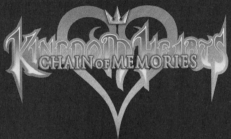

Sora

A boy chosen by the Keyblade—the key for saving the world. In search of his missing friend Riku, Sora continues his journey to return to his Destiny Islands home.

Goofy

Together with Sora and Donald, he is searching for the missing King Mickey. His trademark phrases are "A-hyuck" and "Gawrsh."

Donald Duck

Sora's comrade in the journey. He's a master magician, but once he gets bent out of shape...

CHARACTER & STORY

Sora lives peacefully on the Destiny Islands with his friends Riku and Kairi until they are whisked away to separate worlds in the middle of a mysterious storm. While searching for Riku and Kairi, Sora receives the Keyblade, which he uses to fight the Heartless monsters who are trying to steal people's hearts and to infiltrate the heart of all worlds, Kingdom Hearts. He also meets Donald and Goofy, who are searching for their missing King, Mickey, and they join together to search for their lost friends.

After journeying through numerous worlds, they at last find their friends and discover that a wise man named Ansem created the Heartless and became corrupted in his search for power. Riku, who also has been tempted by darkness, joins with Mickey to close the door to Kingdom Hearts from the inside as Sora closes it from the outside, and Ansem is defeated.

Kairi makes it back home safe, but Sora finds himself parted from her again. As he, Donald, and Goofy renew their search for Riku and the King, they come across the mysterious Castle Oblivion and a hooded figure who cryptically says, "Ahead lies something you need, but to claim it, you must lose something dear," and "In this place, to find is to lose...and to lose is to find." As Sora & co. progress through the castle, they find that they are steadily losing their memories! Riku also awakens in the castle's depths to find that he is not as rid of Ansem and the darkness as he had hoped. The shadowy members of Organization XIII who run the castle also seem to have their own sinister plans for Sora and Riku, plans involving a young girl with a sketchbook...

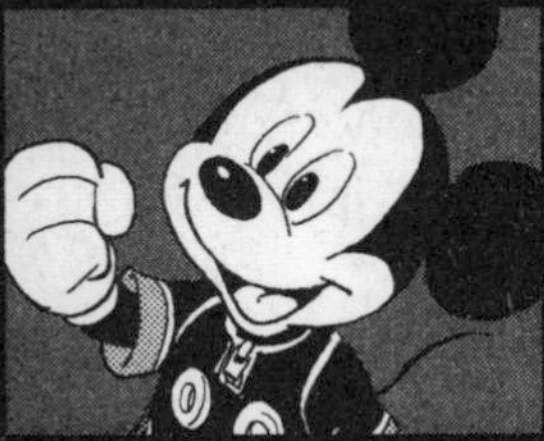

King [Mickey]

King of Disney Castle. He is missing together with Riku.

Naminé

A mysterious girl who is quietly drawing pictures alone in one of the castle rooms.

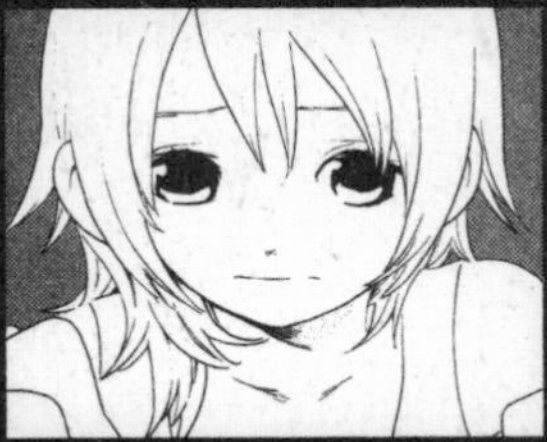

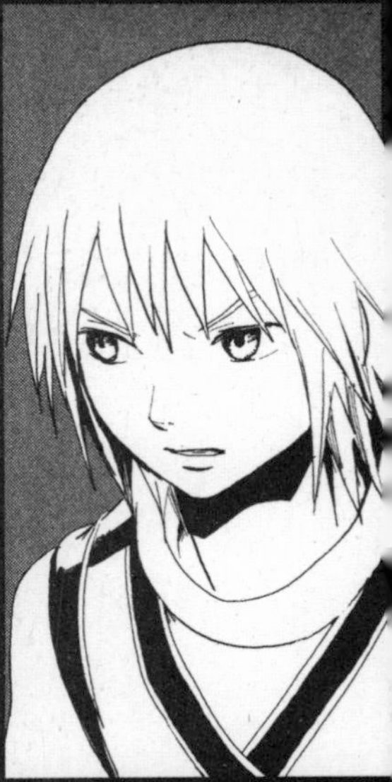

Riku

Sora's best friend. He closes the door from the inside together with the King, and gets left behind in the world of darkness.

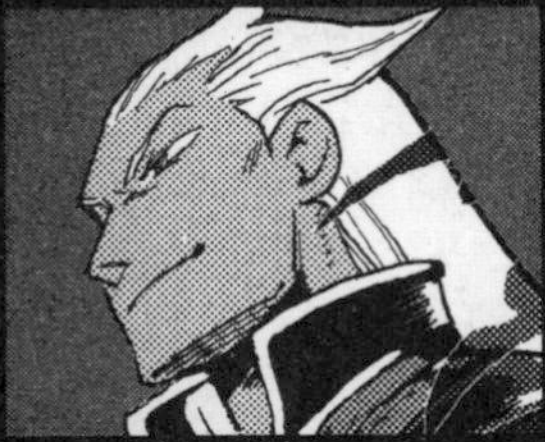

Ansem

The "Seeker of Darkness" who hid in Riku's heart to control him.

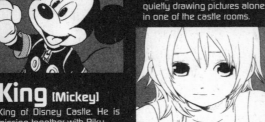

Kairi

Sora's childhood friend. She's waiting on the island for Sora to return.

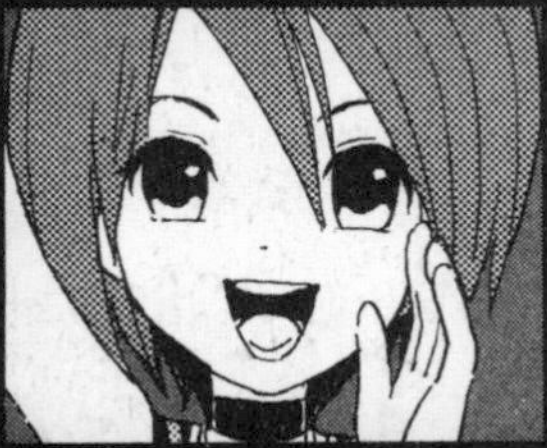

Organization XIII Members

The members of this mysterious organization dress in black robes and search for secrets of the heart...

Underground Members

Zexion

No. 6 in the Organization

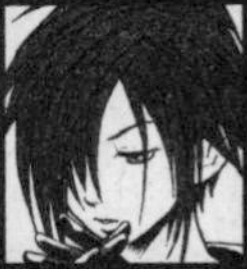

Leader of the Underground Members. Meticulous by nature, the word is that he's a surprisingly domestic type!

Lexaeus

No. 5 in the Organization

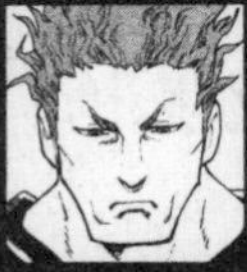

Administers the underground together with Zexion and Vexen. Avid puzzler.

Vexen

No. 4 in the Organization

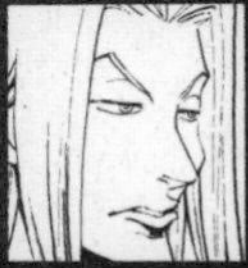

Oldest member of Castle Oblivion. But not necessarily respected by the younger members...

Aboveground Members

Larxene

No. 12 in the Organization

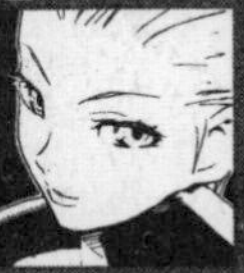

Cold-blooded, temperamental and vicious. Once she flies off the handle, there's no stopping her.

Marluxia

No. 11 in the Organization

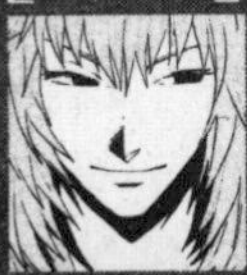

Lord of Castle Oblivion who loves flowers. It seems he's plotting something...

Axel

No. 8 in the Organization

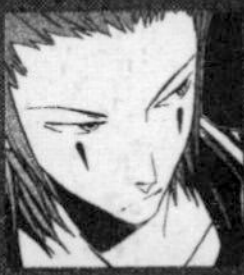

Mysterious individual who appears before Sora from time to time and leaves little bits of advice.

CONTENTS

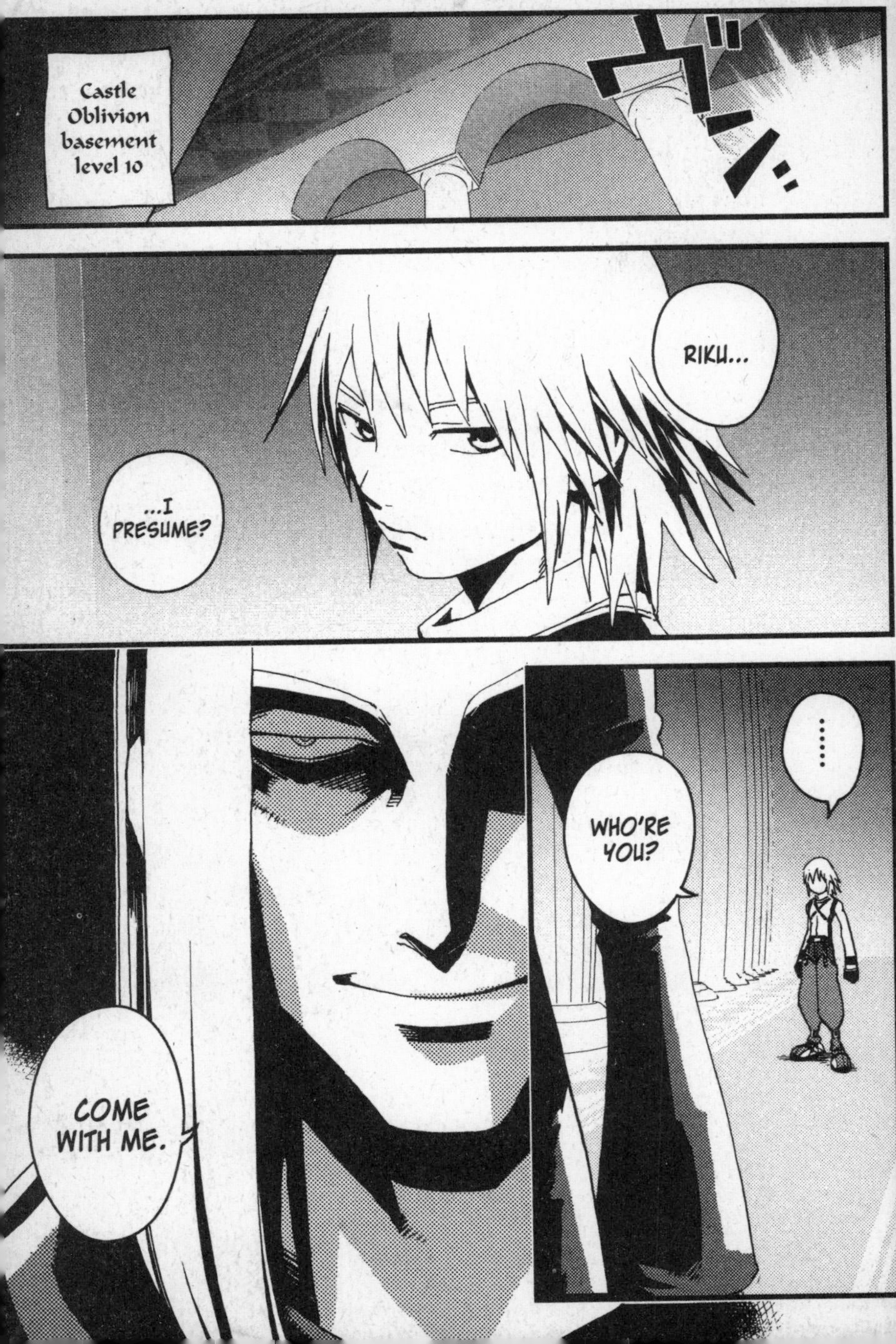
Castle Oblivion basement level 10
RIKU...
...I PRESUME?
......
WHO'RE YOU?
COME WITH ME.

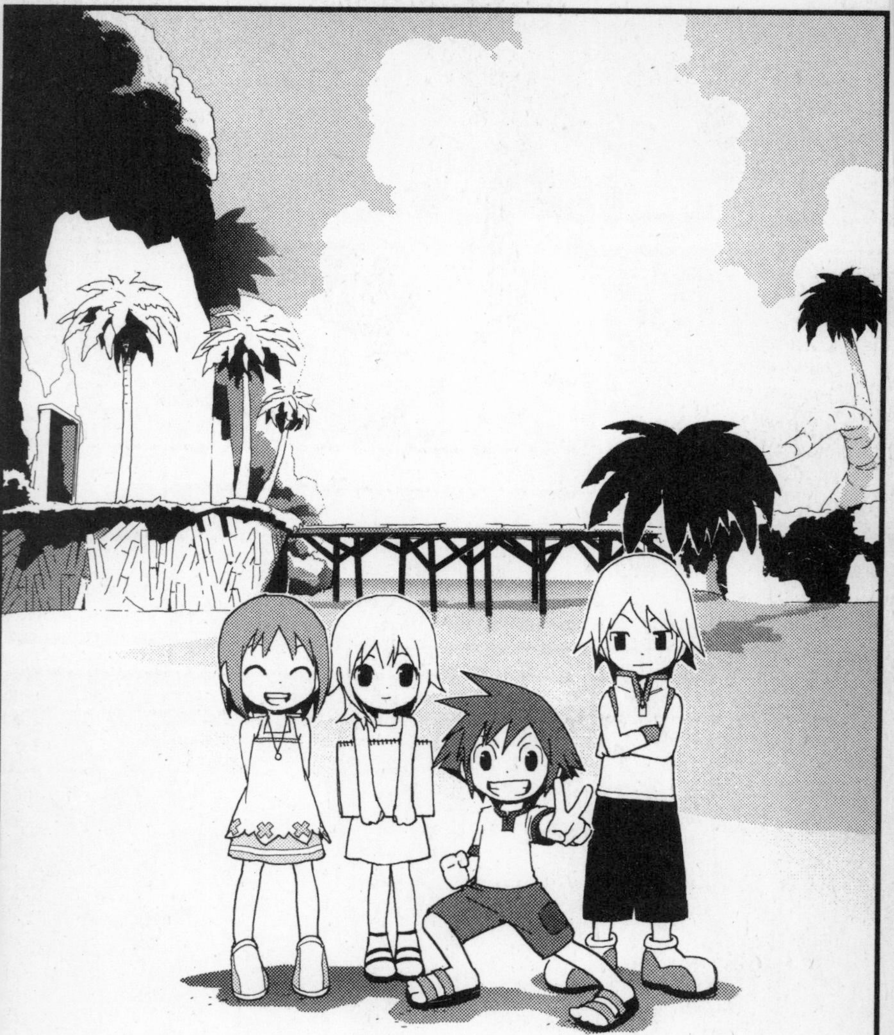

Card 07 Memories

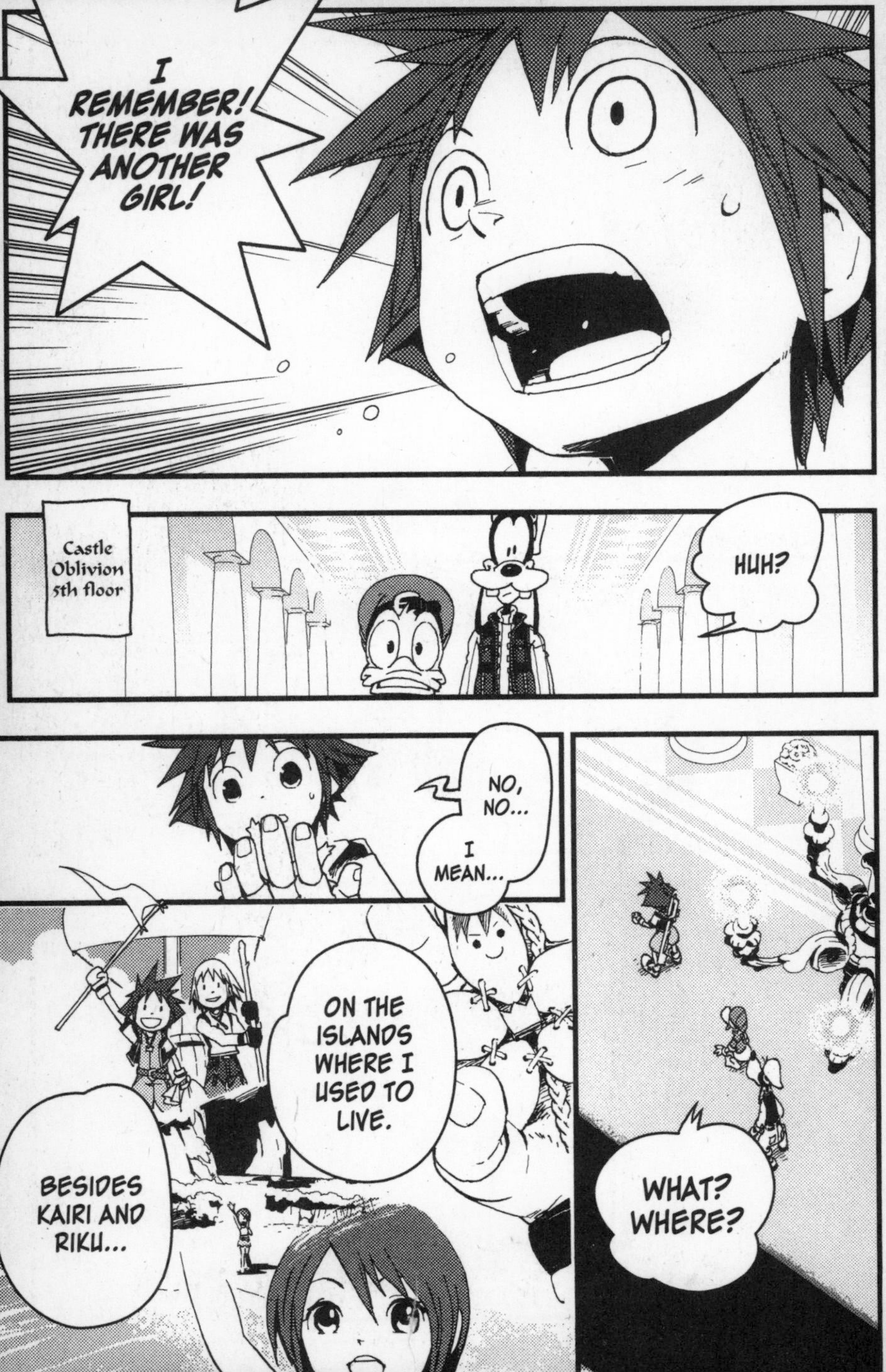
I REMEMBER! THERE WAS ANOTHER GIRL!
HUH?
Castle Oblivion 5th floor
WHAT? WHERE?
NO, NO... I MEAN...
ON THE ISLANDS WHERE I USED TO LIVE.
BESIDES KAIRI AND RIKU...

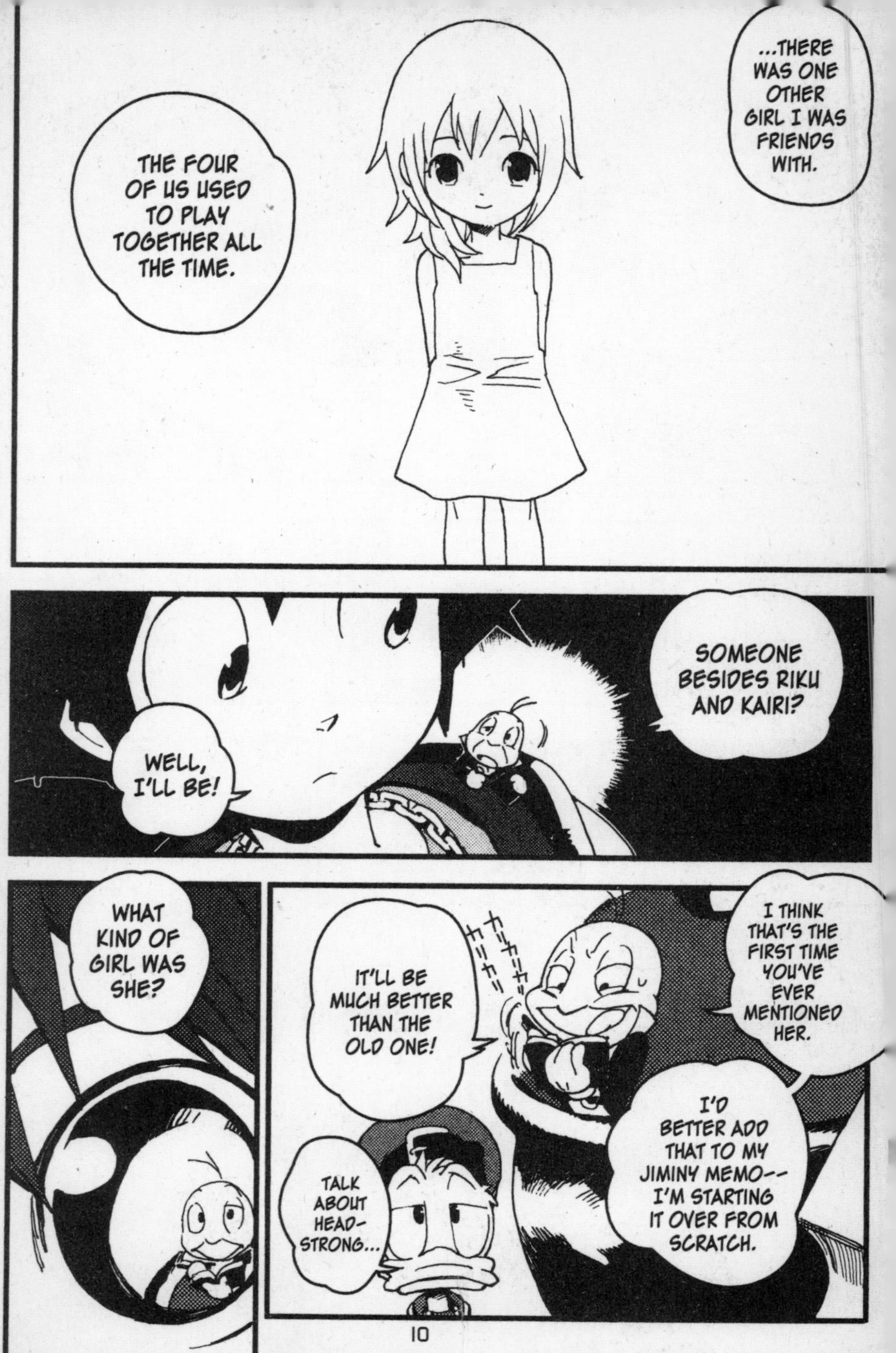
...THERE WAS ONE OTHER GIRL I WAS FRIENDS WITH.
THE FOUR OF US USED TO PLAY TOGETHER ALL THE TIME.
SOMEONE BESIDES RIKU AND KAIRI?
WELL, I'LL BE!
I THINK THAT'S THE FIRST TIME YOU'VE EVER MENTIONED HER.
I'D BETTER ADD THAT TO MY JIMINY MEMO--I'M STARTING IT OVER FROM SCRATCH.
IT'LL BE MUCH BETTER THAN THE OLD ONE!
TALK ABOUT HEAD-STRONG...
WHAT KIND OF GIRL WAS SHE?

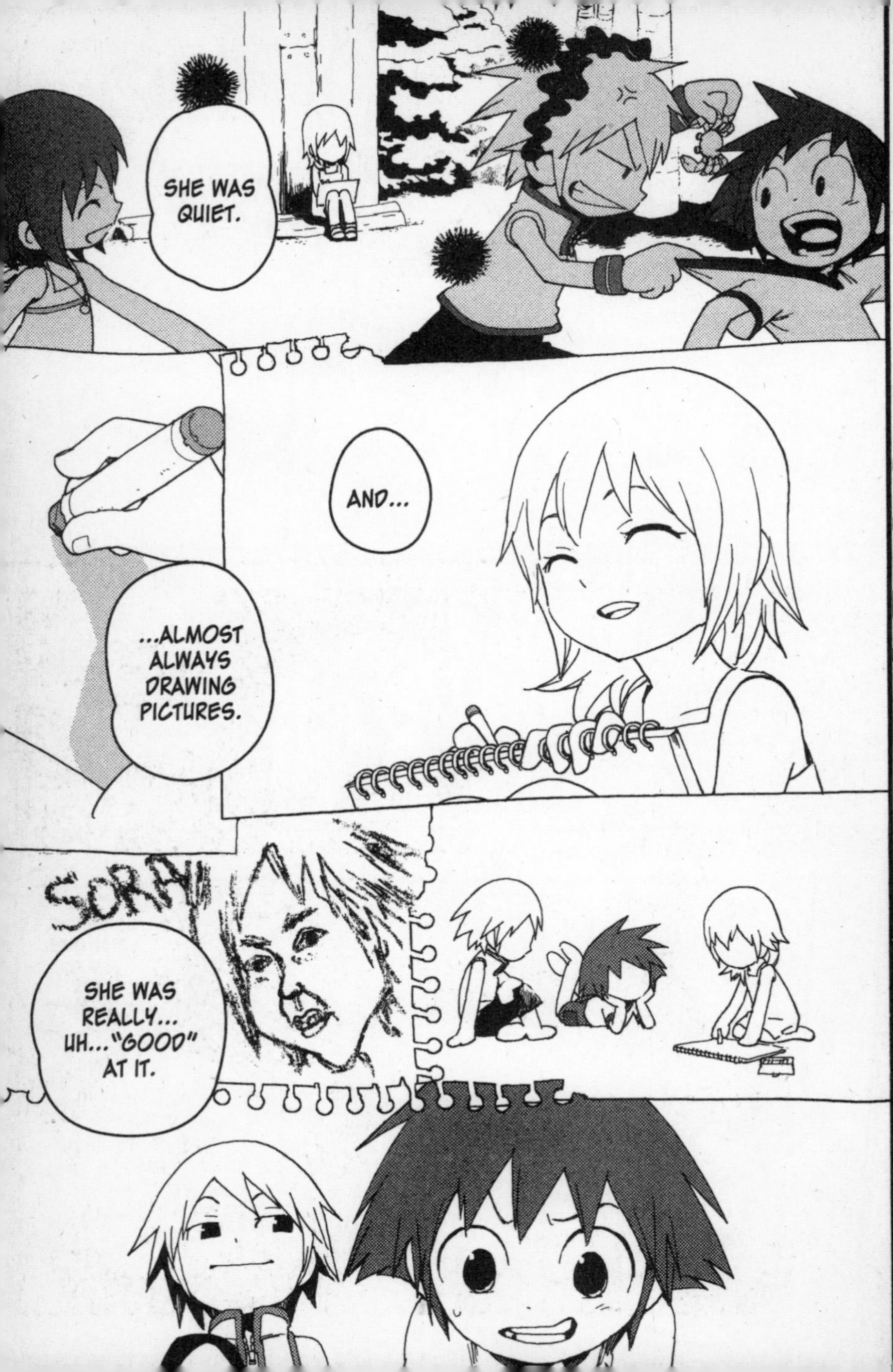
SHE WAS QUIET.
AND...
...ALMOST ALWAYS DRAWING PICTURES.
SORA!!
SHE WAS REALLY... UH..."GOOD" AT IT.

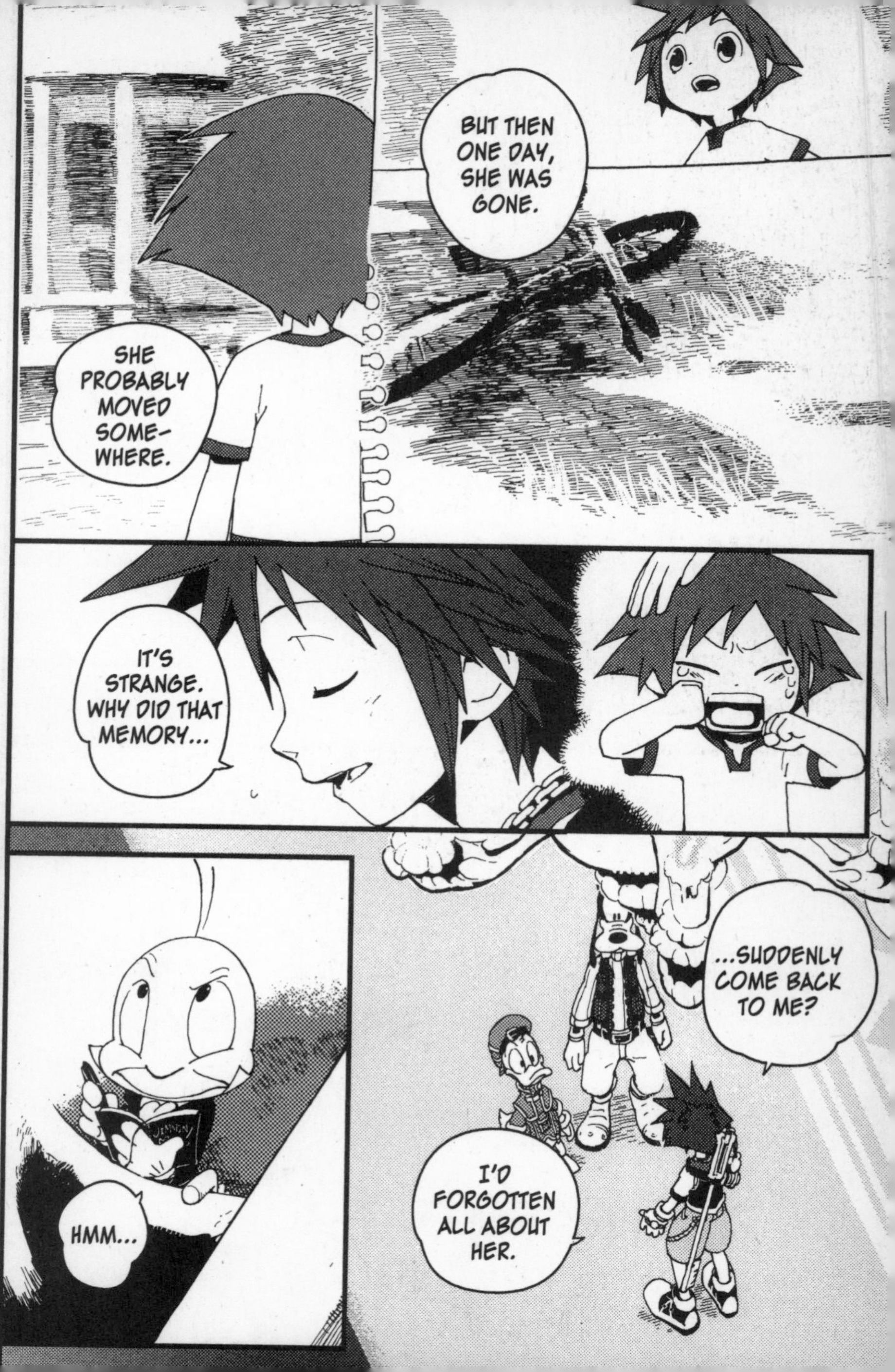
BUT THEN ONE DAY, SHE WAS GONE.
SHE PROBABLY MOVED SOME-WHERE.
IT'S STRANGE. WHY DID THAT MEMORY...
...SUDDENLY COME BACK TO ME?
I'D FORGOTTEN ALL ABOUT HER.
HMM...

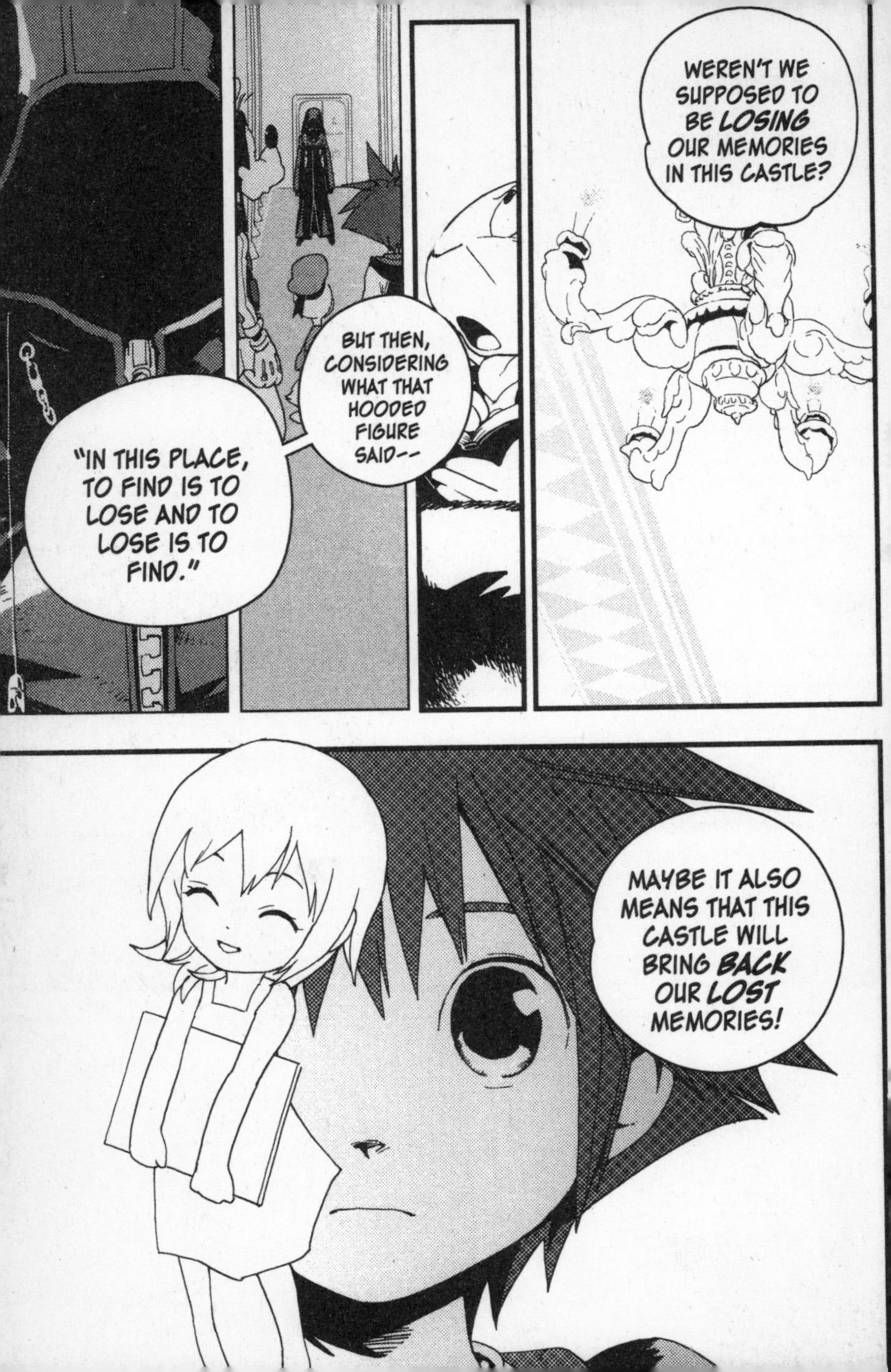
WEREN'T WE SUPPOSED TO BE LOSING OUR MEMORIES IN THIS CASTLE?
BUT THEN, CONSIDERING WHAT THAT HOODED FIGURE SAID--
"IN THIS PLACE, TO FIND IS TO LOSE AND TO LOSE IS TO FIND."
MAYBE IT ALSO MEANS THAT THIS CASTLE WILL BRING BACK OUR LOST MEMORIES!

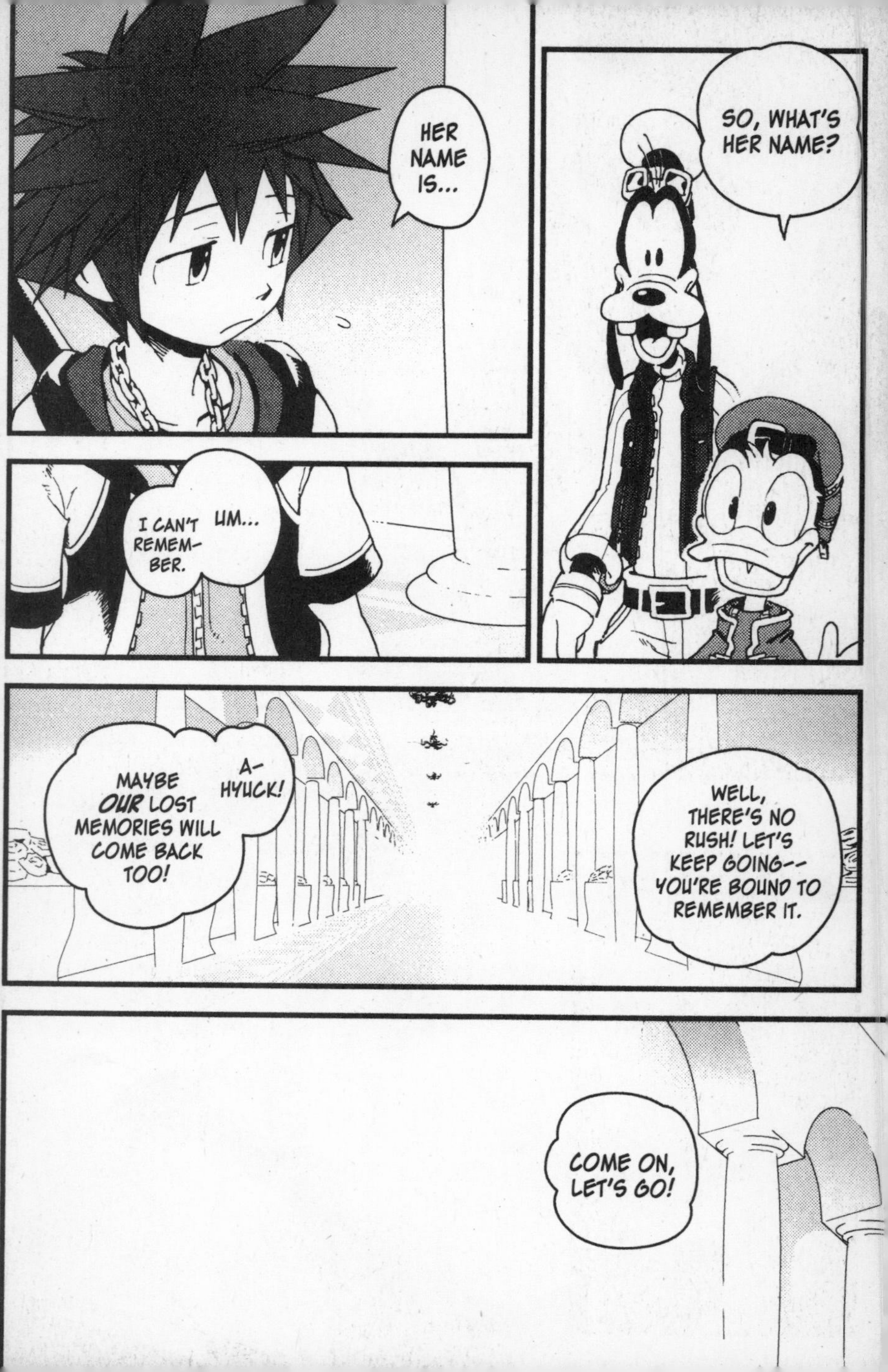
SO, WHAT'S HER NAME?
HER NAME IS...
UM...
I CAN'T REMEMBER.
WELL, THERE'S NO RUSH! LET'S KEEP GOING-- YOU'RE BOUND TO REMEMBER IT.
A-HYUCK!
MAYBE OUR LOST MEMORIES WILL COME BACK TOO!
COME ON, LET'S GO!

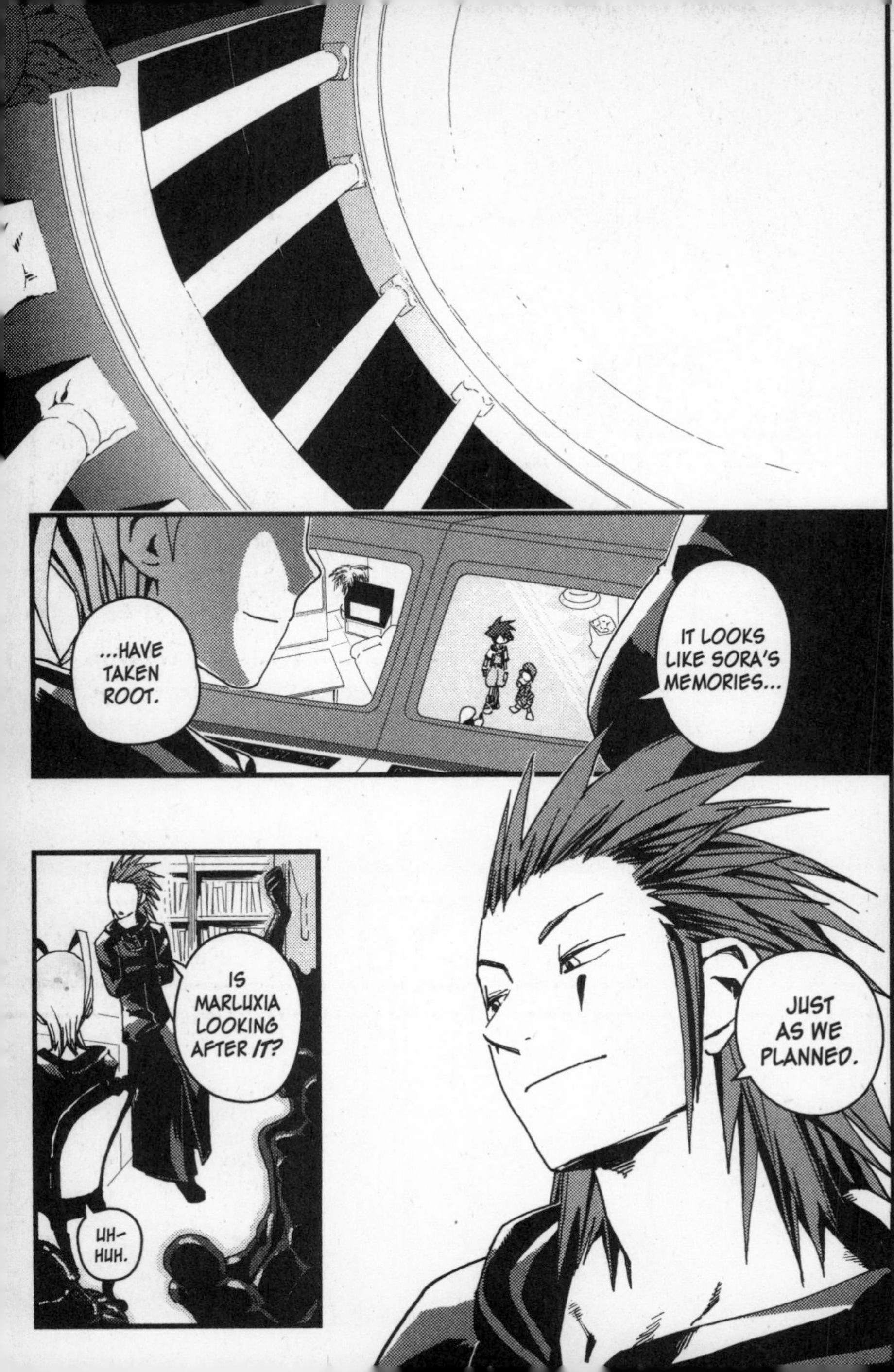
IT LOOKS LIKE SORA'S MEMORIES...
...HAVE TAKEN ROOT.
JUST AS WE PLANNED.
IS MARLUXIA LOOKING AFTER *IT*?
UH-HUH.

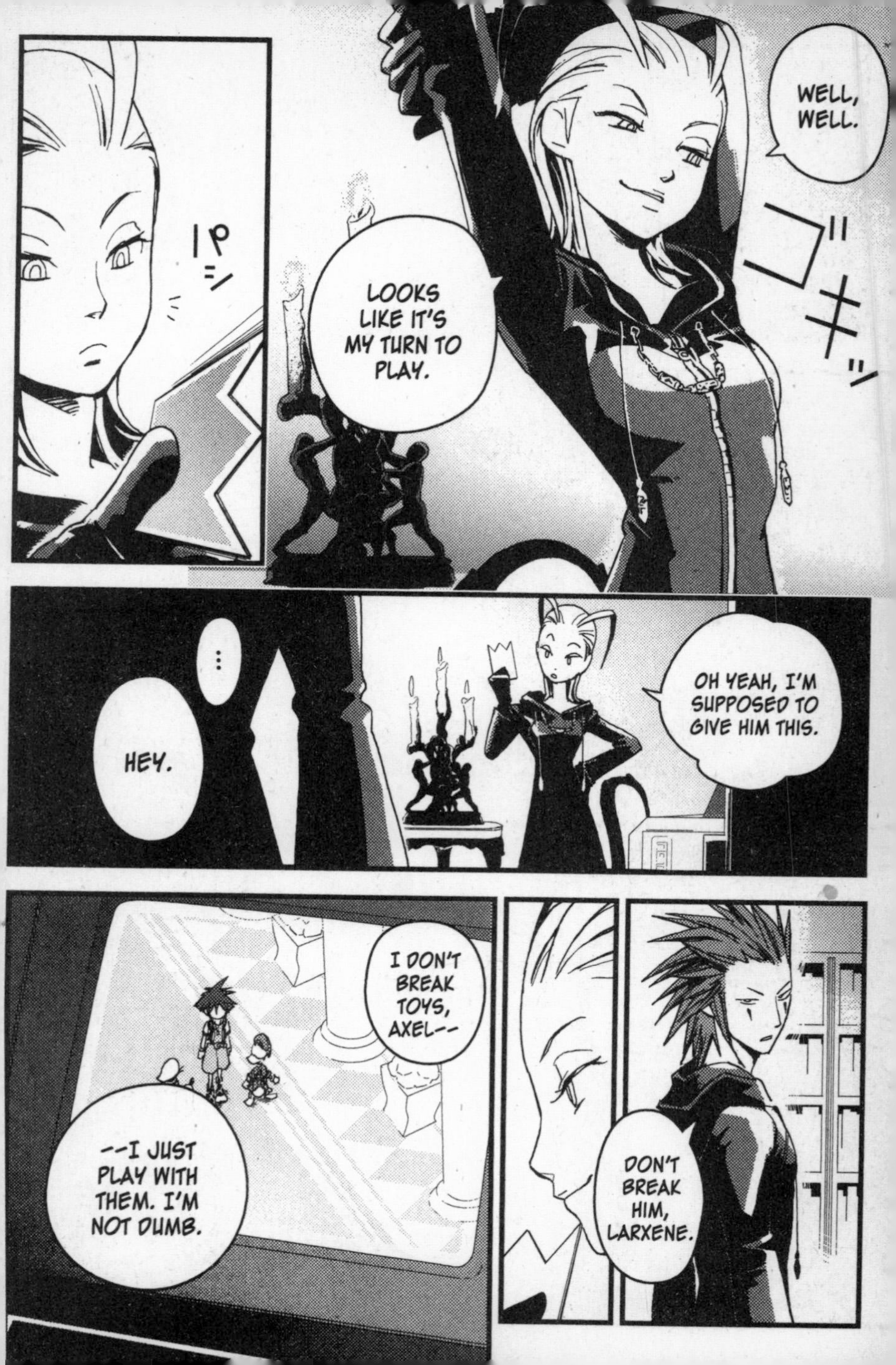
WELL, WELL.
ゴキッ
LOOKS LIKE IT'S MY TURN TO PLAY.
OH YEAH, I'M SUPPOSED TO GIVE HIM THIS.
...
HEY.
DON'T BREAK HIM, LARXENE.
I DON'T BREAK TOYS, AXEL--
--I JUST PLAY WITH THEM. I'M NOT DUMB.

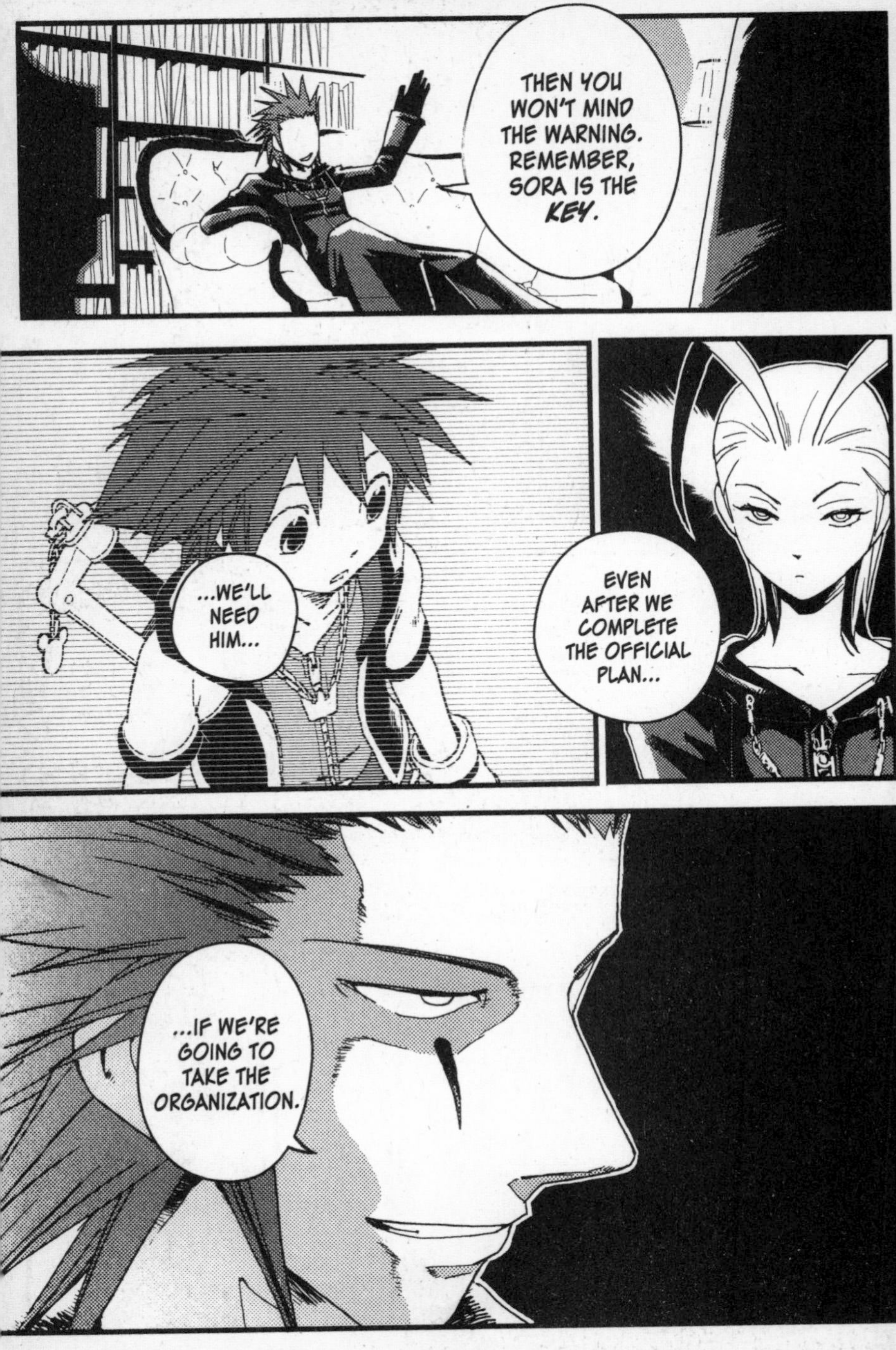
THEN YOU WON'T MIND THE WARNING. REMEMBER, SORA IS THE *KEY*.
EVEN AFTER WE COMPLETE THE OFFICIAL PLAN...
...WE'LL NEED HIM...
...IF WE'RE GOING TO TAKE THE ORGANIZATION.

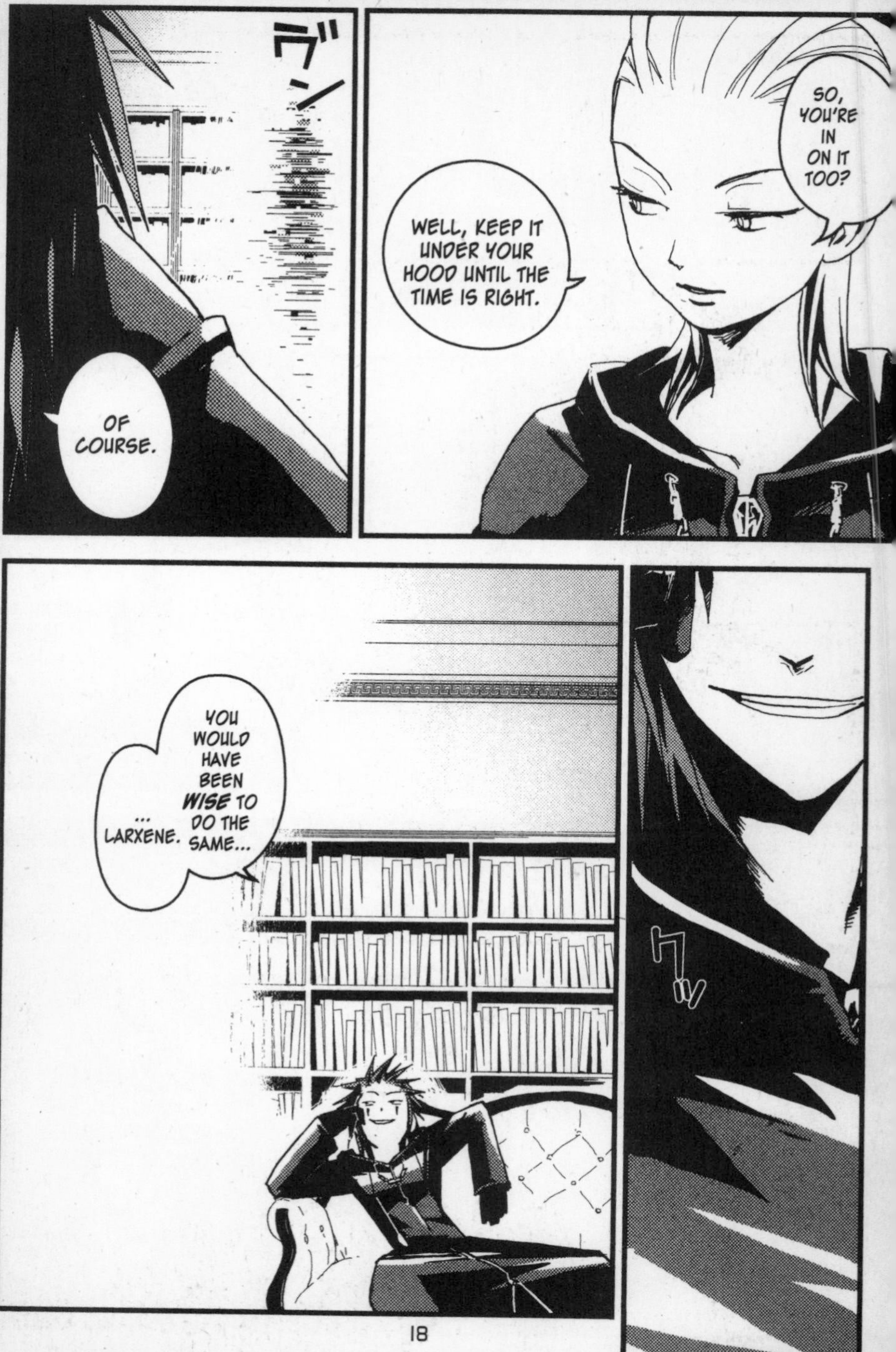
SO, YOU'RE IN ON IT TOO?
WELL, KEEP IT UNDER YOUR HOOD UNTIL THE TIME IS RIGHT.
ヴン
OF COURSE.
YOU WOULD HAVE BEEN **WISE** TO DO THE SAME...
...LARXENE.

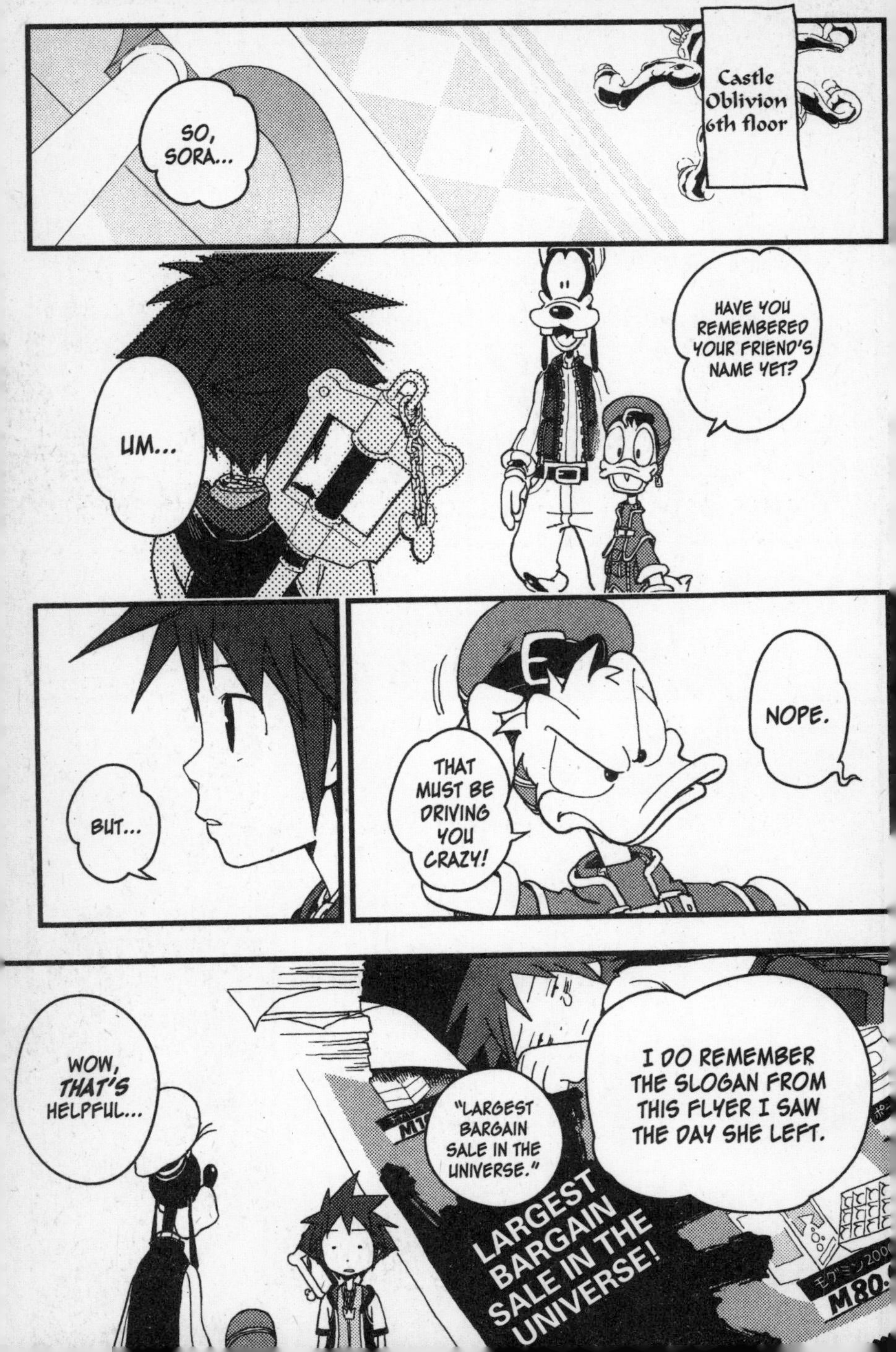
Castle Oblivion 6th floor
SO, SORA...
HAVE YOU REMEMBERED YOUR FRIEND'S NAME YET?
UM...
NOPE.
THAT MUST BE DRIVING YOU CRAZY!
BUT...
I DO REMEMBER THE SLOGAN FROM THIS FLYER I SAW THE DAY SHE LEFT.
"LARGEST BARGAIN SALE IN THE UNIVERSE."
LARGEST BARGAIN SALE IN THE UNIVERSE!
WOW, *THAT'S* HELPFUL...

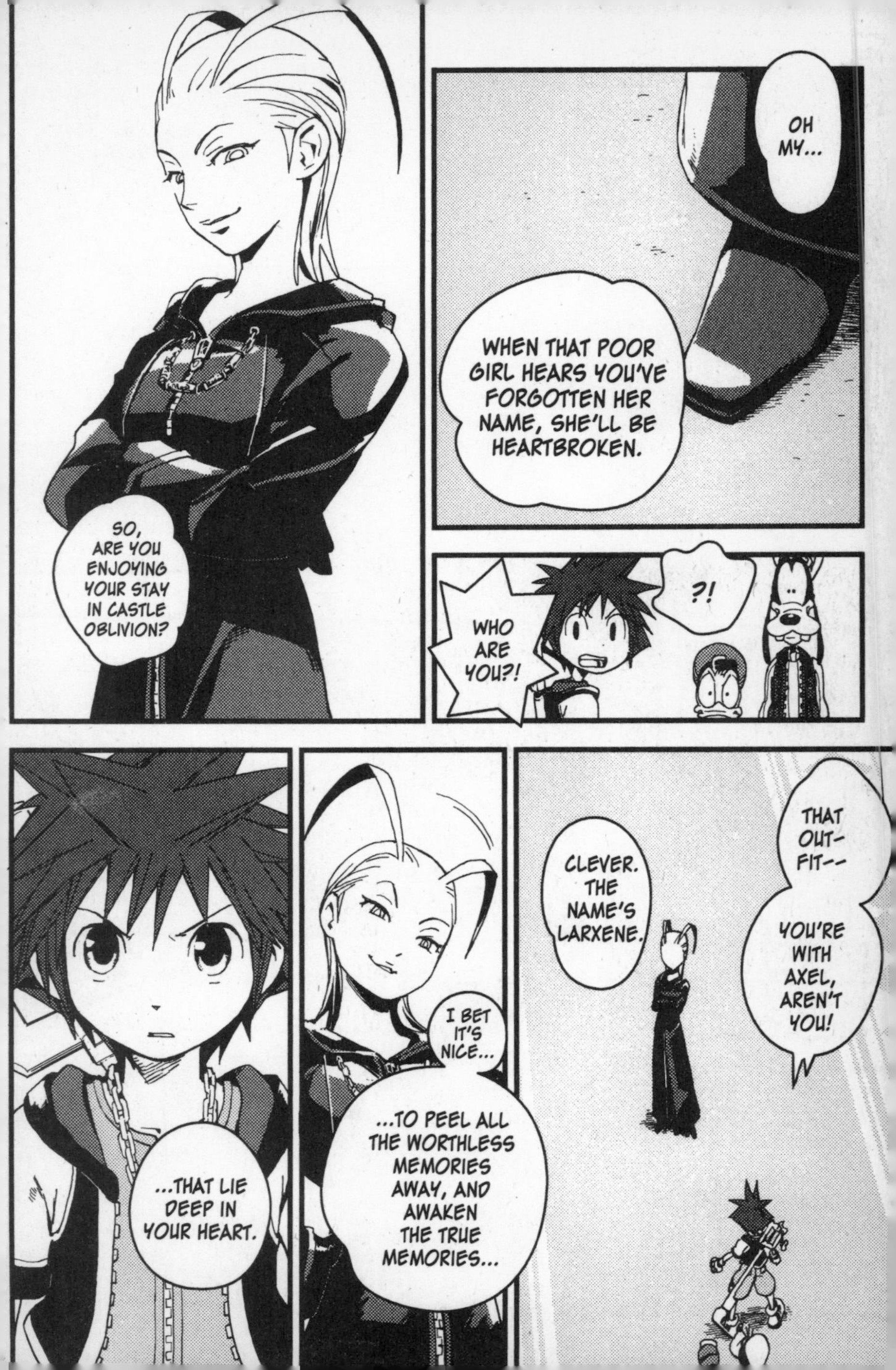
OH MY...
WHEN THAT POOR GIRL HEARS YOU'VE FORGOTTEN HER NAME, SHE'LL BE HEARTBROKEN.
?!
WHO ARE YOU?!
SO, ARE YOU ENJOYING YOUR STAY IN CASTLE OBLIVION?
THAT OUT-FIT--
YOU'RE WITH AXEL, AREN'T YOU!
CLEVER. THE NAME'S LARXENE.
I BET IT'S NICE...
...TO PEEL ALL THE WORTHLESS MEMORIES AWAY, AND AWAKEN THE TRUE MEMORIES...
...THAT LIE DEEP IN YOUR HEART.

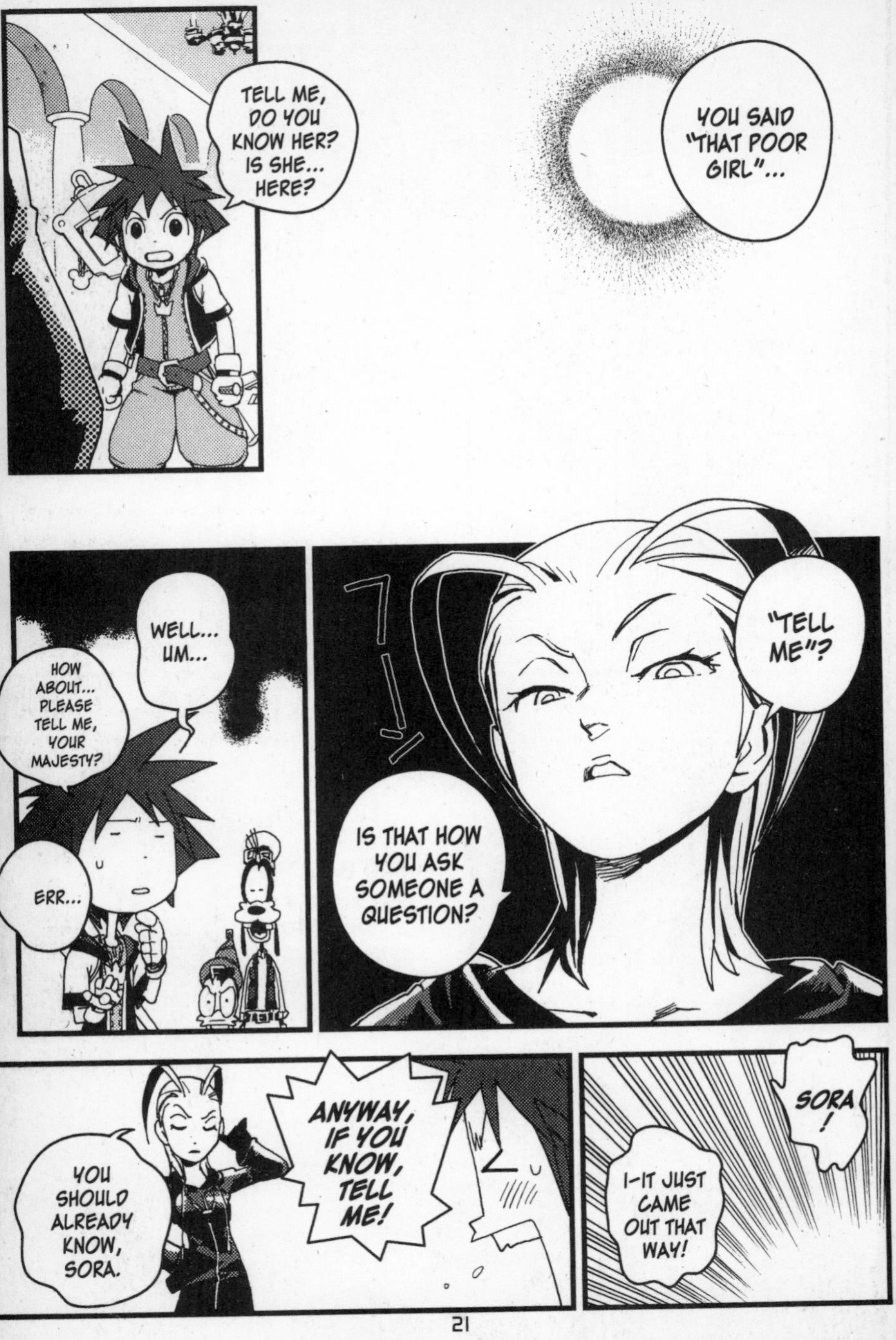
YOU SAID "THAT POOR GIRL"...
TELL ME, DO YOU KNOW HER? IS SHE... HERE?
"TELL ME"?
IS THAT HOW YOU ASK SOMEONE A QUESTION?
WELL... UM...
HOW ABOUT... PLEASE TELL ME, YOUR MAJESTY?
ERR...
SORA!
I-IT JUST CAME OUT THAT WAY!
ANYWAY, IF YOU KNOW, TELL ME!
YOU SHOULD ALREADY KNOW, SORA.

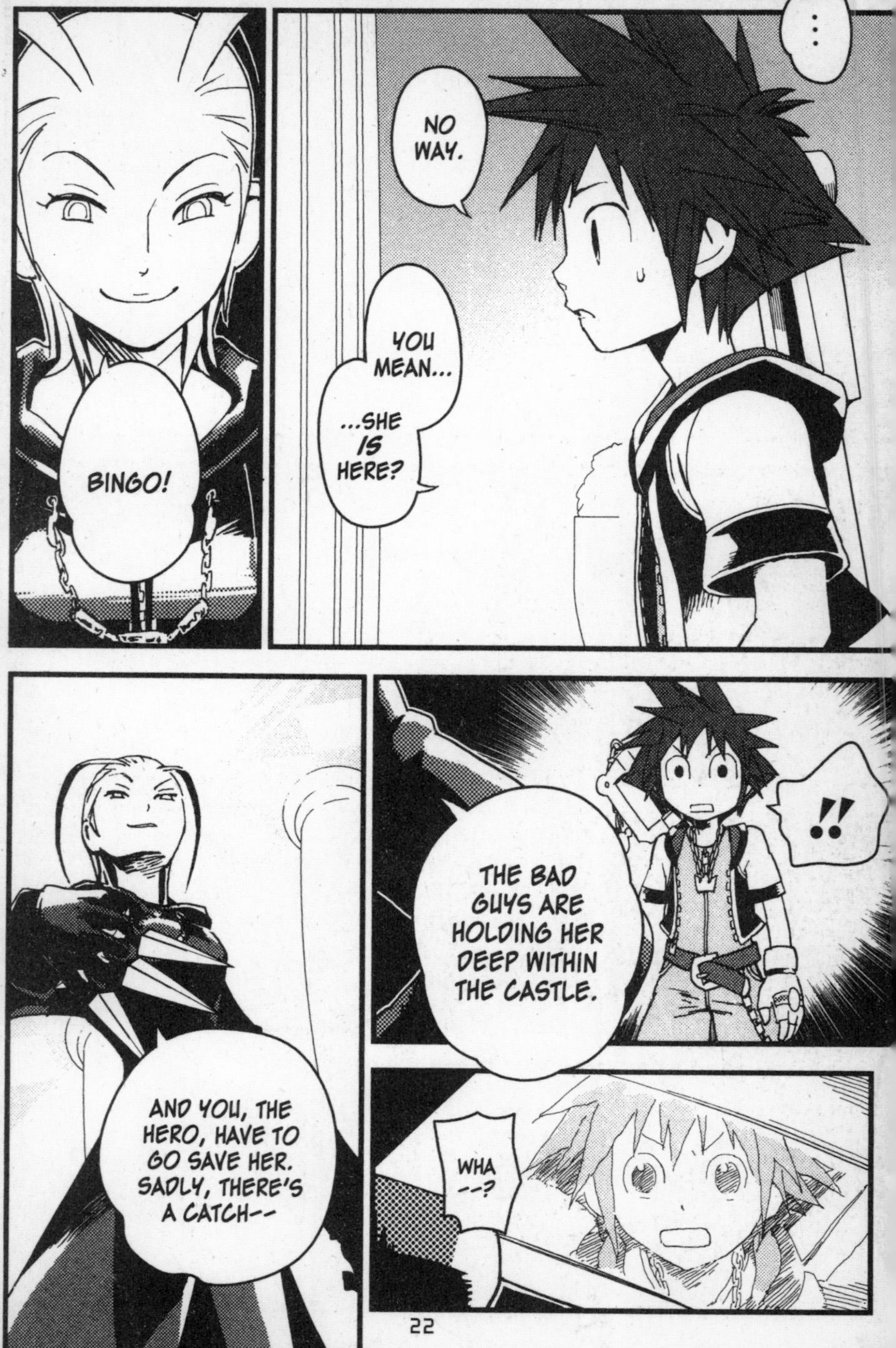

...
NO WAY.
YOU MEAN... ...SHE *IS* HERE?
BINGO!
!!
THE BAD GUYS ARE HOLDING HER DEEP WITHIN THE CASTLE.
WHA--?
AND YOU, THE HERO, HAVE TO GO SAVE HER. SADLY, THERE'S A CATCH--

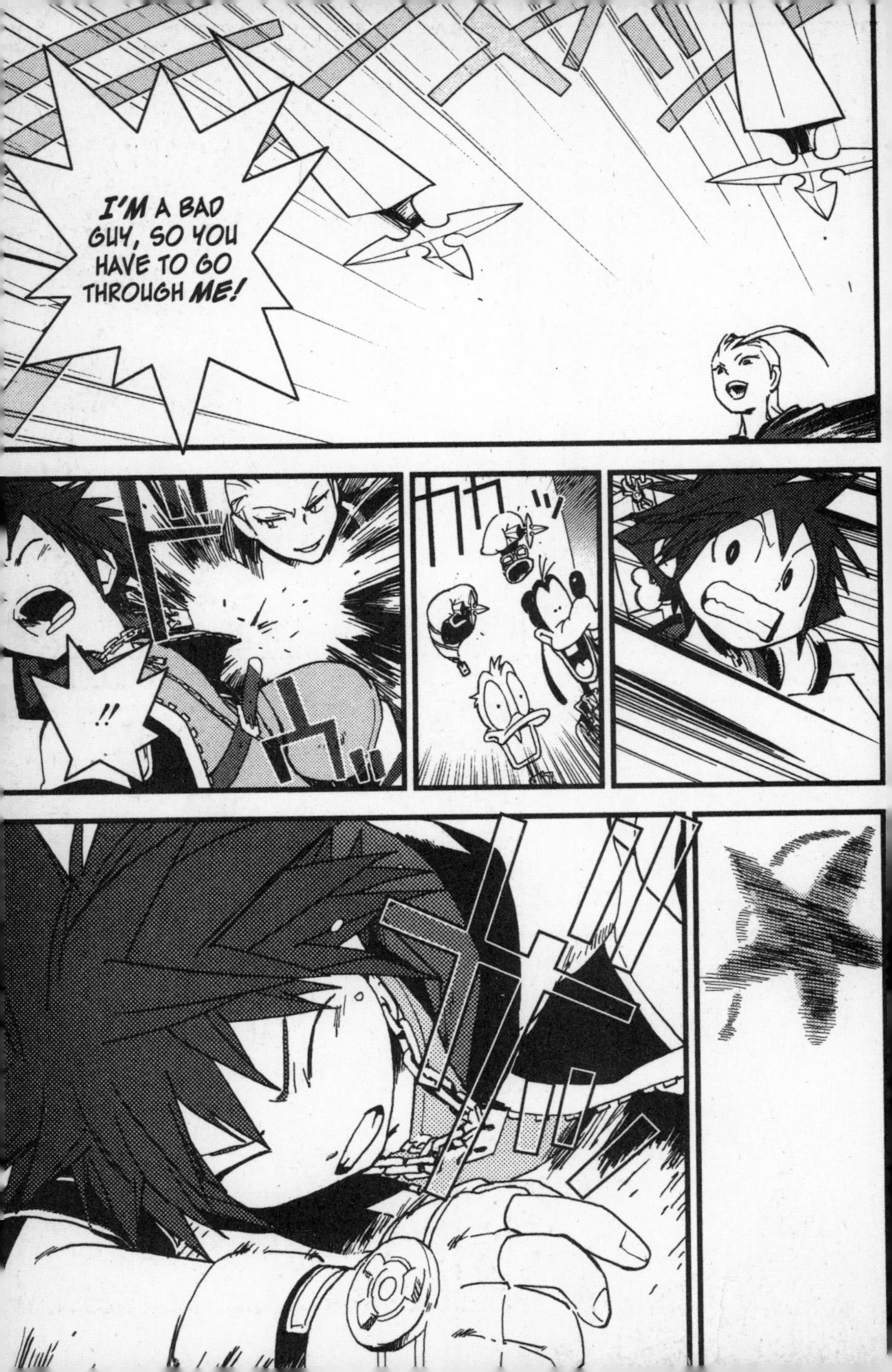
I'M A BAD GUY, SO YOU HAVE TO GO THROUGH ME!
!!

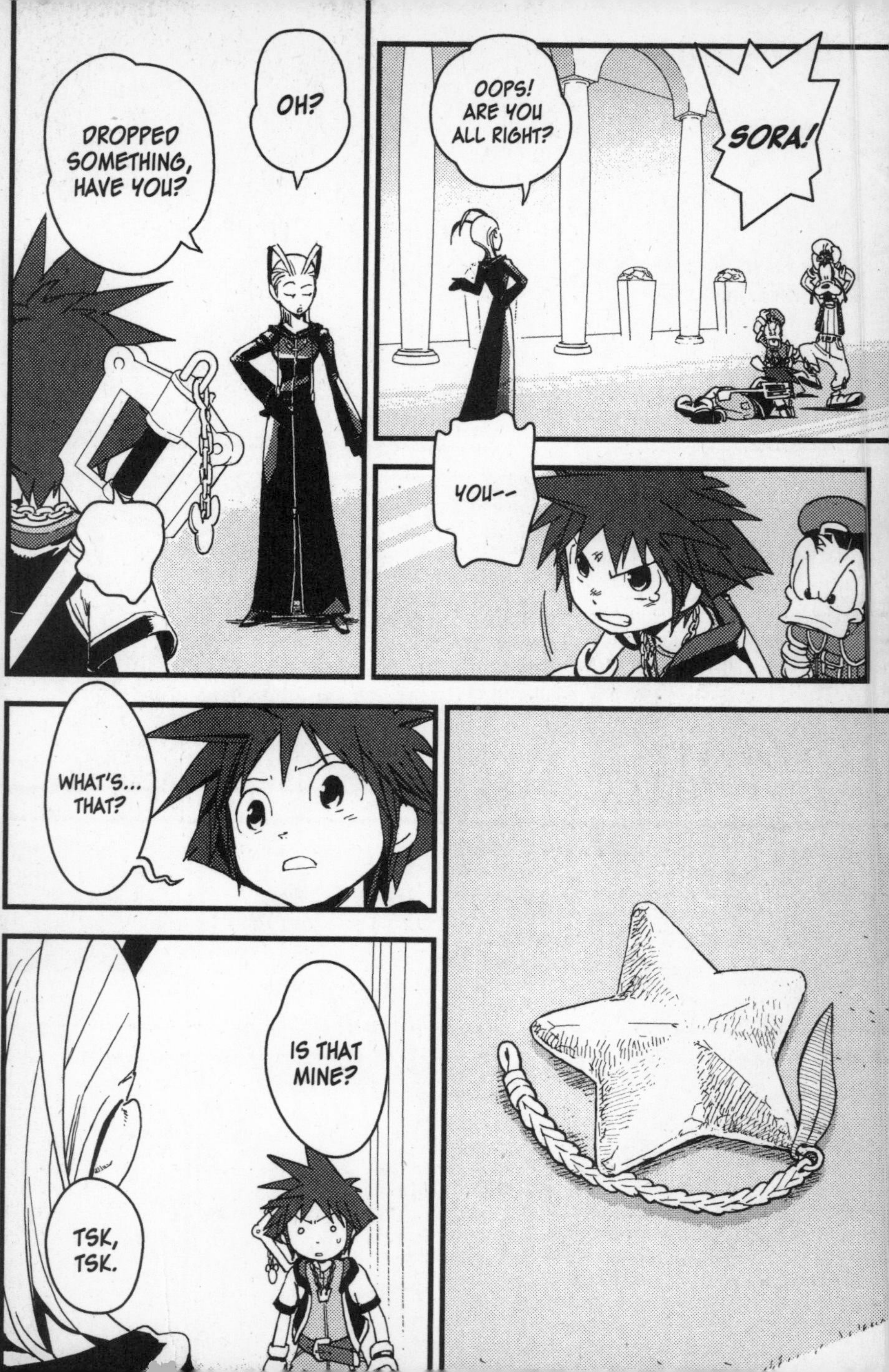
SORA!
OOPS! ARE YOU ALL RIGHT?
YOU--
OH?
DROPPED SOMETHING, HAVE YOU?
WHAT'S... THAT?
IS THAT MINE?
TSK, TSK.

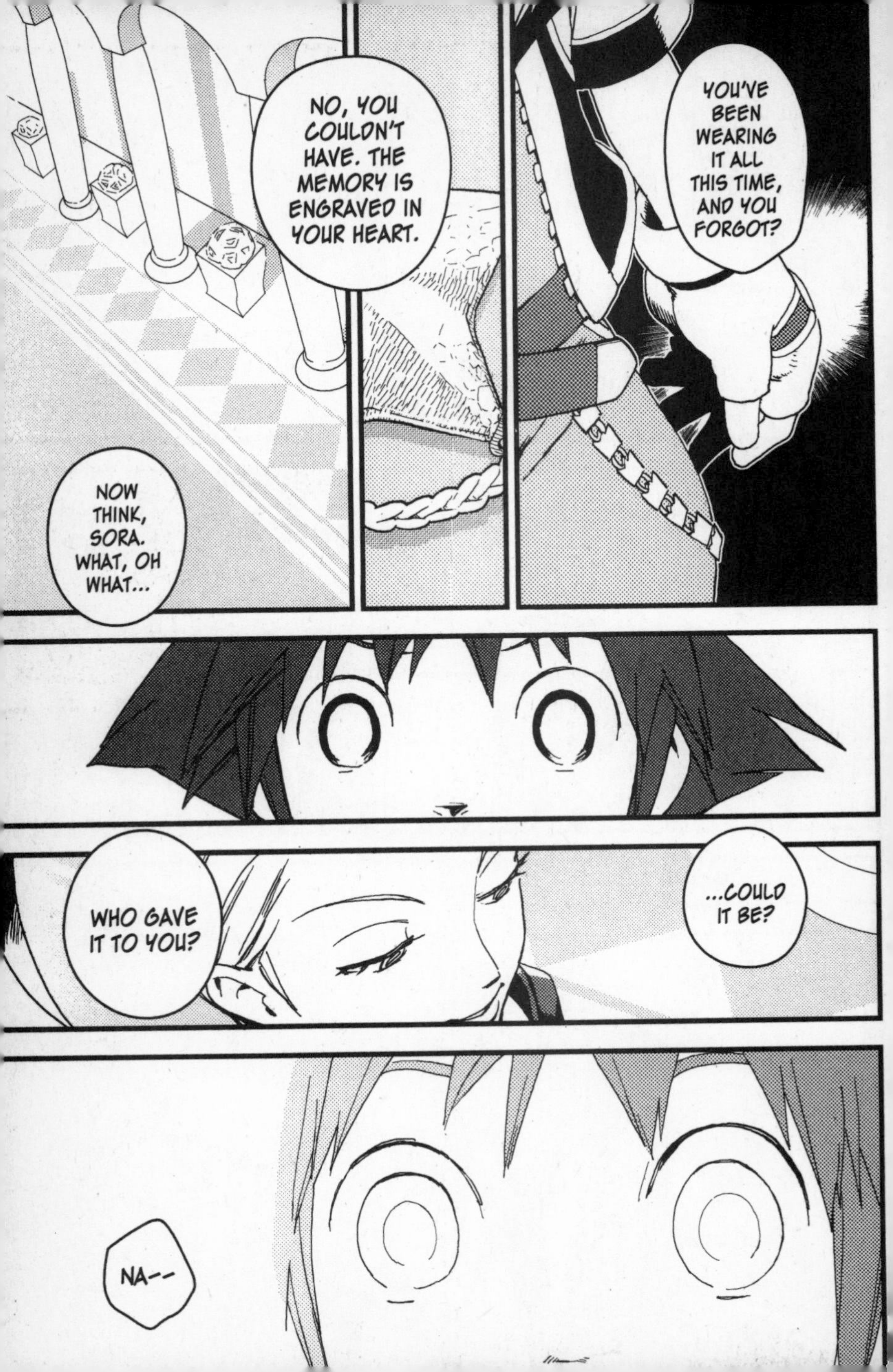
YOU'VE BEEN WEARING IT ALL THIS TIME, AND YOU FORGOT?
NO, YOU COULDN'T HAVE. THE MEMORY IS ENGRAVED IN YOUR HEART.
NOW THINK, SORA. WHAT, OH WHAT...
...COULD IT BE?
WHO GAVE IT TO YOU?
NA--

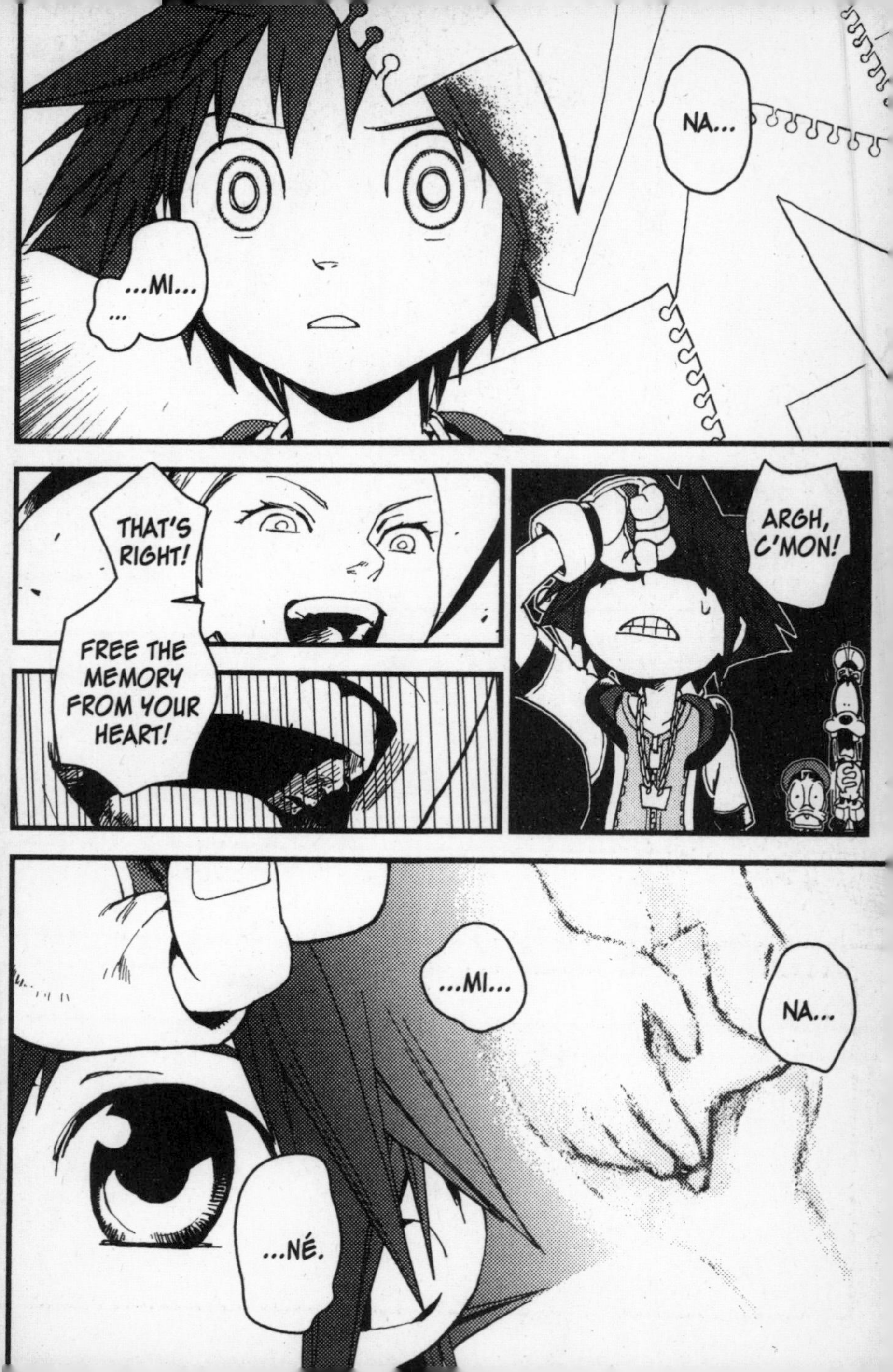
NA...
...MI...
...
ARGH, C'MON!
THAT'S RIGHT!
FREE THE MEMORY FROM YOUR HEART!
NA...
...MI...
...NÉ.

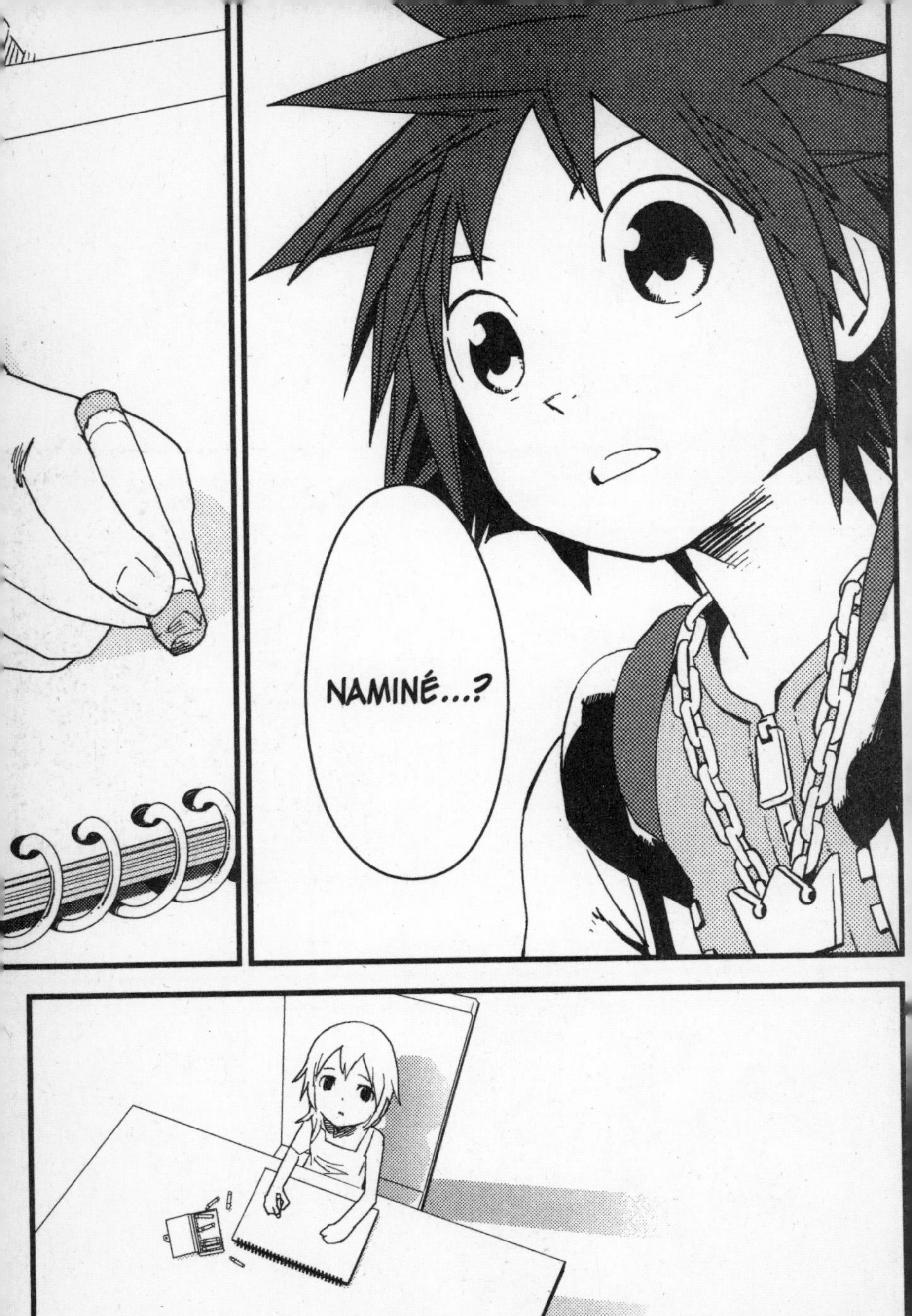
NAMINÉ...?

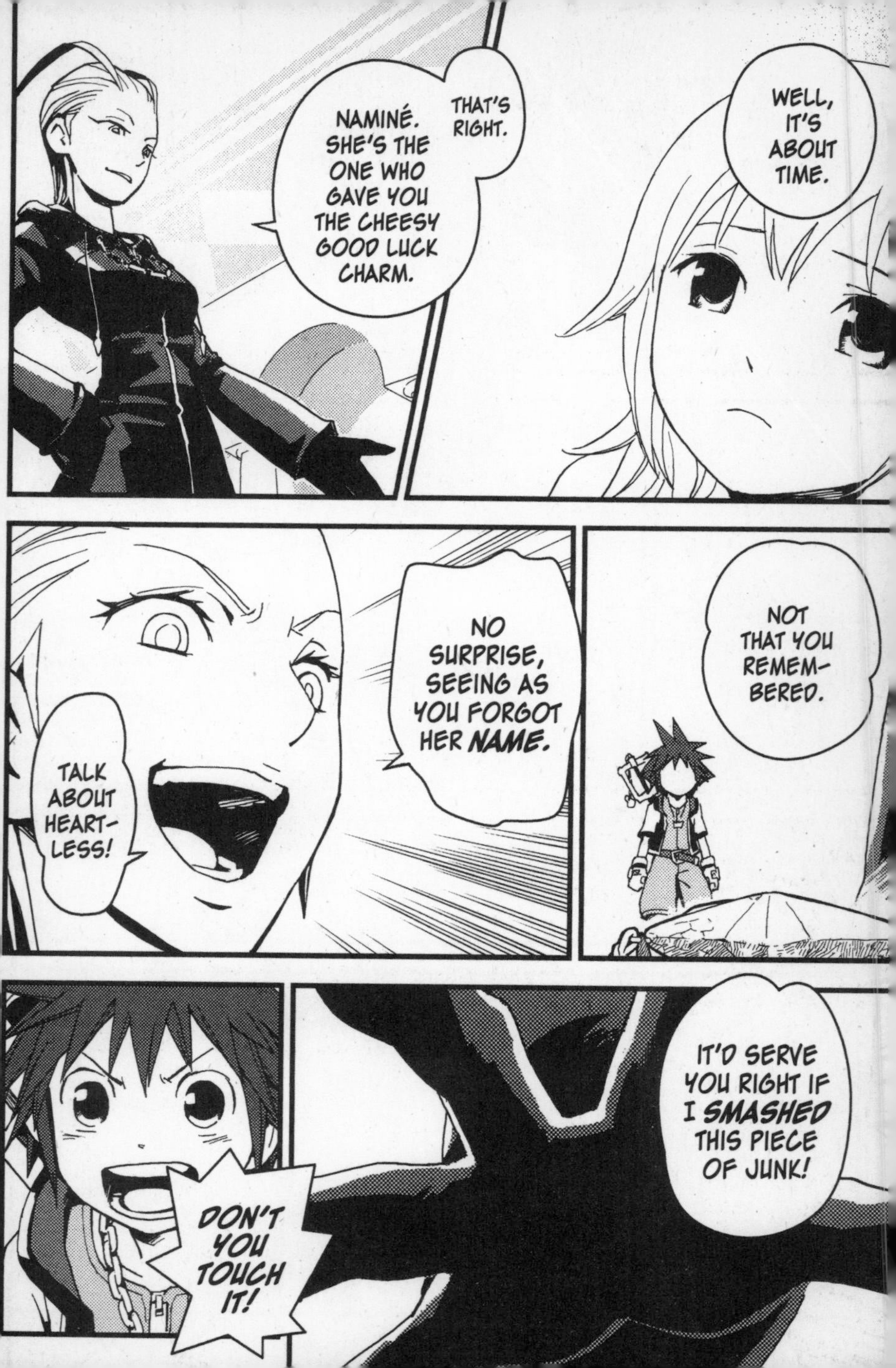
WELL, IT'S ABOUT TIME.
THAT'S RIGHT.
NAMINÉ. SHE'S THE ONE WHO GAVE YOU THE CHEESY GOOD LUCK CHARM.
NOT THAT YOU REMEMBERED.
NO SURPRISE, SEEING AS YOU FORGOT HER *NAME.*
TALK ABOUT HEARTLESS!
IT'D SERVE YOU RIGHT IF I *SMASHED* THIS PIECE OF JUNK!
DON'T YOU TOUCH IT!

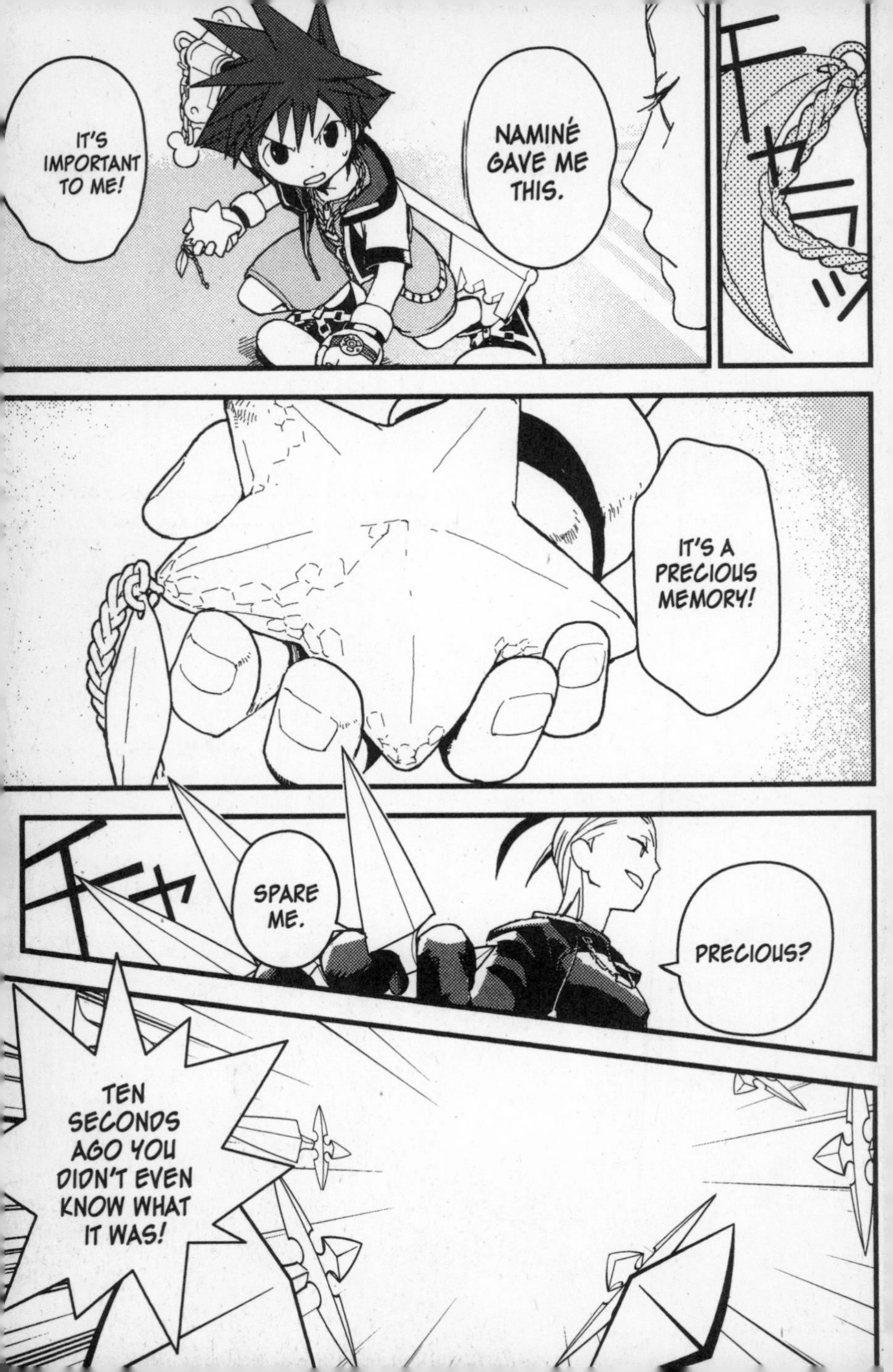
NAMINÉ GAVE ME THIS.
IT'S IMPORTANT TO ME!
IT'S A PRECIOUS MEMORY!
PRECIOUS?
SPARE ME.
TEN SECONDS AGO YOU DIDN'T EVEN KNOW WHAT IT WAS!

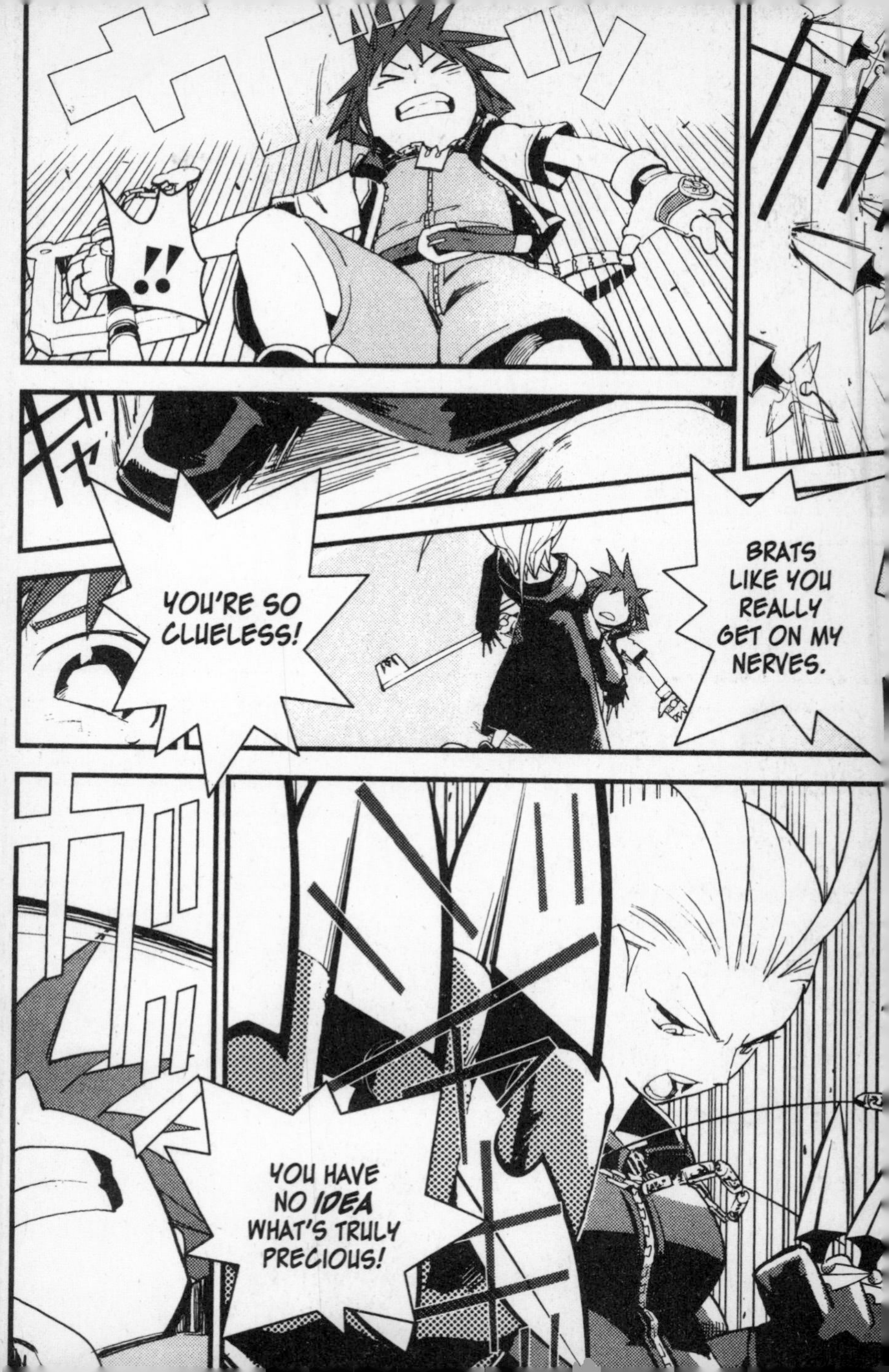
!!
BRATS LIKE YOU REALLY GET ON MY NERVES.
YOU'RE SO CLUELESS!
YOU HAVE NO *IDEA* WHAT'S TRULY PRECIOUS!

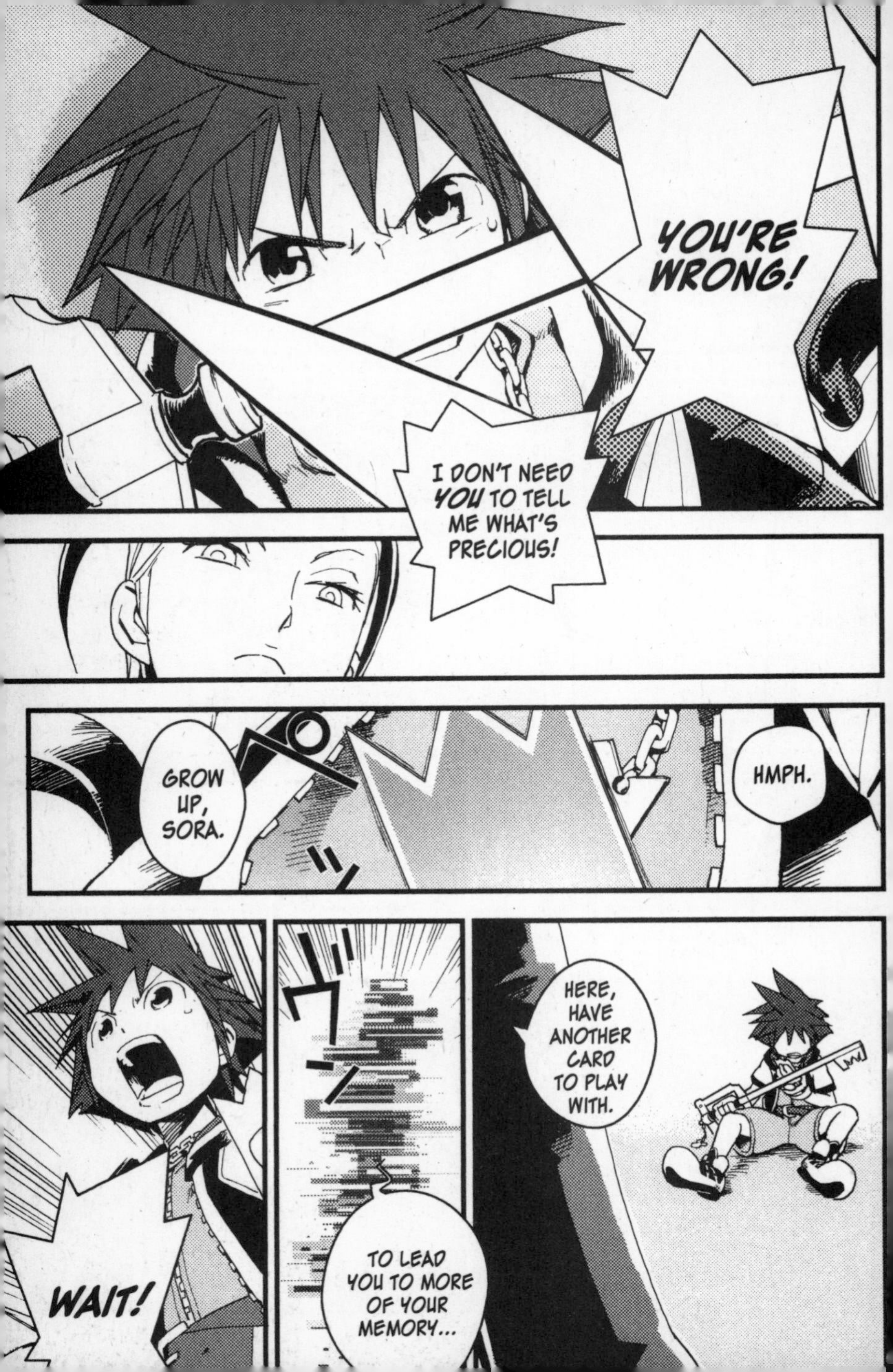
YOU'RE WRONG!
I DON'T NEED YOU TO TELL ME WHAT'S PRECIOUS!
HMPH.
GROW UP, SORA.
HERE, HAVE ANOTHER CARD TO PLAY WITH.
TO LEAD YOU TO MORE OF YOUR MEMORY...
WAIT!

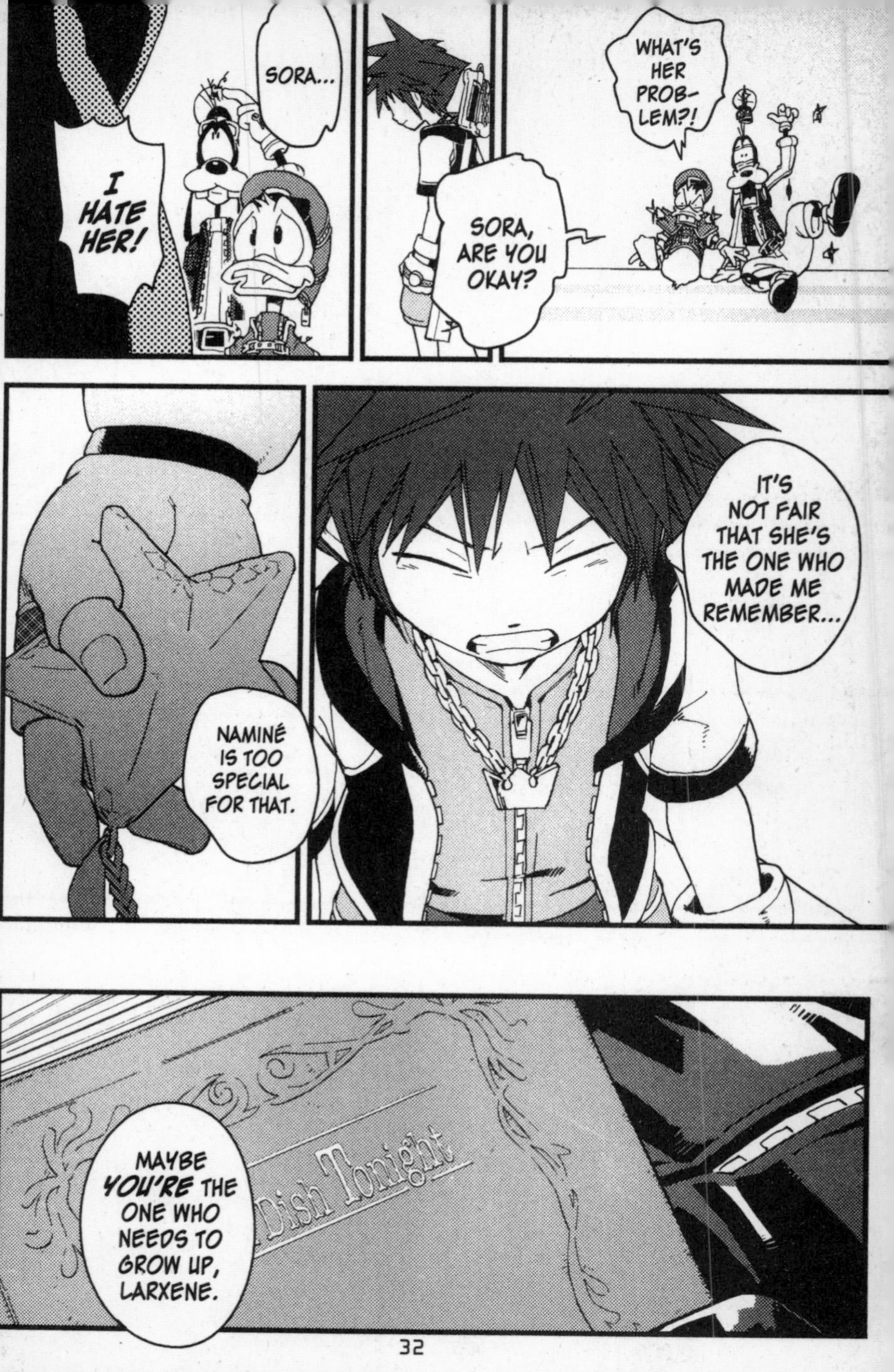
WHAT'S HER PROBLEM?!
SORA, ARE YOU OKAY?
SORA...
I HATE HER!
IT'S NOT FAIR THAT SHE'S THE ONE WHO MADE ME REMEMBER...
NAMINÉ IS TOO SPECIAL FOR THAT.
MAYBE *YOU'RE* THE ONE WHO NEEDS TO GROW UP, LARXENE.
Dish Tonight

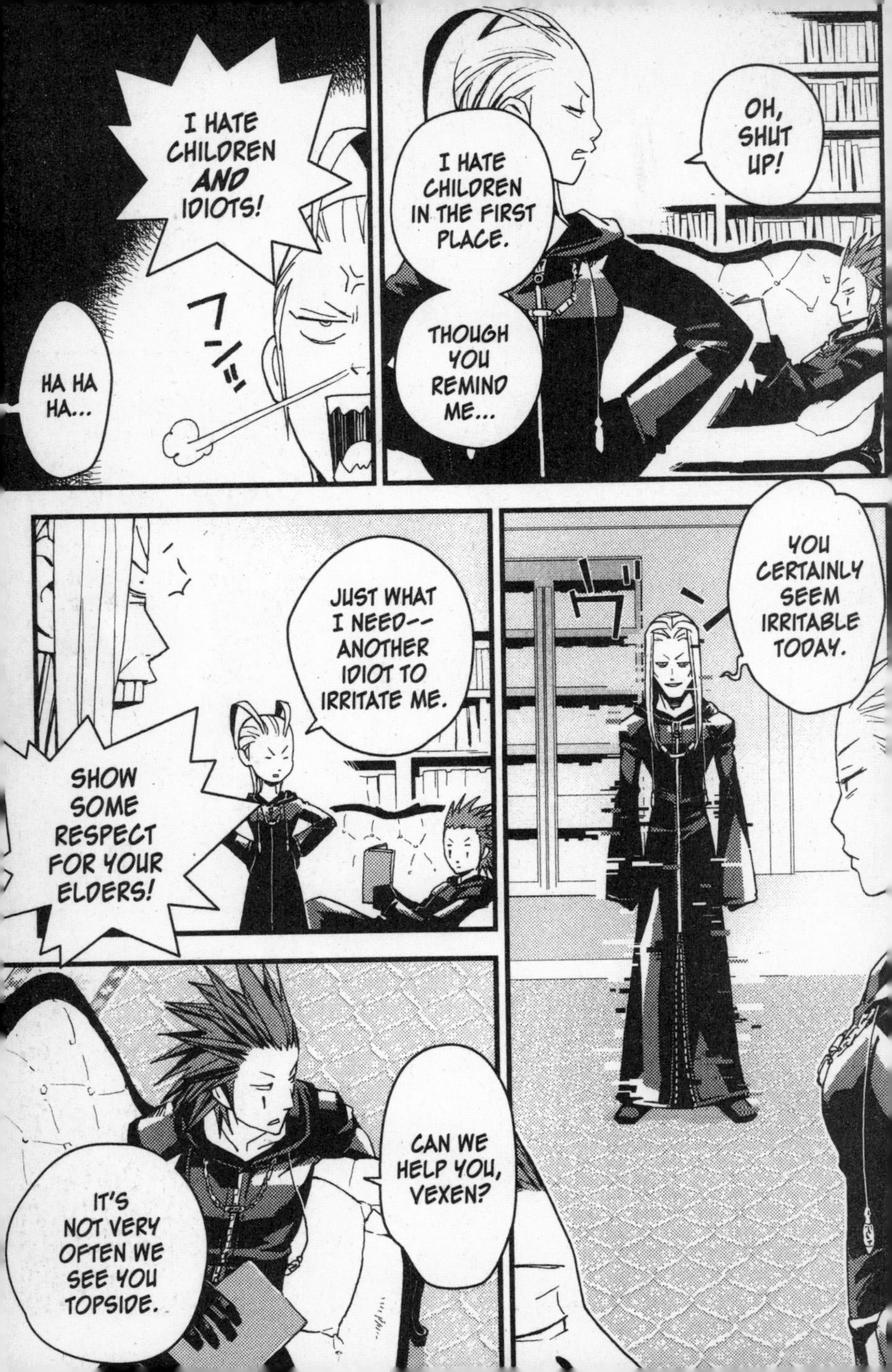

OH, SHUT UP!
I HATE CHILDREN IN THE FIRST PLACE.
THOUGH YOU REMIND ME...
I HATE CHILDREN AND IDIOTS!
HA HA HA...
YOU CERTAINLY SEEM IRRITABLE TODAY.
JUST WHAT I NEED--ANOTHER IDIOT TO IRRITATE ME.
SHOW SOME RESPECT FOR YOUR ELDERS!
CAN WE HELP YOU, VEXEN?
IT'S NOT VERY OFTEN WE SEE YOU TOPSIDE.

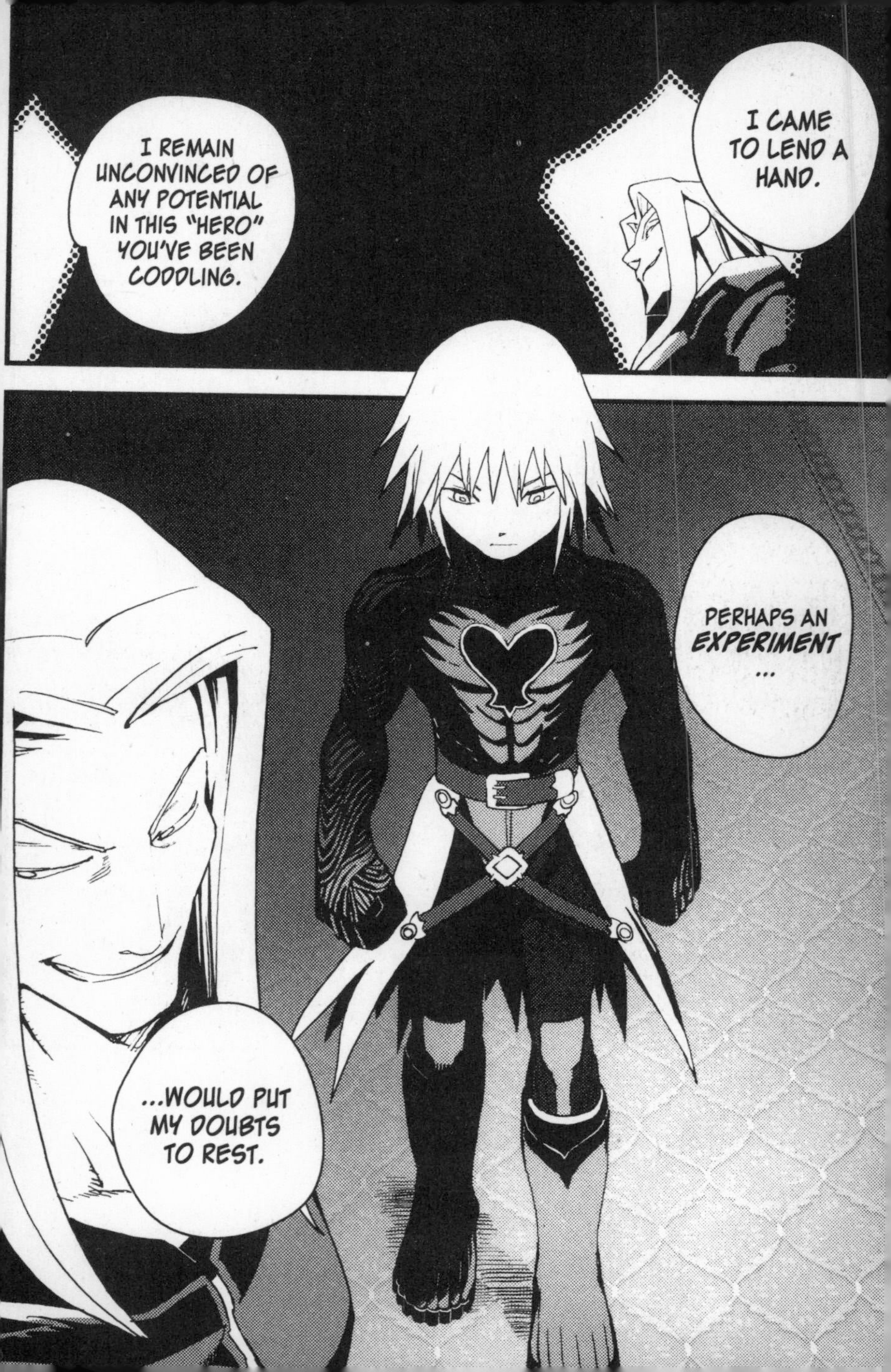
I CAME TO LEND A HAND.
I REMAIN UNCONVINCED OF ANY POTENTIAL IN THIS "HERO" YOU'VE BEEN CODDLING.
PERHAPS AN *EXPERIMENT* ...
...WOULD PUT MY DOUBTS TO REST.

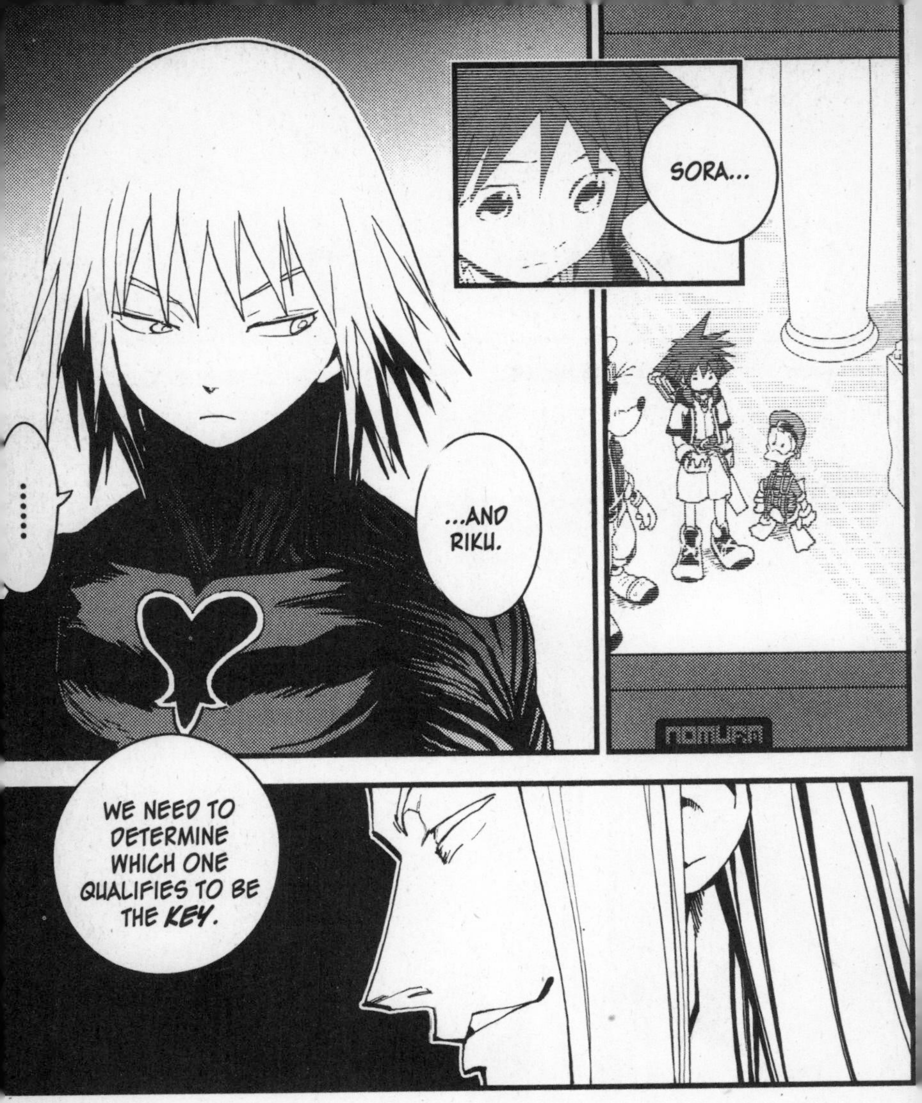
SORA...
...AND RIKU.
......
WE NEED TO DETERMINE WHICH ONE QUALIFIES TO BE THE *KEY*.

Card 08 Promise

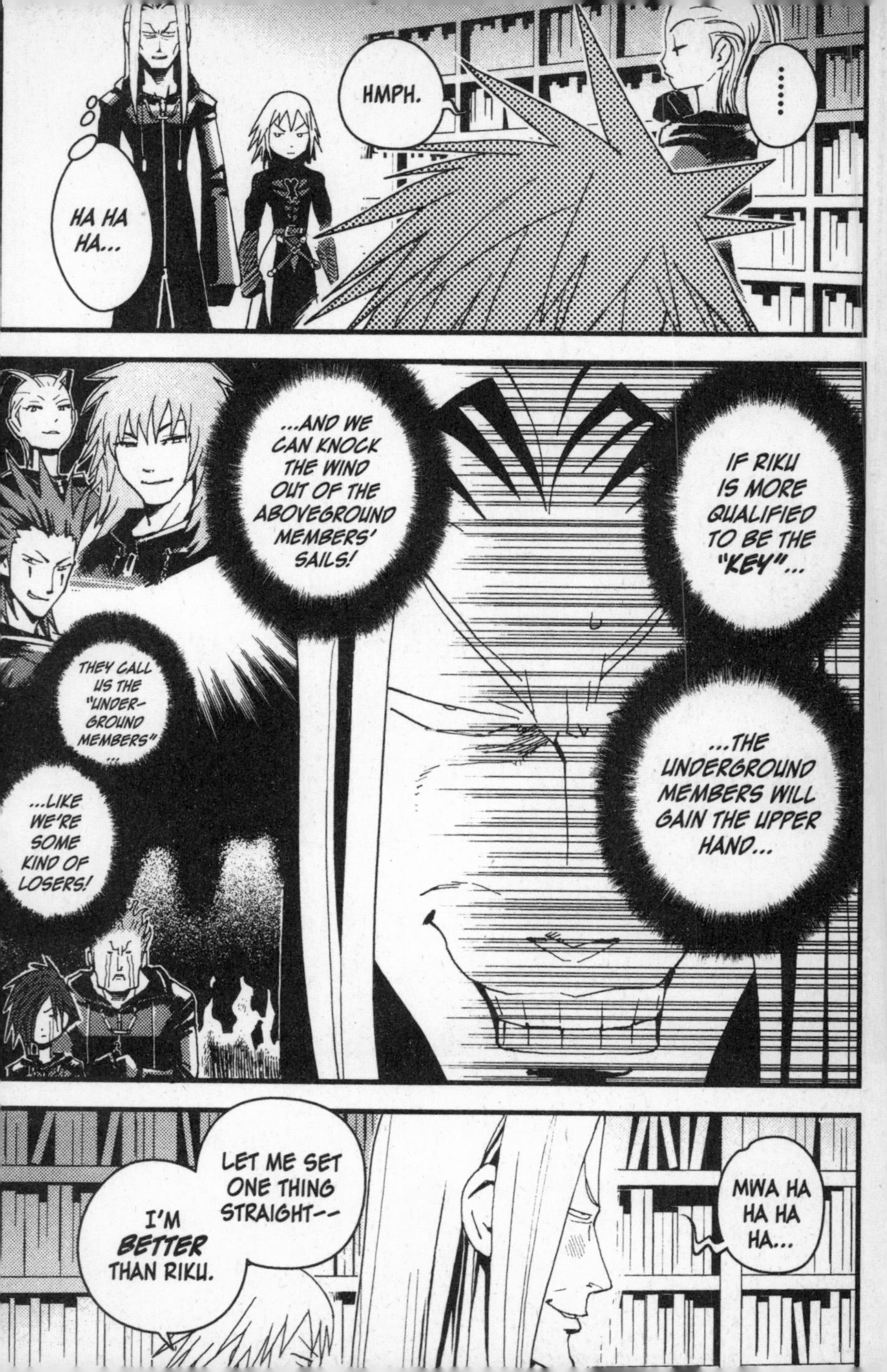
......
HMPH.
HA HA HA...
IF RIKU IS MORE QUALIFIED TO BE THE "KEY"...
...THE UNDERGROUND MEMBERS WILL GAIN THE UPPER HAND...
...AND WE CAN KNOCK THE WIND OUT OF THE ABOVEGROUND MEMBERS' SAILS!
THEY CALL US THE "UNDER-GROUND MEMBERS"...
...LIKE WE'RE SOME KIND OF LOSERS!
MWA HA HA HA HA...
LET ME SET ONE THING STRAIGHT--
I'M BETTER THAN RIKU.

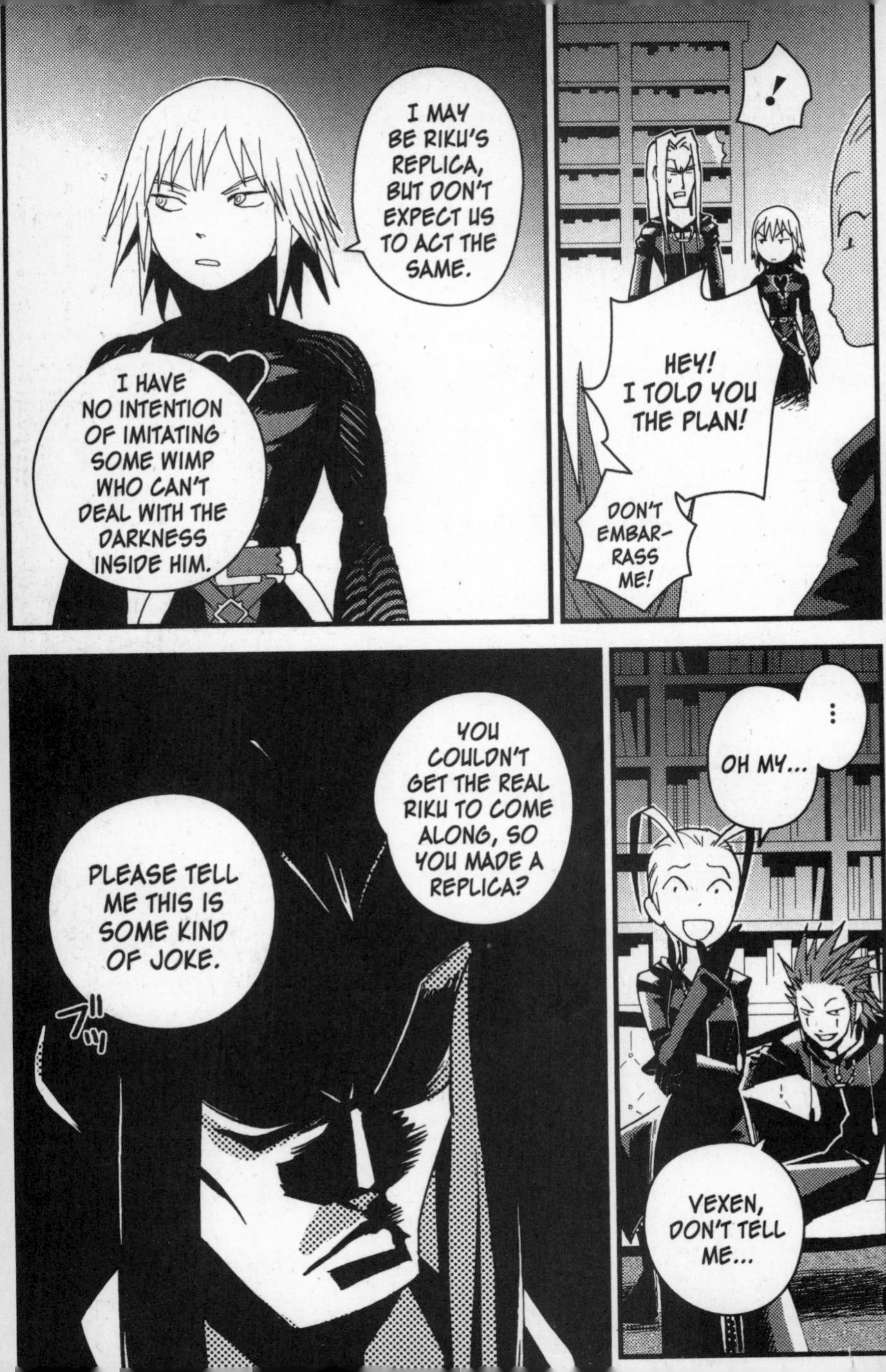
!
HEY! I TOLD YOU THE PLAN!
DON'T EMBARRASS ME!
I MAY BE RIKU'S REPLICA, BUT DON'T EXPECT US TO ACT THE SAME.
I HAVE NO INTENTION OF IMITATING SOME WIMP WHO CAN'T DEAL WITH THE DARKNESS INSIDE HIM.
...
OH MY...
VEXEN, DON'T TELL ME...
YOU COULDN'T GET THE REAL RIKU TO COME ALONG, SO YOU MADE A REPLICA?
PLEASE TELL ME THIS IS SOME KIND OF JOKE.

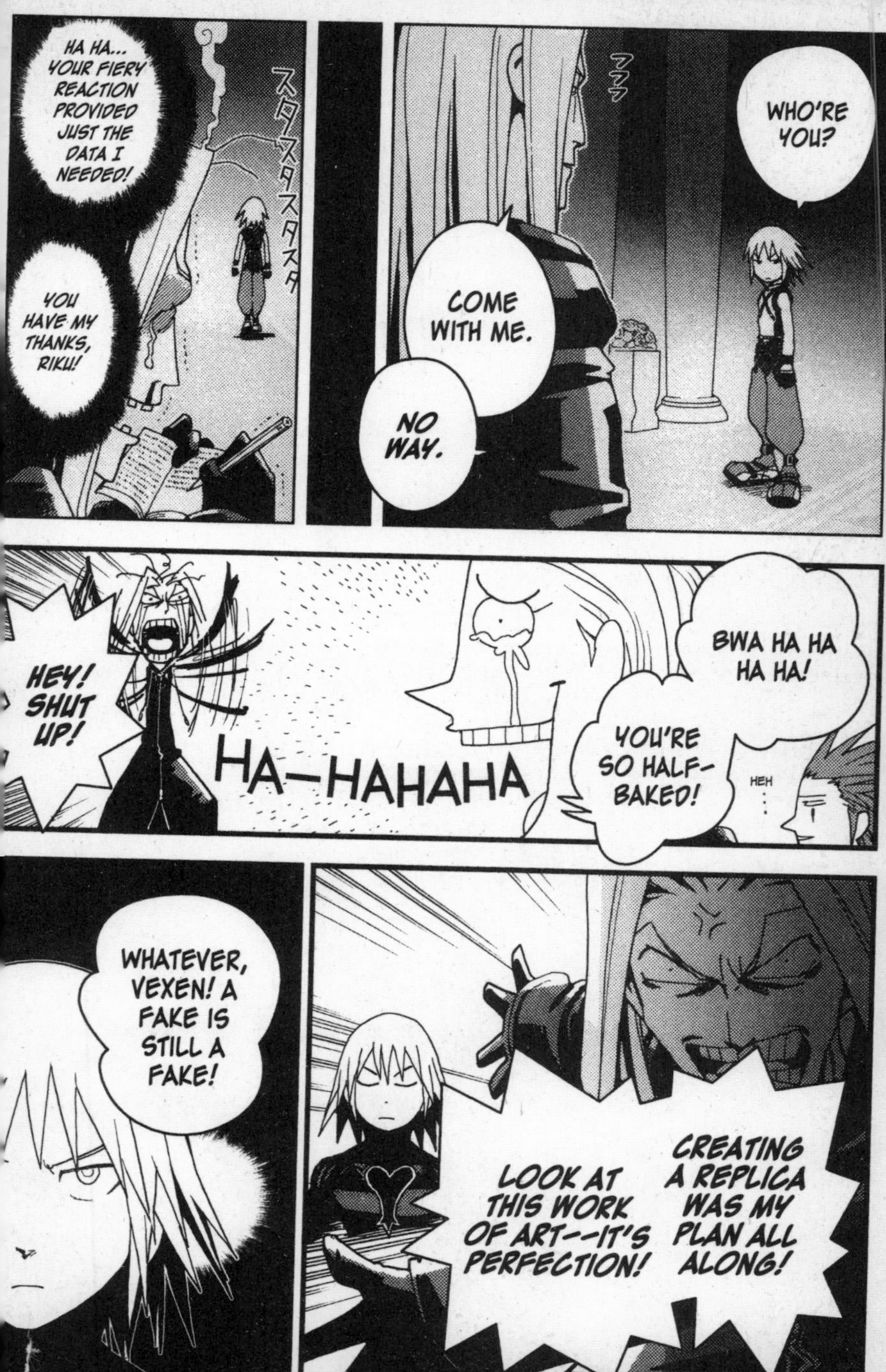
WHO'RE YOU?
フフフ
COME WITH ME.
NO WAY.
スタスタスタスタ
HA HA... YOUR FIERY REACTION PROVIDED JUST THE DATA I NEEDED!
YOU HAVE MY THANKS, RIKU!
BWA HA HA HA HA!
HEH...
YOU'RE SO HALF-BAKED!
HA-HAHAHA
HEY! SHUT UP!
CREATING A REPLICA WAS MY PLAN ALL ALONG!
LOOK AT THIS WORK OF ART--IT'S PERFECTION!
WHATEVER, VEXEN! A FAKE IS STILL A FAKE!

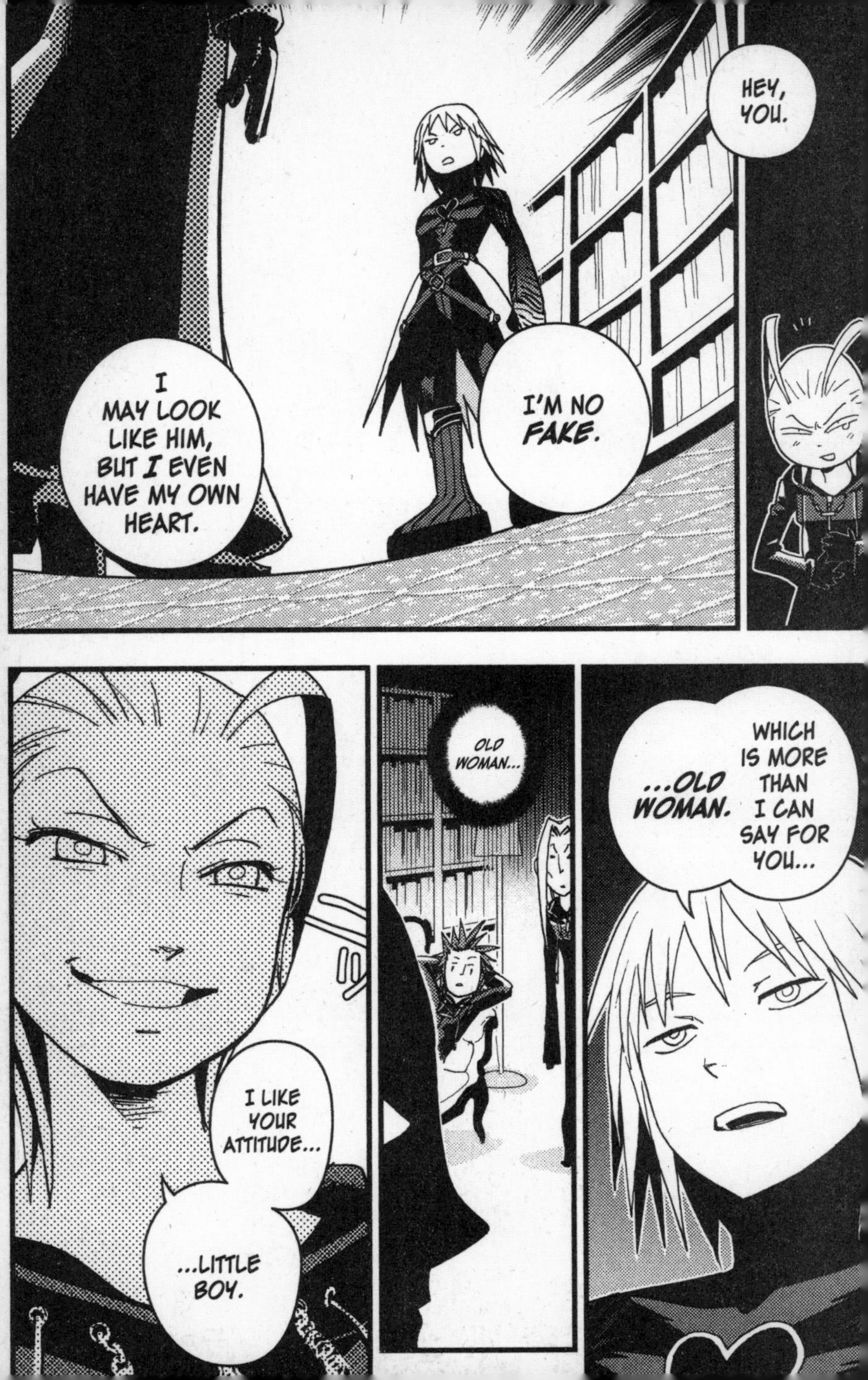
HEY, YOU.
I'M NO FAKE.
I MAY LOOK LIKE HIM, BUT I EVEN HAVE MY OWN HEART.
WHICH IS MORE THAN I CAN SAY FOR YOU...
...OLD WOMAN.
OLD WOMAN...
I LIKE YOUR ATTITUDE...
...LITTLE BOY.

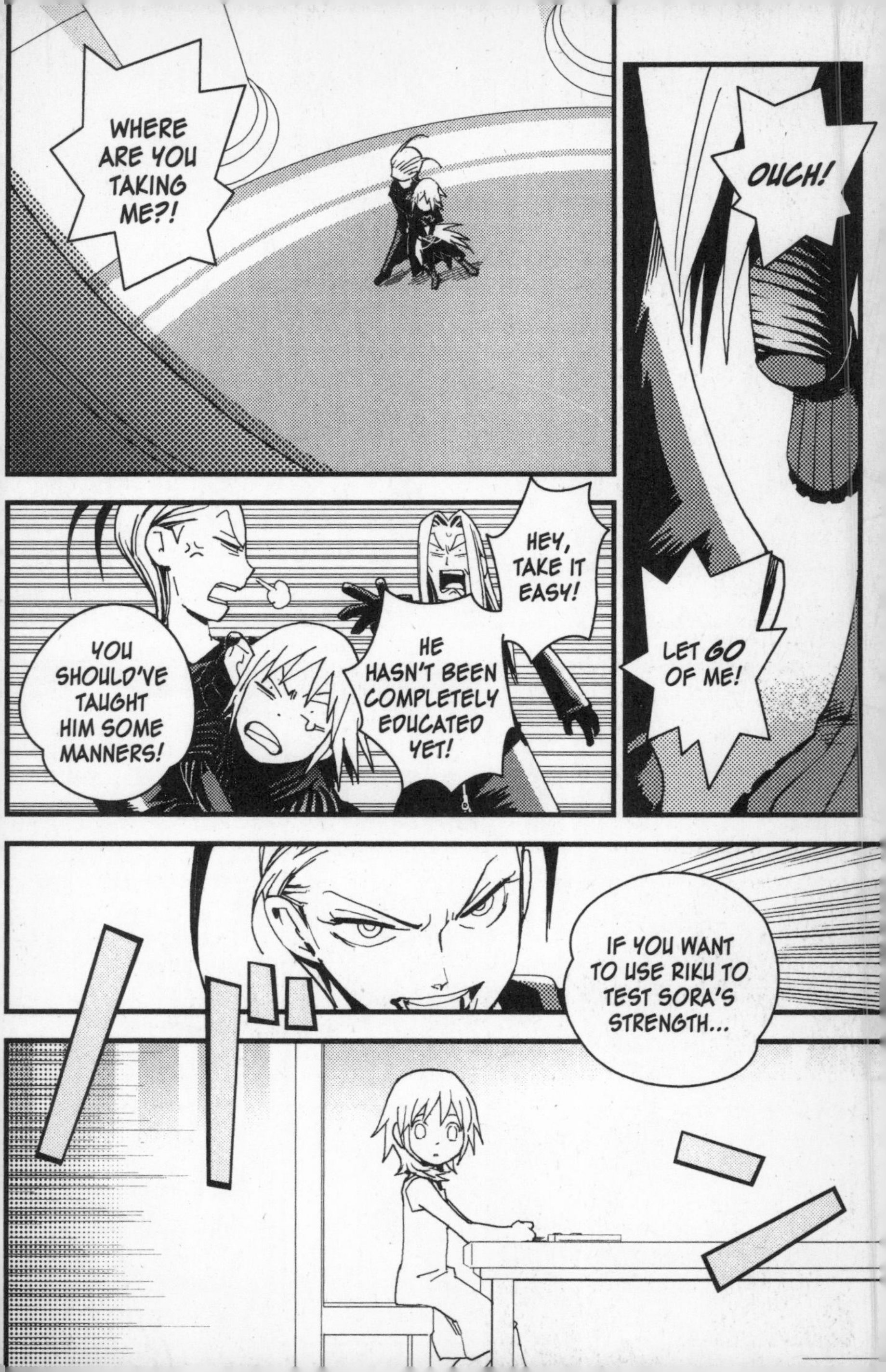
OUCH!
LET GO OF ME!
WHERE ARE YOU TAKING ME?!
HEY, TAKE IT EASY!
HE HASN'T BEEN COMPLETELY EDUCATED YET!
YOU SHOULD'VE TAUGHT HIM SOME MANNERS!
IF YOU WANT TO USE RIKU TO TEST SORA'S STRENGTH...

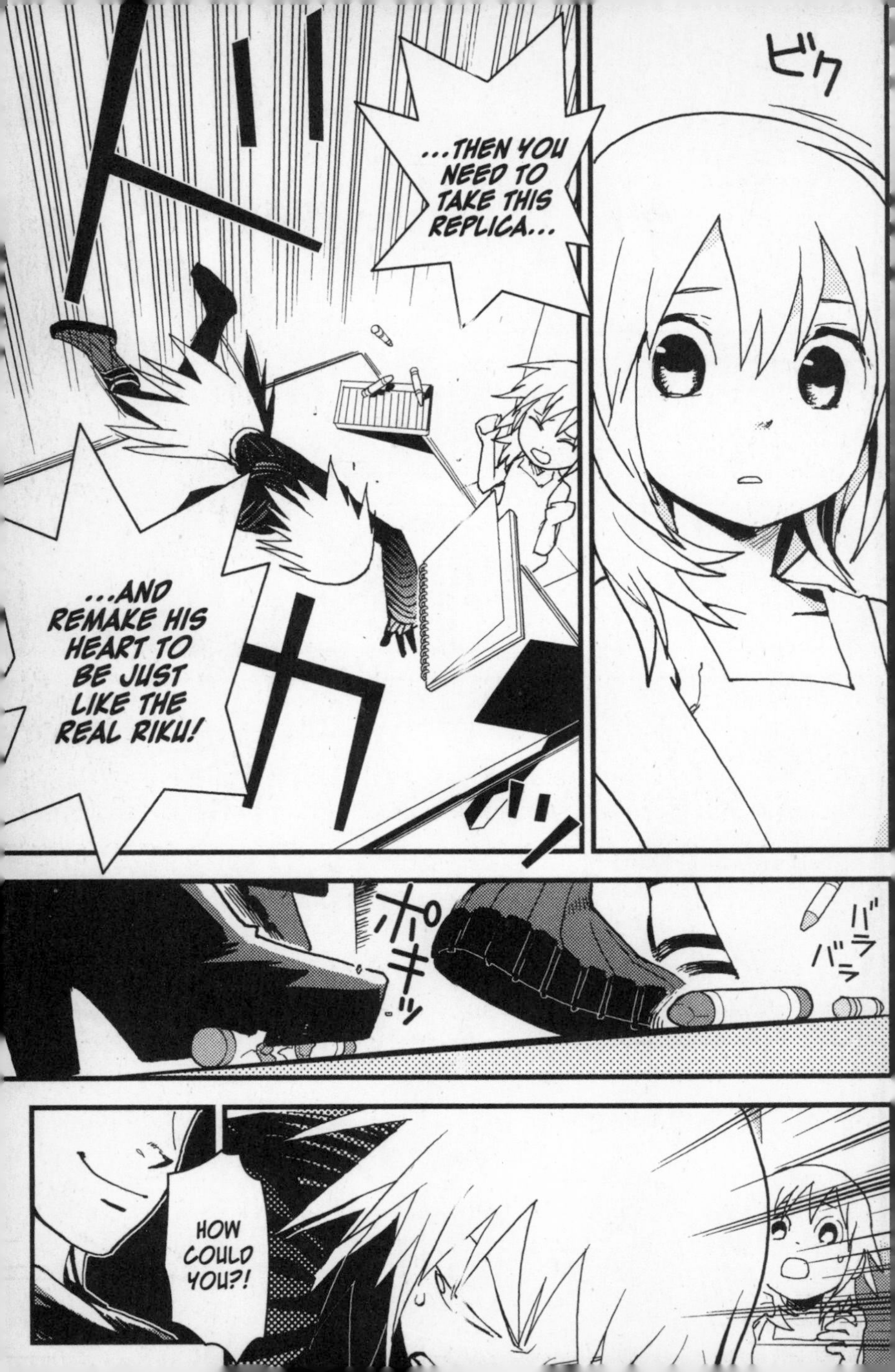
ビク
...THEN YOU NEED TO TAKE THIS REPLICA...
ドカッ
...AND REMAKE HIS HEART TO BE JUST LIKE THE REAL RIKU!
バラバラ
ポキッ
HOW COULD YOU?!

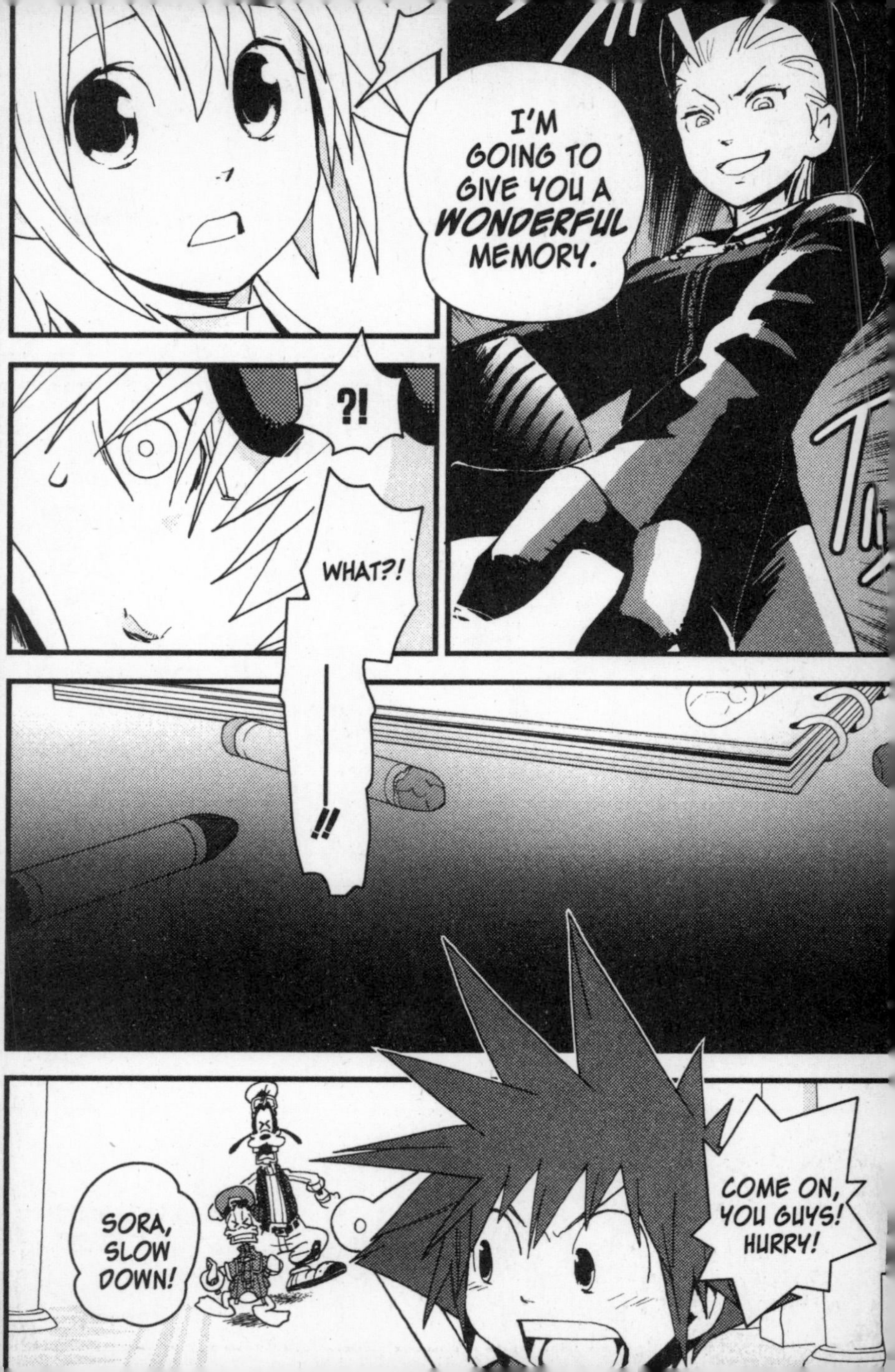

I'M GOING TO GIVE YOU A WONDERFUL MEMORY.
?!
WHAT?!
!!
COME ON, YOU GUYS! HURRY!
SORA, SLOW DOWN!

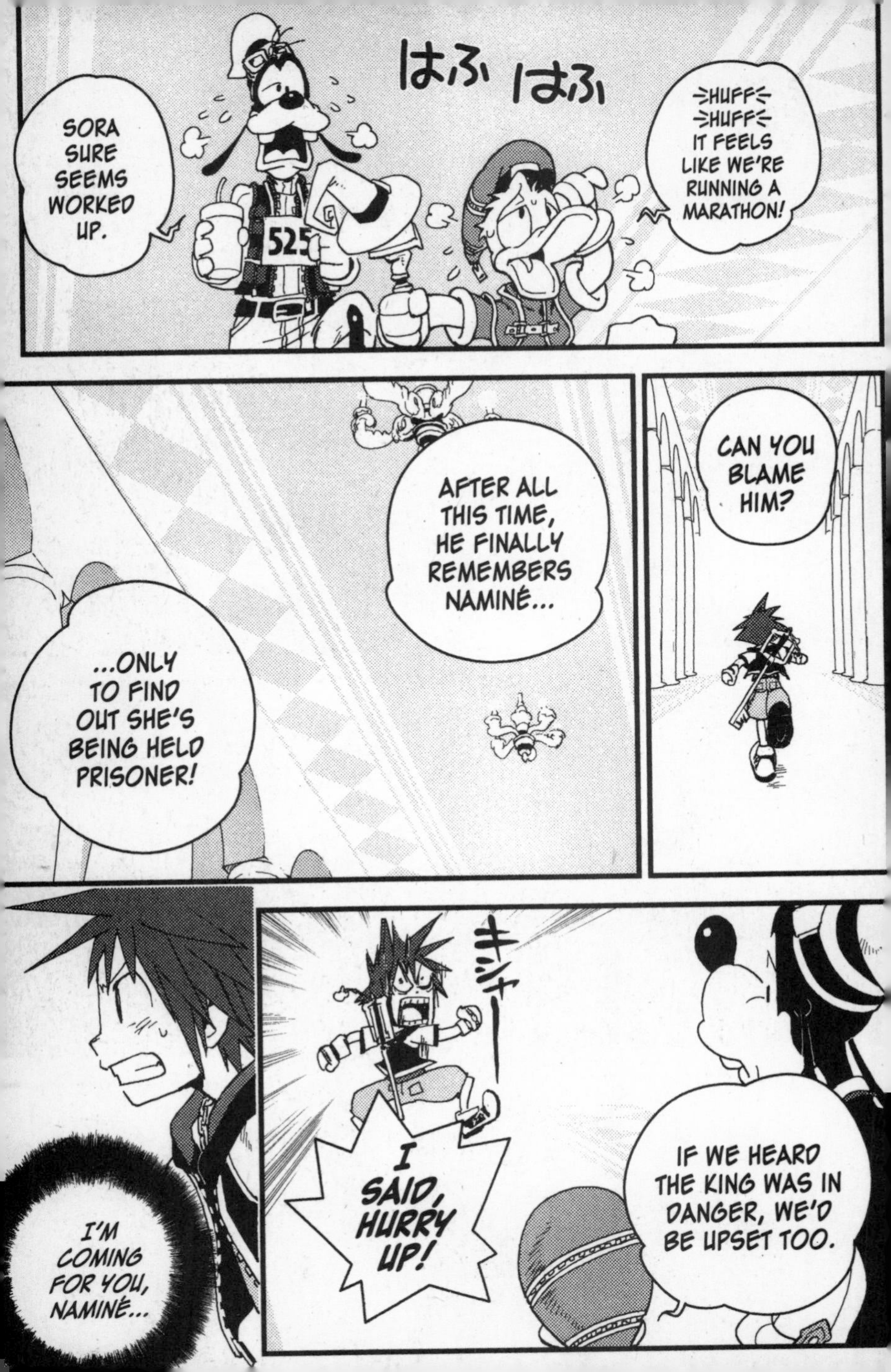

≡HUFF≡ ≡HUFF≡ IT FEELS LIKE WE'RE RUNNING A MARATHON!
はふ はふ
SORA SURE SEEMS WORKED UP.
525
CAN YOU BLAME HIM?
AFTER ALL THIS TIME, HE FINALLY REMEMBERS NAMINÉ...
...ONLY TO FIND OUT SHE'S BEING HELD PRISONER!
キシャー
IF WE HEARD THE KING WAS IN DANGER, WE'D BE UPSET TOO.
I SAID, HURRY UP!
I'M COMING FOR YOU, NAMINÉ...

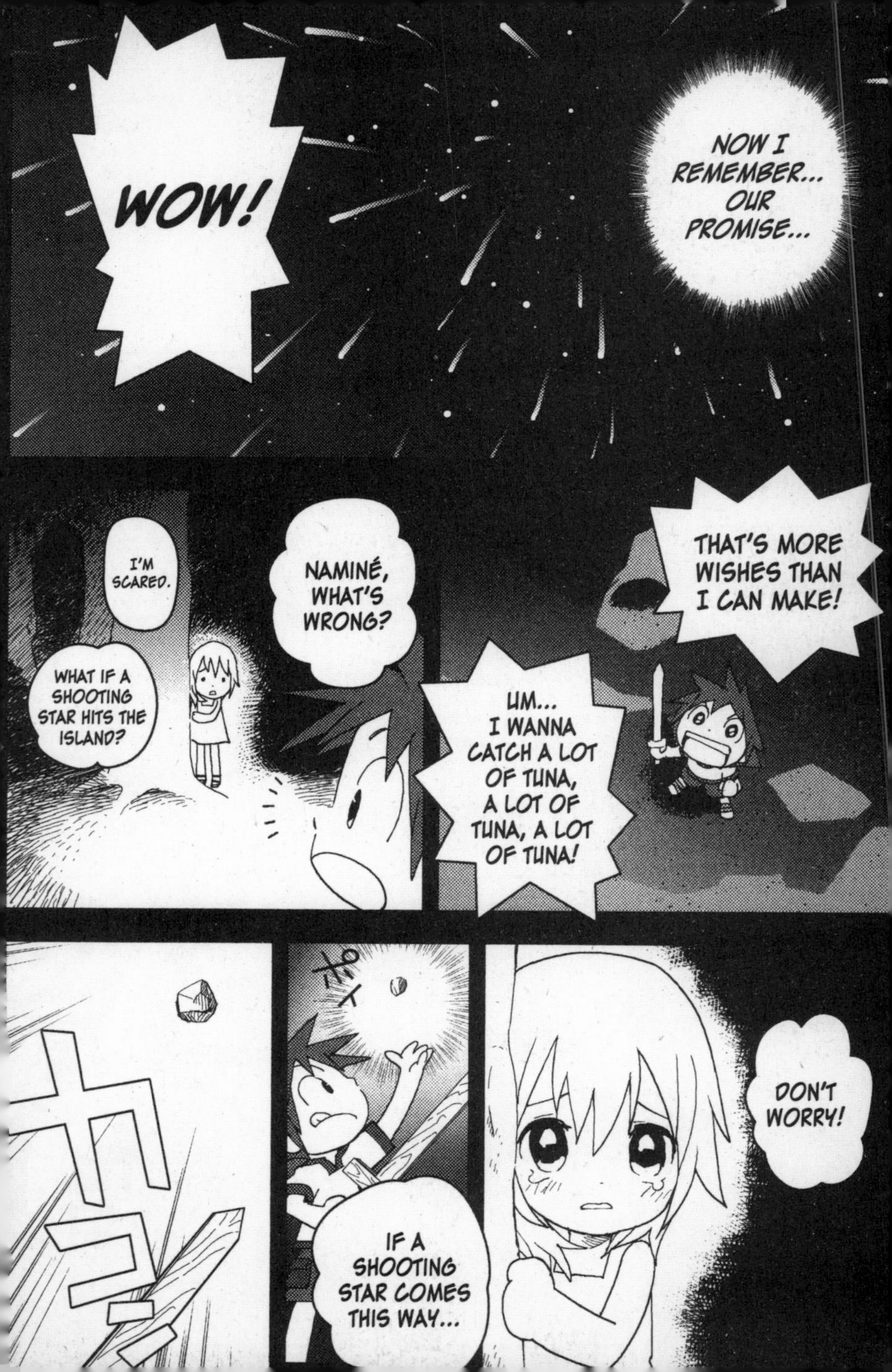
NOW I REMEMBER... OUR PROMISE...
WOW!
THAT'S MORE WISHES THAN I CAN MAKE!
UM... I WANNA CATCH A LOT OF TUNA, A LOT OF TUNA, A LOT OF TUNA!
NAMINÉ, WHAT'S WRONG?
I'M SCARED.
WHAT IF A SHOOTING STAR HITS THE ISLAND?
DON'T WORRY!
IF A SHOOTING STAR COMES THIS WAY...

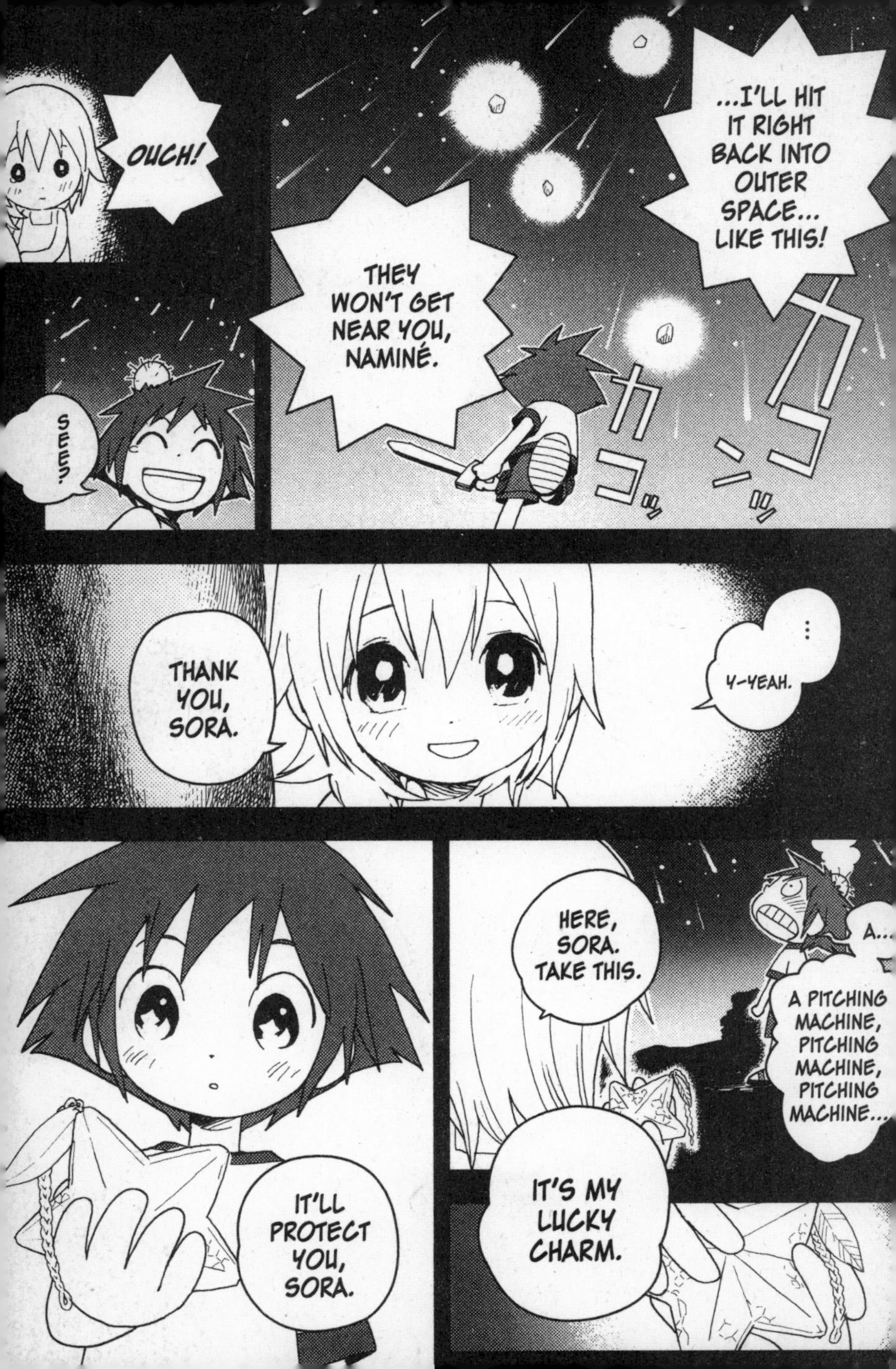
...I'LL HIT IT RIGHT BACK INTO OUTER SPACE... LIKE THIS!
カコーンッ
THEY WON'T GET NEAR YOU, NAMINÉ.
カコッ
OUCH!
SEES?
... Y-YEAH.
THANK YOU, SORA.
A...
A PITCHING MACHINE, PITCHING MACHINE, PITCHING MACHINE...
HERE, SORA. TAKE THIS.
IT'S MY LUCKY CHARM.
IT'LL PROTECT YOU, SORA.

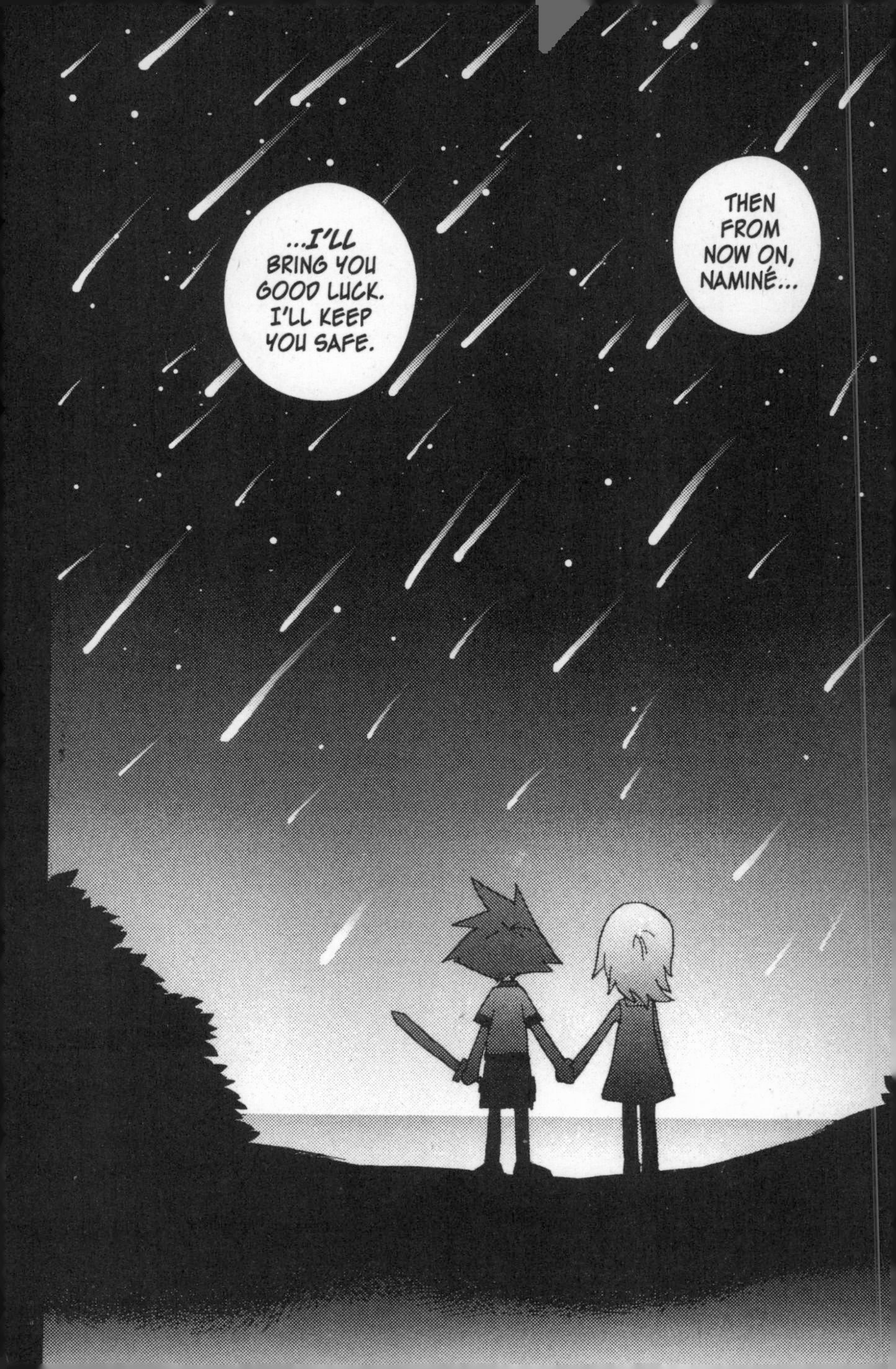
THEN FROM NOW ON, NAMINÉ...
...I'LL BRING YOU GOOD LUCK. I'LL KEEP YOU SAFE.

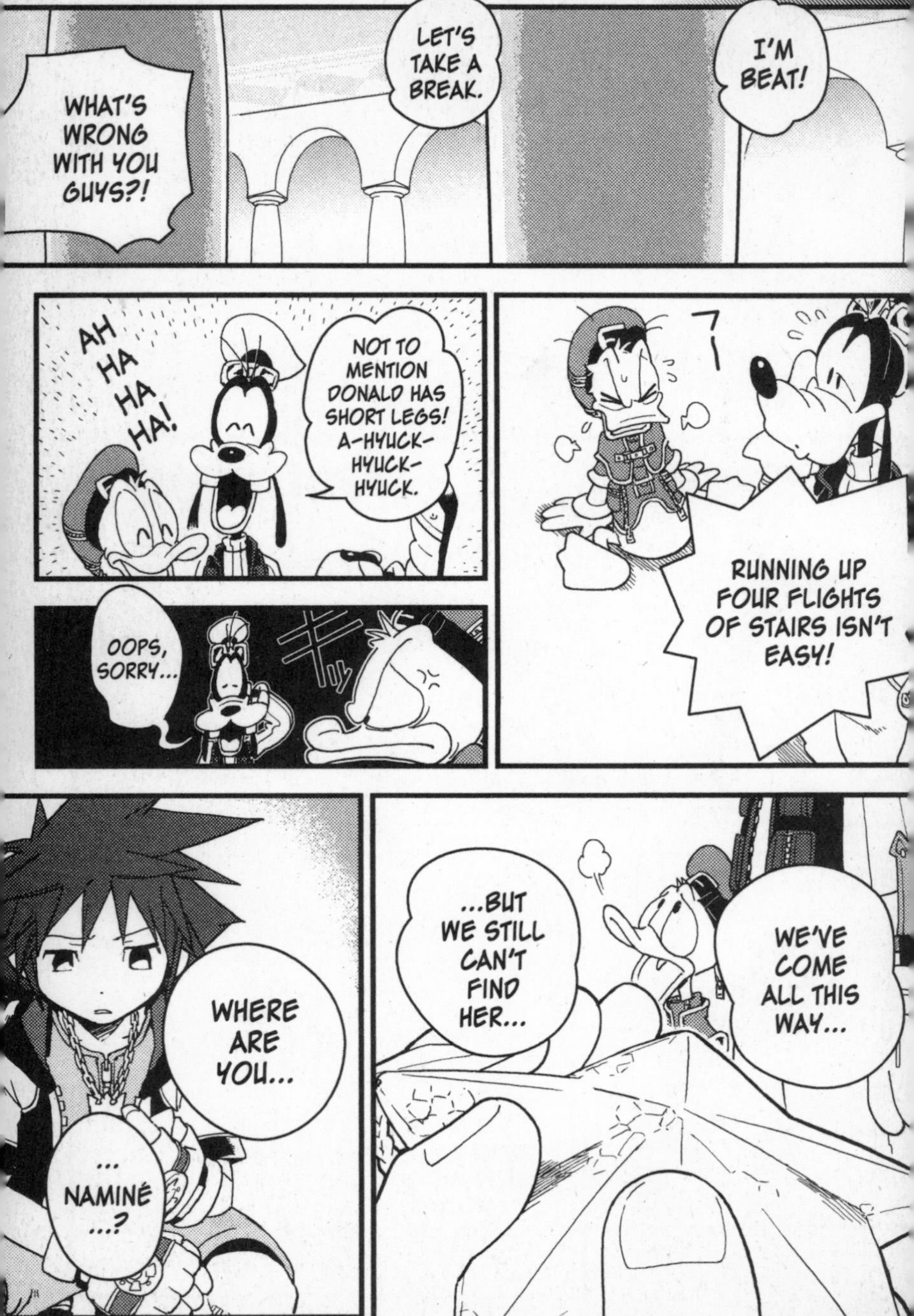
I'M BEAT!
LET'S TAKE A BREAK.
WHAT'S WRONG WITH YOU GUYS?!
RUNNING UP FOUR FLIGHTS OF STAIRS ISN'T EASY!
NOT TO MENTION DONALD HAS SHORT LEGS! A-HYUCK-HYUCK-HYUCK.
AH HA HA HA!
OOPS, SORRY...
WE'VE COME ALL THIS WAY...
...BUT WE STILL CAN'T FIND HER...
WHERE ARE YOU...
... NAMINÉ ...?

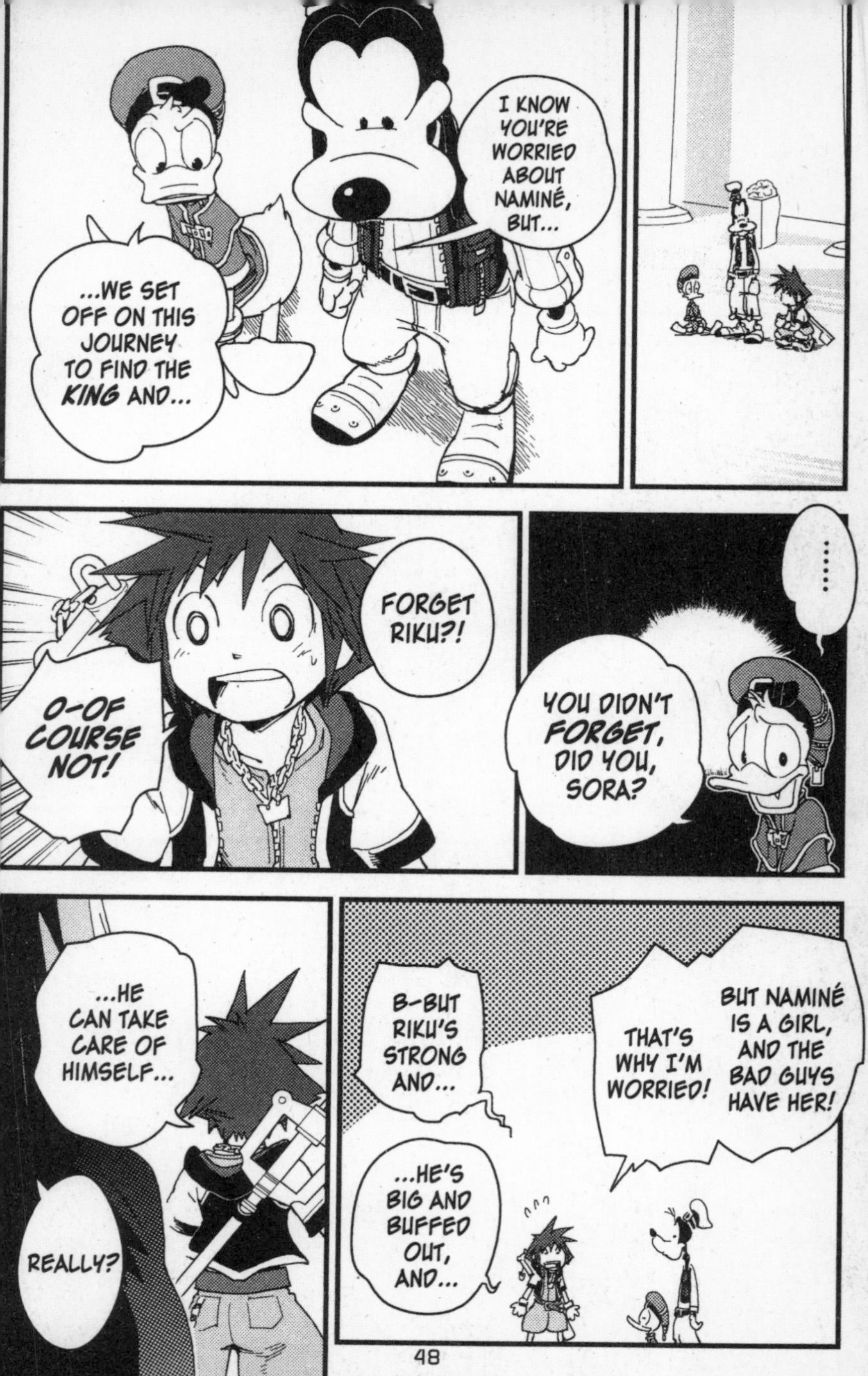
I KNOW YOU'RE WORRIED ABOUT NAMINÉ, BUT...
...WE SET OFF ON THIS JOURNEY TO FIND THE KING AND...
......
YOU DIDN'T FORGET, DID YOU, SORA?
FORGET RIKU?!
O-OF COURSE NOT!
BUT NAMINÉ IS A GIRL, AND THE BAD GUYS HAVE HER!
THAT'S WHY I'M WORRIED!
B-BUT RIKU'S STRONG AND...
...HE'S BIG AND BUFFED OUT, AND...
...HE CAN TAKE CARE OF HIMSELF...
REALLY?

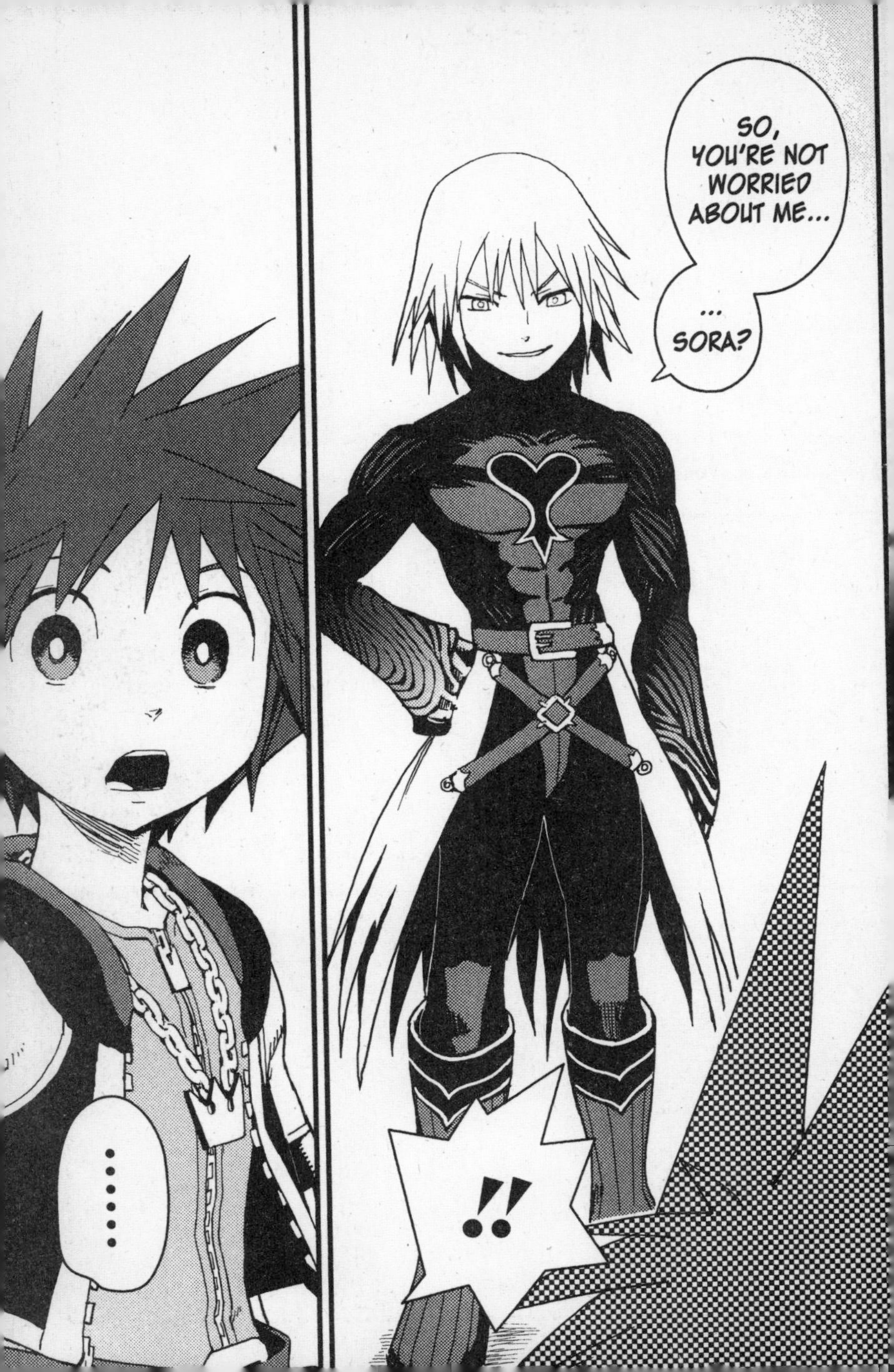
SO, YOU'RE NOT WORRIED ABOUT ME...
... SORA?
!!
......

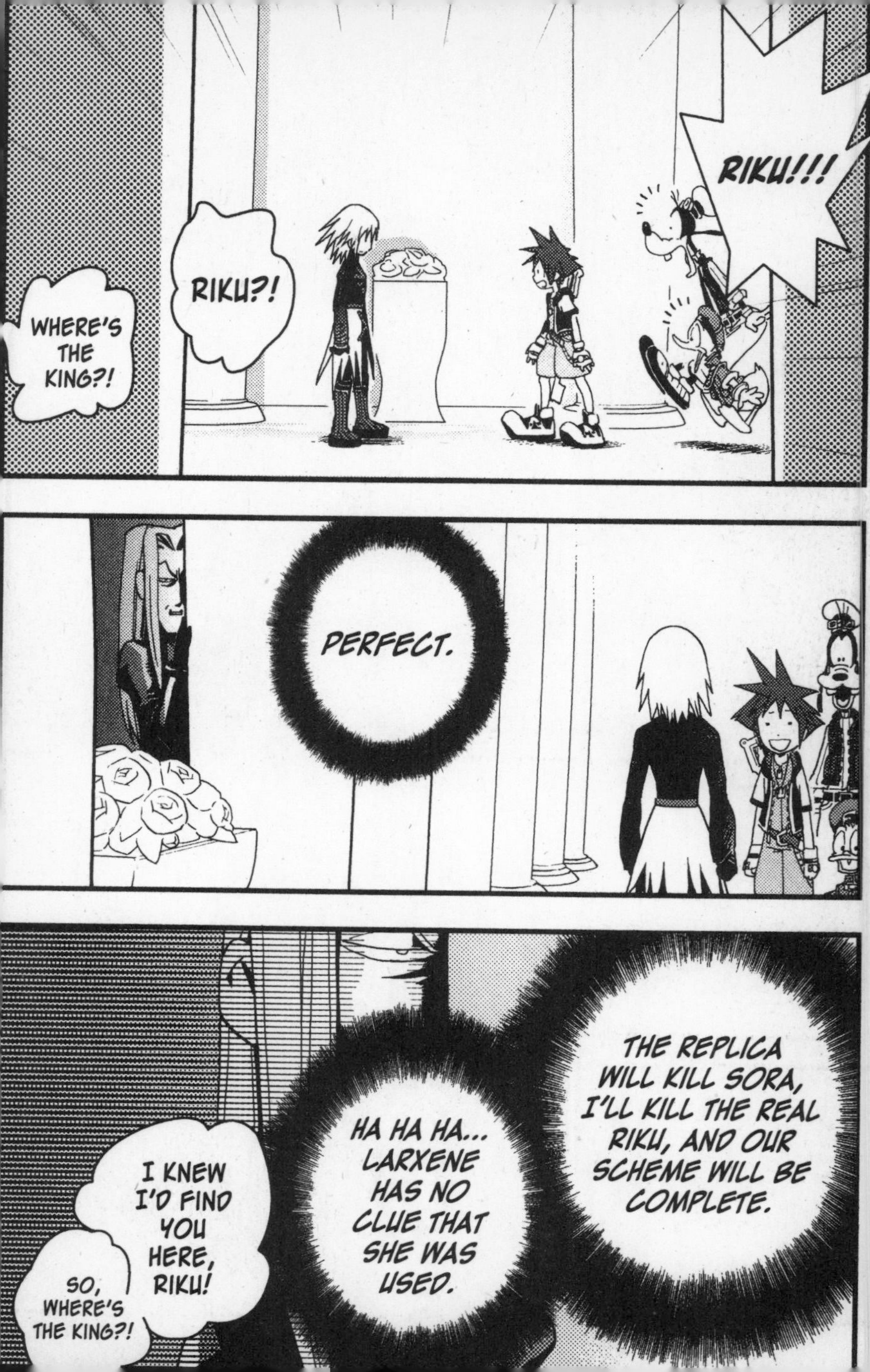
RIKU!!!
RIKU?!
WHERE'S THE KING?!
PERFECT.
THE REPLICA WILL KILL SORA, I'LL KILL THE REAL RIKU, AND OUR SCHEME WILL BE COMPLETE.
HA HA HA... LARXENE HAS NO CLUE THAT SHE WAS USED.
I KNEW I'D FIND YOU HERE, RIKU!
SO, WHERE'S THE KING?!

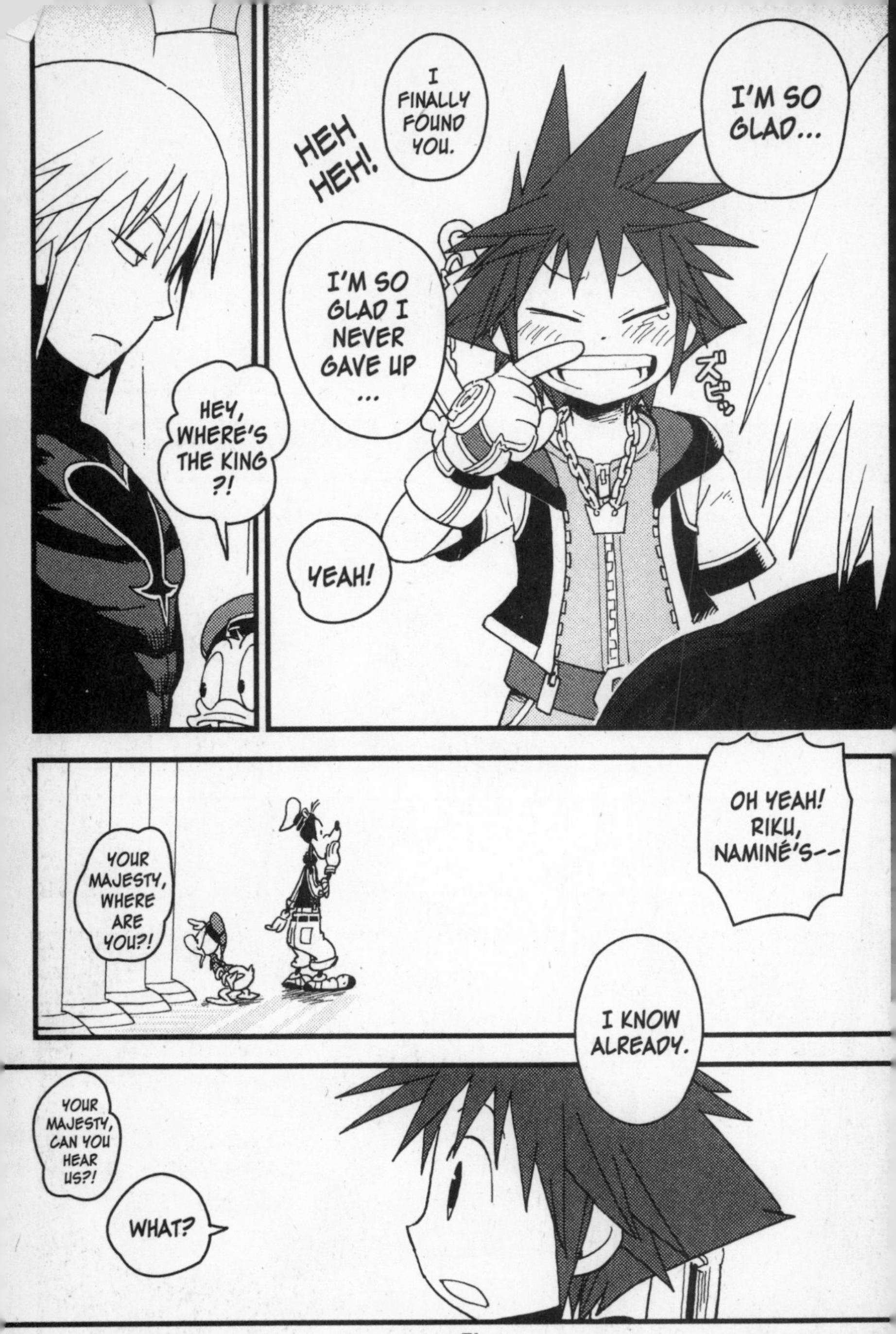
I'M SO GLAD...
I FINALLY FOUND YOU.
HEH HEH!
I'M SO GLAD I NEVER GAVE UP ...
YEAH!
HEY, WHERE'S THE KING ?!
OH YEAH! RIKU, NAMINÉ'S--
YOUR MAJESTY, WHERE ARE YOU?!
I KNOW ALREADY.
YOUR MAJESTY, CAN YOU HEAR US?!
WHAT?

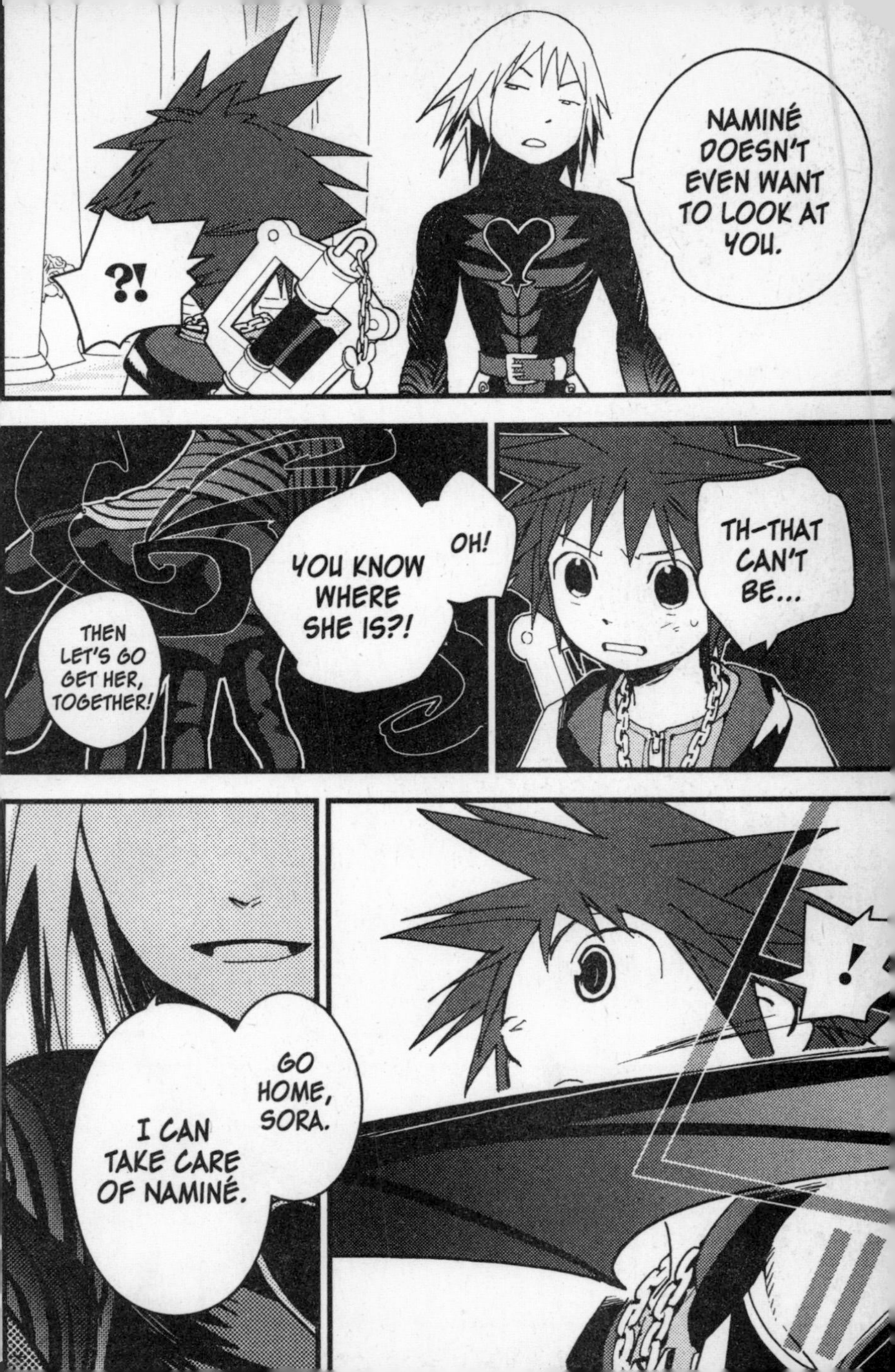
NAMINÉ DOESN'T EVEN WANT TO LOOK AT YOU.
?!
TH-THAT CAN'T BE...
OH!
YOU KNOW WHERE SHE IS?!
THEN LET'S GO GET HER, TOGETHER!
!
GO HOME, SORA.
I CAN TAKE CARE OF NAMINÉ.

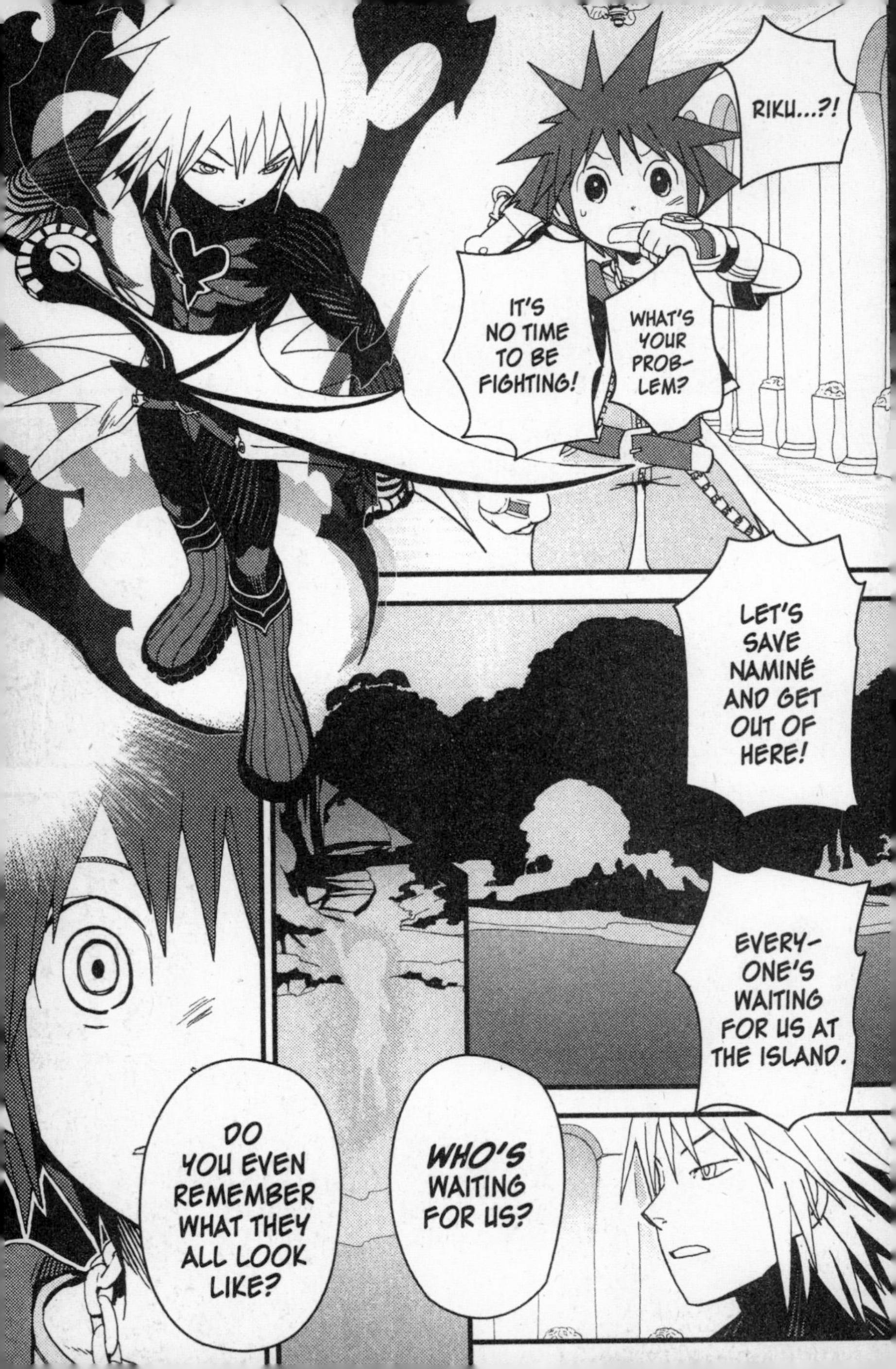
RIKU...?!
WHAT'S YOUR PROB-LEM?
IT'S NO TIME TO BE FIGHTING!
LET'S SAVE NAMINÉ AND GET OUT OF HERE!
EVERY-ONE'S WAITING FOR US AT THE ISLAND.
WHO'S WAITING FOR US?
DO YOU EVEN REMEMBER WHAT THEY ALL LOOK LIKE?

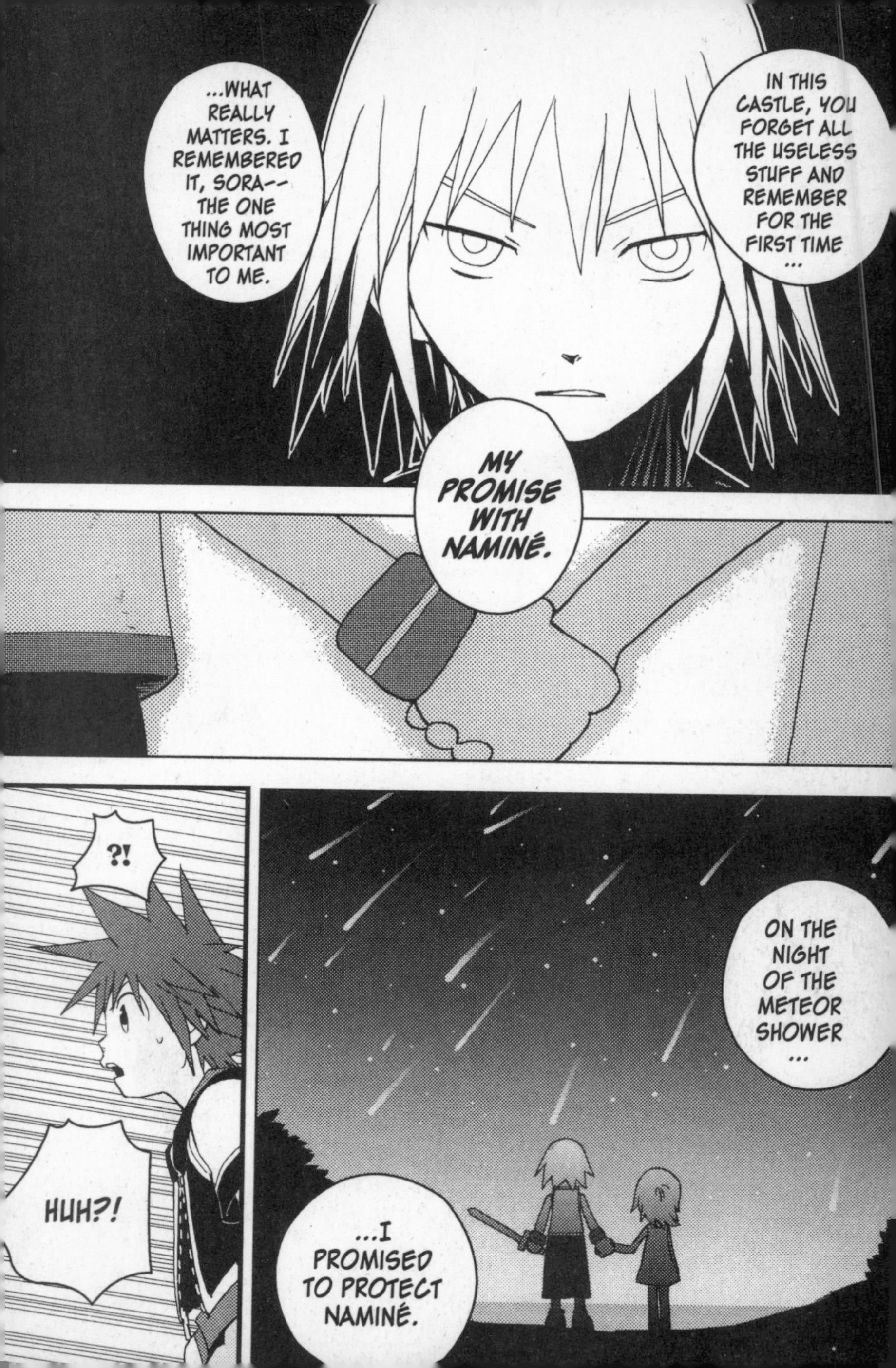
IN THIS CASTLE, YOU FORGET ALL THE USELESS STUFF AND REMEMBER FOR THE FIRST TIME ...
...WHAT REALLY MATTERS. I REMEMBERED IT, SORA-- THE ONE THING MOST IMPORTANT TO ME.
MY PROMISE WITH NAMINÉ.
ON THE NIGHT OF THE METEOR SHOWER ...
...I PROMISED TO PROTECT NAMINÉ.
?!
HUH?!

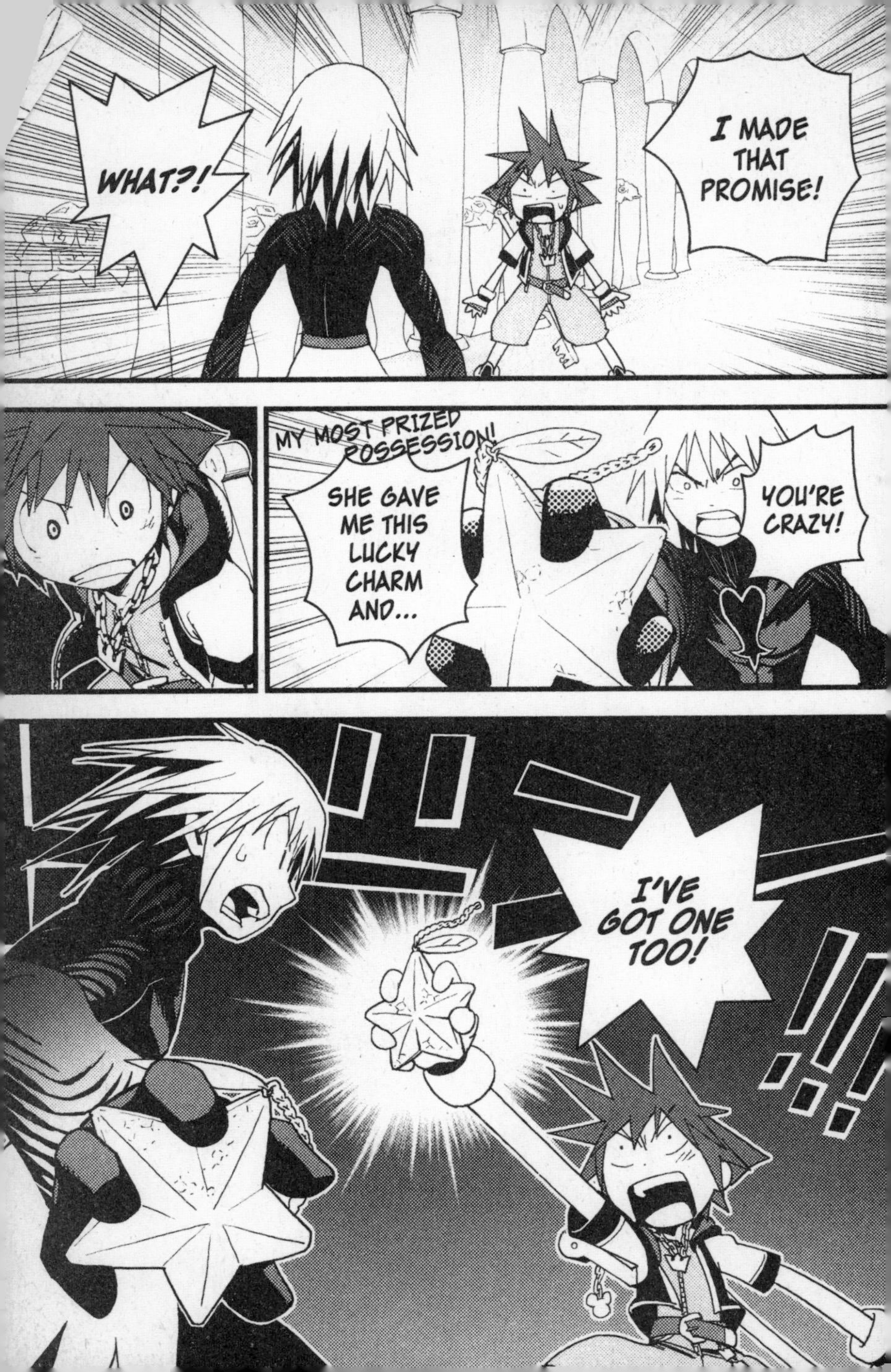
I MADE THAT PROMISE!
WHAT?!
YOU'RE CRAZY!
SHE GAVE ME THIS LUCKY CHARM AND...
MY MOST PRIZED POSSESSION!
I'VE GOT ONE TOO!

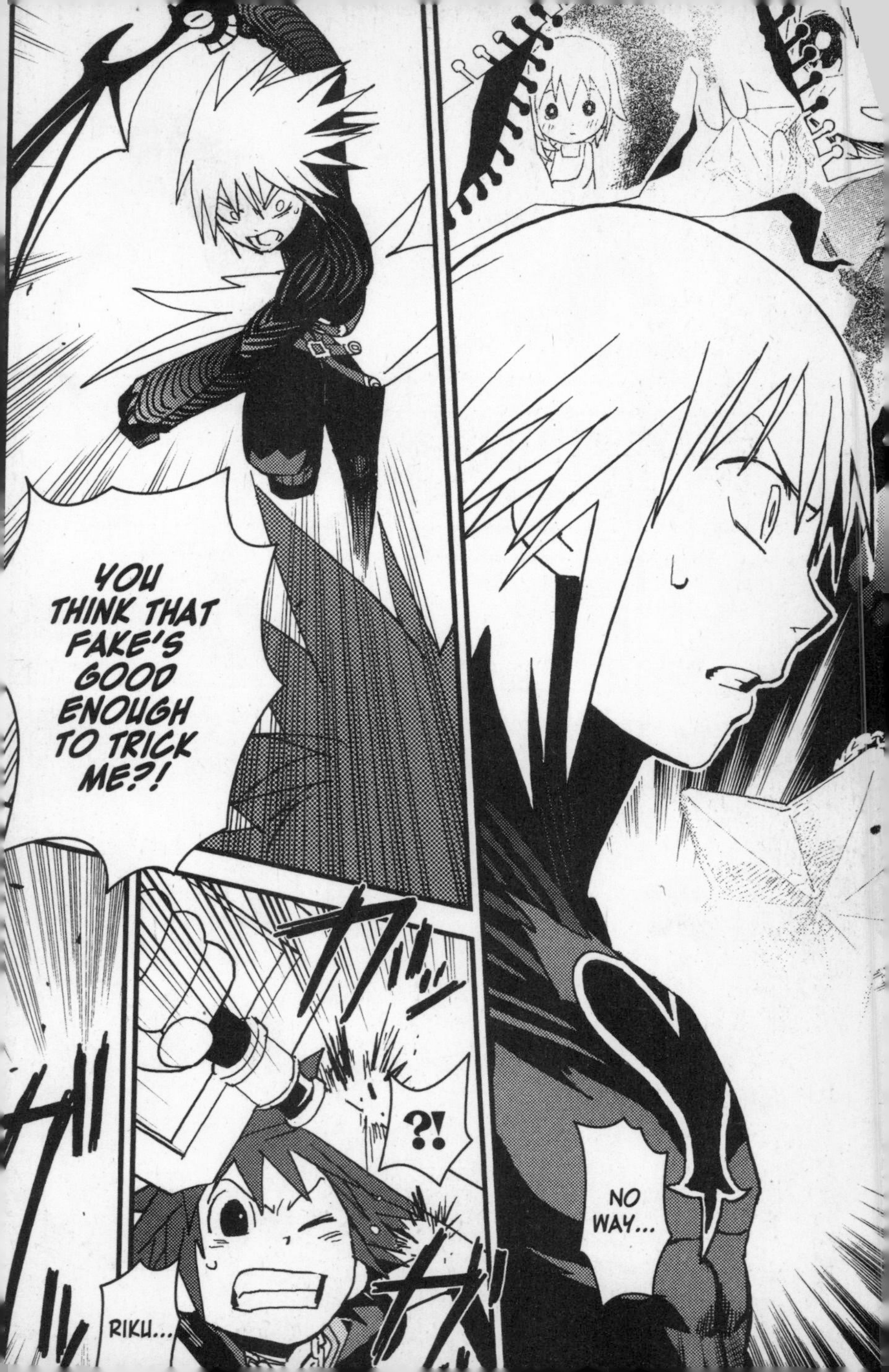
NO WAY...
YOU THINK THAT FAKE'S GOOD ENOUGH TO TRICK ME?!
?!
RIKU...

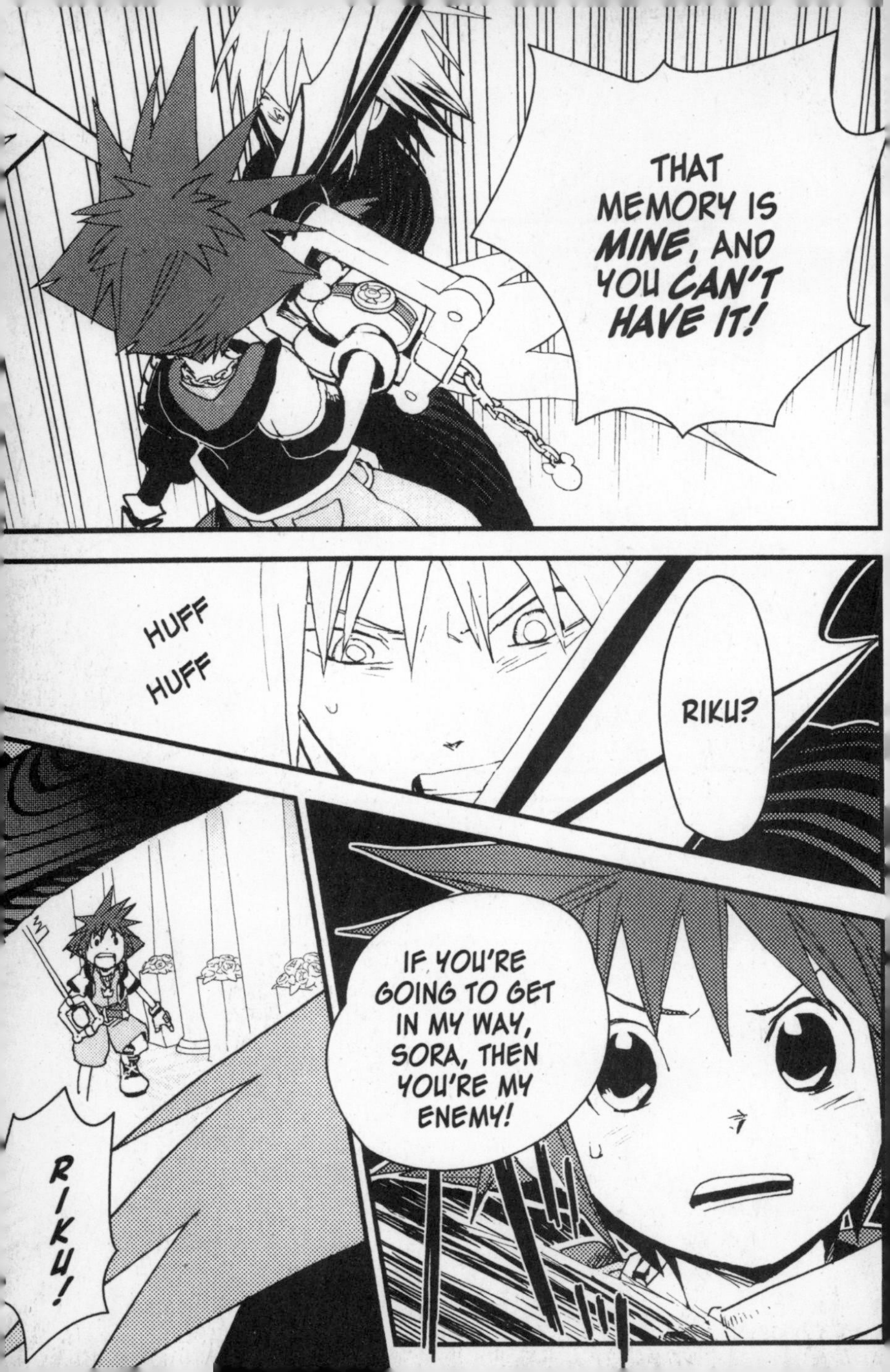
THAT MEMORY IS MINE, AND YOU CAN'T HAVE IT!
HUFF HUFF
RIKU?
IF YOU'RE GOING TO GET IN MY WAY, SORA, THEN YOU'RE MY ENEMY!
RIKU!

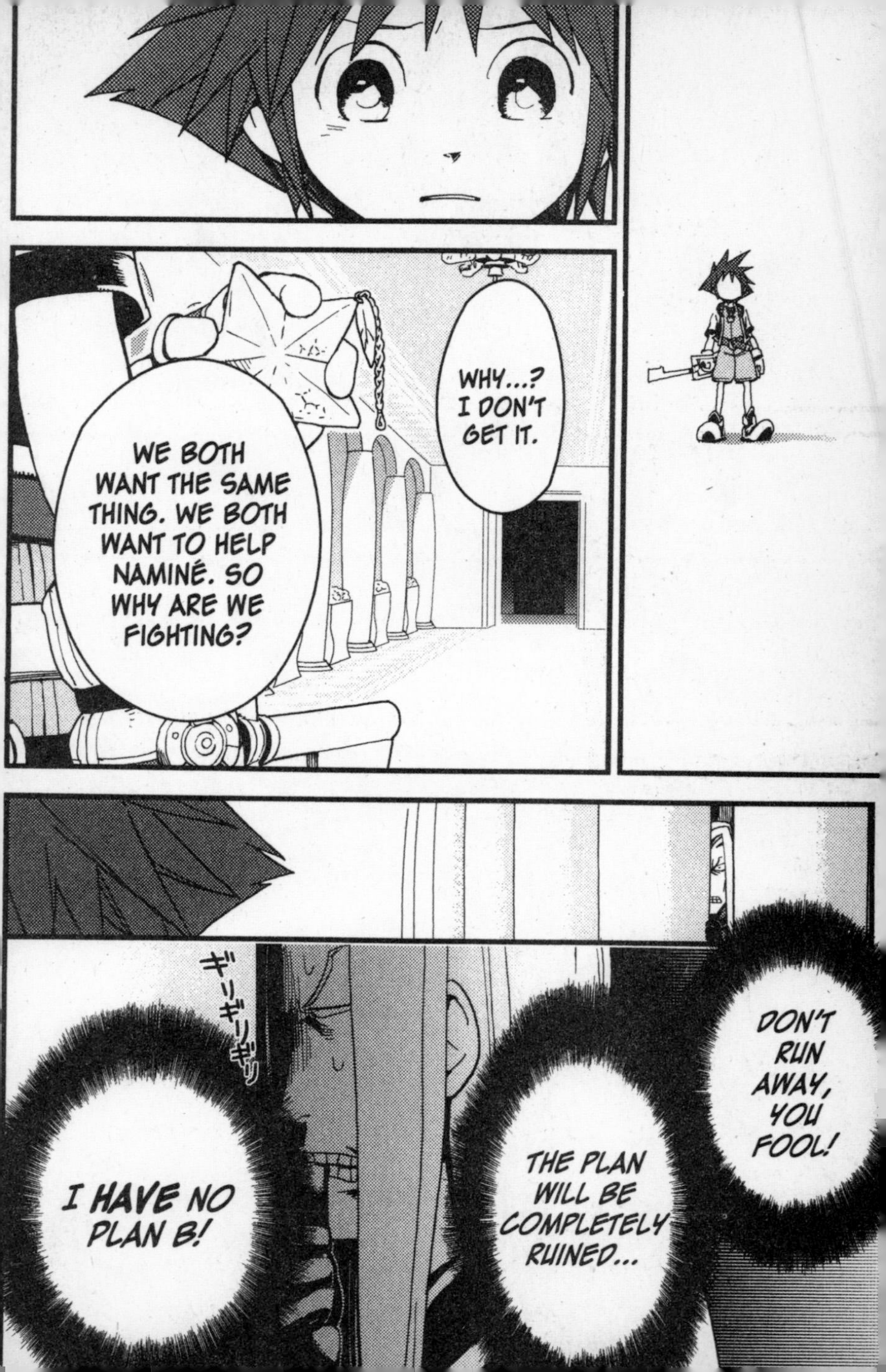
WHY...? I DON'T GET IT.
WE BOTH WANT THE SAME THING. WE BOTH WANT TO HELP NAMINÉ. SO WHY ARE WE FIGHTING?
DON'T RUN AWAY, YOU FOOL!
THE PLAN WILL BE COMPLETELY RUINED...
ギリギリギリ
I **HAVE** NO PLAN B!

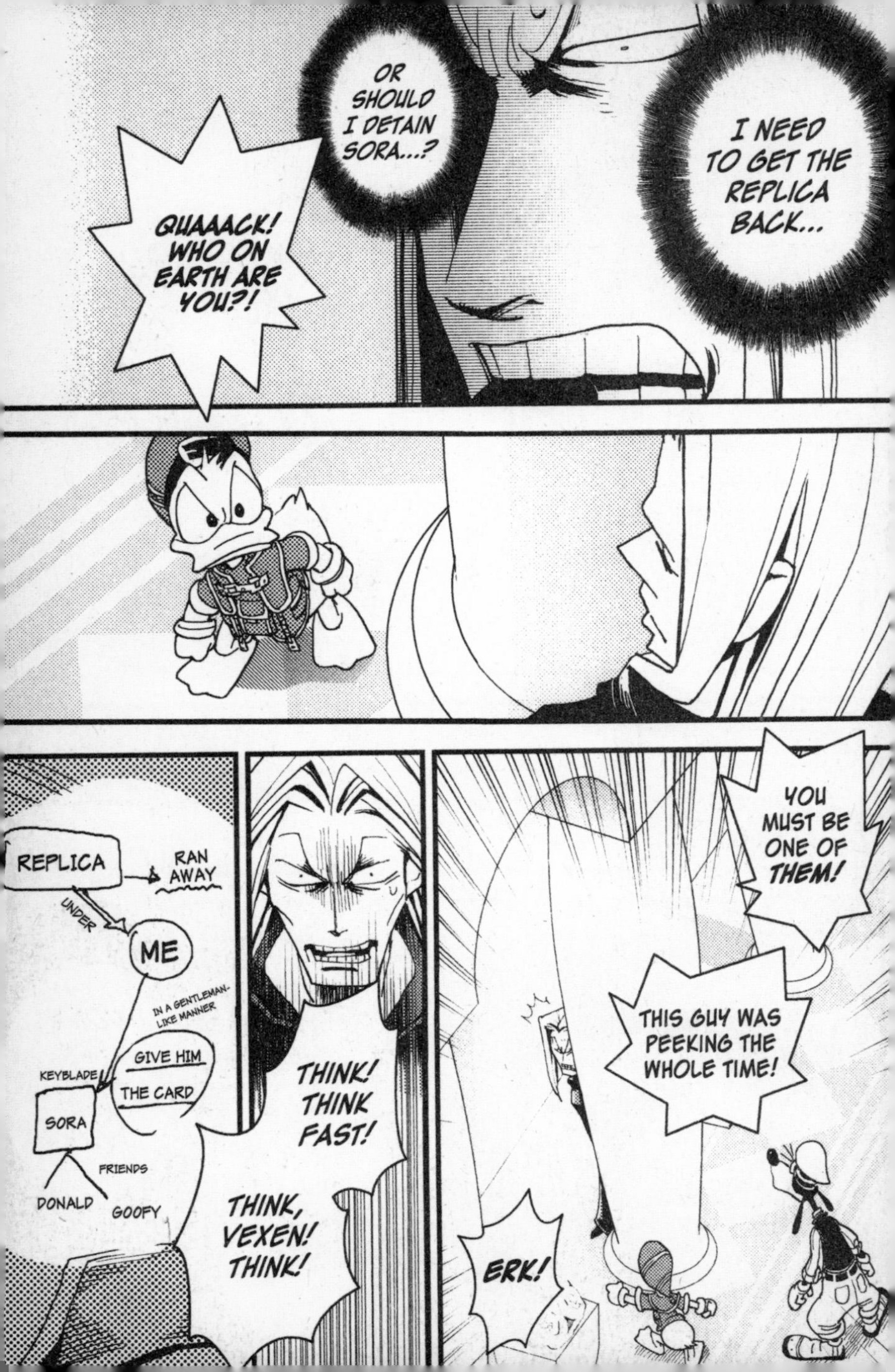
I NEED TO GET THE REPLICA BACK...
OR SHOULD I DETAIN SORA...?
QUAAACK! WHO ON EARTH ARE YOU?!
YOU MUST BE ONE OF THEM!
THIS GUY WAS PEEKING THE WHOLE TIME!
ERK!
THINK! THINK FAST!
THINK, VEXEN! THINK!
REPLICA
RAN AWAY
UNDER
ME
IN A GENTLEMAN-LIKE MANNER
GIVE HIM
THE CARD
KEYBLADE
SORA
FRIENDS
DONALD
GOOFY

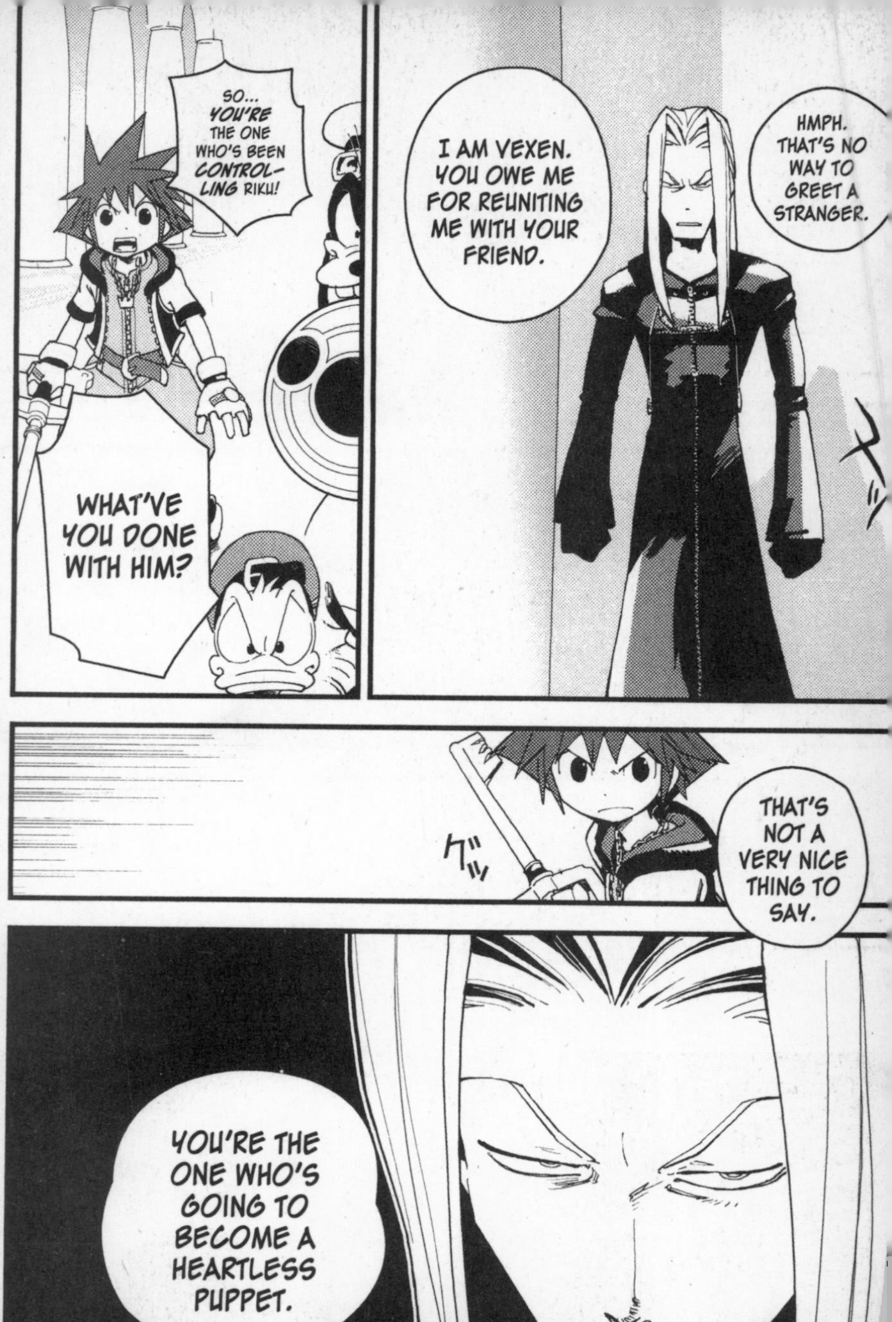
HMPH. THAT'S NO WAY TO GREET A STRANGER.
I AM VEXEN. YOU OWE ME FOR REUNITING ME WITH YOUR FRIEND.
SO... YOU'RE THE ONE WHO'S BEEN CONTROL-LING RIKU!
WHAT'VE YOU DONE WITH HIM?
THAT'S NOT A VERY NICE THING TO SAY.
YOU'RE THE ONE WHO'S GOING TO BECOME A HEARTLESS PUPPET.

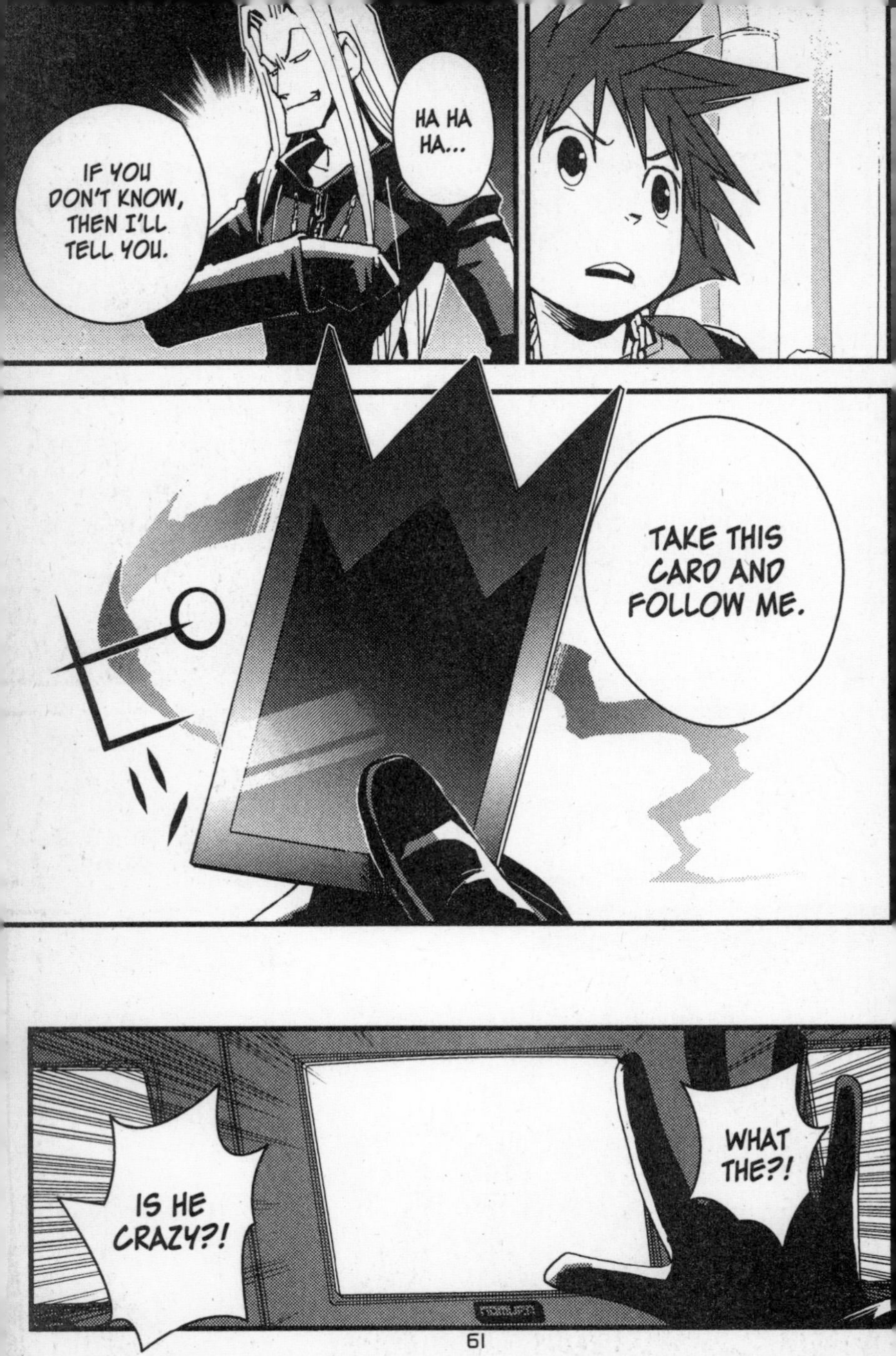
HA HA HA...
IF YOU DON'T KNOW, THEN I'LL TELL YOU.
TAKE THIS CARD AND FOLLOW ME.
WHAT THE?!
IS HE CRAZY?!

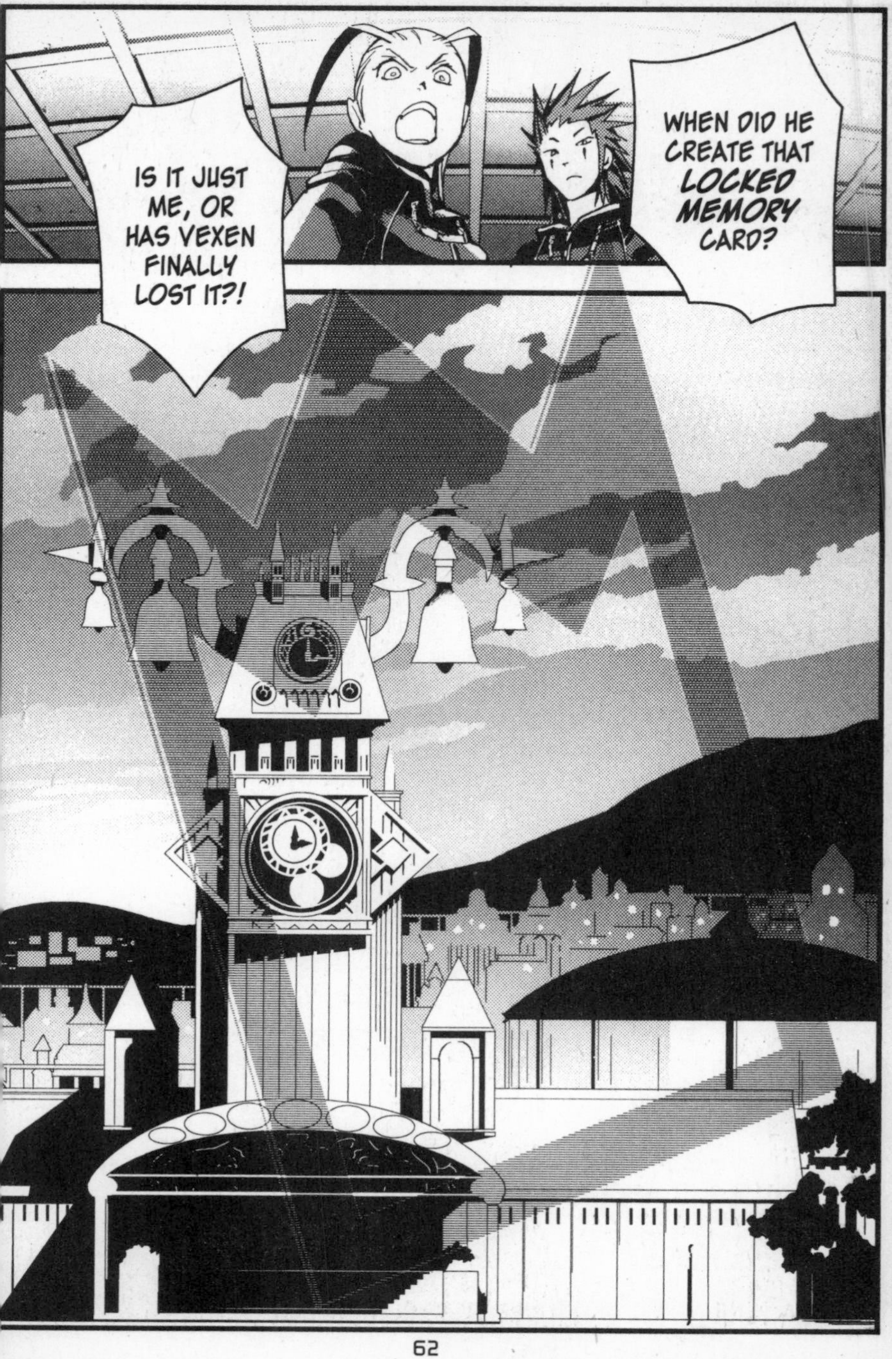
WHEN DID HE CREATE THAT *LOCKED MEMORY* CARD?
IS IT JUST ME, OR HAS VEXEN FINALLY LOST IT?!

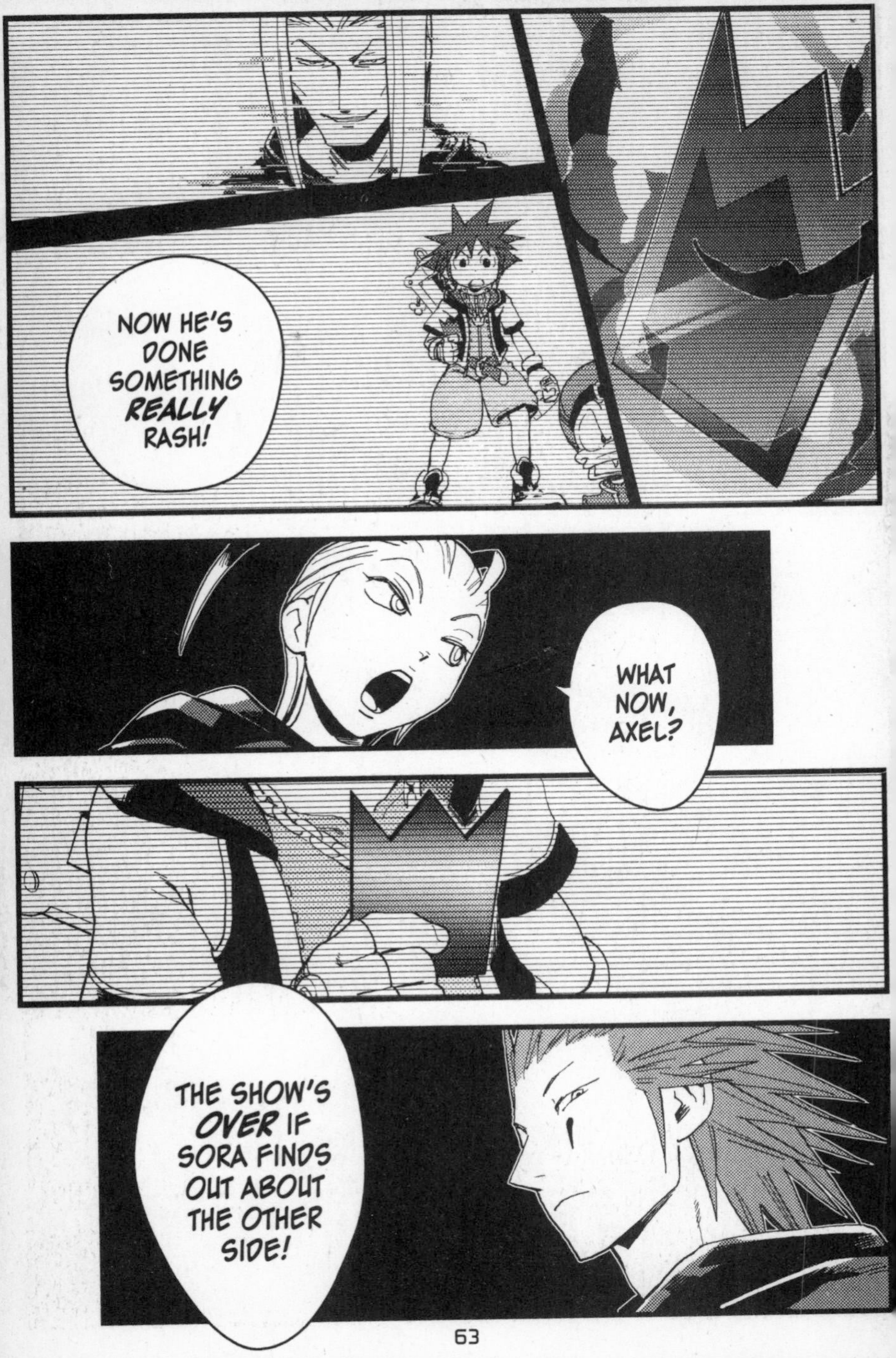
NOW HE'S DONE SOMETHING REALLY RASH!
WHAT NOW, AXEL?
THE SHOW'S OVER IF SORA FINDS OUT ABOUT THE OTHER SIDE!

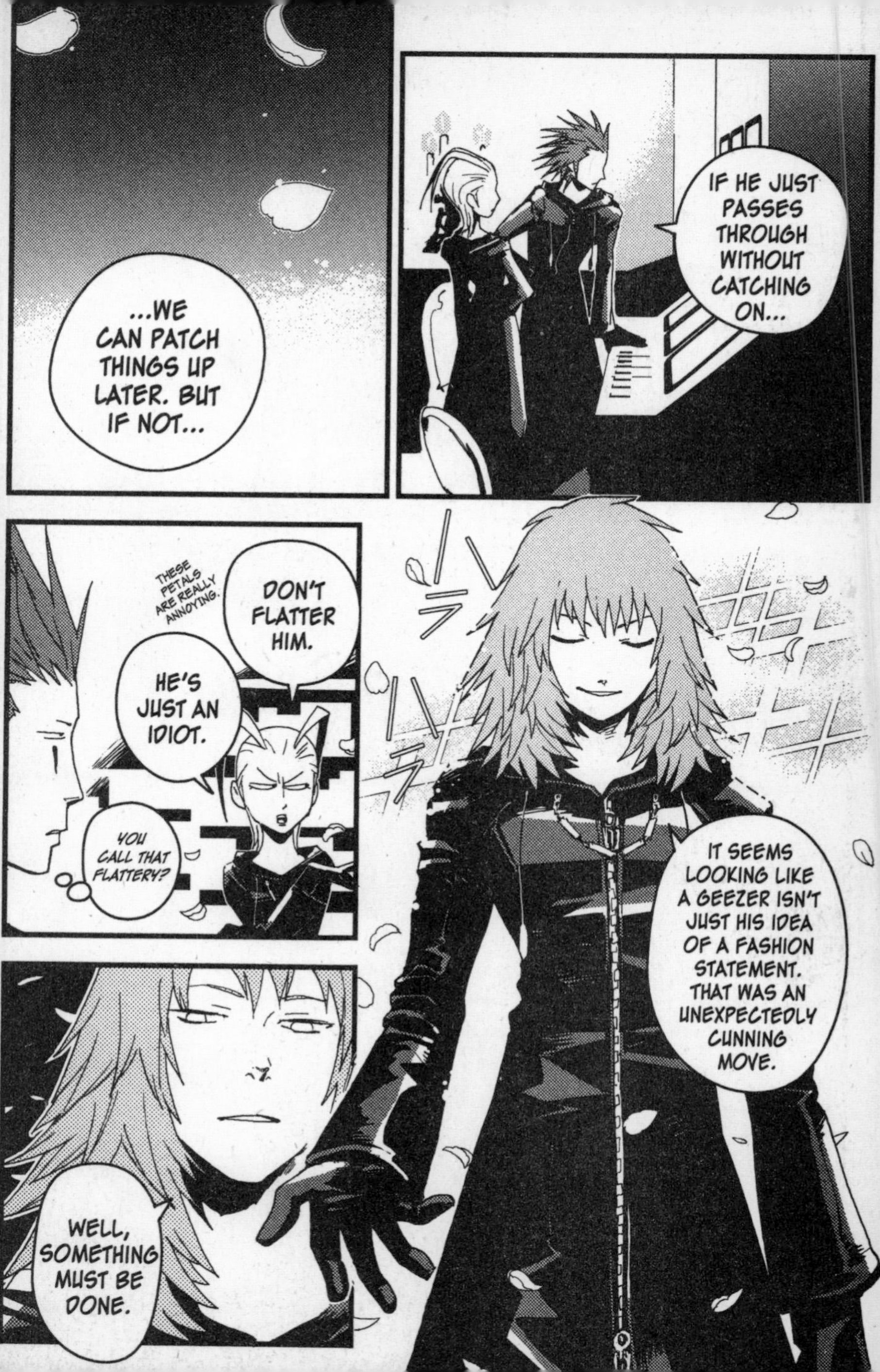
IF HE JUST PASSES THROUGH WITHOUT CATCHING ON...
...WE CAN PATCH THINGS UP LATER. BUT IF NOT...
IT SEEMS LOOKING LIKE A GEEZER ISN'T JUST HIS IDEA OF A FASHION STATEMENT. THAT WAS AN UNEXPECTEDLY CUNNING MOVE.
DON'T FLATTER HIM.
THESE PETALS ARE REALLY ANNOYING.
HE'S JUST AN IDIOT.
YOU CALL THAT FLATTERY?
WELL, SOMETHING MUST BE DONE.

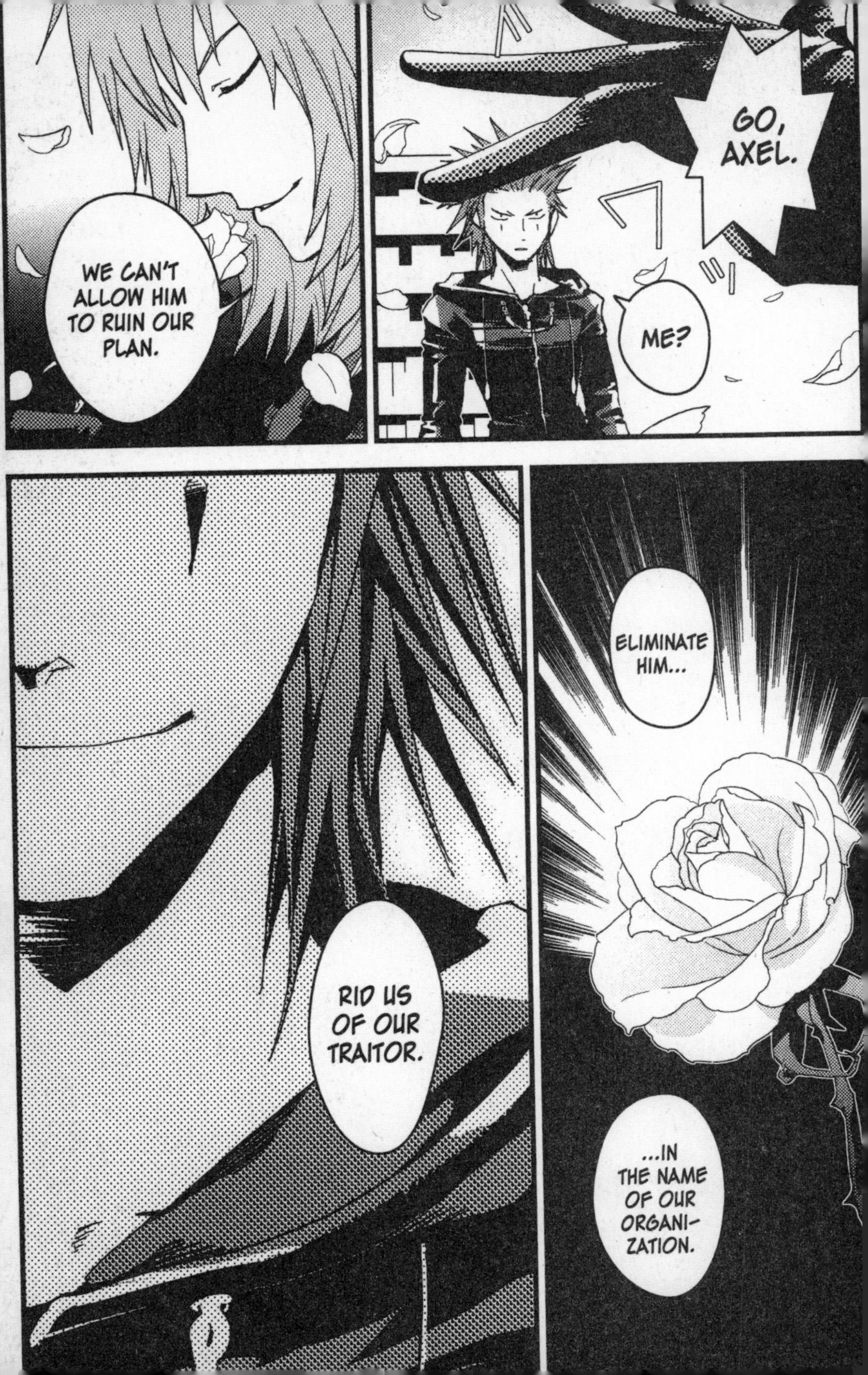
GO, AXEL.
ME?
WE CAN'T ALLOW HIM TO RUIN OUR PLAN.
ELIMINATE HIM...
...IN THE NAME OF OUR ORGANI-ZATION.
RID US OF OUR TRAITOR.

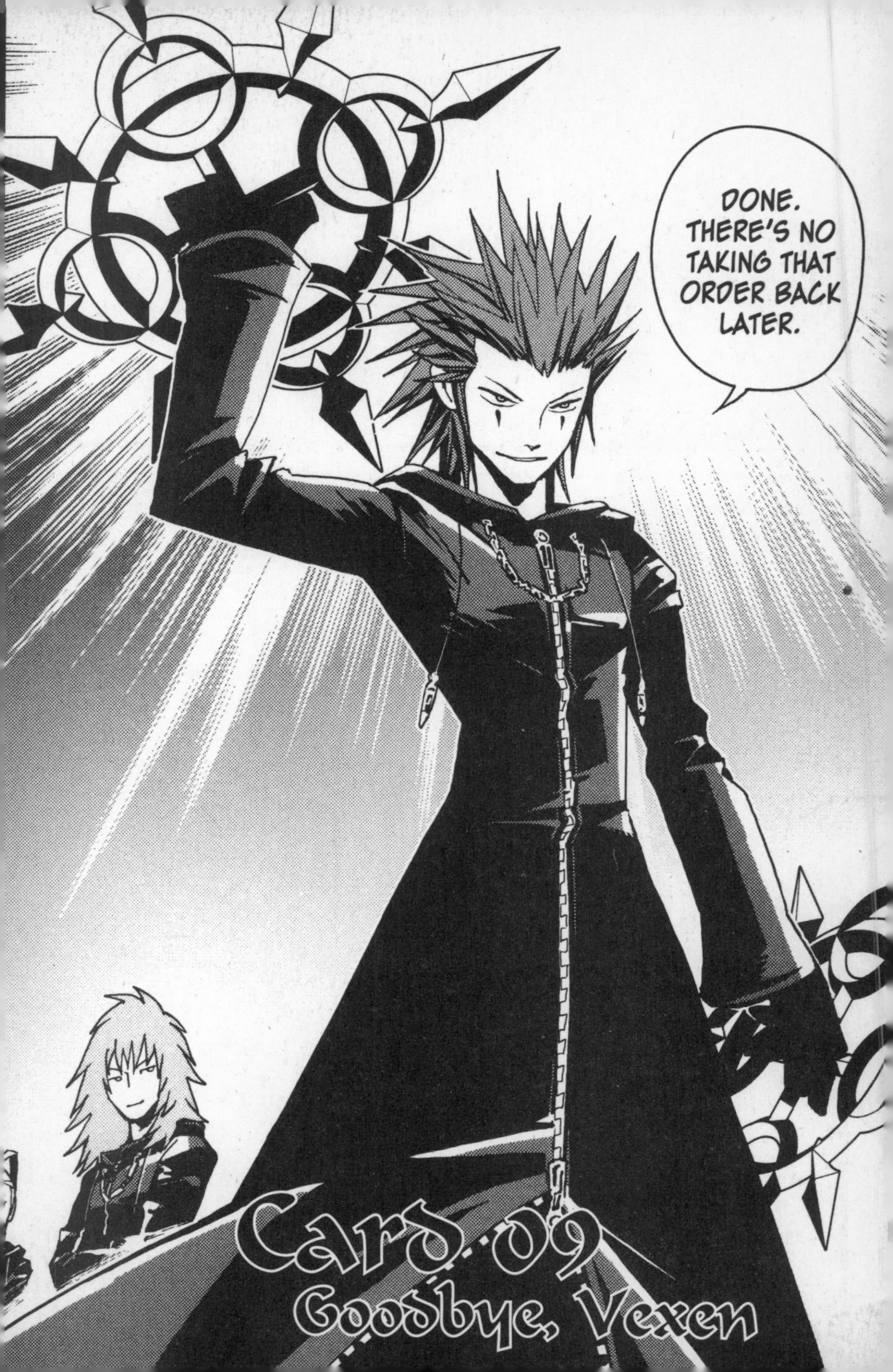
DONE. THERE'S NO TAKING THAT ORDER BACK LATER.
Card 09
Goodbye, Vexen

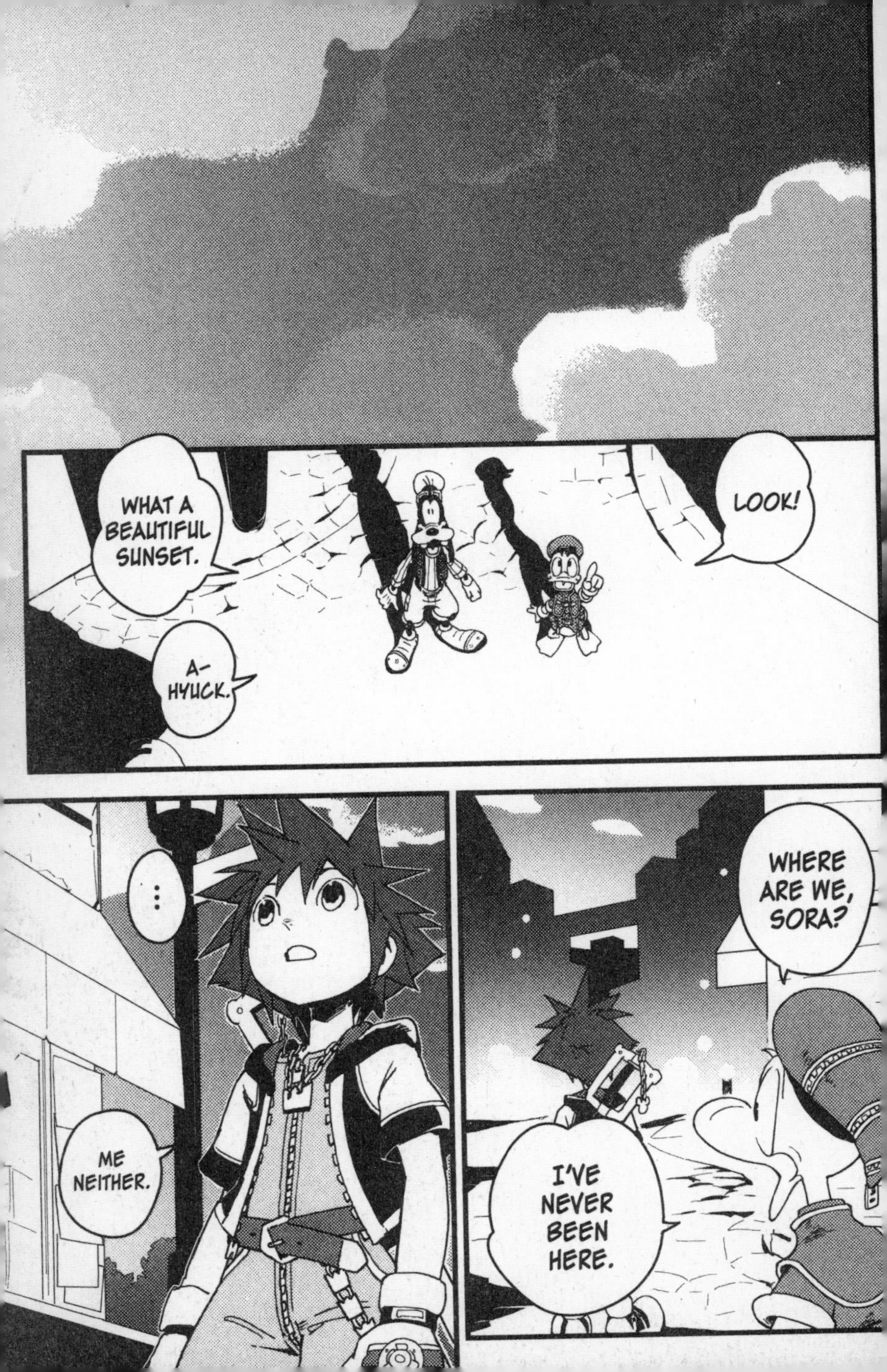
LOOK!
WHAT A BEAUTIFUL SUNSET.
A-HYUCK.
WHERE ARE WE, SORA?
I'VE NEVER BEEN HERE.
...
ME NEITHER.

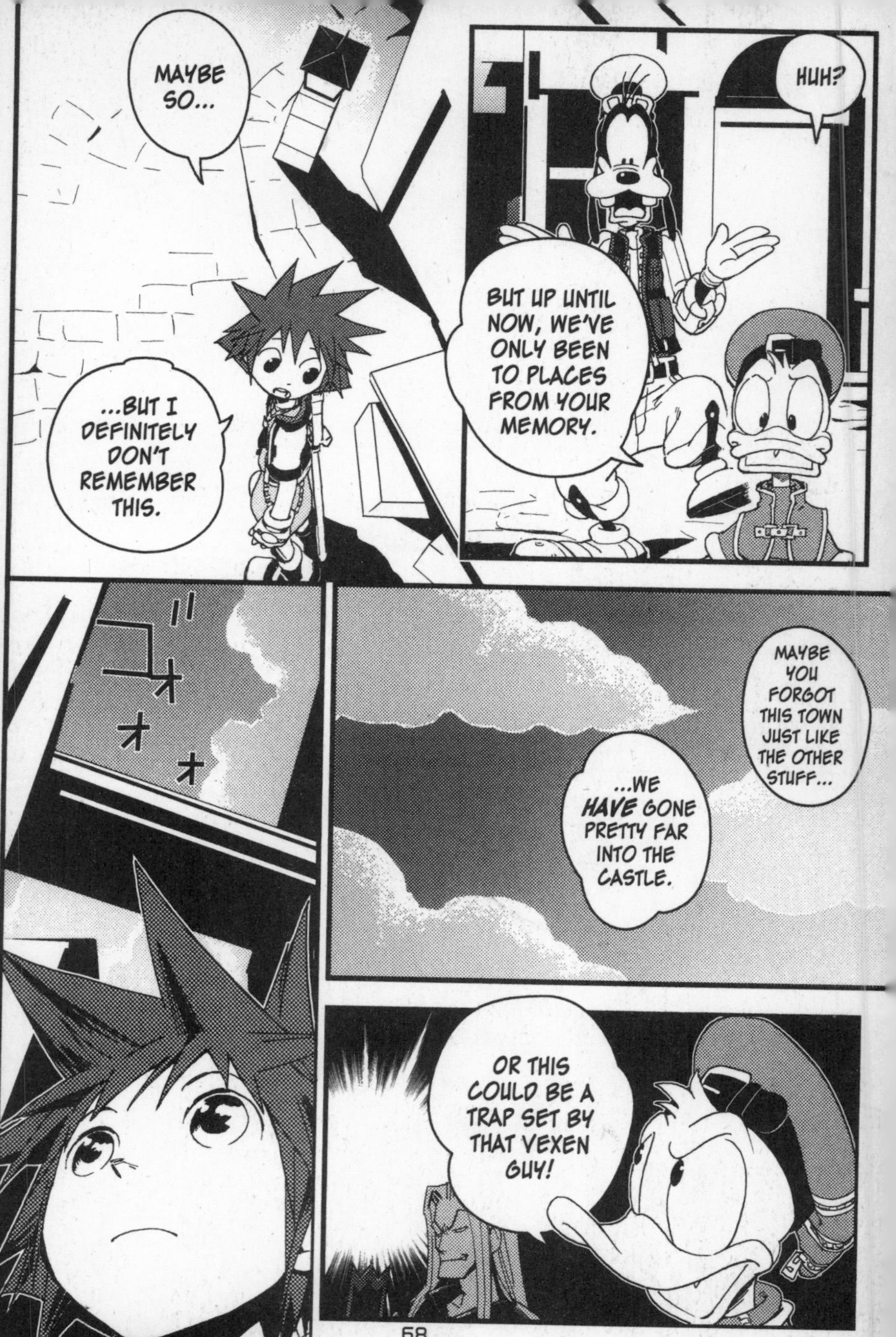
HUH?
BUT UP UNTIL NOW, WE'VE ONLY BEEN TO PLACES FROM YOUR MEMORY.
MAYBE SO...
...BUT I DEFINITELY DON'T REMEMBER THIS.
MAYBE YOU FORGOT THIS TOWN JUST LIKE THE OTHER STUFF...
...WE HAVE GONE PRETTY FAR INTO THE CASTLE.
OR THIS COULD BE A TRAP SET BY THAT VEXEN GUY!
ゴオオオ

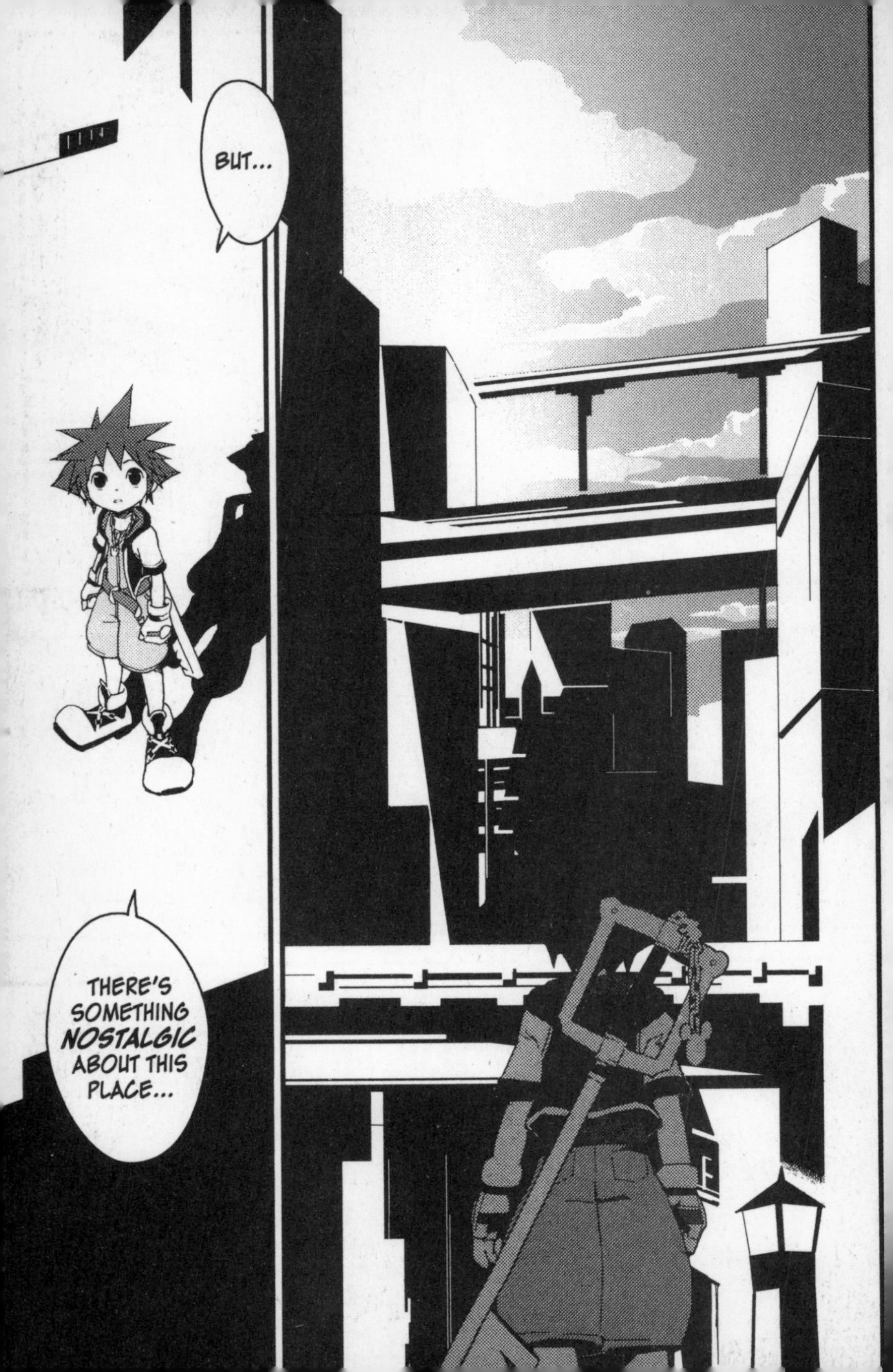
BUT...
THERE'S SOMETHING NOSTALGIC ABOUT THIS PLACE...

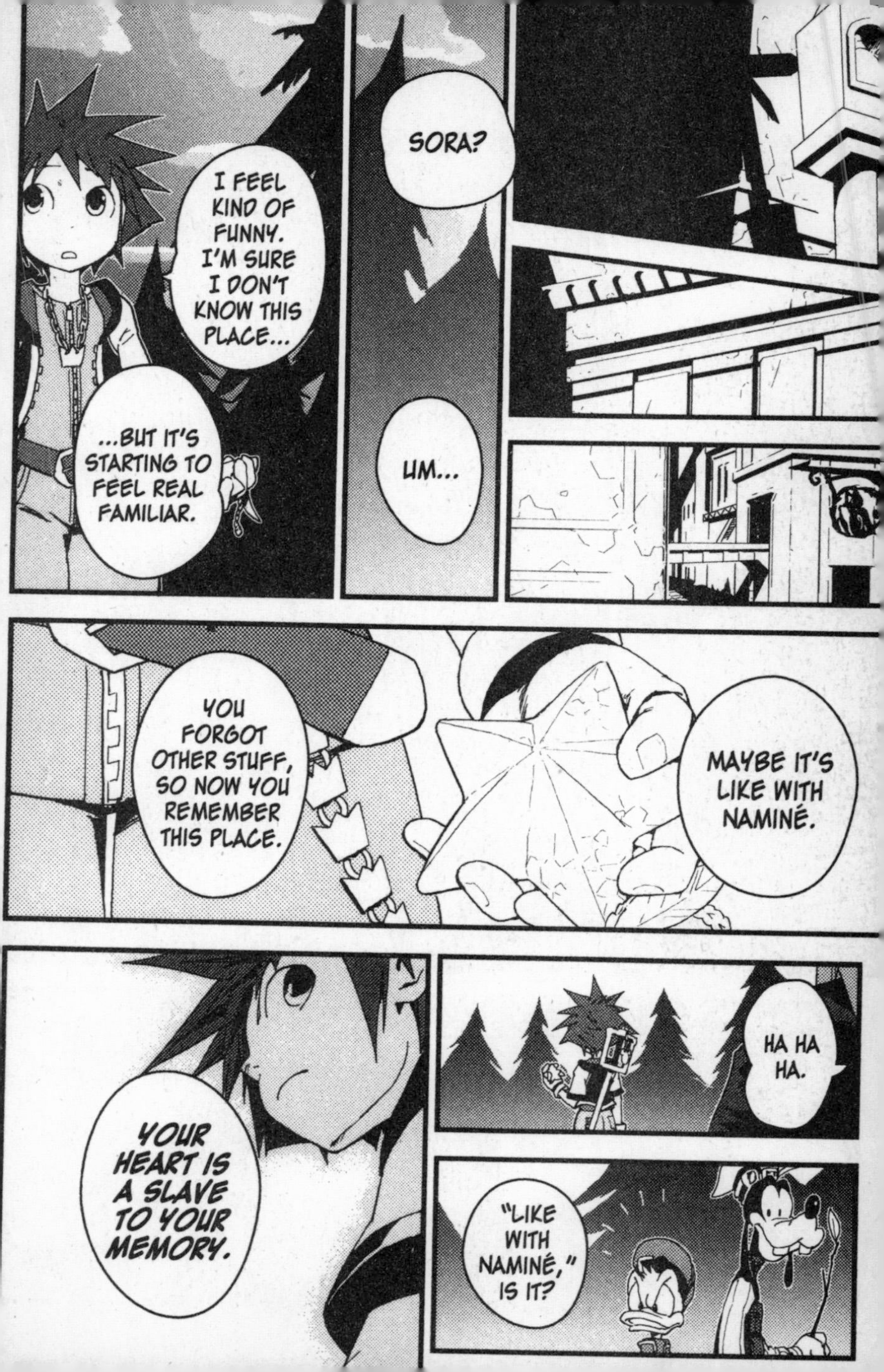
SORA?
UM...
I FEEL KIND OF FUNNY. I'M SURE I DON'T KNOW THIS PLACE...
...BUT IT'S STARTING TO FEEL REAL FAMILIAR.
MAYBE IT'S LIKE WITH NAMINÉ.
YOU FORGOT OTHER STUFF, SO NOW YOU REMEMBER THIS PLACE.
HA HA HA.
"LIKE WITH NAMINÉ," IS IT?
YOUR HEART IS A SLAVE TO YOUR MEMORY.

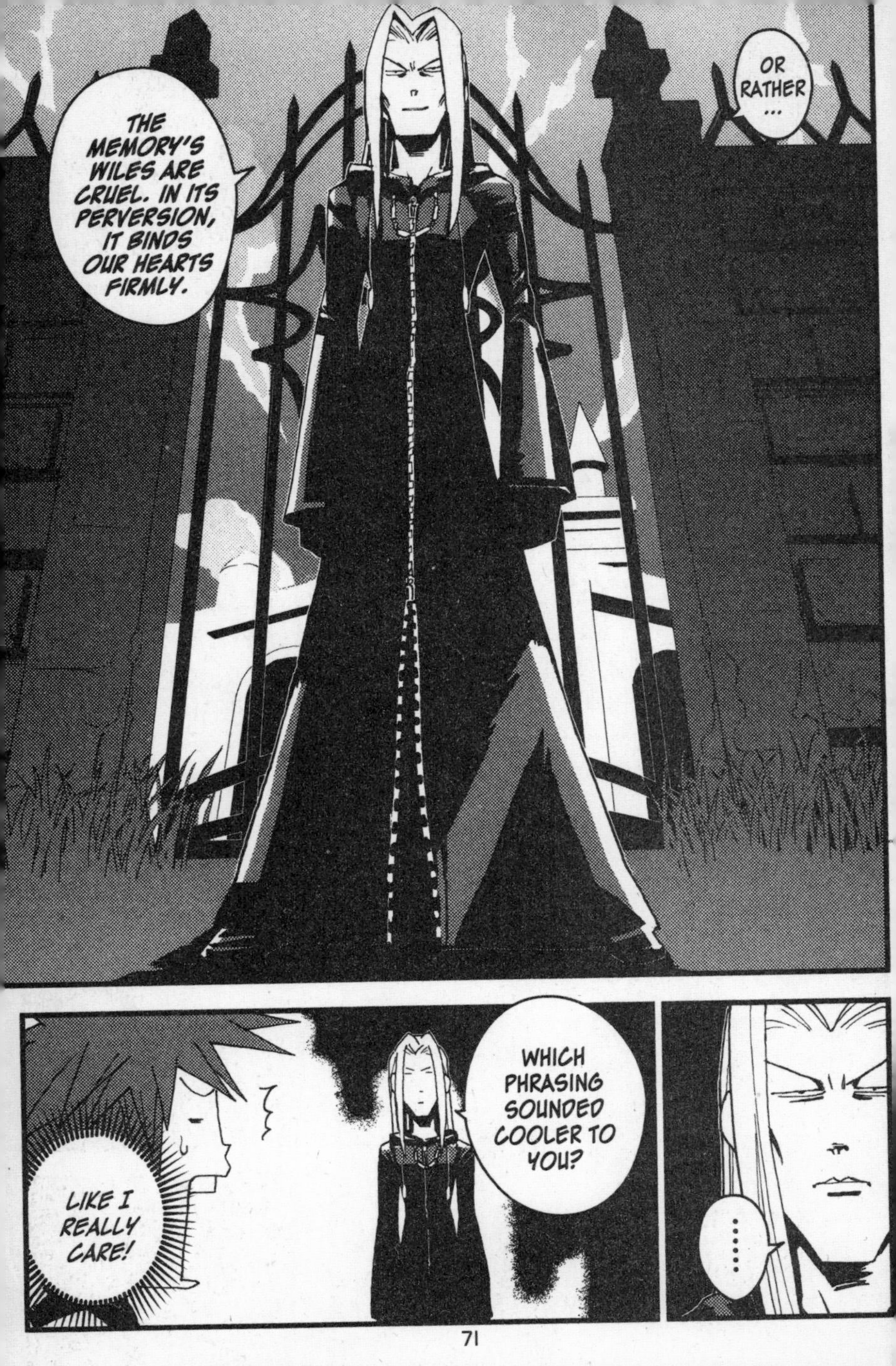
OR RATHER ...
THE MEMORY'S WILES ARE CRUEL. IN ITS PERVERSION, IT BINDS OUR HEARTS FIRMLY.
......
WHICH PHRASING SOUNDED COOLER TO YOU?
LIKE I REALLY CARE!

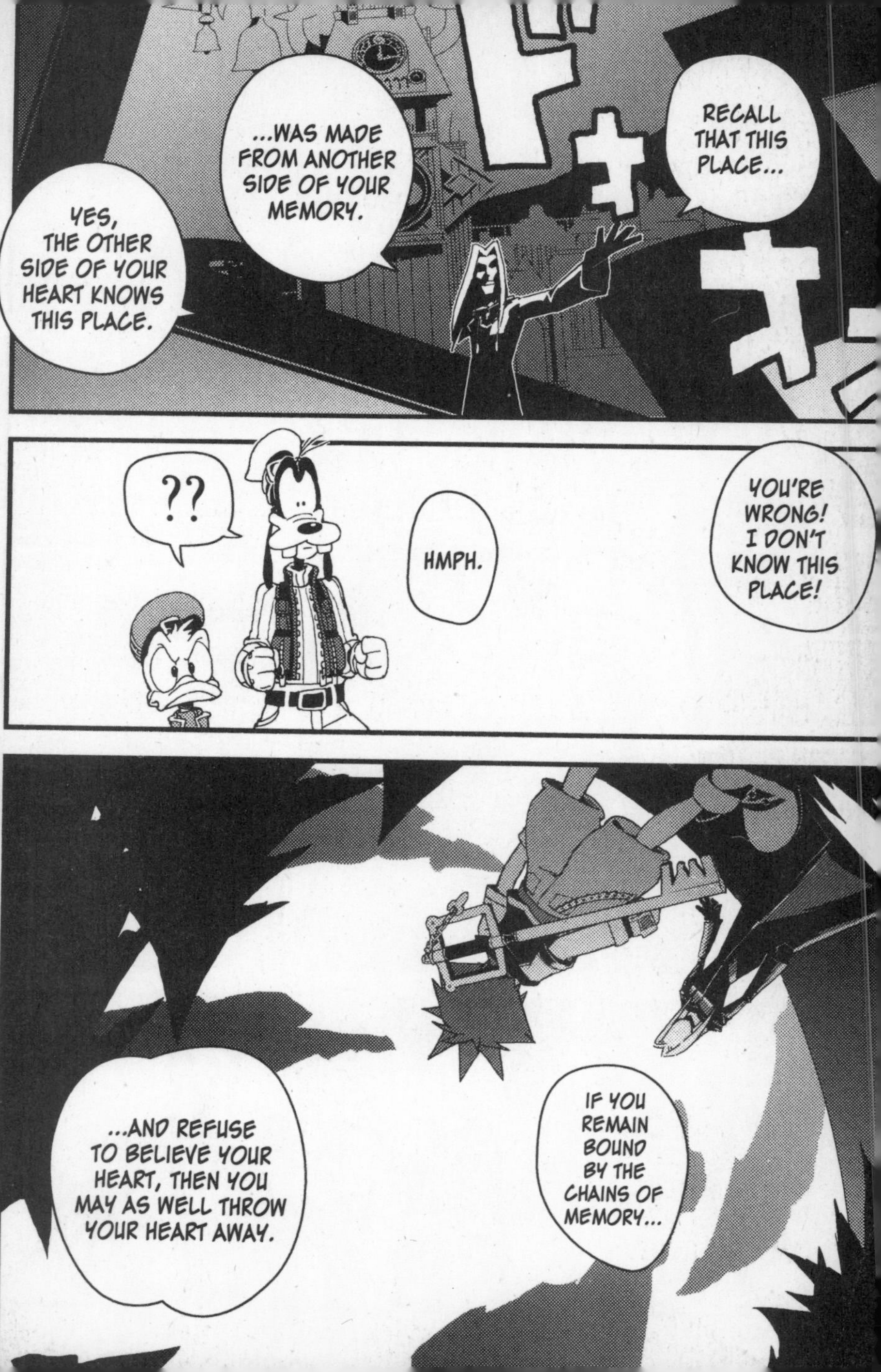
RECALL THAT THIS PLACE...
...WAS MADE FROM ANOTHER SIDE OF YOUR MEMORY.
YES, THE OTHER SIDE OF YOUR HEART KNOWS THIS PLACE.
YOU'RE WRONG! I DON'T KNOW THIS PLACE!
HMPH.
??
IF YOU REMAIN BOUND BY THE CHAINS OF MEMORY...
...AND REFUSE TO BELIEVE YOUR HEART, THEN YOU MAY AS WELL THROW YOUR HEART AWAY.

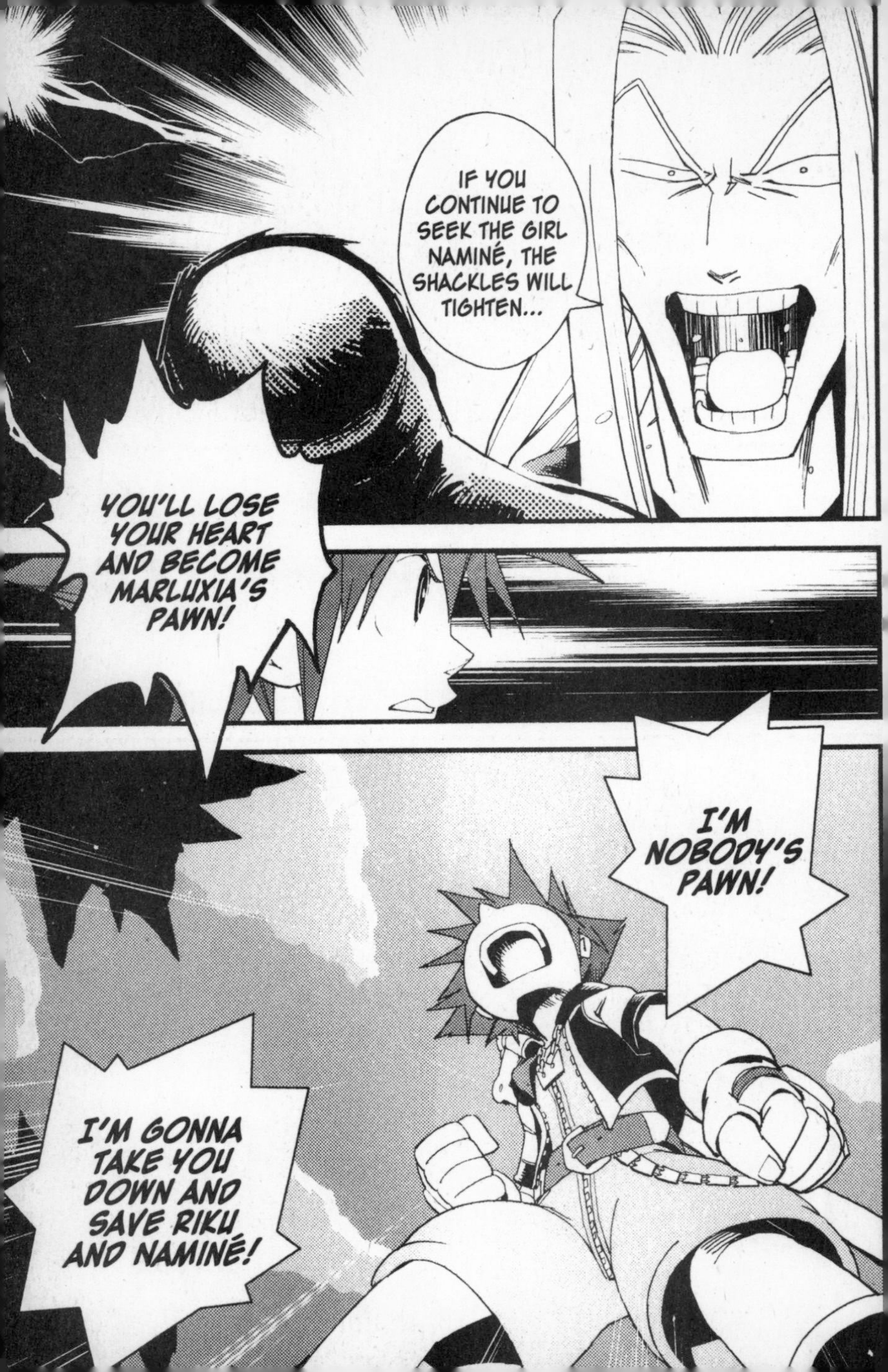
IF YOU CONTINUE TO SEEK THE GIRL NAMINÉ, THE SHACKLES WILL TIGHTEN...
YOU'LL LOSE YOUR HEART AND BECOME MARLUXIA'S PAWN!
I'M NOBODY'S PAWN!
I'M GONNA TAKE YOU DOWN AND SAVE RIKU AND NAMINÉ!

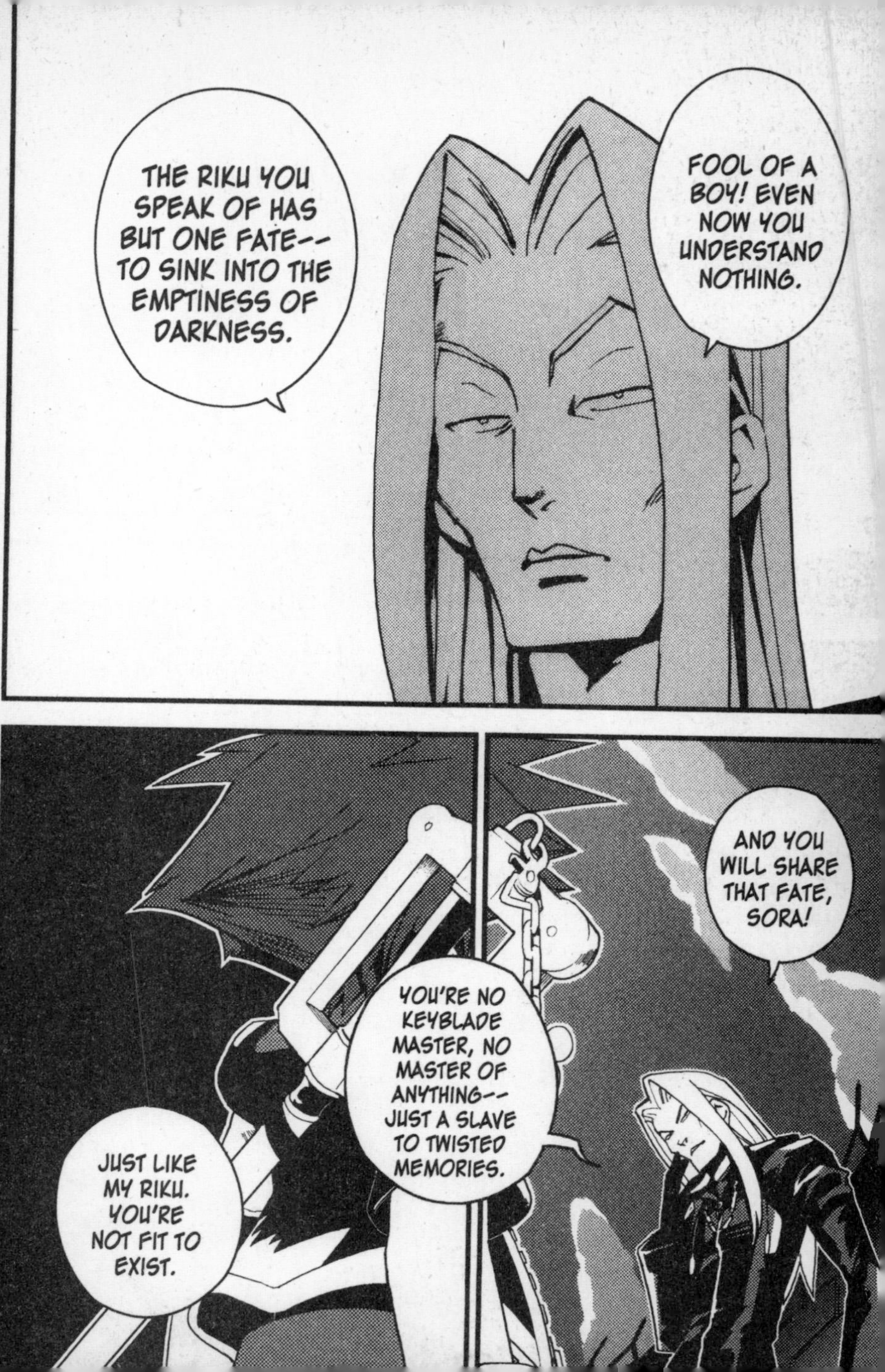
FOOL OF A BOY! EVEN NOW YOU UNDERSTAND NOTHING.
THE RIKU YOU SPEAK OF HAS BUT ONE FATE-- TO SINK INTO THE EMPTINESS OF DARKNESS.
AND YOU WILL SHARE THAT FATE, SORA!
YOU'RE NO KEYBLADE MASTER, NO MASTER OF ANYTHING-- JUST A SLAVE TO TWISTED MEMORIES.
JUST LIKE MY RIKU. YOU'RE NOT FIT TO EXIST.

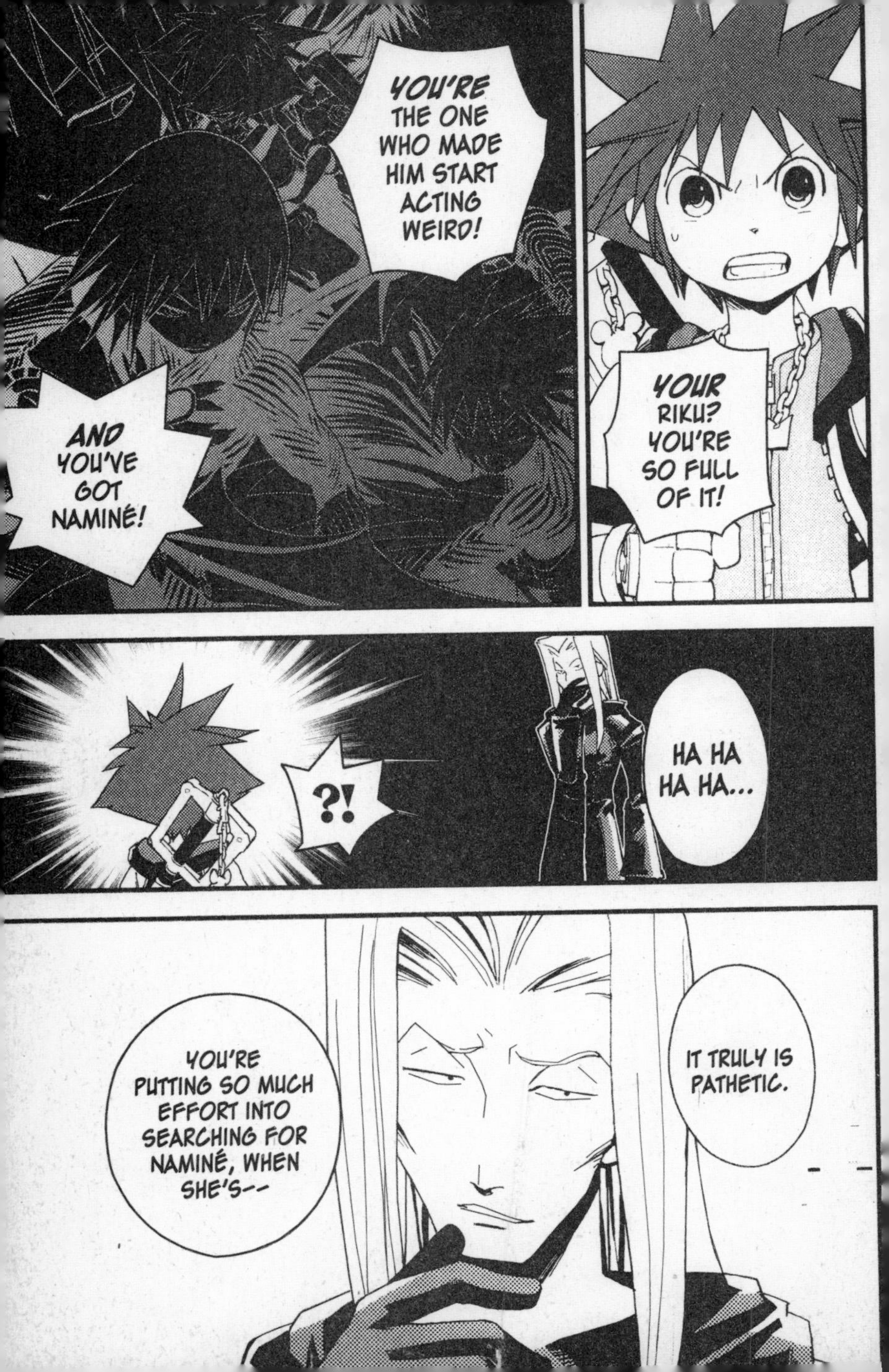
YOUR RIKU? YOU'RE SO FULL OF IT!
YOU'RE THE ONE WHO MADE HIM START ACTING WEIRD!
AND YOU'VE GOT NAMINÉ!
HA HA HA HA...
?!
IT TRULY IS PATHETIC.
YOU'RE PUTTING SO MUCH EFFORT INTO SEARCHING FOR NAMINÉ, WHEN SHE'S--

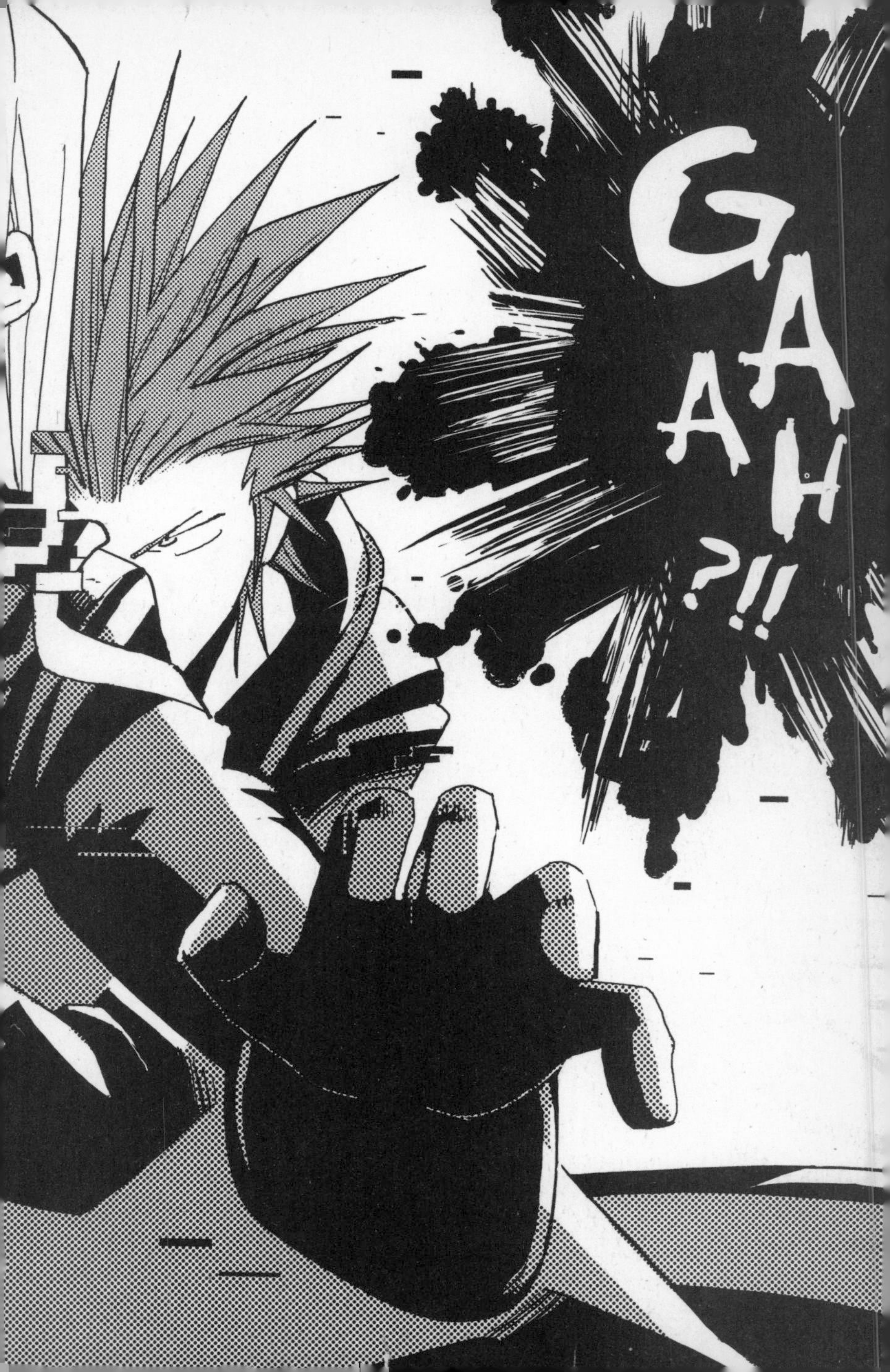
GAAAH?!!

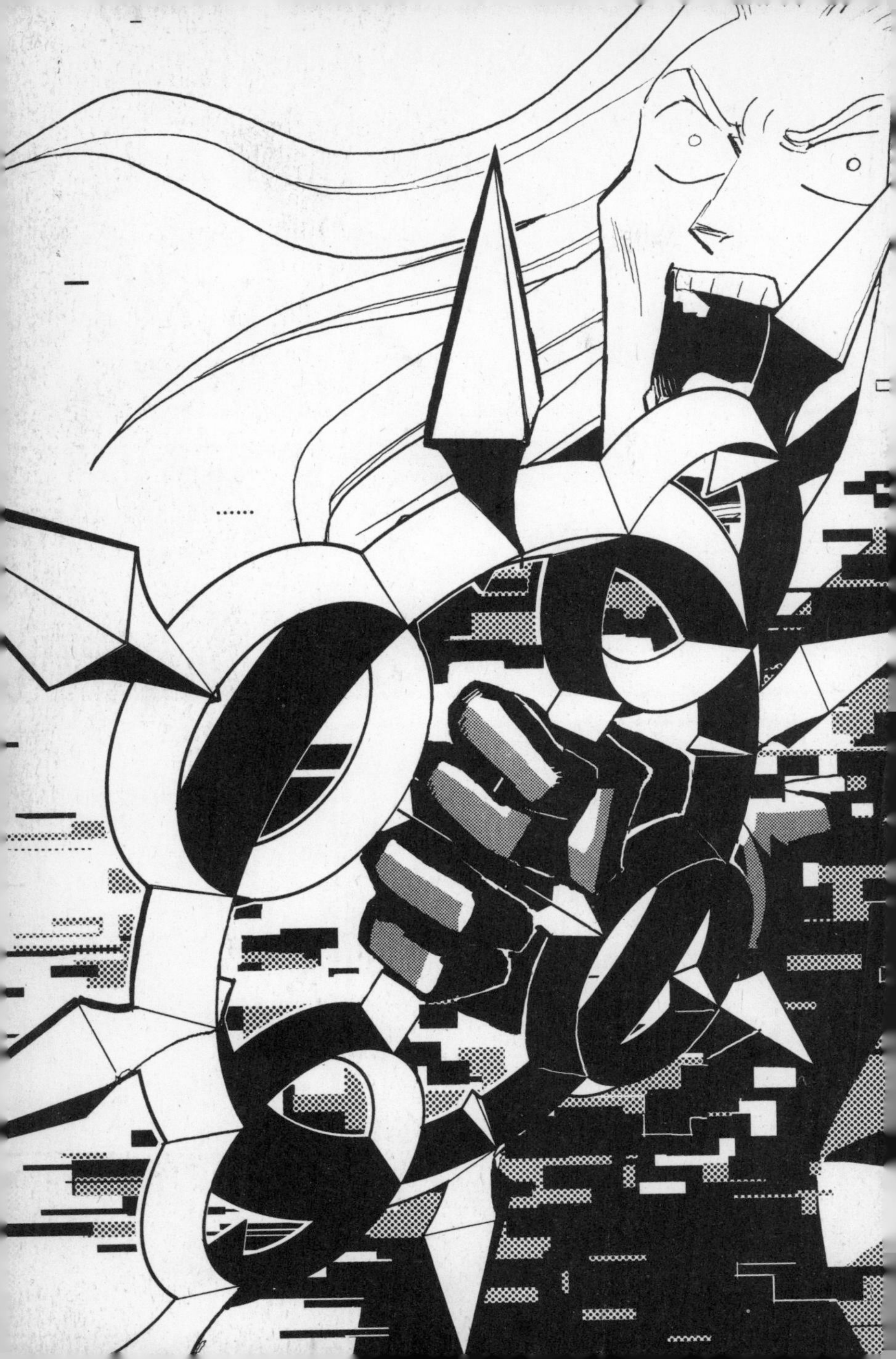
......

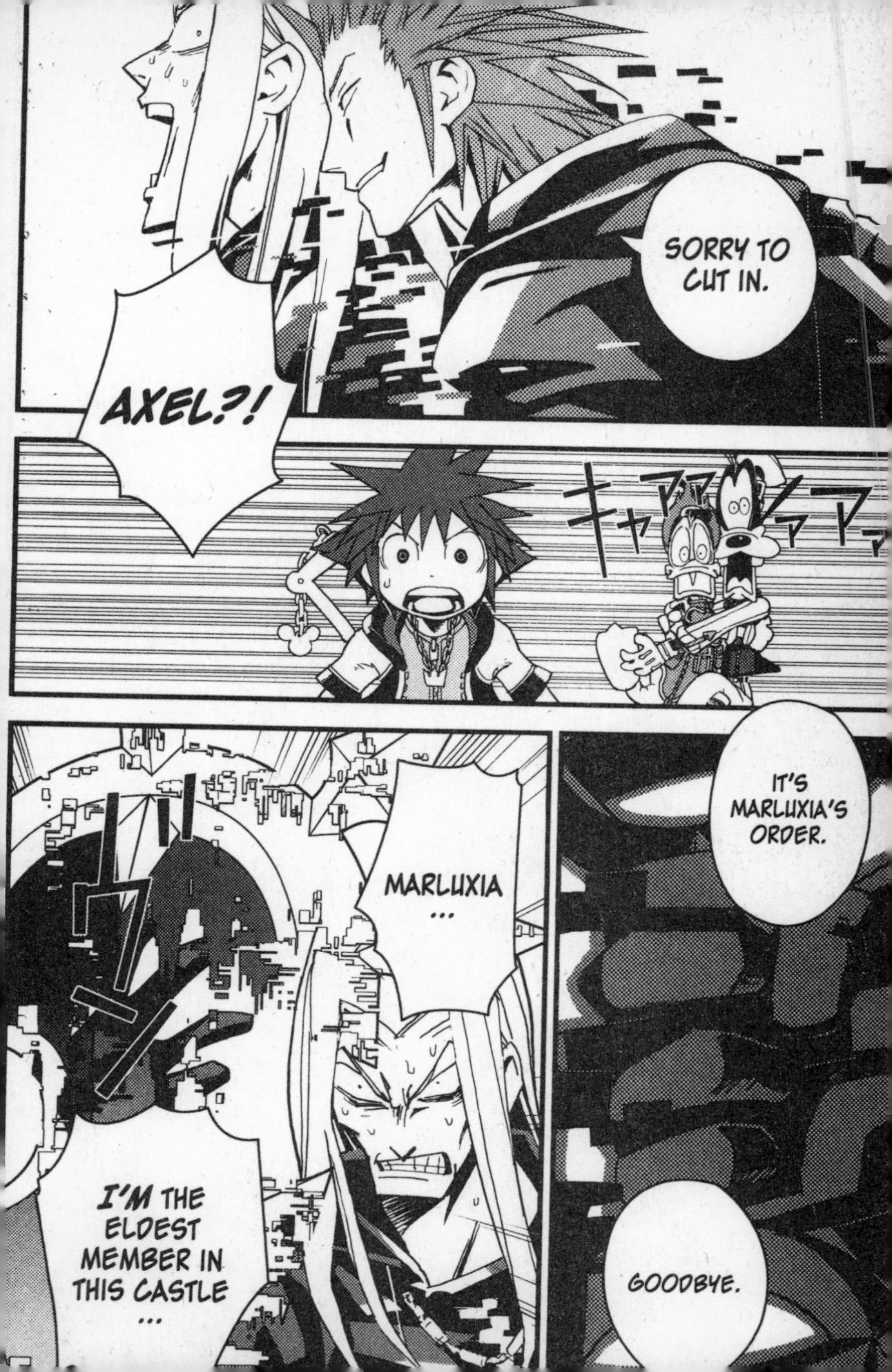
SORRY TO CUT IN.
AXEL?!
キャアアァァァ
IT'S MARLUXIA'S ORDER.
GOODBYE.
MARLUXIA ...
I'M THE ELDEST MEMBER IN THIS CASTLE ...

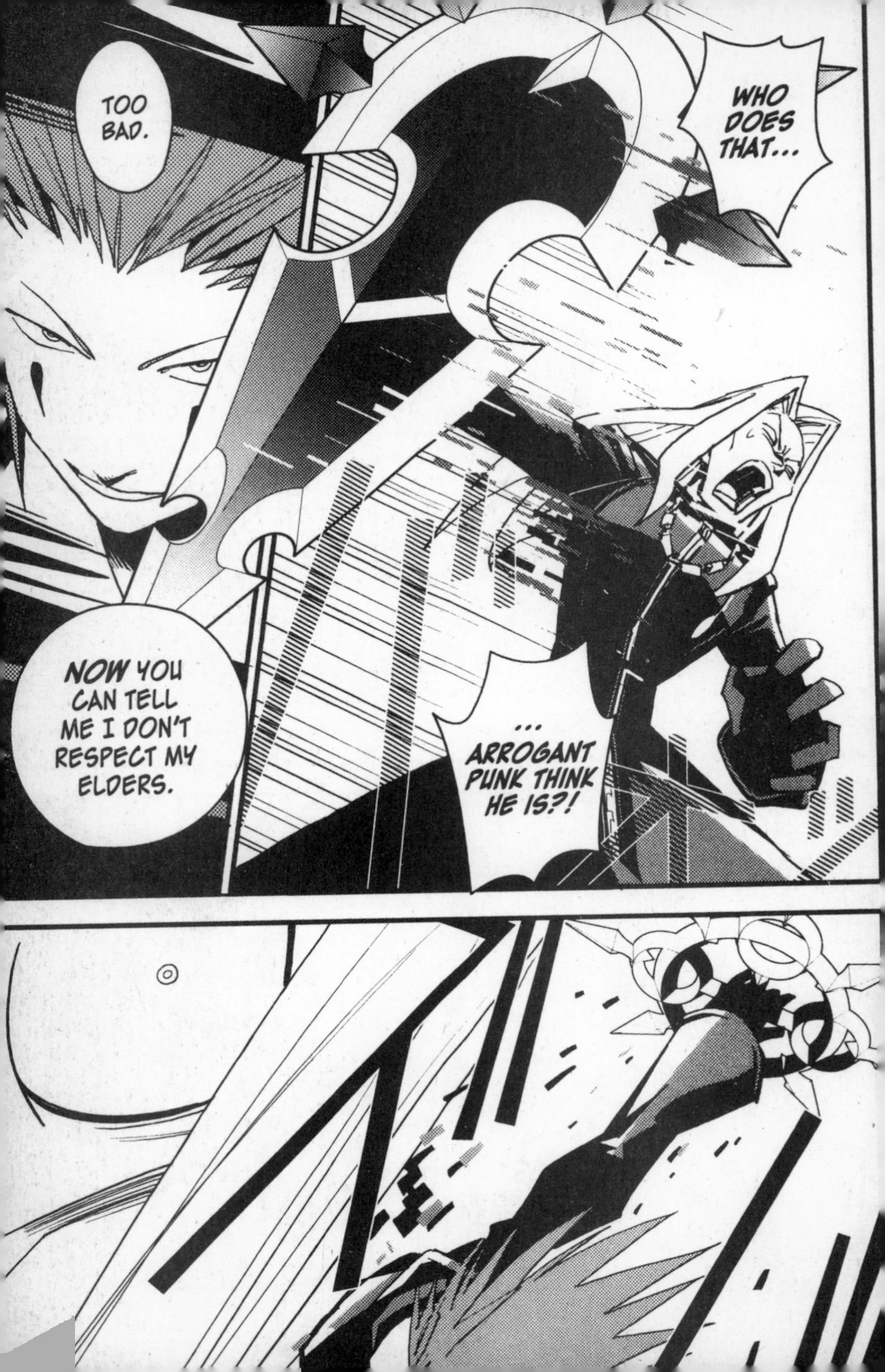
WHO DOES THAT...
TOO BAD.
...ARROGANT PUNK THINK HE IS?!
NOW YOU CAN TELL ME I DON'T RESPECT MY ELDERS.

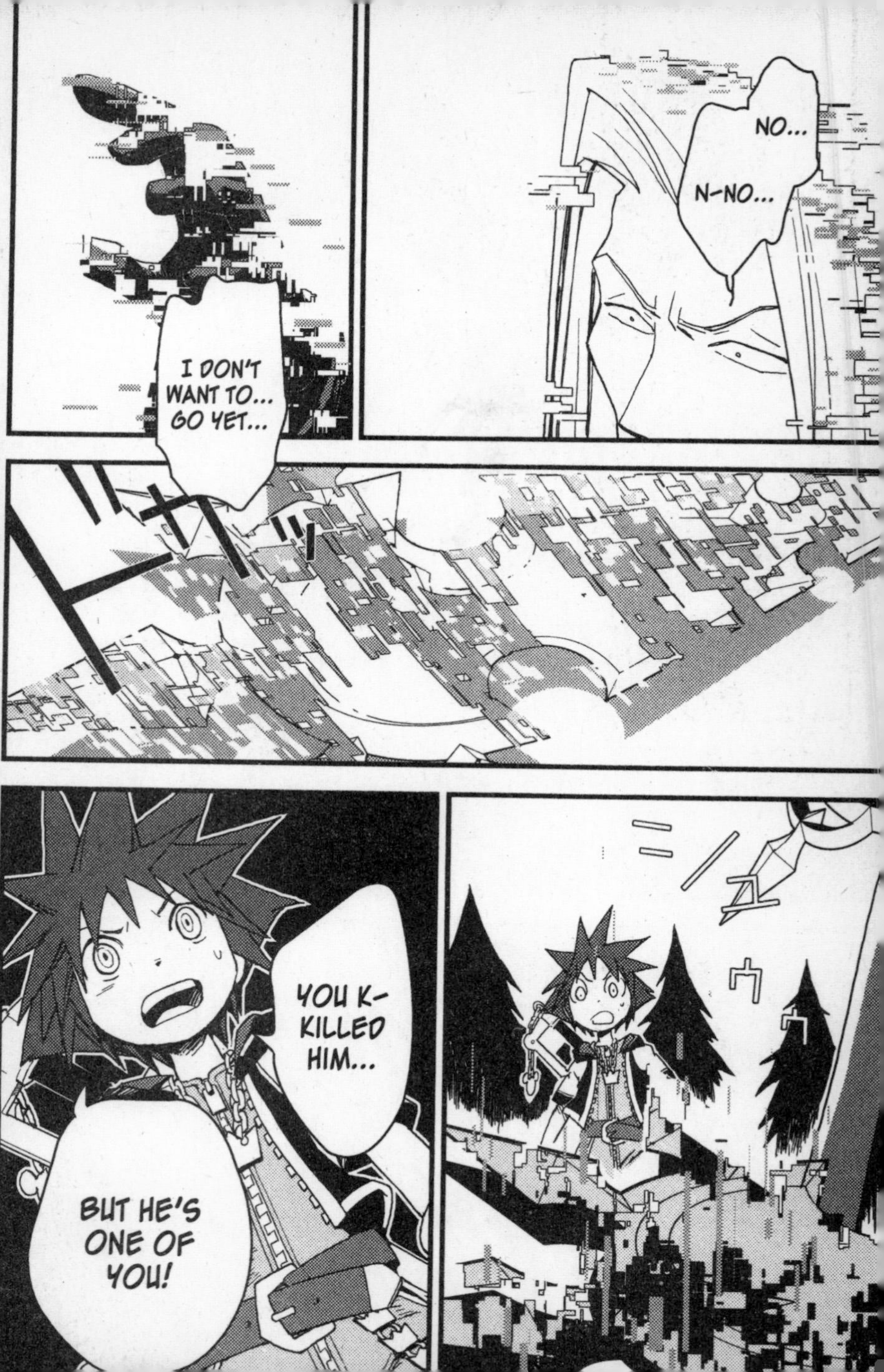
NO...
N-NO...
I DON'T WANT TO... GO YET...
YOU K-KILLED HIM...
BUT HE'S ONE OF YOU!

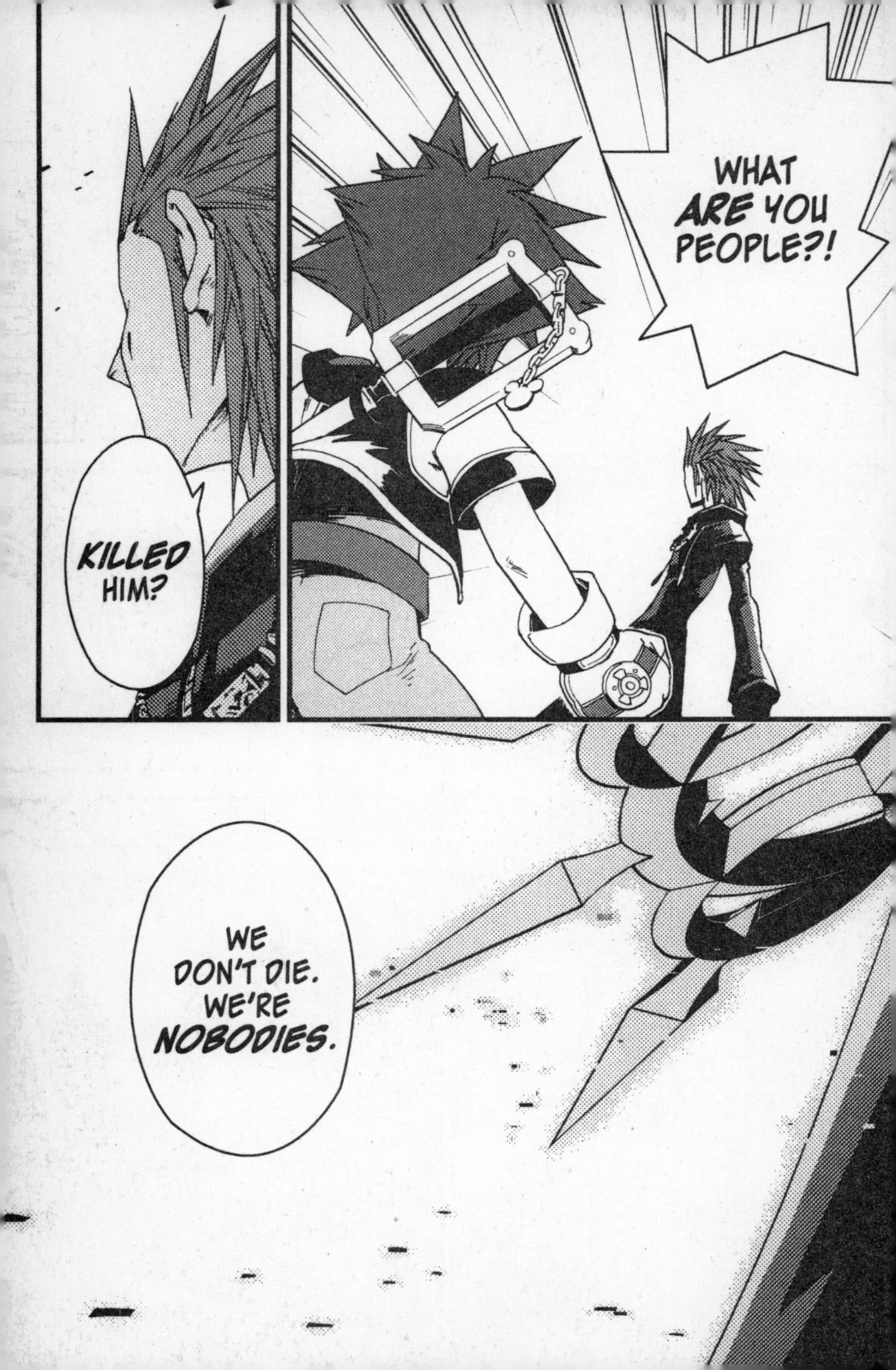
WHAT ARE YOU PEOPLE?!
KILLED HIM?
WE DON'T DIE. WE'RE NOBODIES.

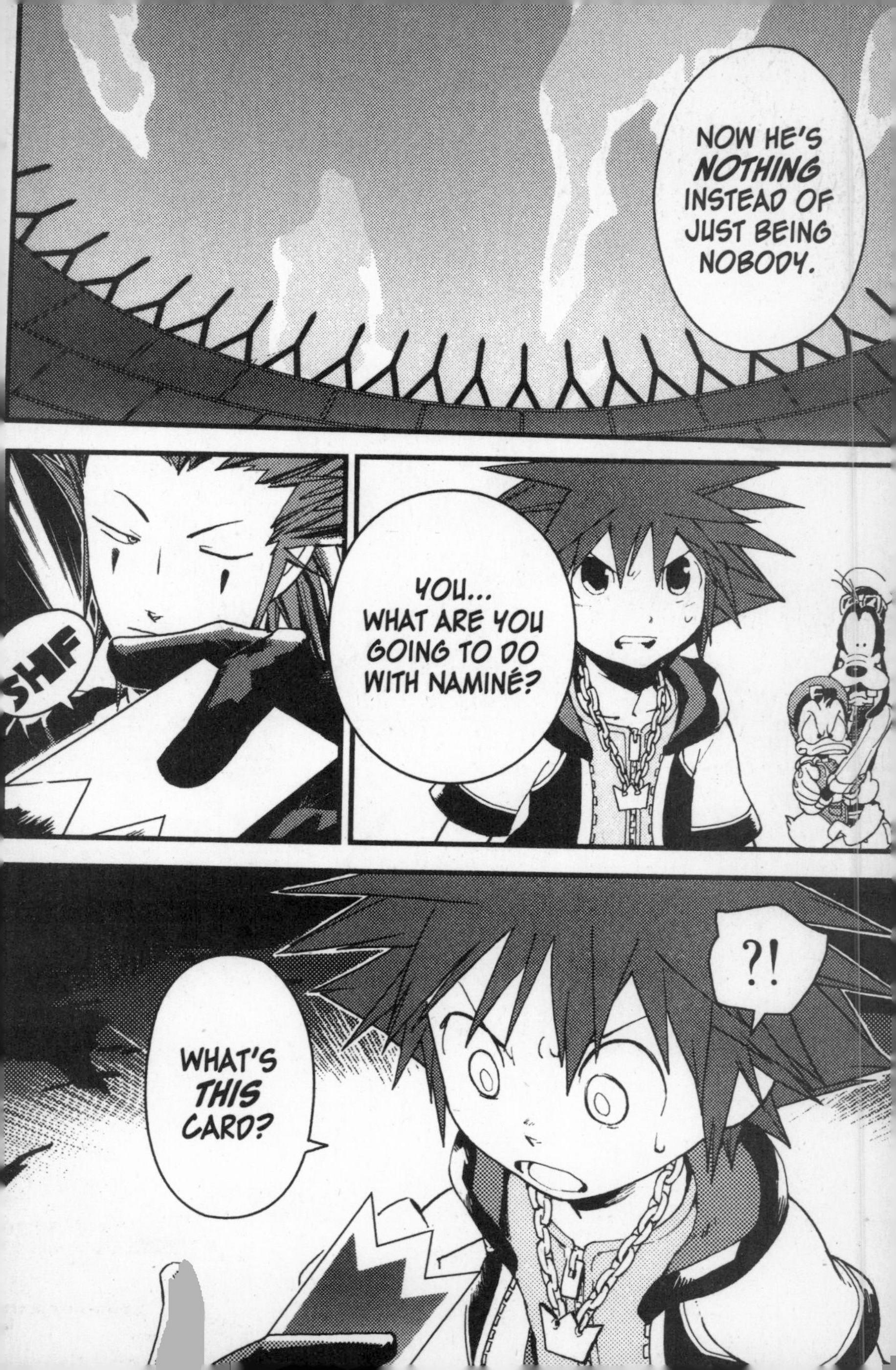
NOW HE'S NOTHING INSTEAD OF JUST BEING NOBODY.
YOU... WHAT ARE YOU GOING TO DO WITH NAMINÉ?
SHF
?!
WHAT'S THIS CARD?

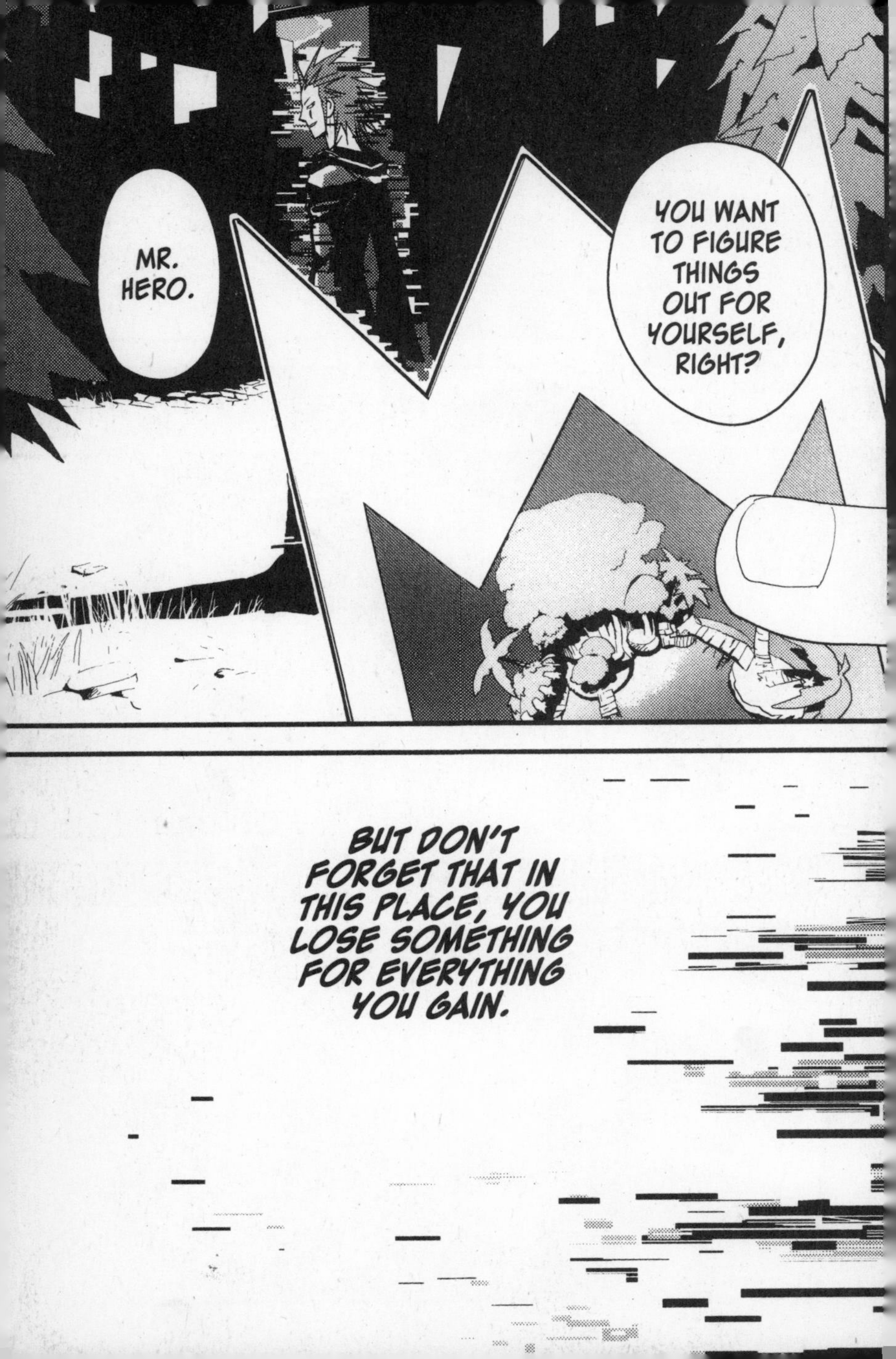
YOU WANT TO FIGURE THINGS OUT FOR YOURSELF, RIGHT?
MR. HERO.
BUT DON'T FORGET THAT IN THIS PLACE, YOU LOSE SOMETHING FOR EVERYTHING YOU GAIN.

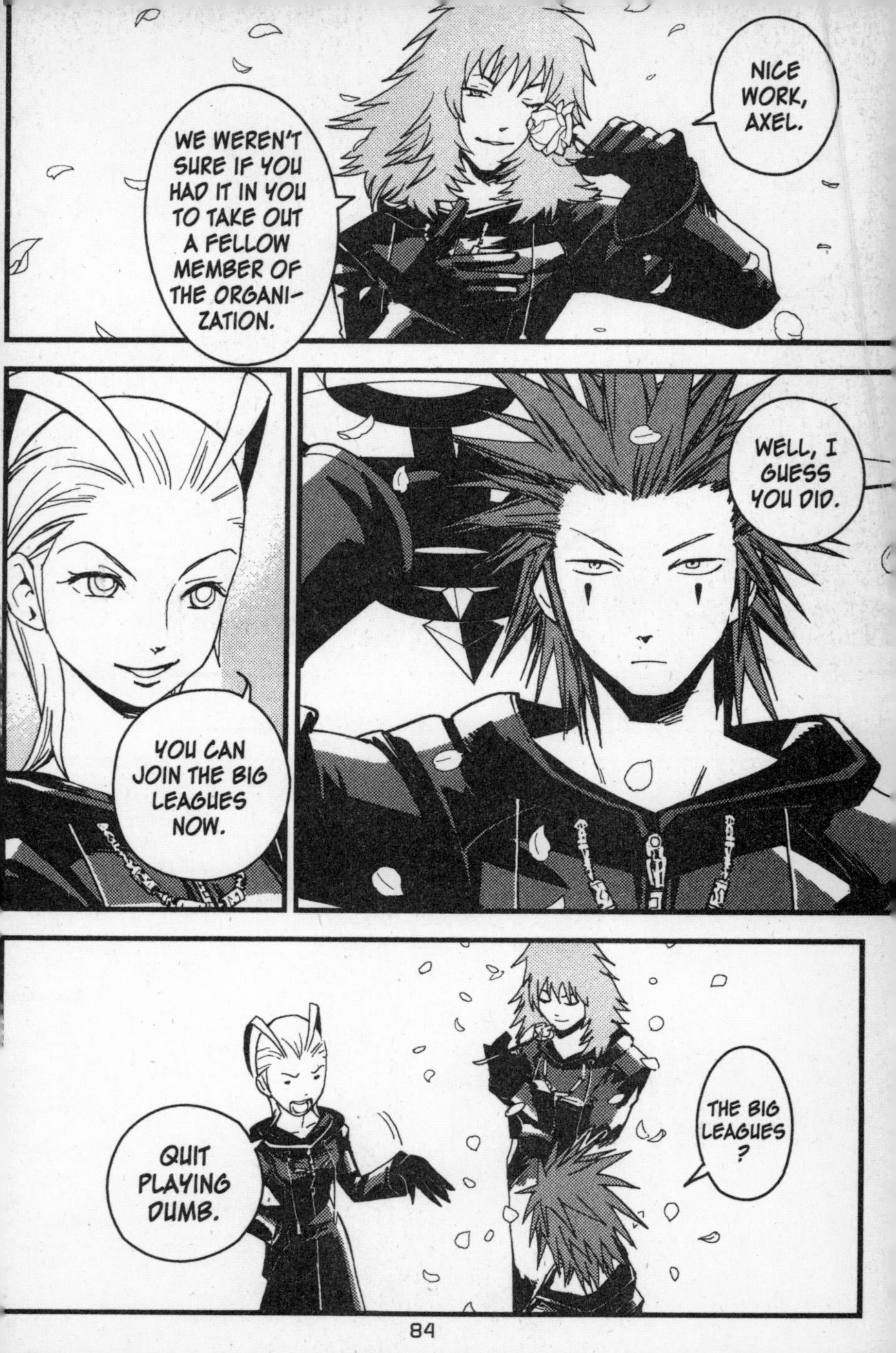
NICE WORK, AXEL.
WE WEREN'T SURE IF YOU HAD IT IN YOU TO TAKE OUT A FELLOW MEMBER OF THE ORGANI-ZATION.
WELL, I GUESS YOU DID.
YOU CAN JOIN THE BIG LEAGUES NOW.
THE BIG LEAGUES?
QUIT PLAYING DUMB.

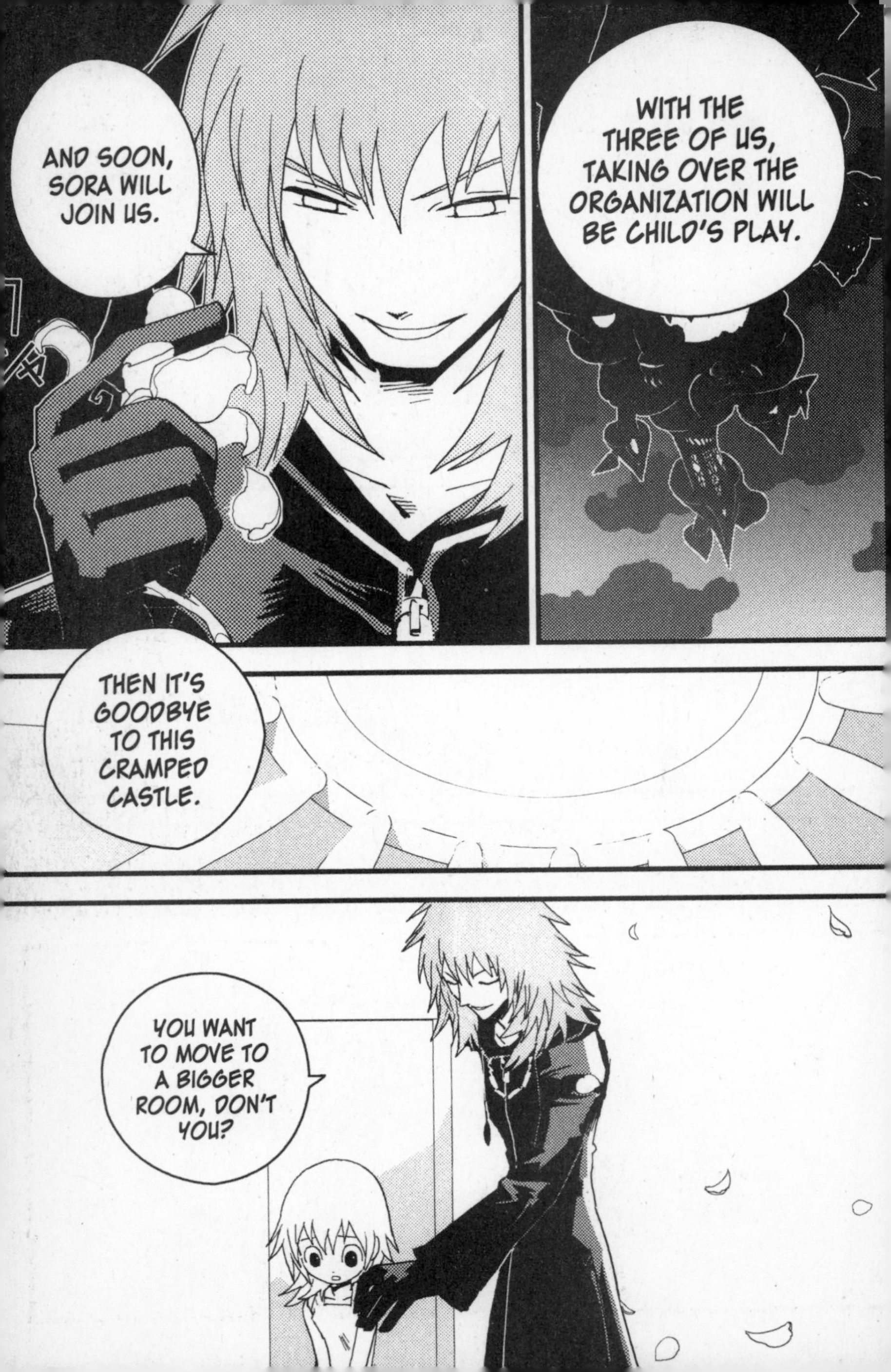
WITH THE THREE OF US, TAKING OVER THE ORGANIZATION WILL BE CHILD'S PLAY.
AND SOON, SORA WILL JOIN US.
THEN IT'S GOODBYE TO THIS CRAMPED CASTLE.
YOU WANT TO MOVE TO A BIGGER ROOM, DON'T YOU?

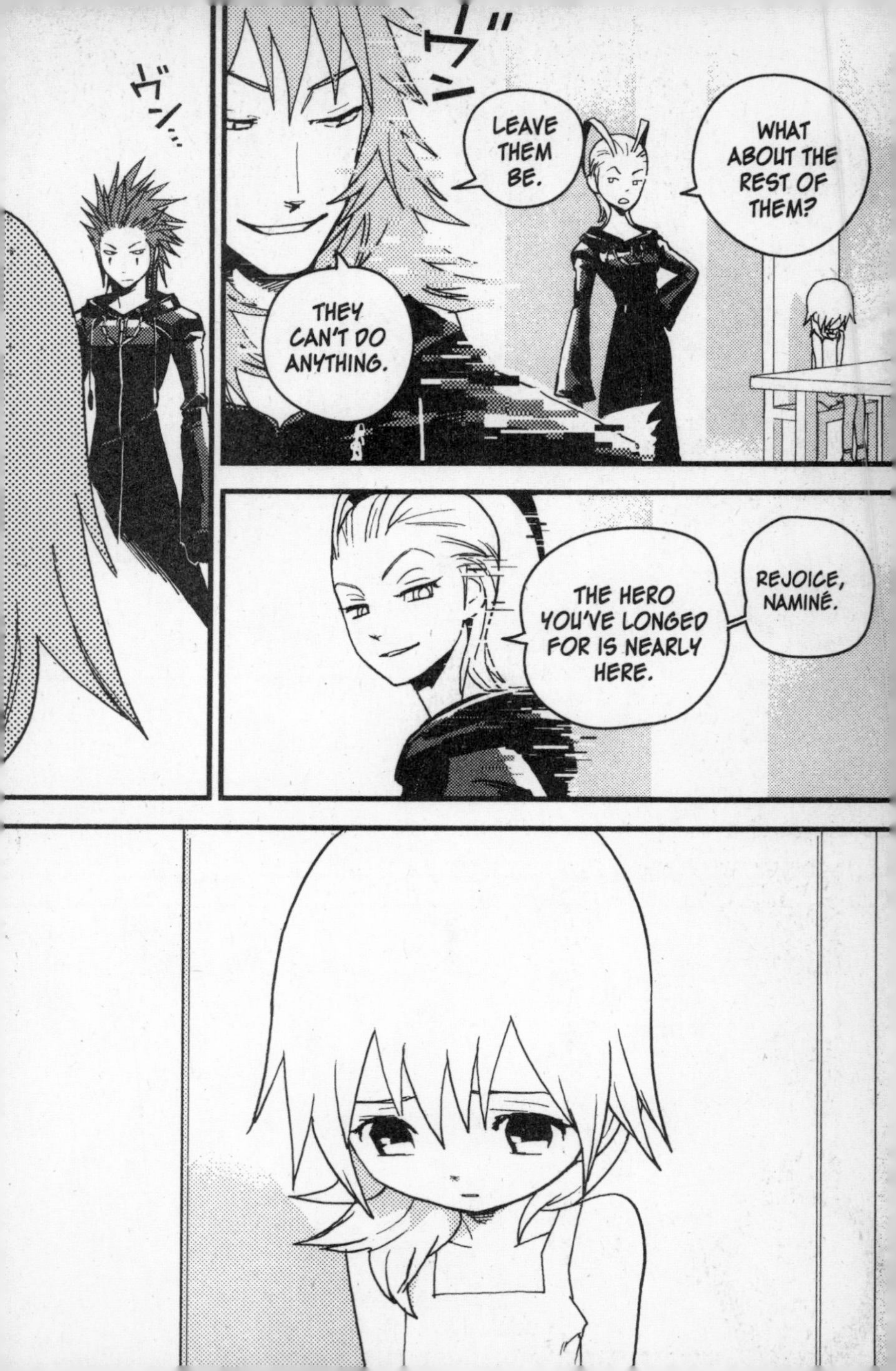
WHAT ABOUT THE REST OF THEM?
ヴン
LEAVE THEM BE.
THEY CAN'T DO ANYTHING.
REJOICE, NAMINÉ.
THE HERO YOU'VE LONGED FOR IS NEARLY HERE.
ヴン…

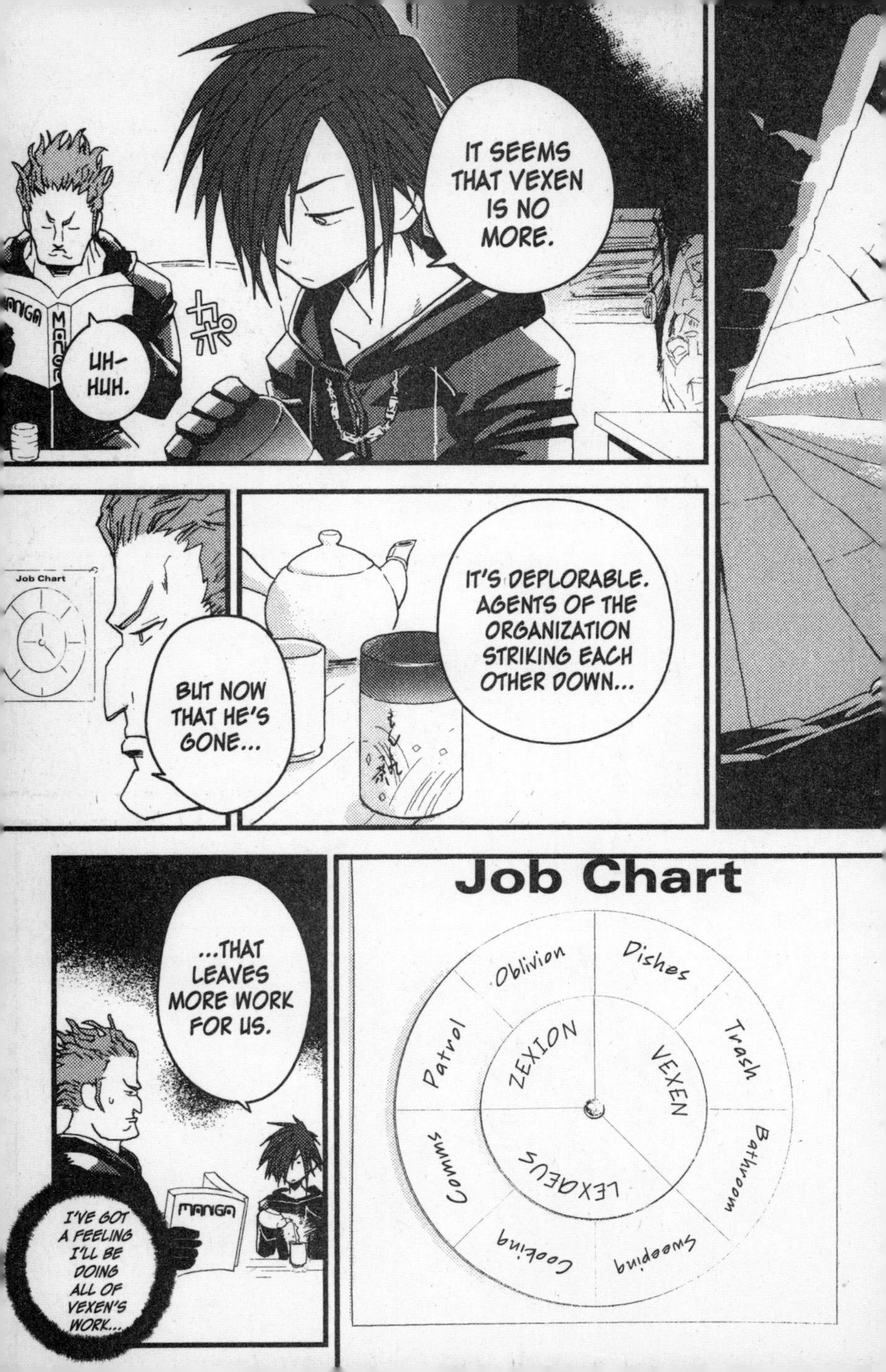
IT SEEMS THAT VEXEN IS NO MORE.
MANGA
UH-HUH.
IT'S DEPLORABLE. AGENTS OF THE ORGANIZATION STRIKING EACH OTHER DOWN...
Job Chart
BUT NOW THAT HE'S GONE...
Job Chart
Oblivion
Dishes
Trash
Bathroom
Sweeping
Cooking
Comms
Patrol
ZEXION
VEXEN
LEXAEUS
...THAT LEAVES MORE WORK FOR US.
MANGA
I'VE GOT A FEELING I'LL BE DOING ALL OF VEXEN'S WORK...

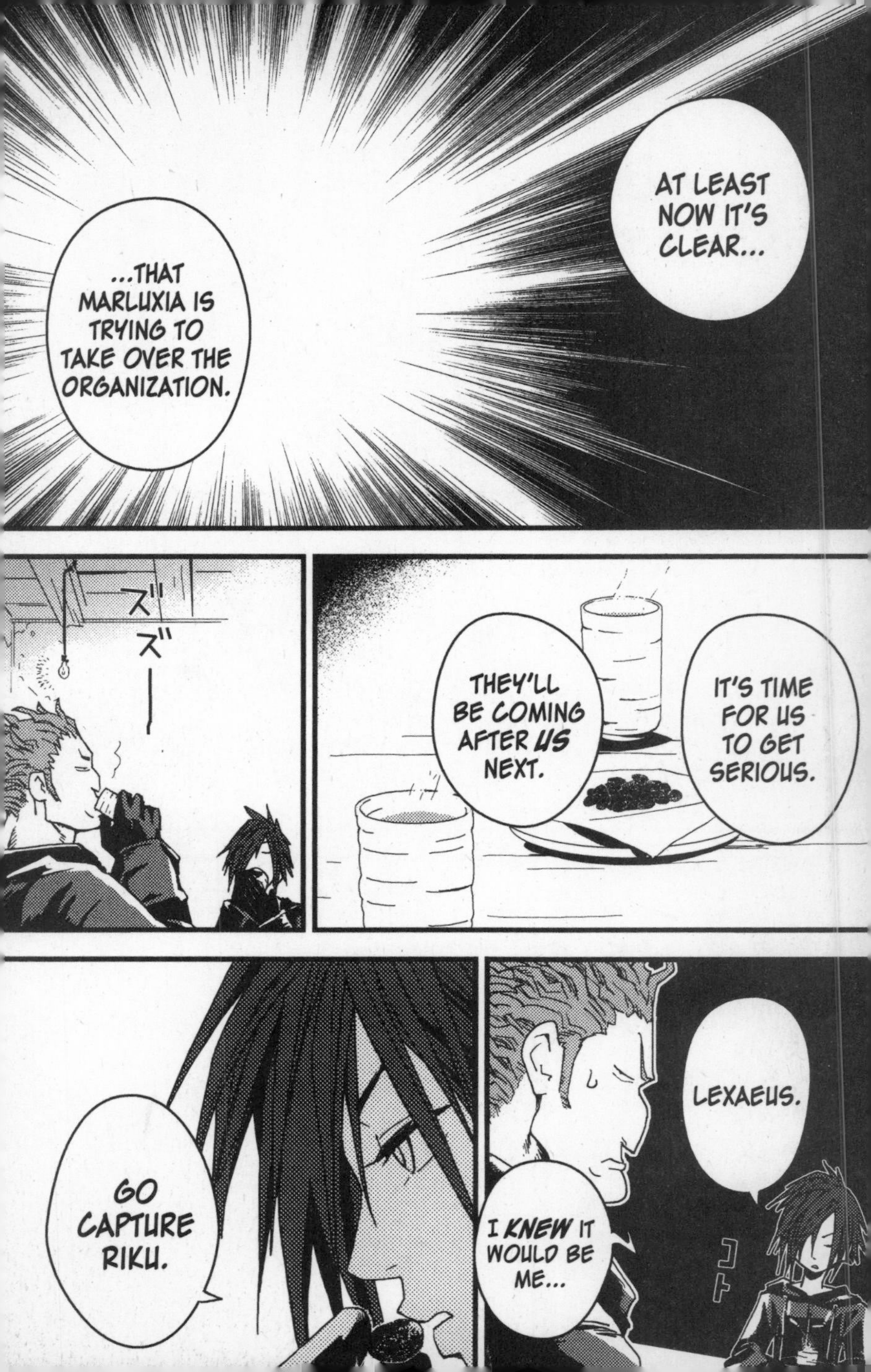
AT LEAST NOW IT'S CLEAR...
...THAT MARLUXIA IS TRYING TO TAKE OVER THE ORGANIZATION.
IT'S TIME FOR US TO GET SERIOUS.
THEY'LL BE COMING AFTER *US* NEXT.
ズズー
LEXAEUS.
コト
I *KNEW* IT WOULD BE ME...
GO CAPTURE RIKU.

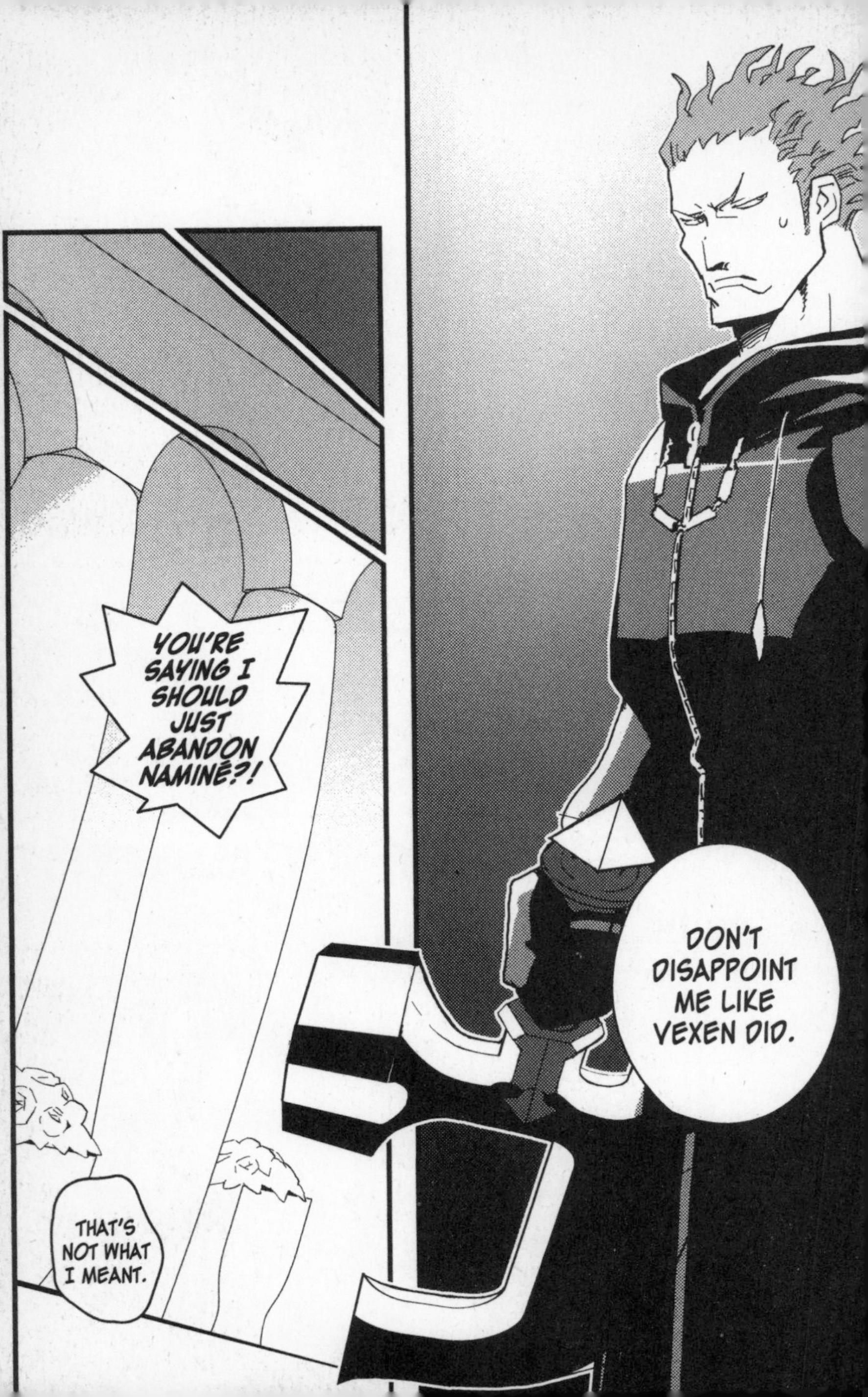
DON'T DISAPPOINT ME LIKE VEXEN DID.
YOU'RE SAYING I SHOULD JUST ABANDON NAMINÉ?!
THAT'S NOT WHAT I MEANT.

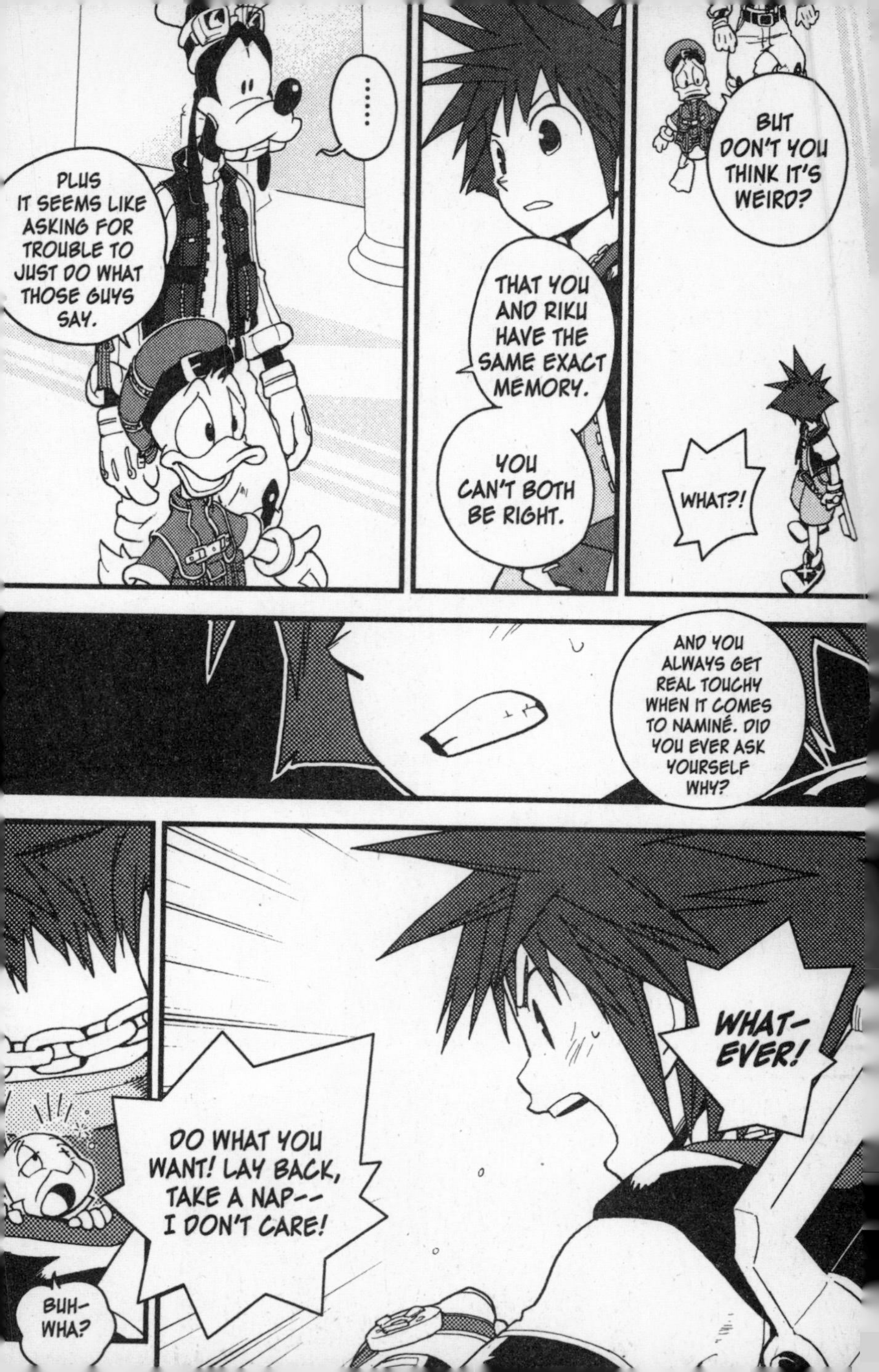
BUT DON'T YOU THINK IT'S WEIRD?
WHAT?!
THAT YOU AND RIKU HAVE THE SAME EXACT MEMORY.
YOU CAN'T BOTH BE RIGHT.
......
PLUS IT SEEMS LIKE ASKING FOR TROUBLE TO JUST DO WHAT THOSE GUYS SAY.
AND YOU ALWAYS GET REAL TOUCHY WHEN IT COMES TO NAMINÉ. DID YOU EVER ASK YOURSELF WHY?
WHAT-EVER!
DO WHAT YOU WANT! LAY BACK, TAKE A NAP-- I DON'T CARE!
BUH-WHA?

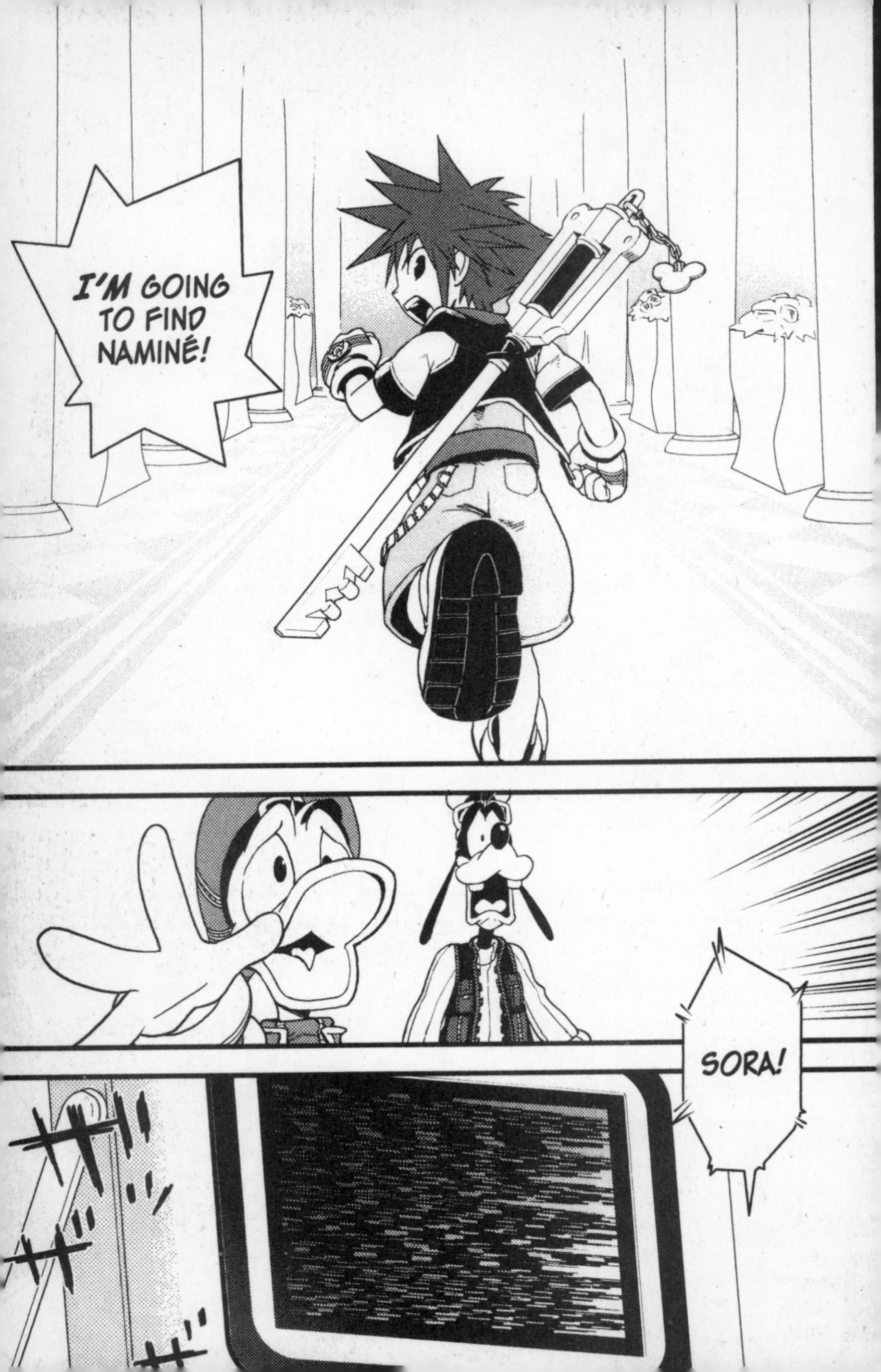
I'M GOING TO FIND NAMINÉ!
SORA!

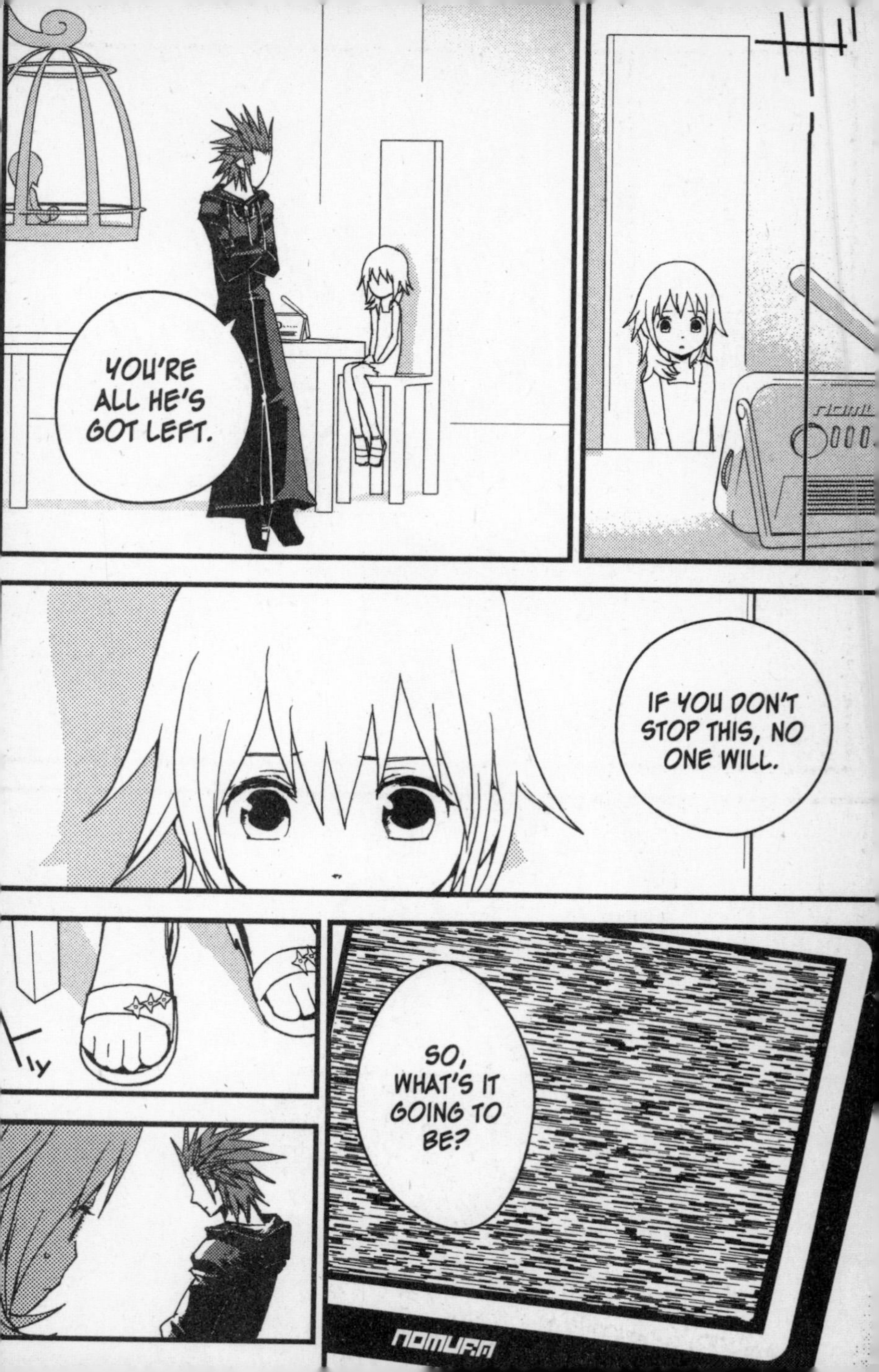
YOU'RE ALL HE'S GOT LEFT.
IF YOU DON'T STOP THIS, NO ONE WILL.
SO, WHAT'S IT GOING TO BE?

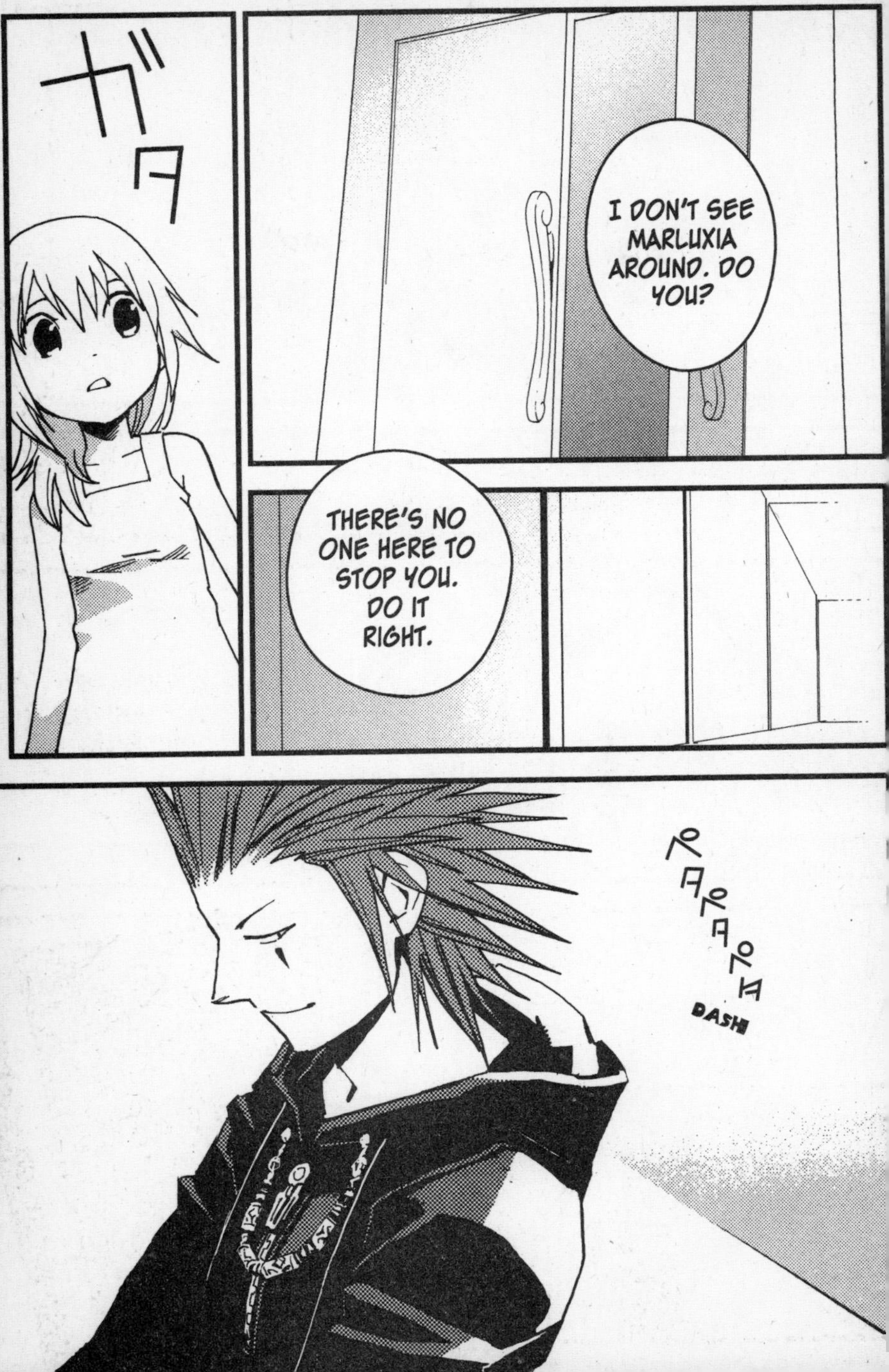
I DON'T SEE MARLUXIA AROUND. DO YOU?
THERE'S NO ONE HERE TO STOP YOU. DO IT RIGHT.
ガタ
DASH

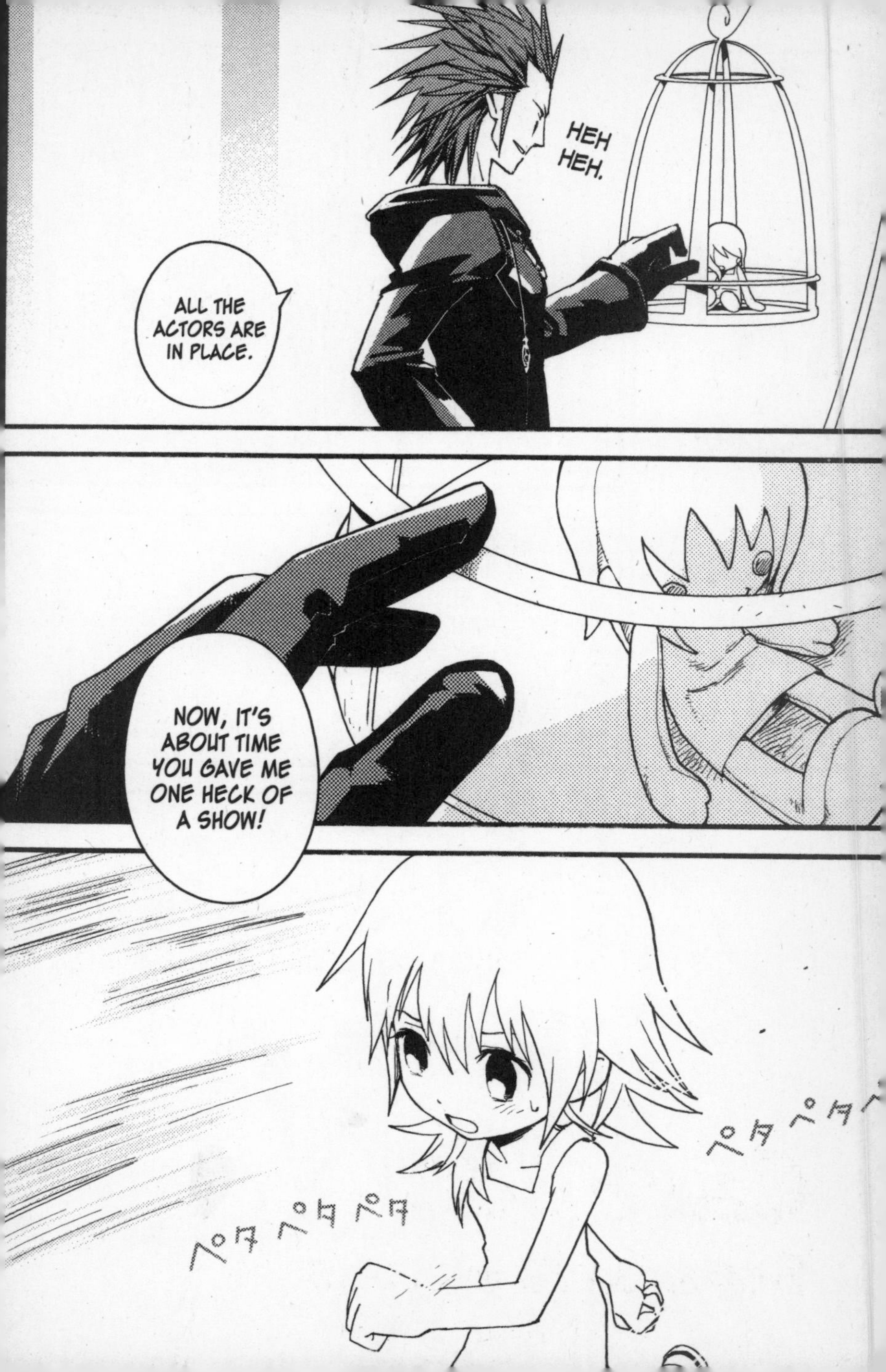
HEH HEH.
ALL THE ACTORS ARE IN PLACE.
NOW, IT'S ABOUT TIME YOU GAVE ME ONE HECK OF A SHOW!
ペタペタ
ペタペタペタ

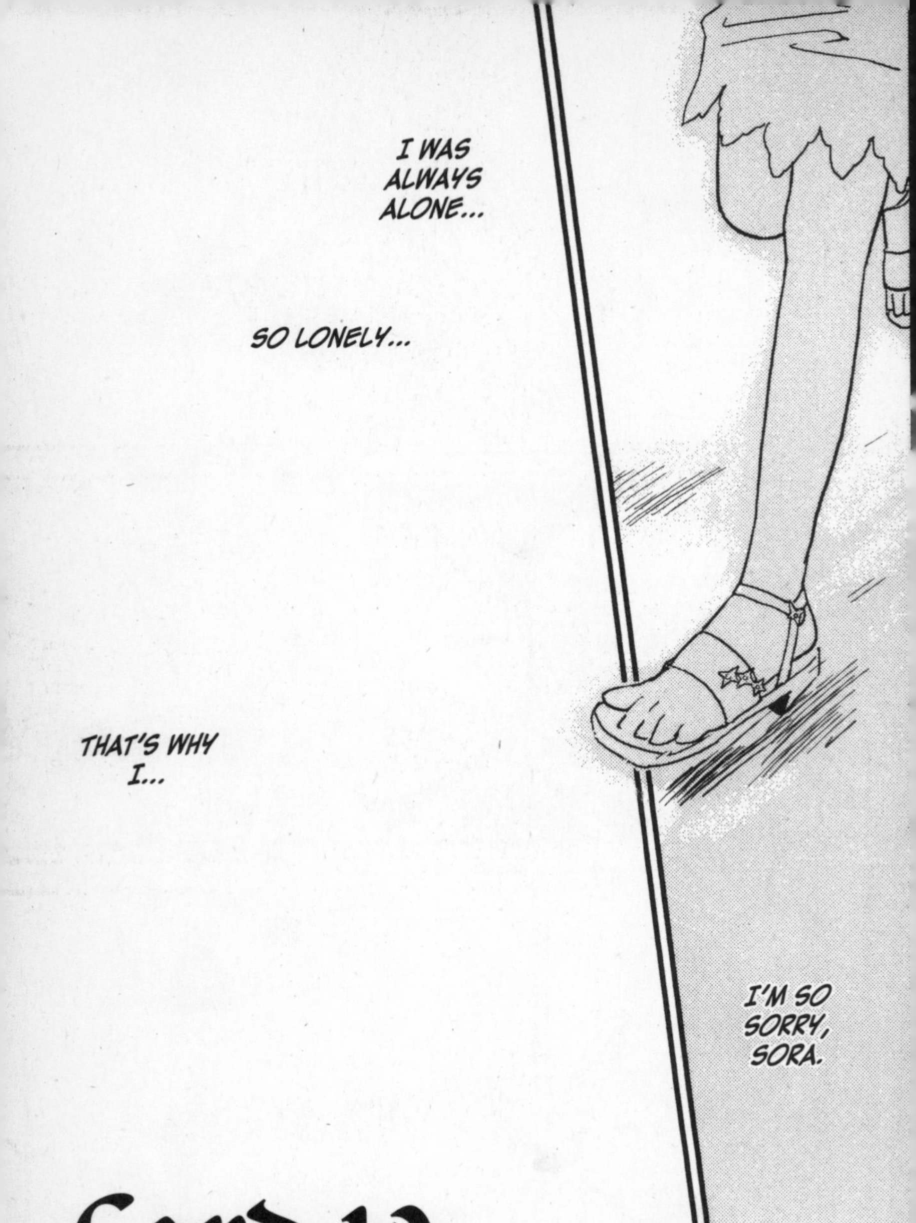
I WAS ALWAYS ALONE...
SO LONELY...
THAT'S WHY I...
I'M SO SORRY, SORA.

Card 10
Separated Hearts

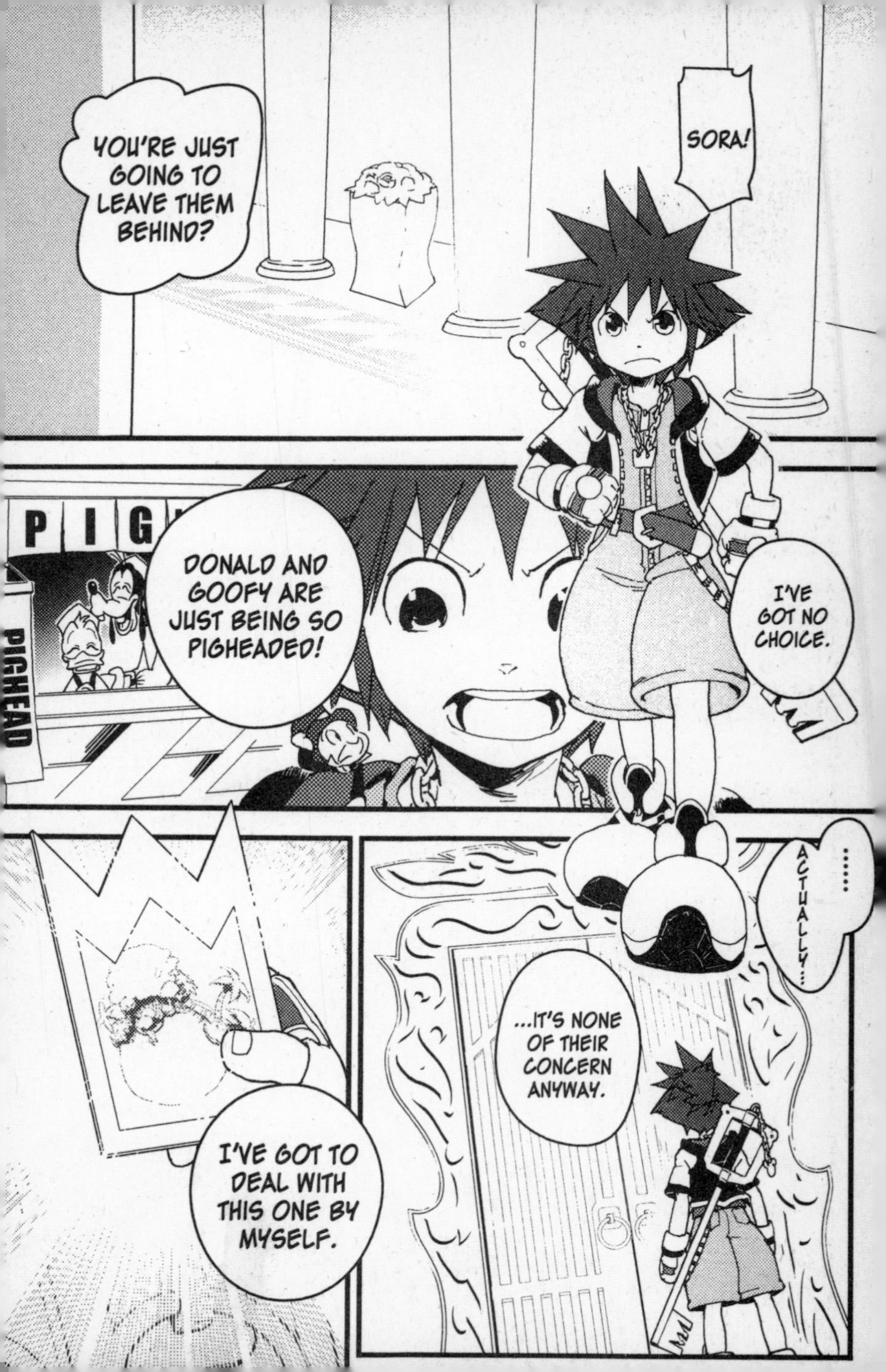
SORA!
YOU'RE JUST GOING TO LEAVE THEM BEHIND?
I'VE GOT NO CHOICE.
DONALD AND GOOFY ARE JUST BEING SO PIGHEADED!
PIG
PIGHEAD
ACTUALLY......
...IT'S NONE OF THEIR CONCERN ANYWAY.
I'VE GOT TO DEAL WITH THIS ONE BY MYSELF.

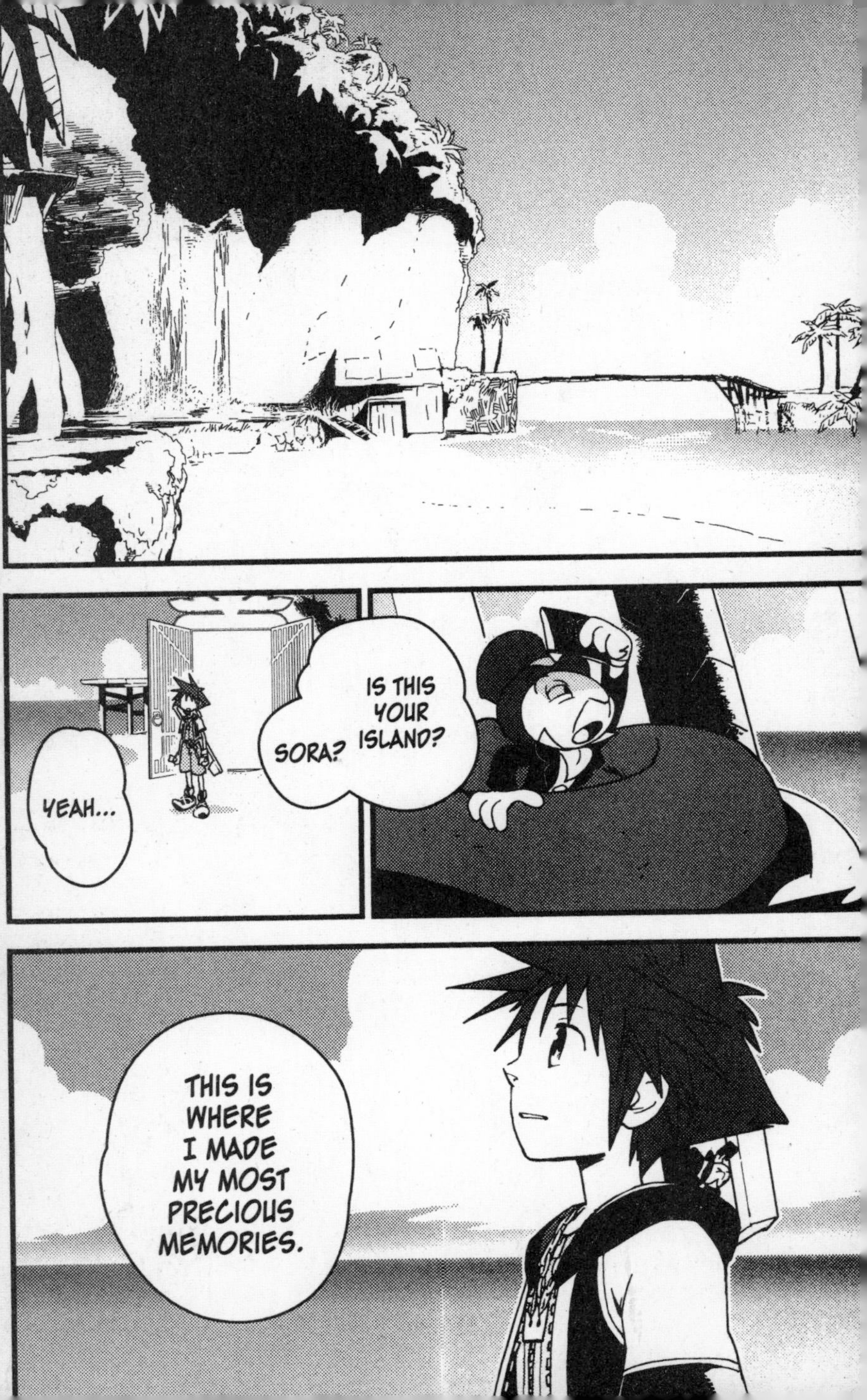
IS THIS YOUR ISLAND?
SORA?
YEAH...
THIS IS WHERE I MADE MY MOST PRECIOUS MEMORIES.

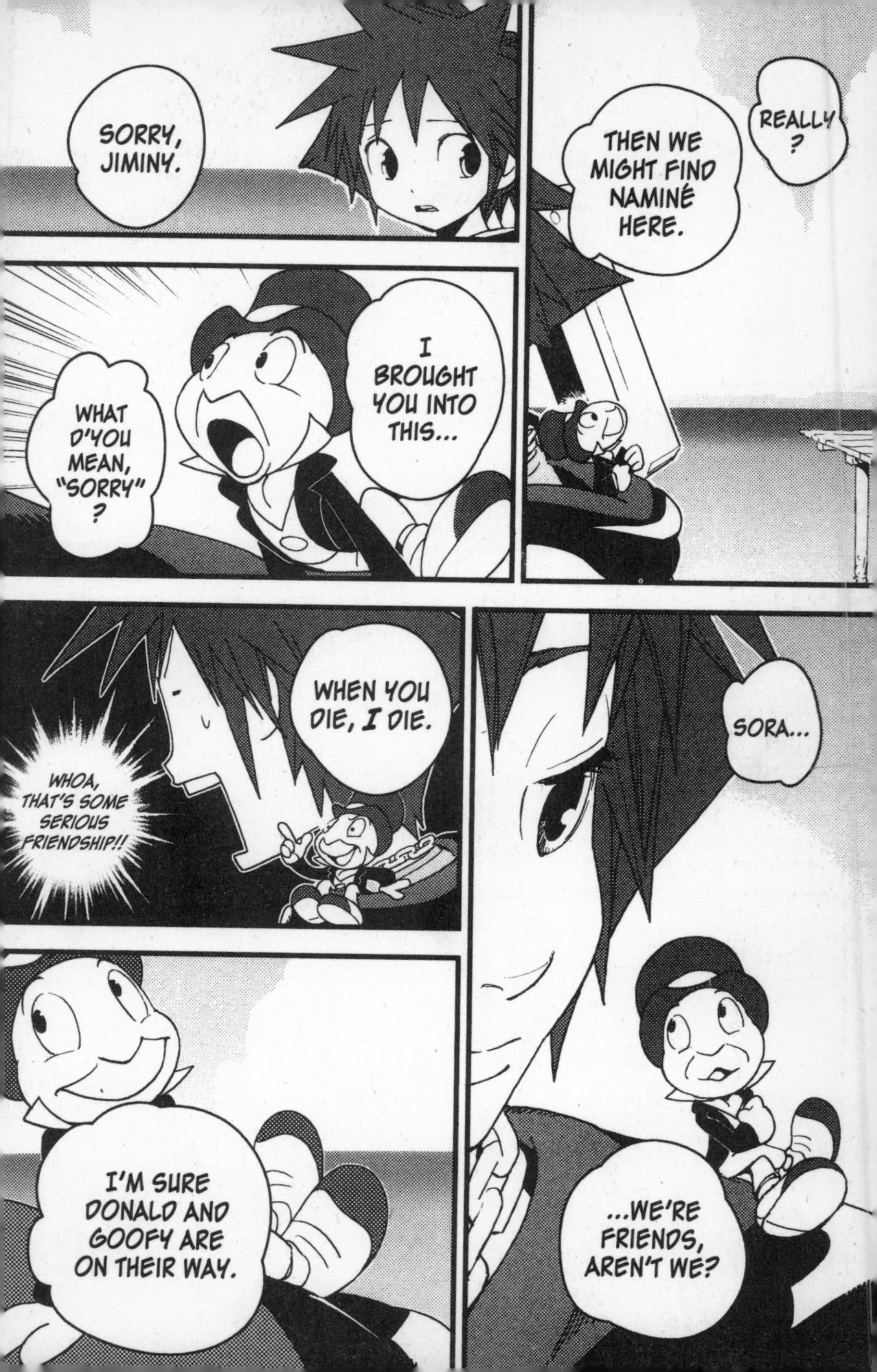
REALLY?
THEN WE MIGHT FIND NAMINÉ HERE.
SORRY, JIMINY.
I BROUGHT YOU INTO THIS...
WHAT D'YOU MEAN, "SORRY"?
SORA...
...WE'RE FRIENDS, AREN'T WE?
WHEN YOU DIE, *I* DIE.
WHOA, THAT'S SOME SERIOUS FRIENDSHIP!!
I'M SURE DONALD AND GOOFY ARE ON THEIR WAY.

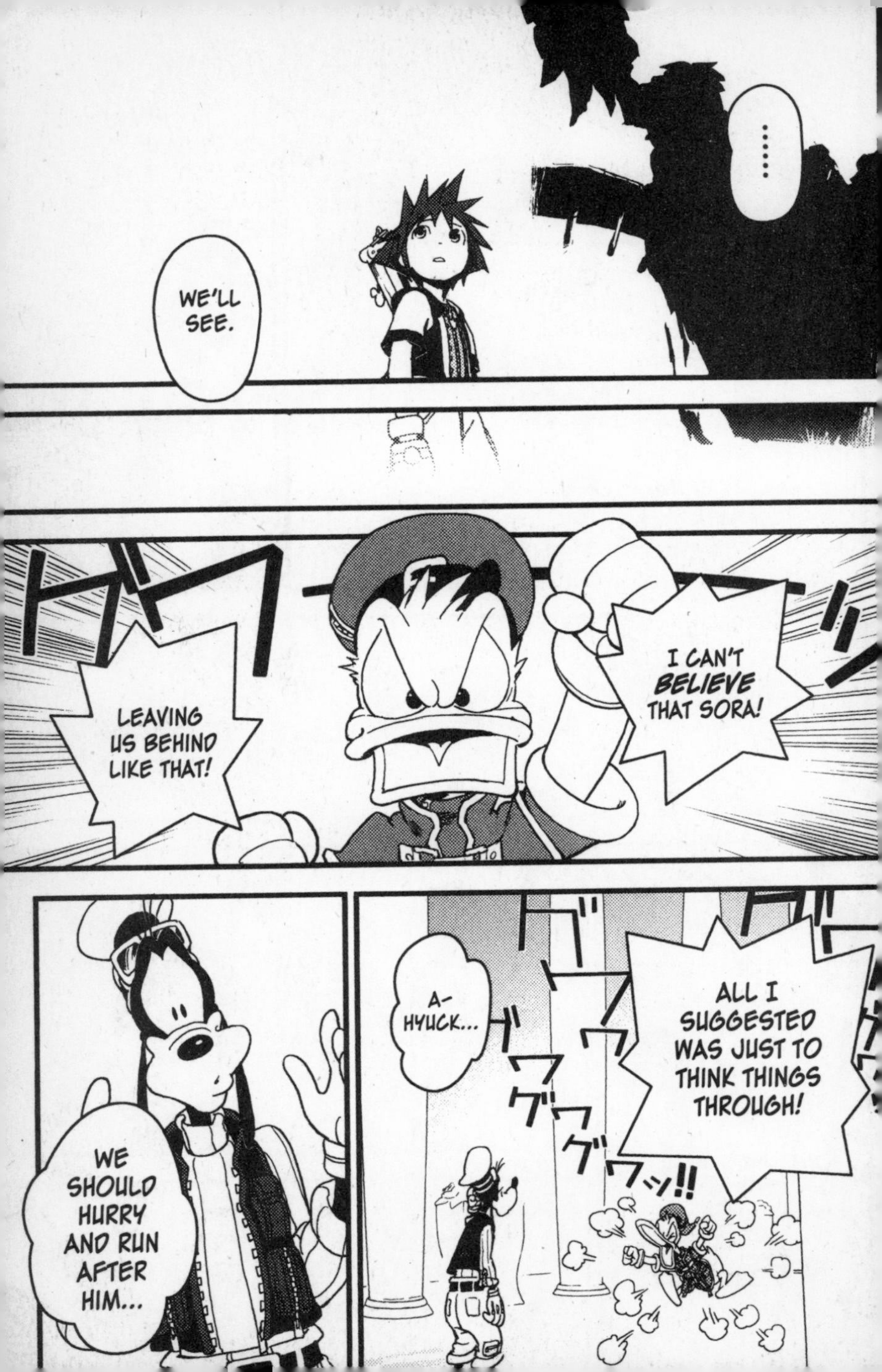
......
WE'LL SEE.
I CAN'T *BELIEVE* THAT SORA!
LEAVING US BEHIND LIKE THAT!
ALL I SUGGESTED WAS JUST TO THINK THINGS THROUGH!
A-HYUCK...
WE SHOULD HURRY AND RUN AFTER HIM...

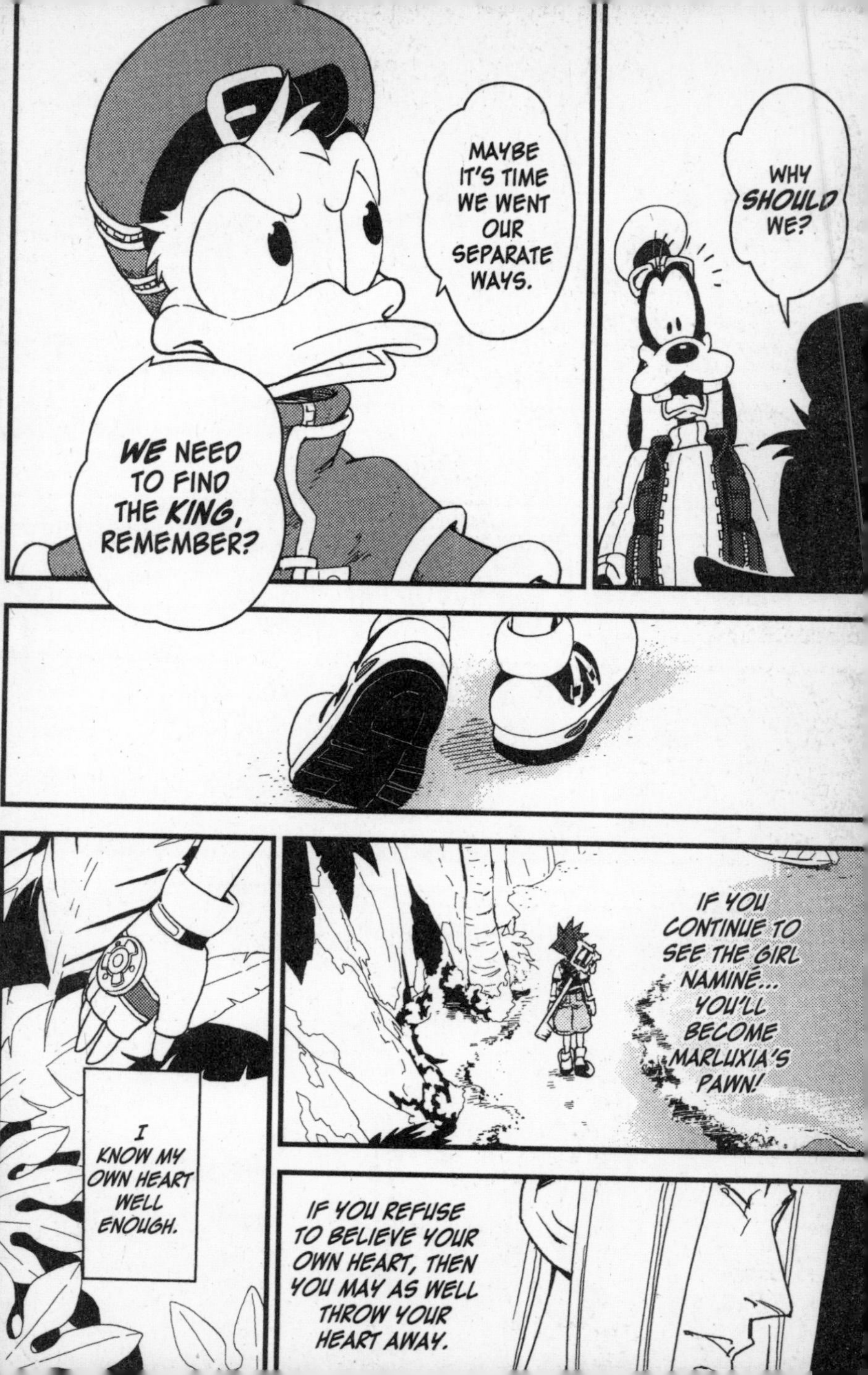
WHY SHOULD WE?
MAYBE IT'S TIME WE WENT OUR SEPARATE WAYS.
WE NEED TO FIND THE KING, REMEMBER?
IF YOU CONTINUE TO SEE THE GIRL NAMINÉ... YOU'LL BECOME MARLUXIA'S PAWN!
IF YOU REFUSE TO BELIEVE YOUR OWN HEART, THEN YOU MAY AS WELL THROW YOUR HEART AWAY.
I KNOW MY OWN HEART WELL ENOUGH.

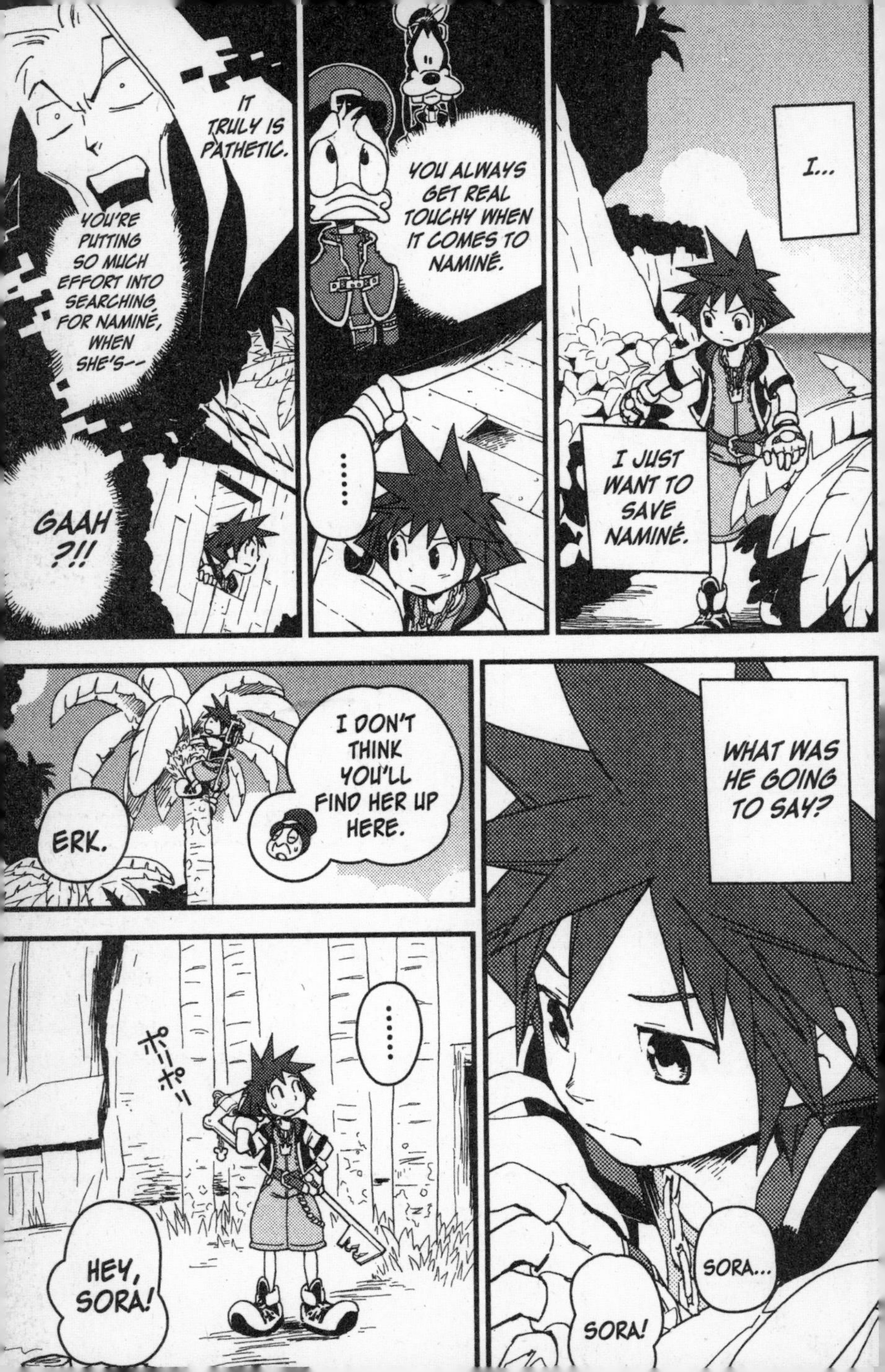
I...
I JUST WANT TO SAVE NAMINÉ.
YOU ALWAYS GET REAL TOUCHY WHEN IT COMES TO NAMINÉ.
......
IT TRULY IS PATHETIC.
YOU'RE PUTTING SO MUCH EFFORT INTO SEARCHING FOR NAMINÉ, WHEN SHE'S--
GAAH ?!!
WHAT WAS HE GOING TO SAY?
SORA...
SORA!
I DON'T THINK YOU'LL FIND HER UP HERE.
ERK.
......
ポリポリ
HEY, SORA!

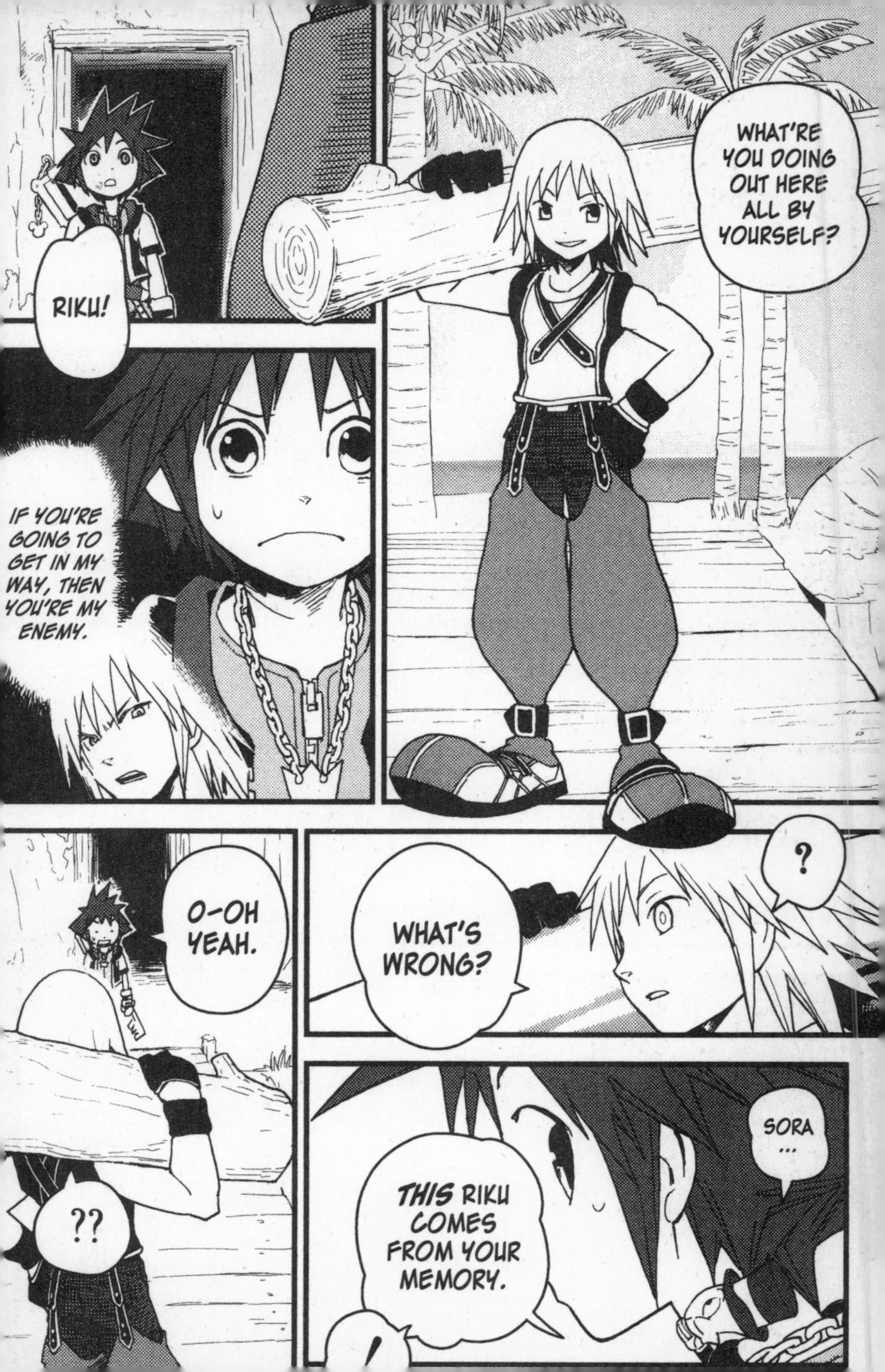
WHAT'RE YOU DOING OUT HERE ALL BY YOURSELF?
RIKU!
IF YOU'RE GOING TO GET IN MY WAY, THEN YOU'RE MY ENEMY.
?
WHAT'S WRONG?
SORA ...
THIS RIKU COMES FROM YOUR MEMORY.
O-OH YEAH.
??

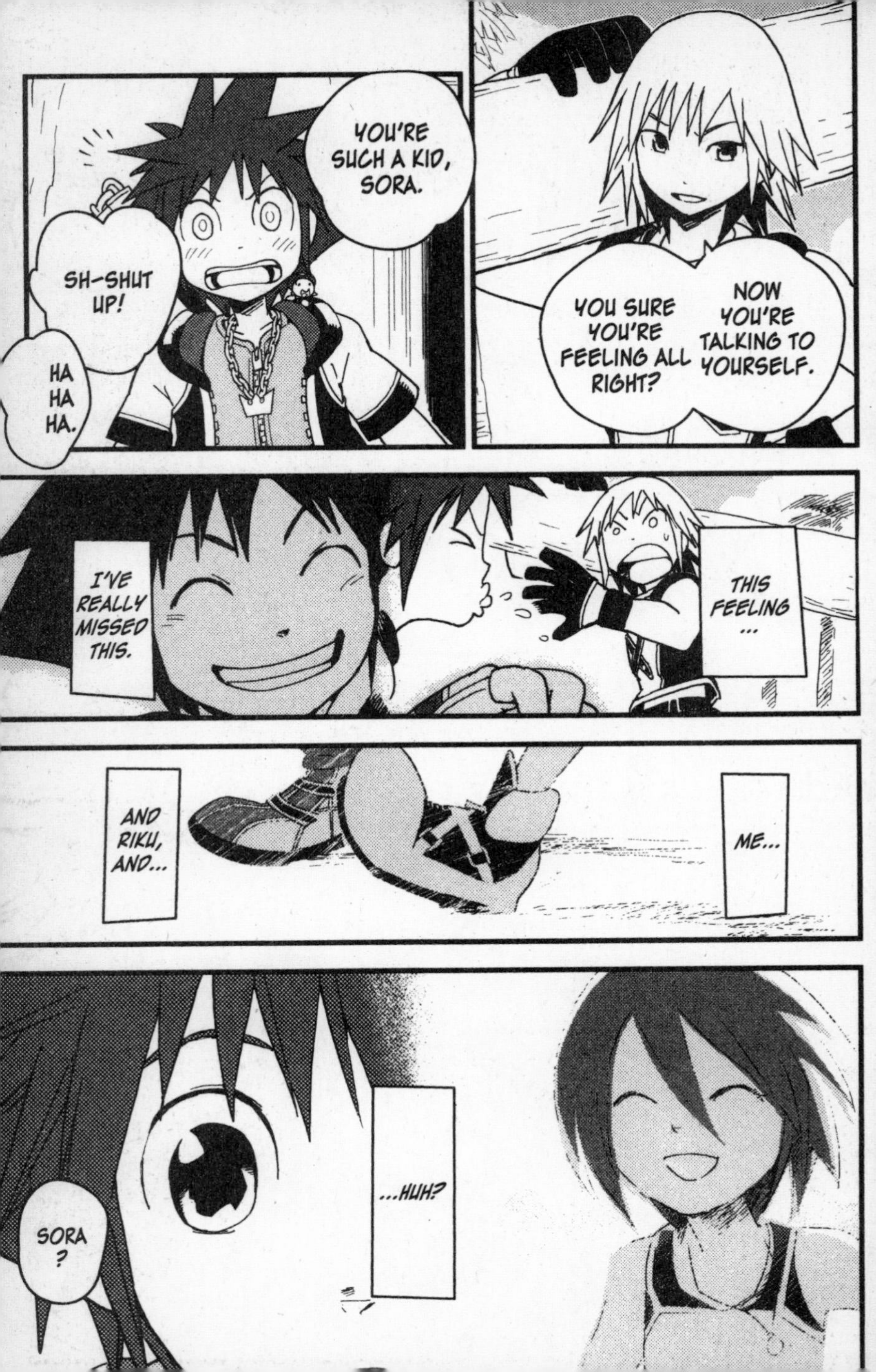
NOW YOU'RE TALKING TO YOURSELF.
YOU SURE YOU'RE FEELING ALL RIGHT?
YOU'RE SUCH A KID, SORA.
SH-SHUT UP!
HA HA HA.
THIS FEELING...
I'VE REALLY MISSED THIS.
ME...
AND RIKU, AND...
...HUH?
SORA?

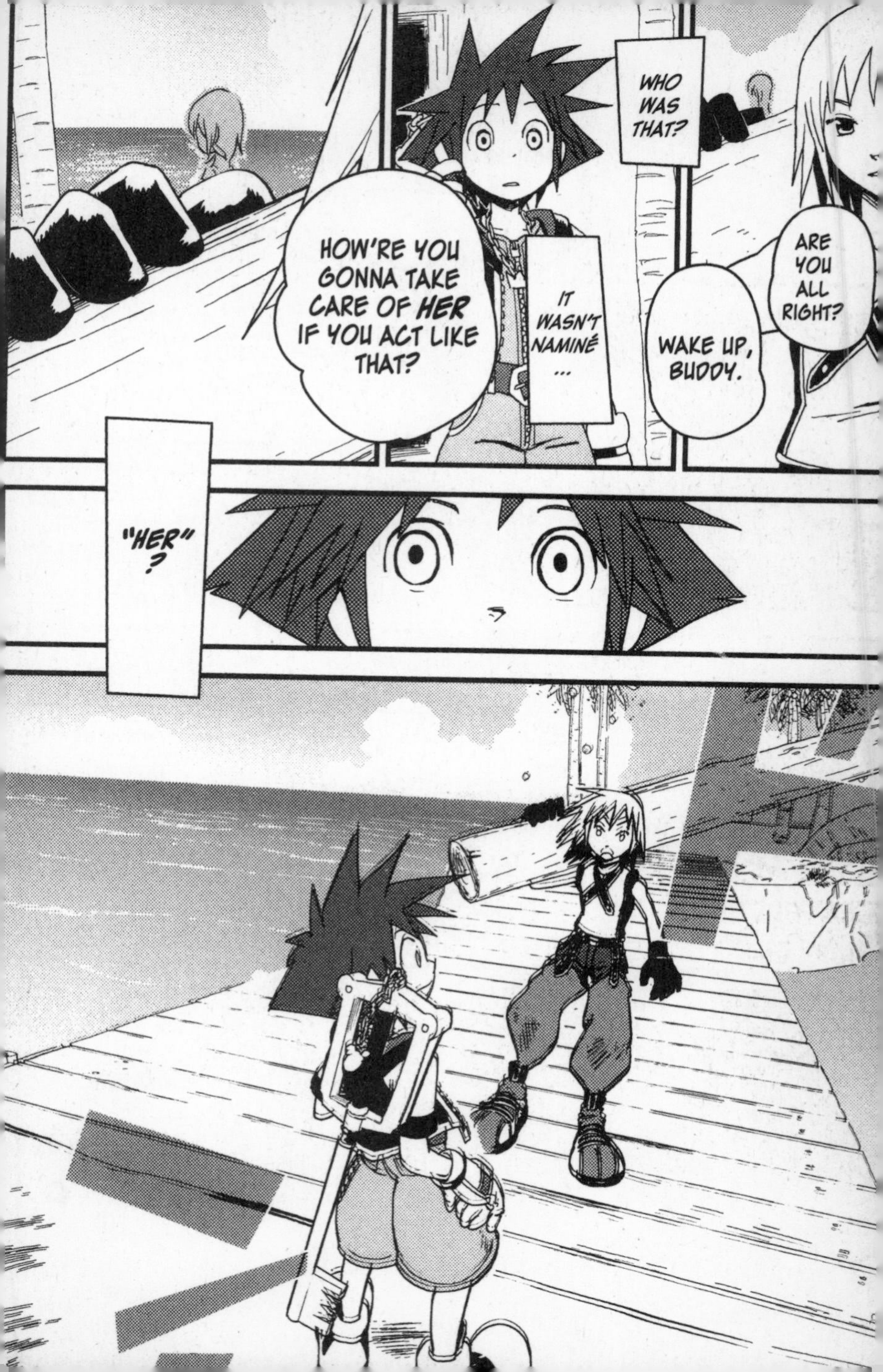
WHO WAS THAT?
ARE YOU ALL RIGHT?
WAKE UP, BUDDY.
IT WASN'T NAMINÉ ...
HOW'RE YOU GONNA TAKE CARE OF **HER** IF YOU ACT LIKE THAT?
"HER" ?

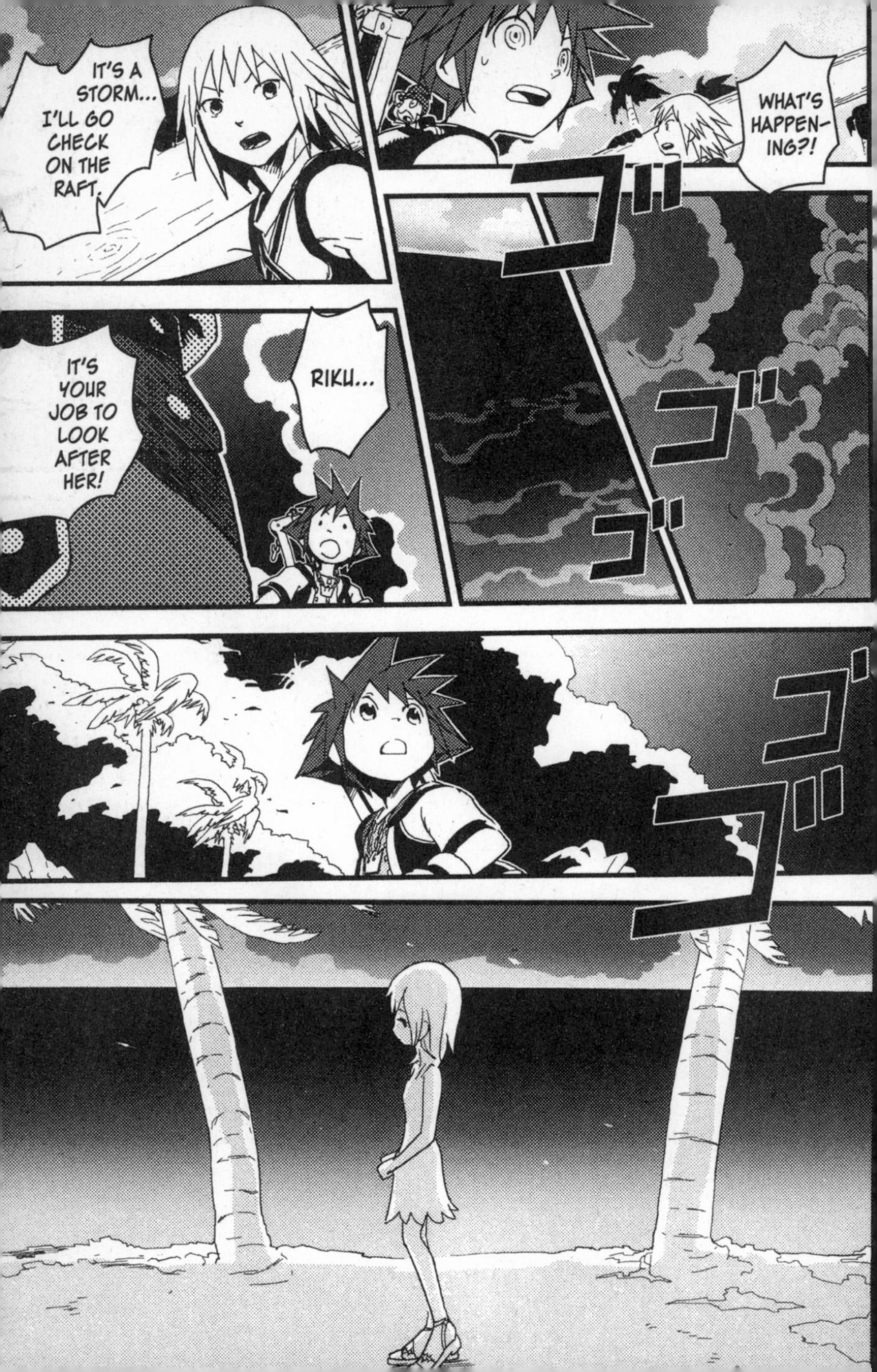
WHAT'S HAPPEN-ING?!
IT'S A STORM... I'LL GO CHECK ON THE RAFT.
ゴ
ゴ
ゴ
RIKU...
IT'S YOUR JOB TO LOOK AFTER HER!
ゴ
ゴ

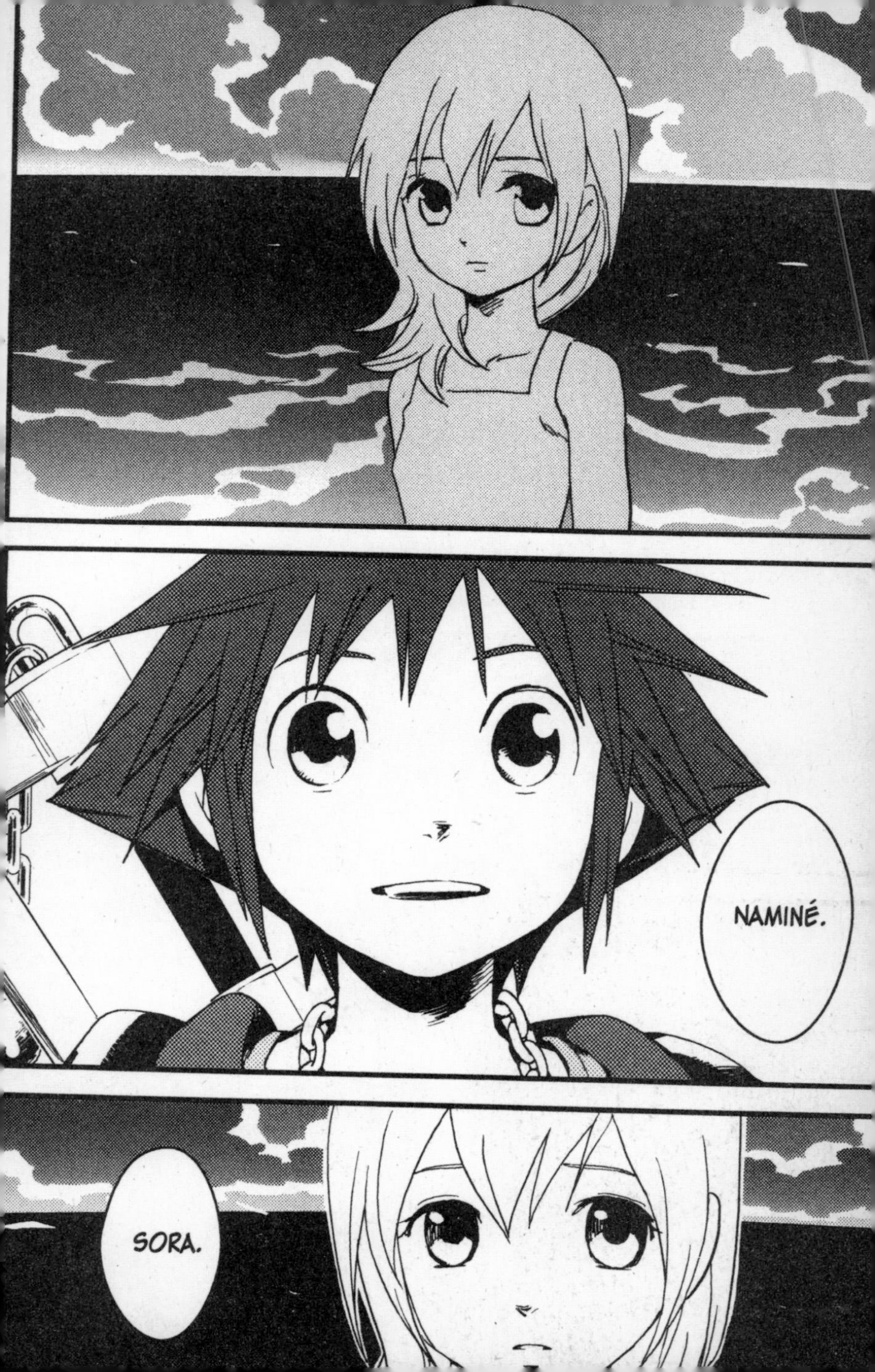
NAMINÉ.
SORA.

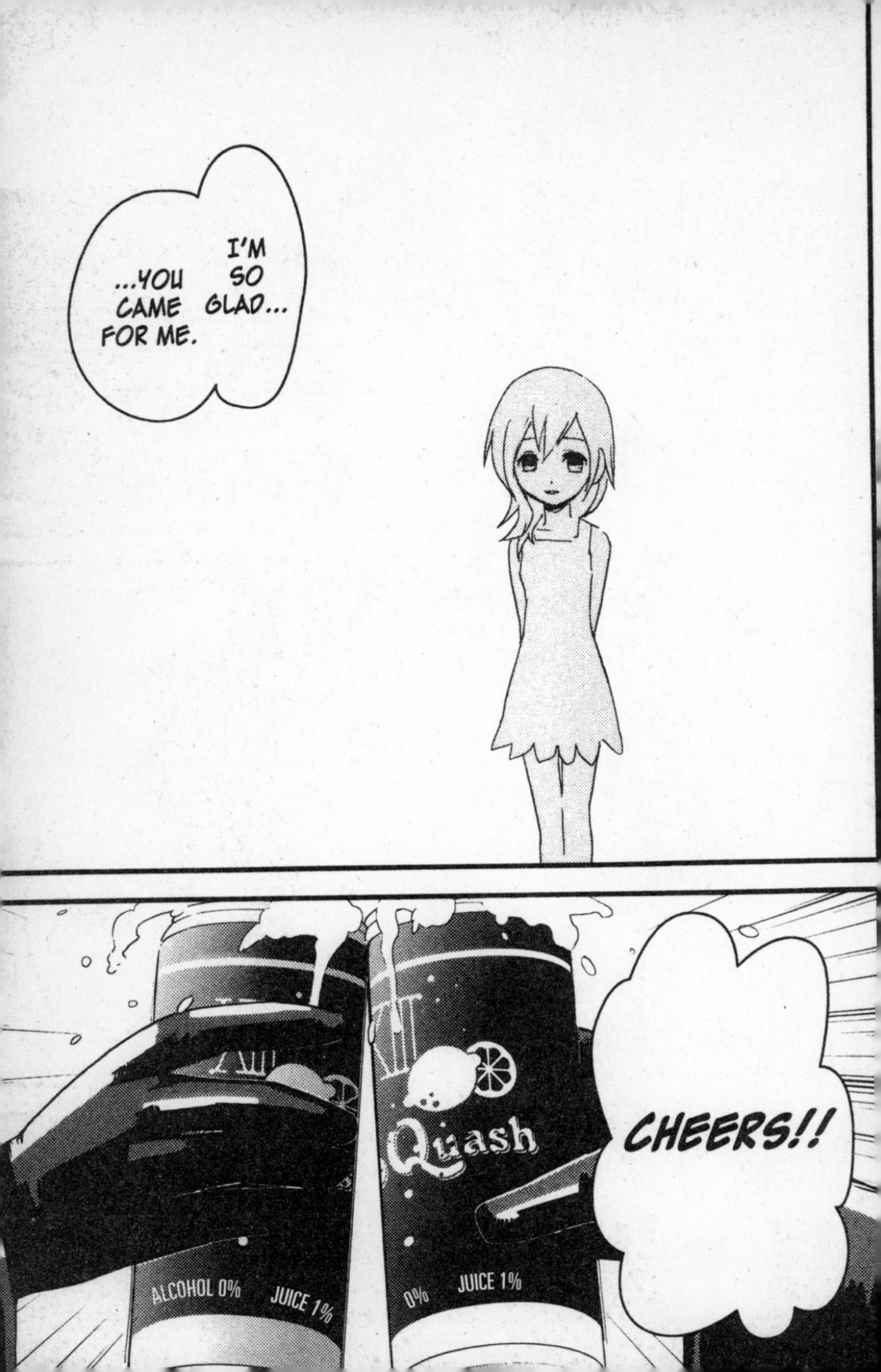
I'M SO GLAD... ...YOU CAME FOR ME.
CHEERS!!
Quash
0% JUICE 1%
ALCOHOL 0% JUICE 1%

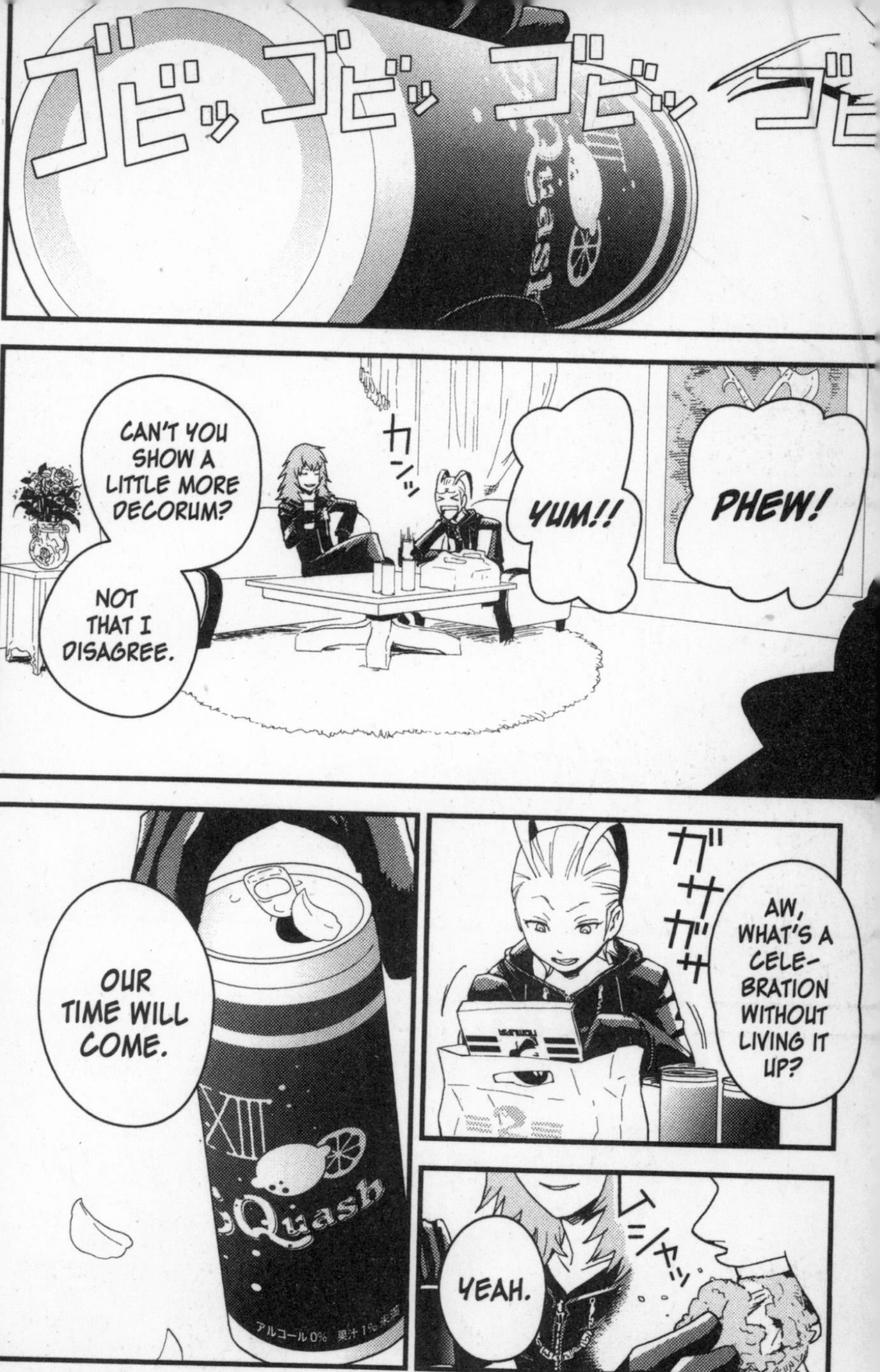
ゴビッ ゴビッ ゴビッ ゴビ
PHEW!
YUM!!
カンッ
CAN'T YOU SHOW A LITTLE MORE DECORUM?
NOT THAT I DISAGREE.
ガサガサ
AW, WHAT'S A CELE-BRATION WITHOUT LIVING IT UP?
ムシャッ
YEAH.
OUR TIME WILL COME.
XIII
SQuash
アルコール0% 果汁1%未満

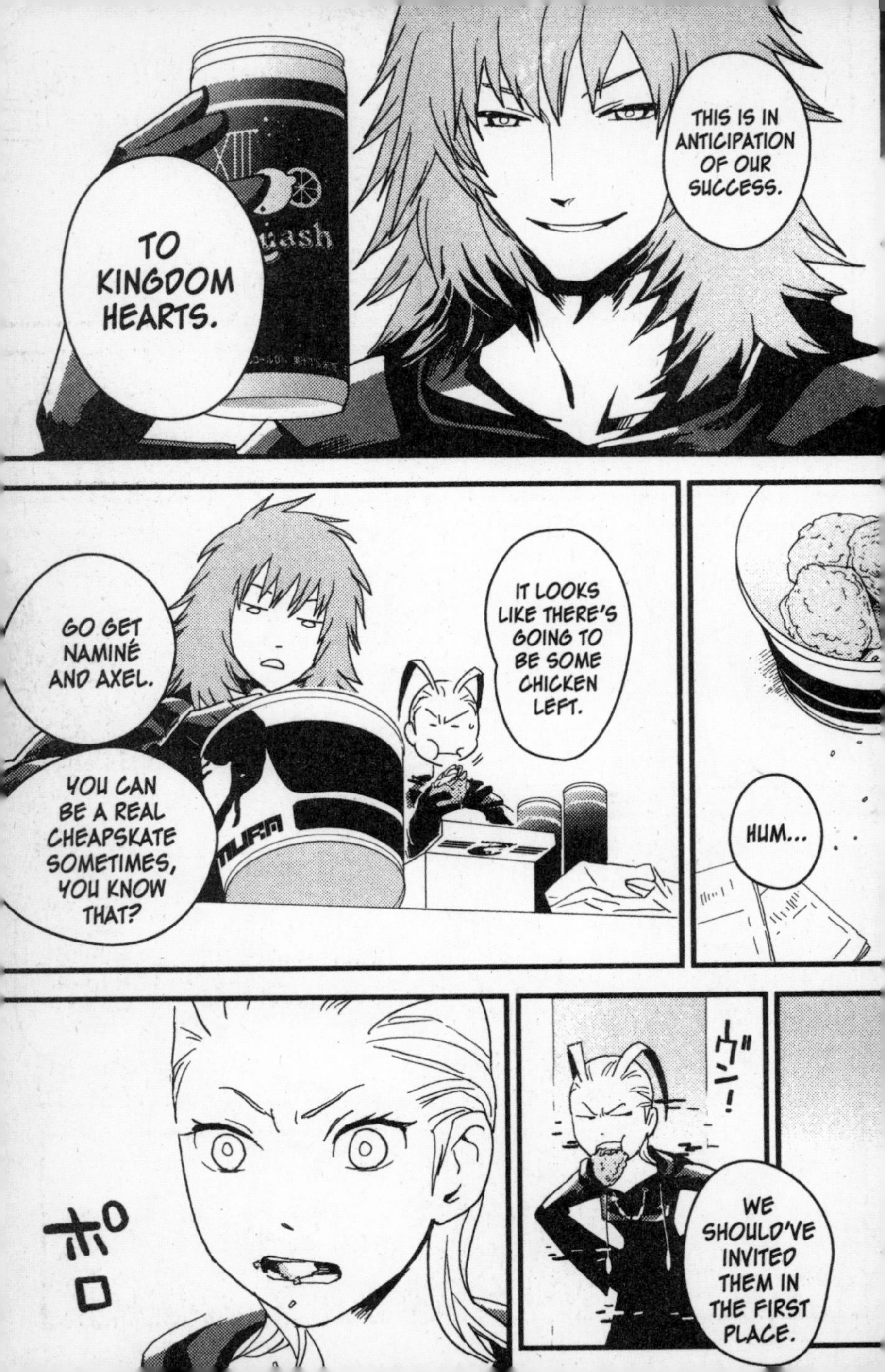
THIS IS IN ANTICIPATION OF OUR SUCCESS.
TO KINGDOM HEARTS.
HUM...
IT LOOKS LIKE THERE'S GOING TO BE SOME CHICKEN LEFT.
GO GET NAMINÉ AND AXEL.
YOU CAN BE A REAL CHEAPSKATE SOMETIMES, YOU KNOW THAT?
ウン!
WE SHOULD'VE INVITED THEM IN THE FIRST PLACE.
ポロ

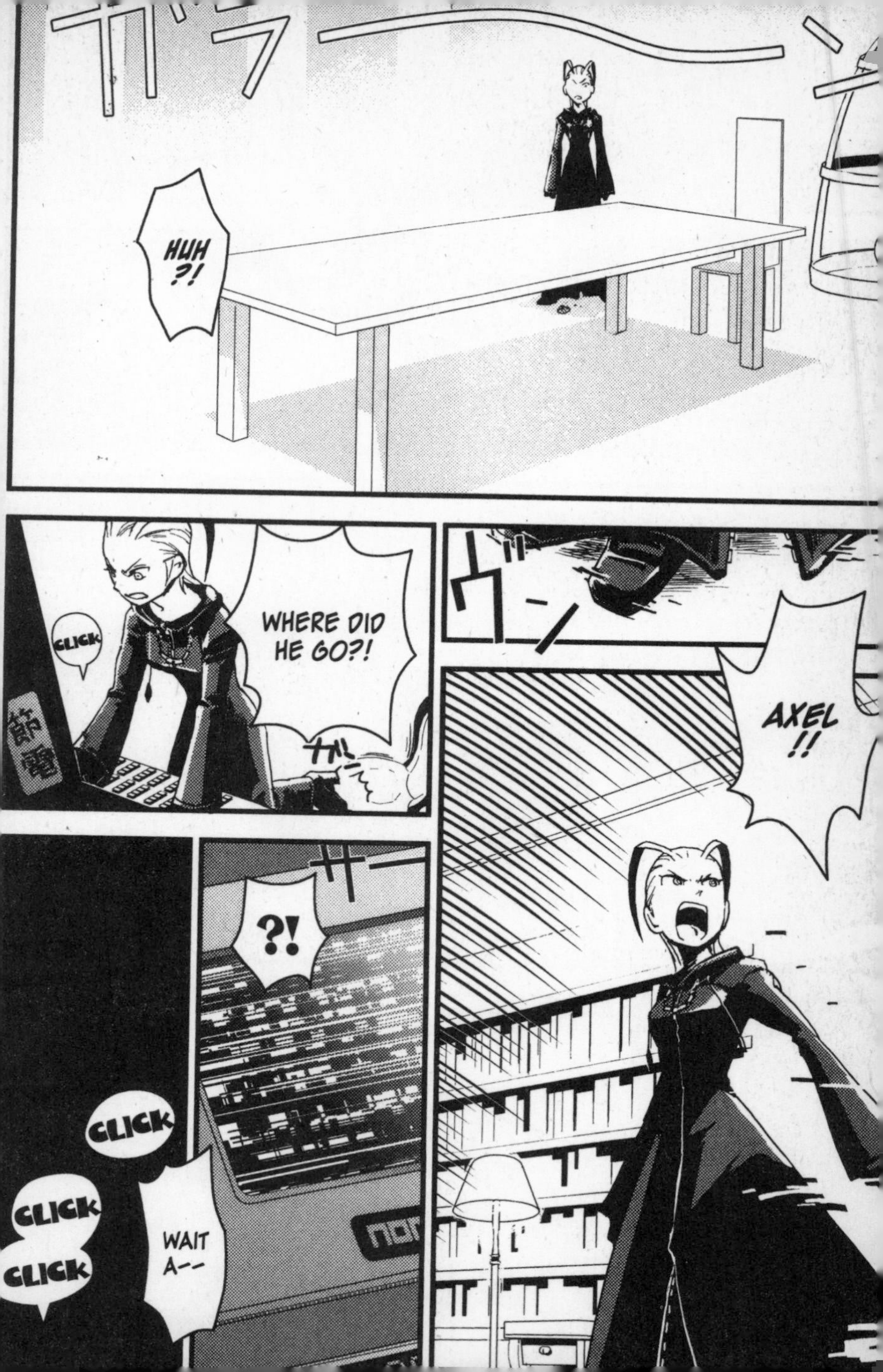
HUH ?!
WHERE DID HE GO?!
CLICK
節電
?!
WAIT A--
CLICK
CLICK
CLICK
AXEL !!

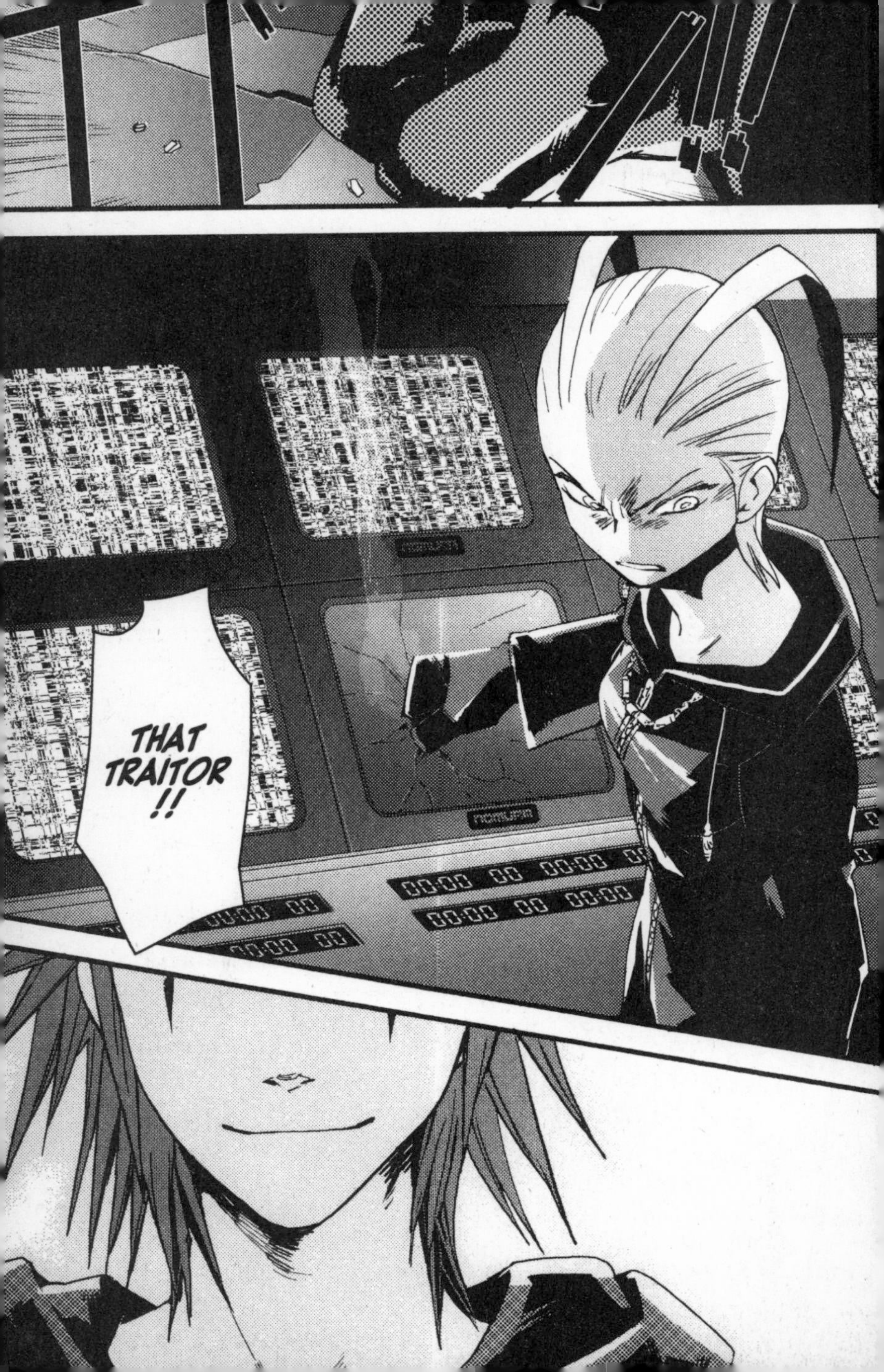
THAT TRAITOR !!

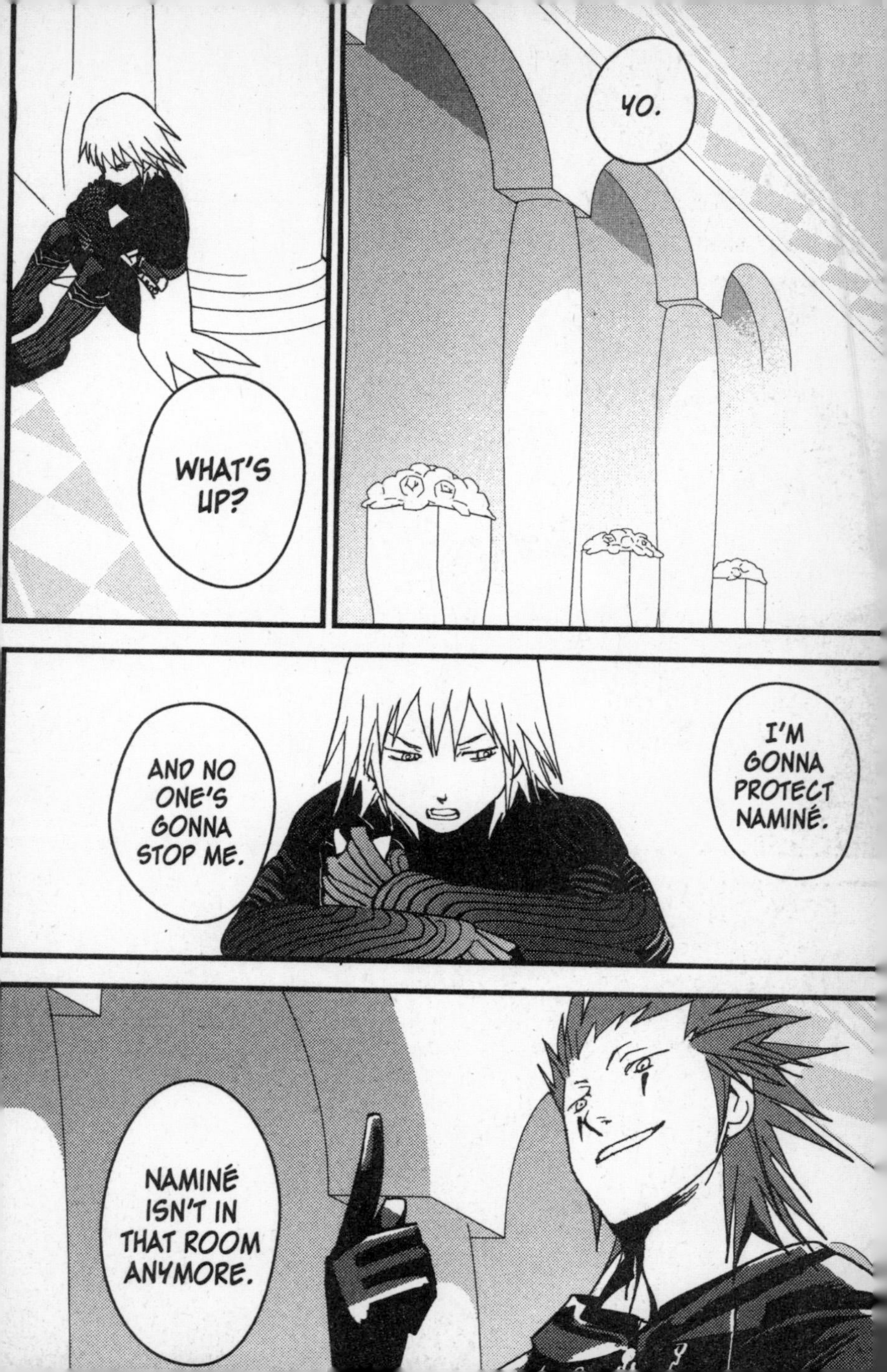
YO.
WHAT'S UP?
I'M GONNA PROTECT NAMINÉ.
AND NO ONE'S GONNA STOP ME.
NAMINÉ ISN'T IN THAT ROOM ANYMORE.

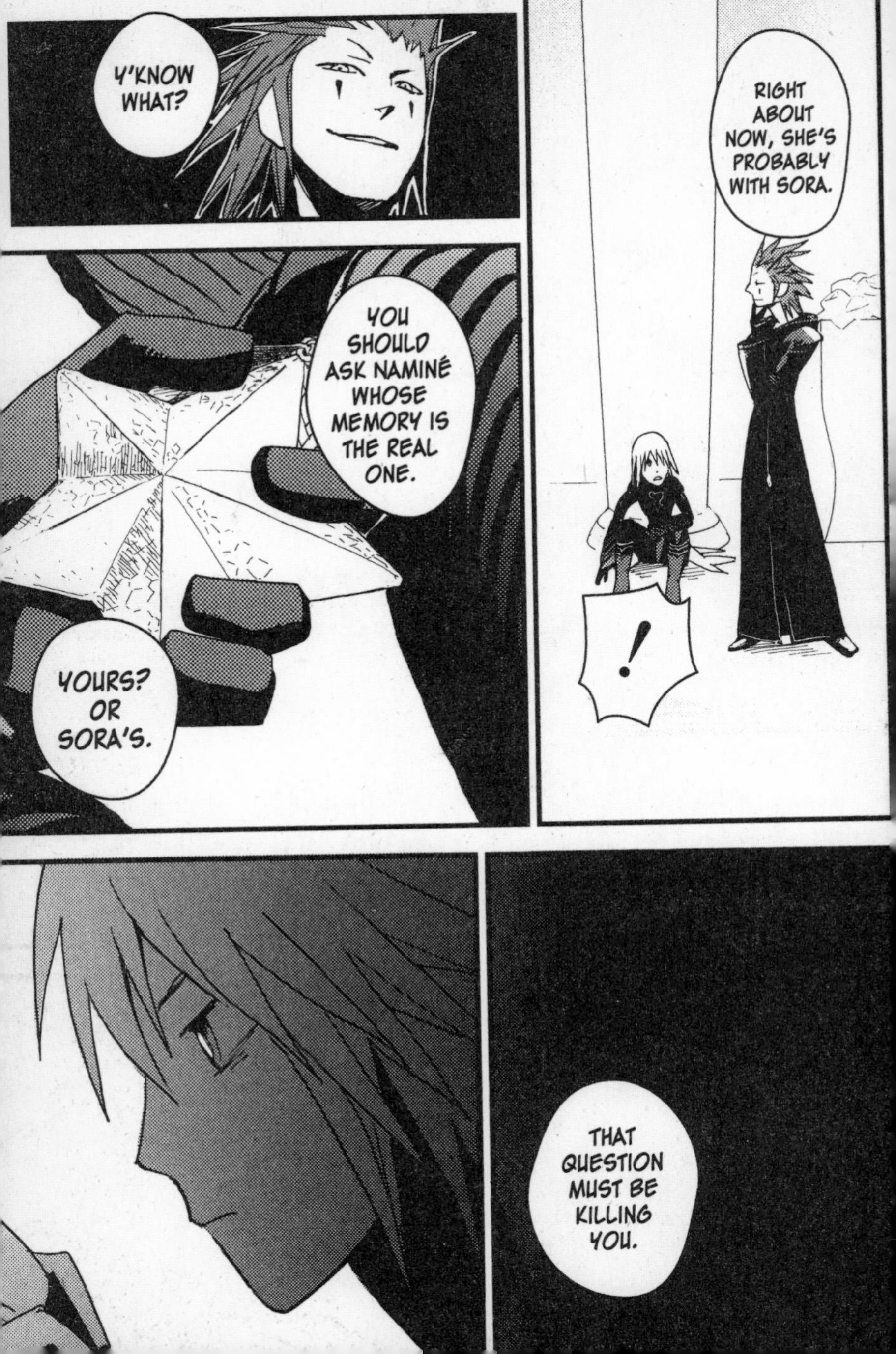
RIGHT ABOUT NOW, SHE'S PROBABLY WITH SORA.
!
Y'KNOW WHAT?
YOU SHOULD ASK NAMINÉ WHOSE MEMORY IS THE REAL ONE.
YOURS? OR SORA'S.
THAT QUESTION MUST BE KILLING YOU.

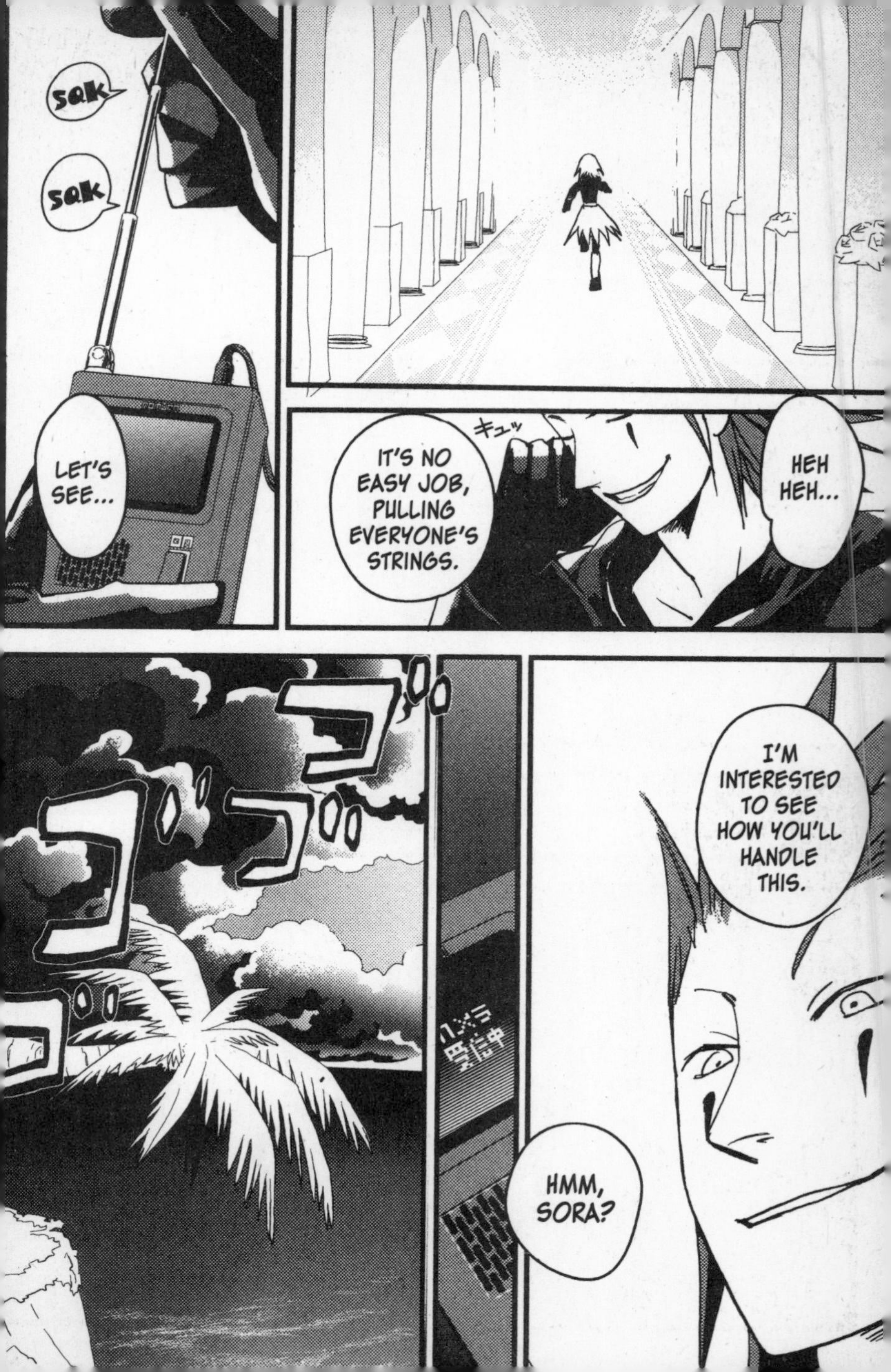
HEH HEH...
キュッ
IT'S NO EASY JOB, PULLING EVERYONE'S STRINGS.
SQK
SQK
LET'S SEE...
I'M INTERESTED TO SEE HOW YOU'LL HANDLE THIS.
HMM, SORA?

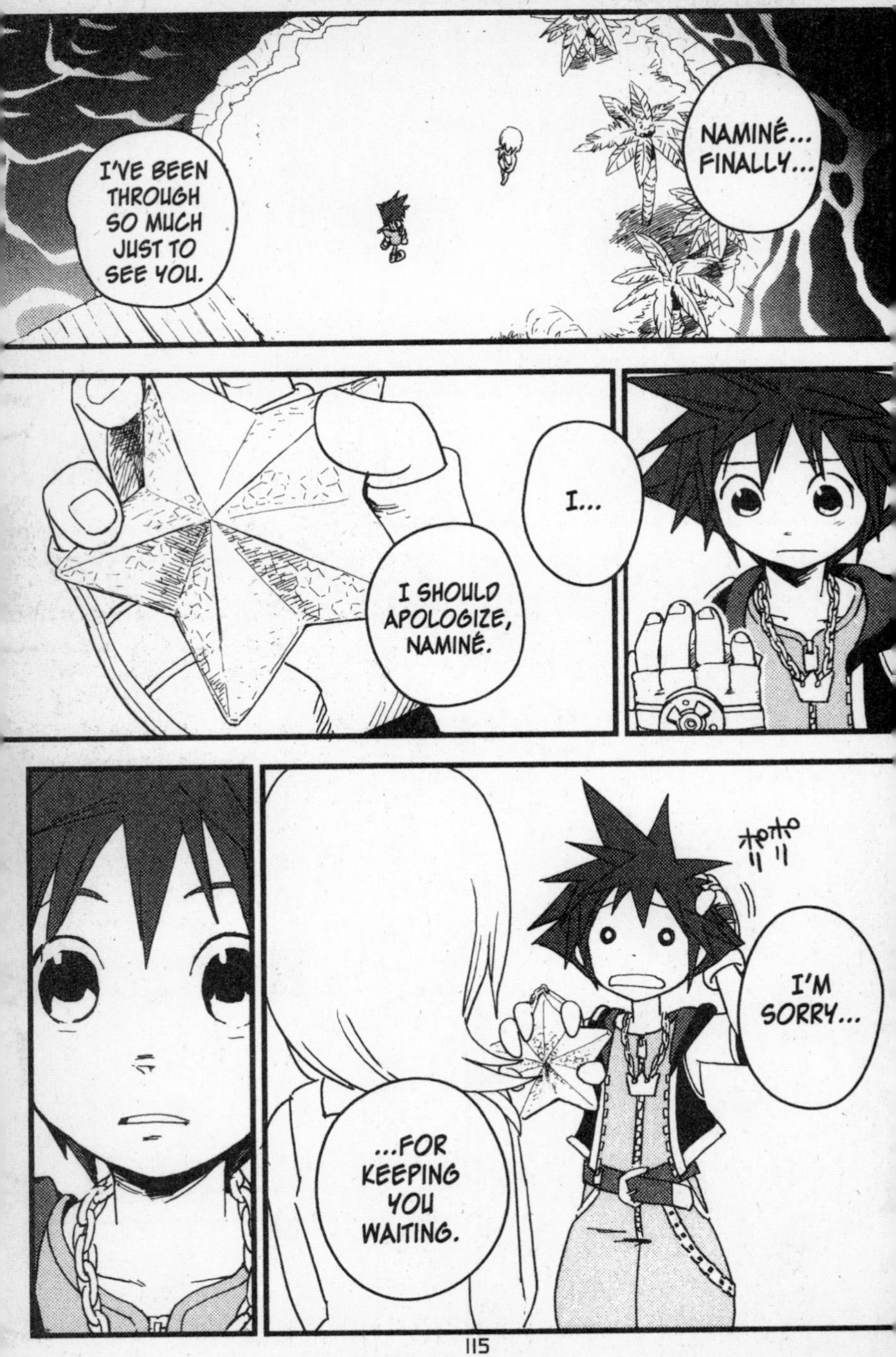
NAMINÉ... FINALLY...
I'VE BEEN THROUGH SO MUCH JUST TO SEE YOU.
I...
I SHOULD APOLOGIZE, NAMINÉ.
I'M SORRY...
...FOR KEEPING YOU WAITING.

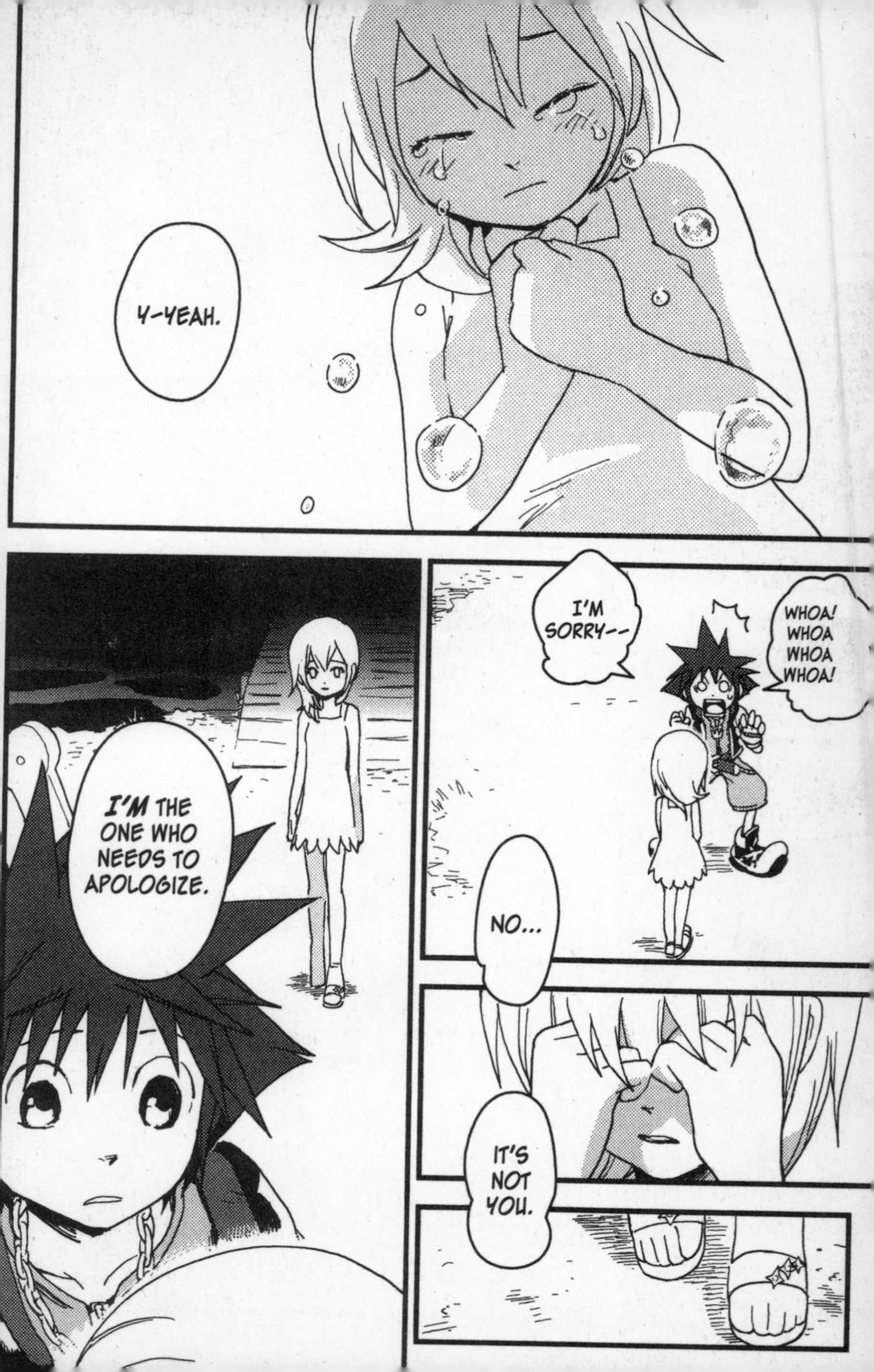
Y-YEAH.
I'M SORRY--
WHOA! WHOA WHOA WHOA!
NO...
IT'S NOT YOU.
I'M THE ONE WHO NEEDS TO APOLOGIZE.

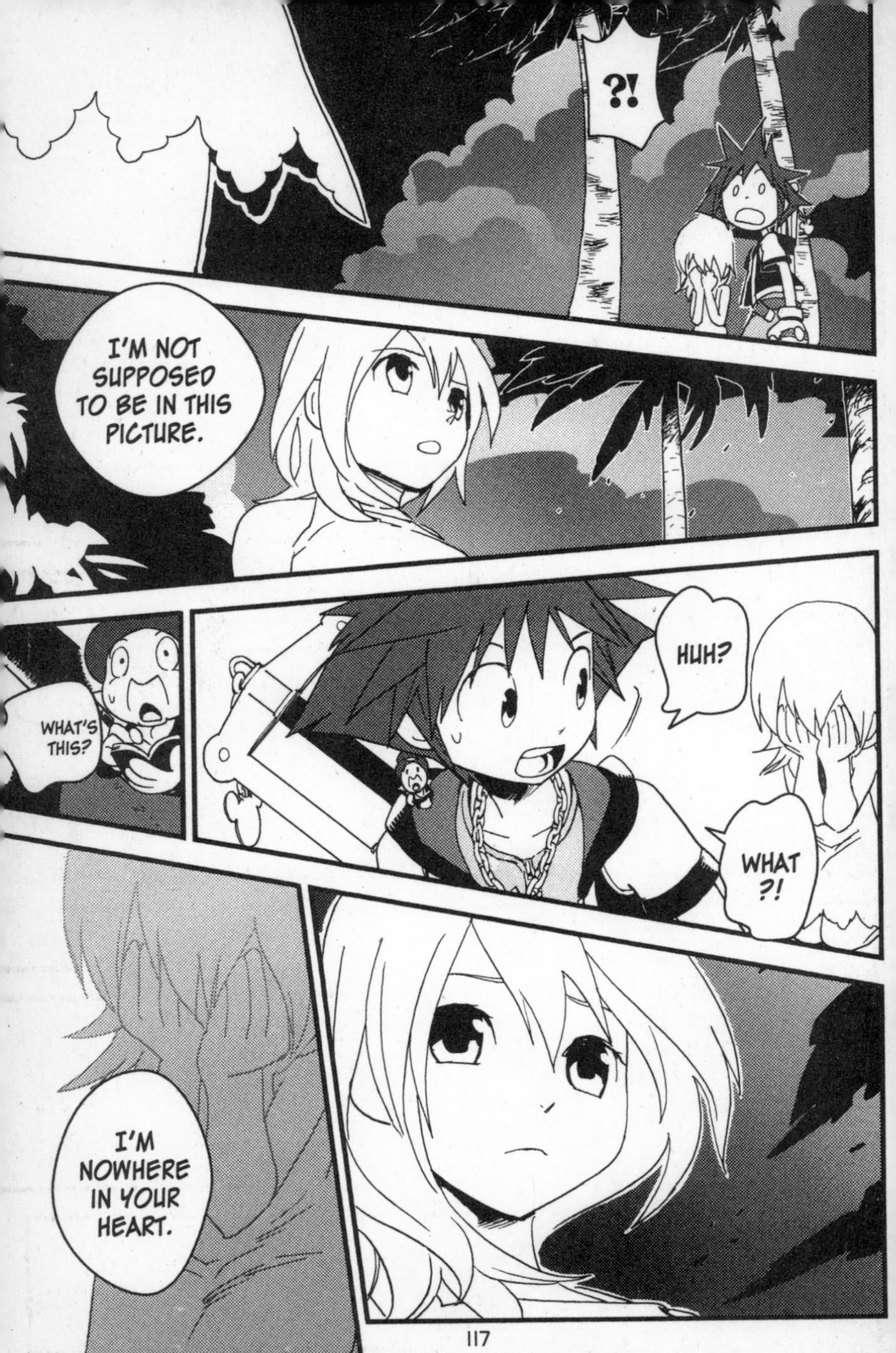
?!
I'M NOT SUPPOSED TO BE IN THIS PICTURE.
HUH?
WHAT ?!
WHAT'S THIS?
I'M NOWHERE IN YOUR HEART.

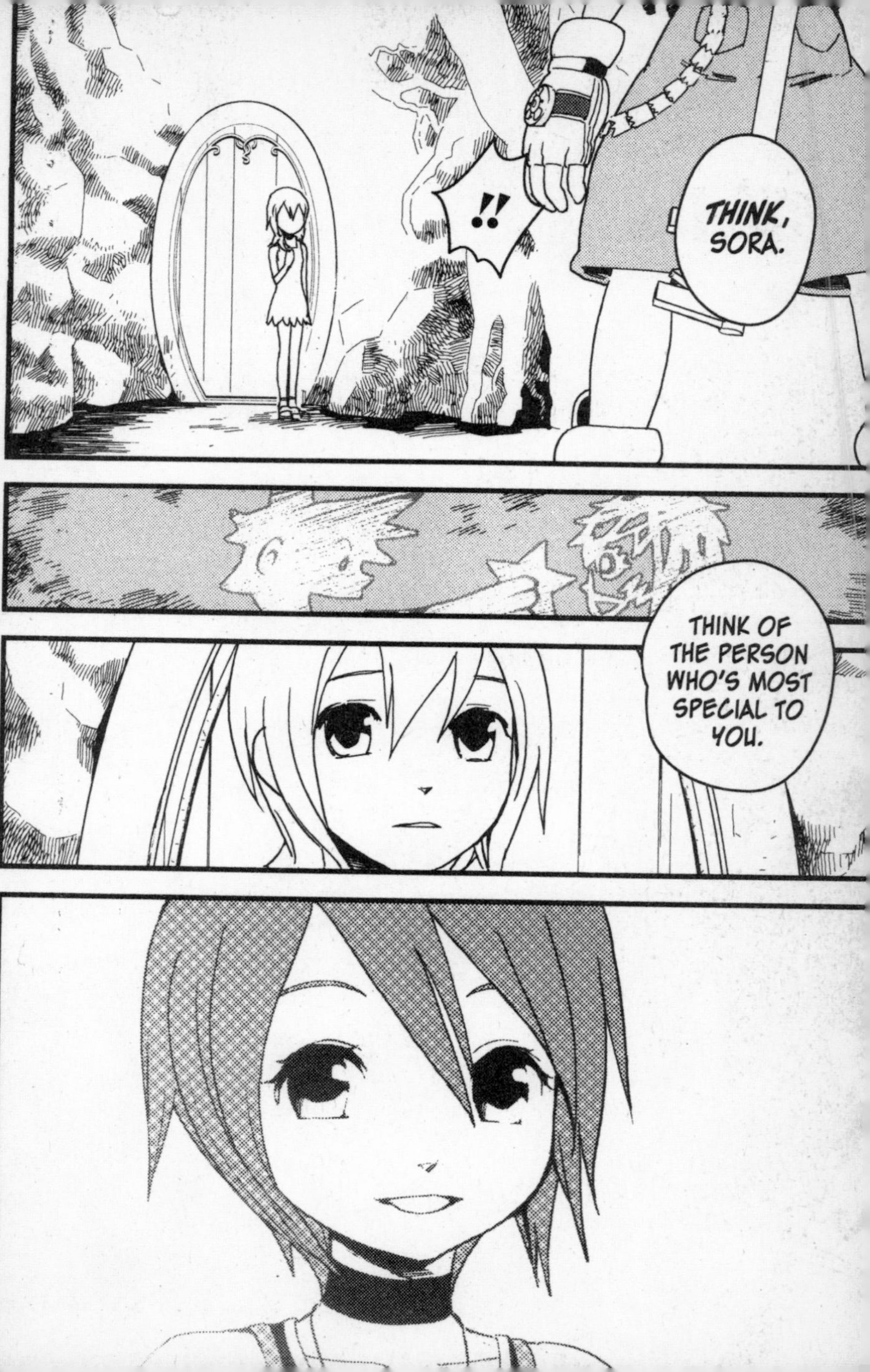
THINK, SORA.
!!
THINK OF THE PERSON WHO'S MOST SPECIAL TO YOU.

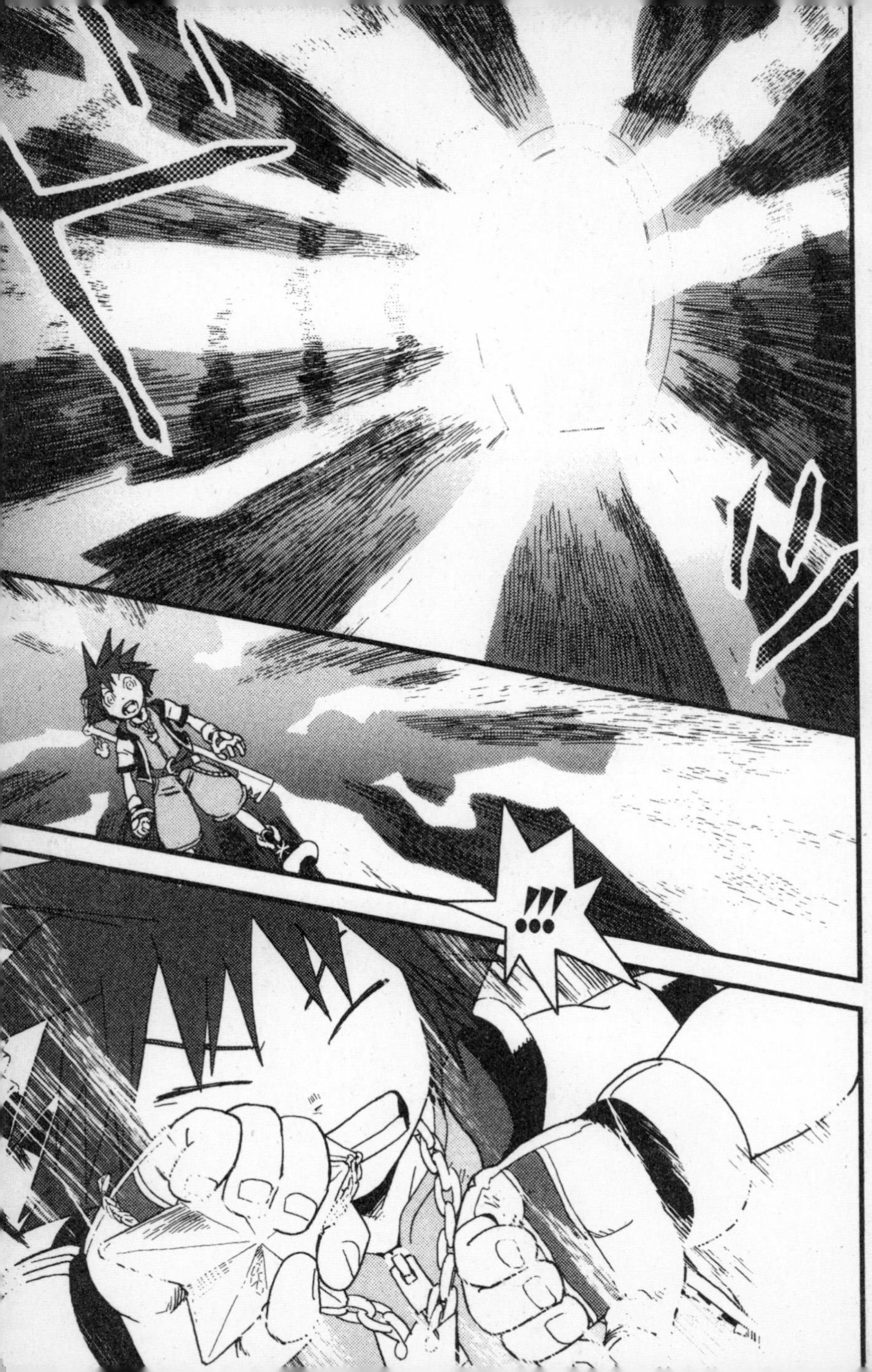
!!!

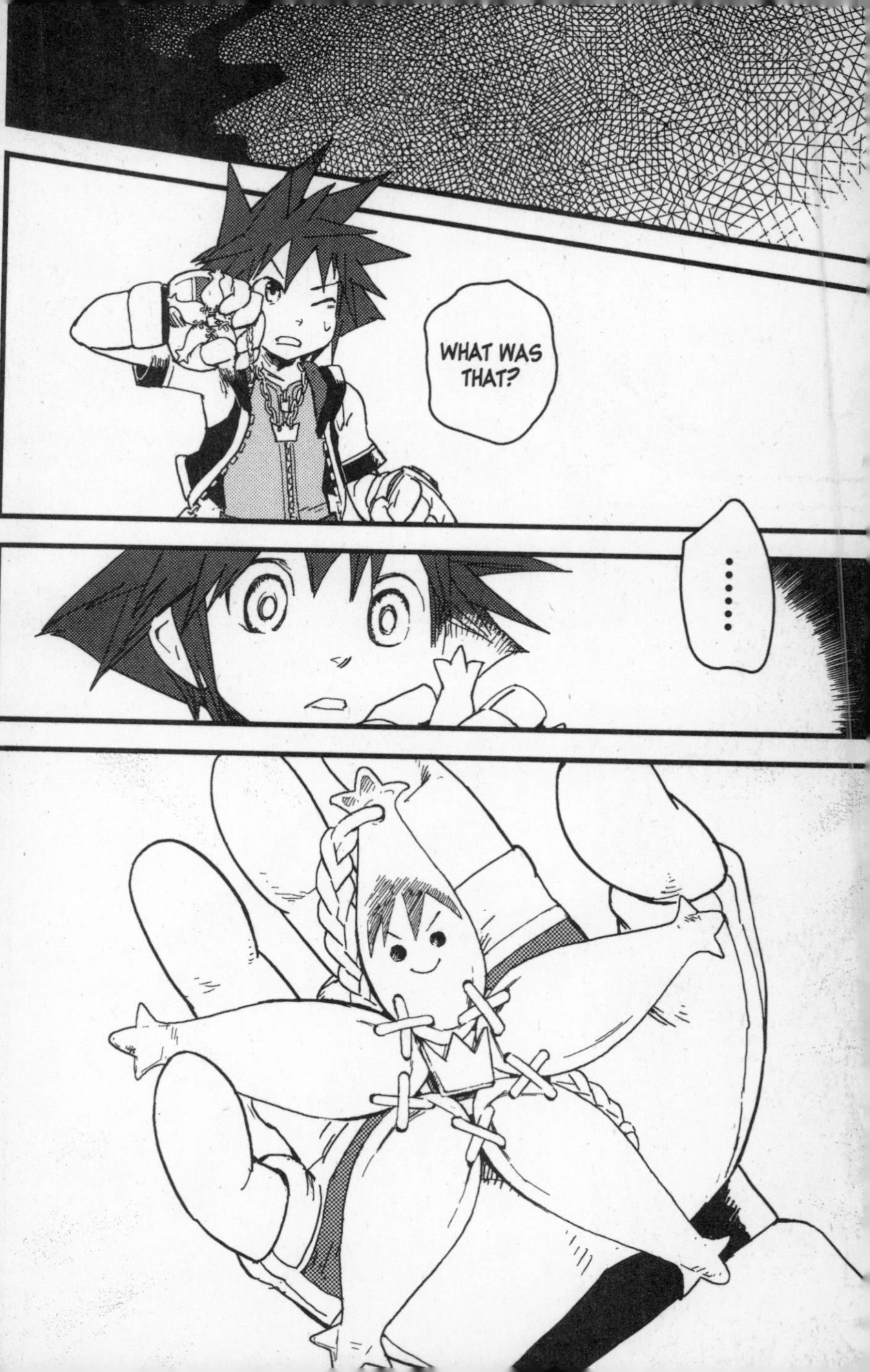
WHAT WAS THAT?
......

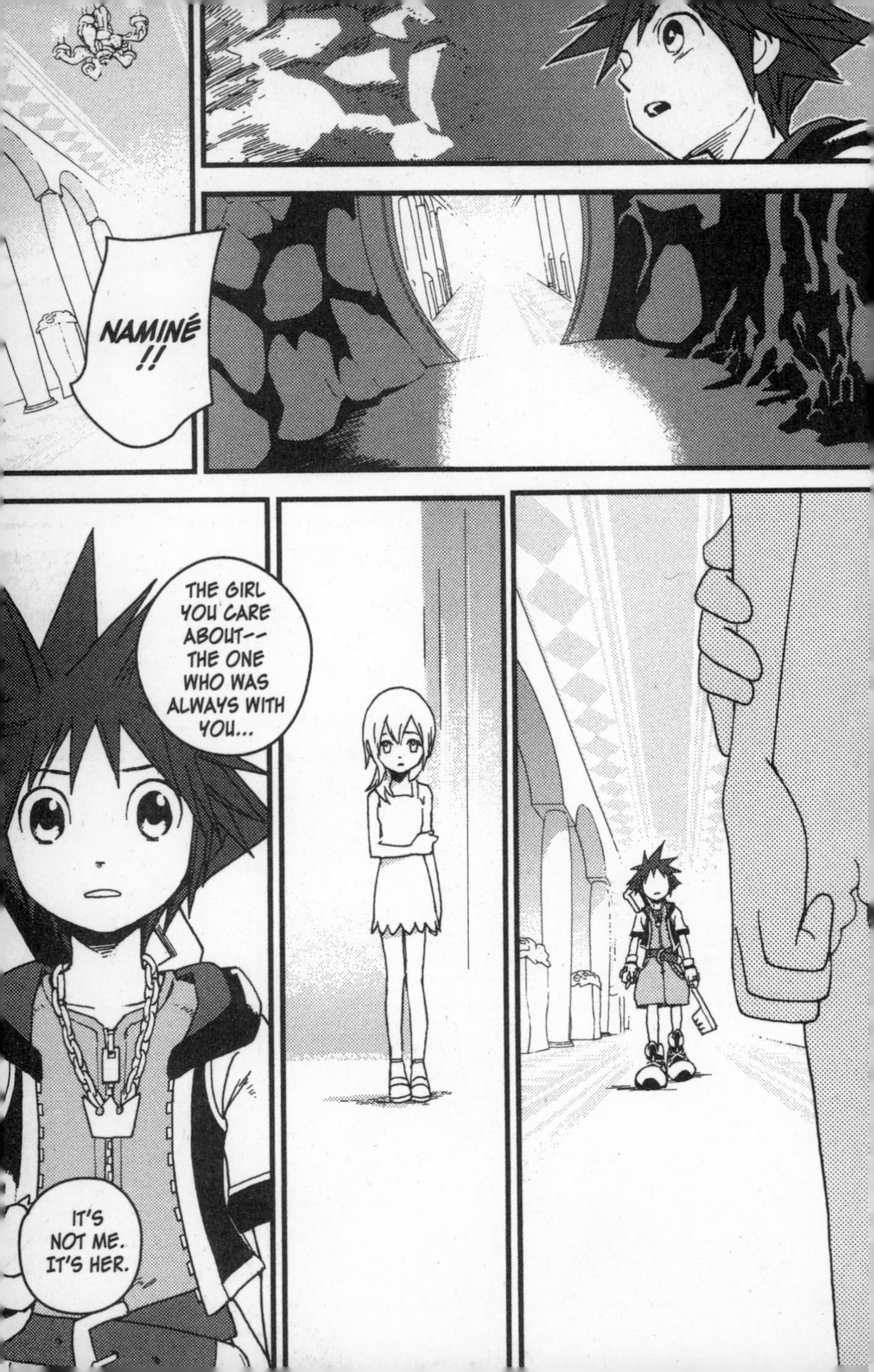
NAMINÉ !!
THE GIRL YOU CARE ABOUT-- THE ONE WHO WAS ALWAYS WITH YOU...
IT'S NOT ME. IT'S HER.

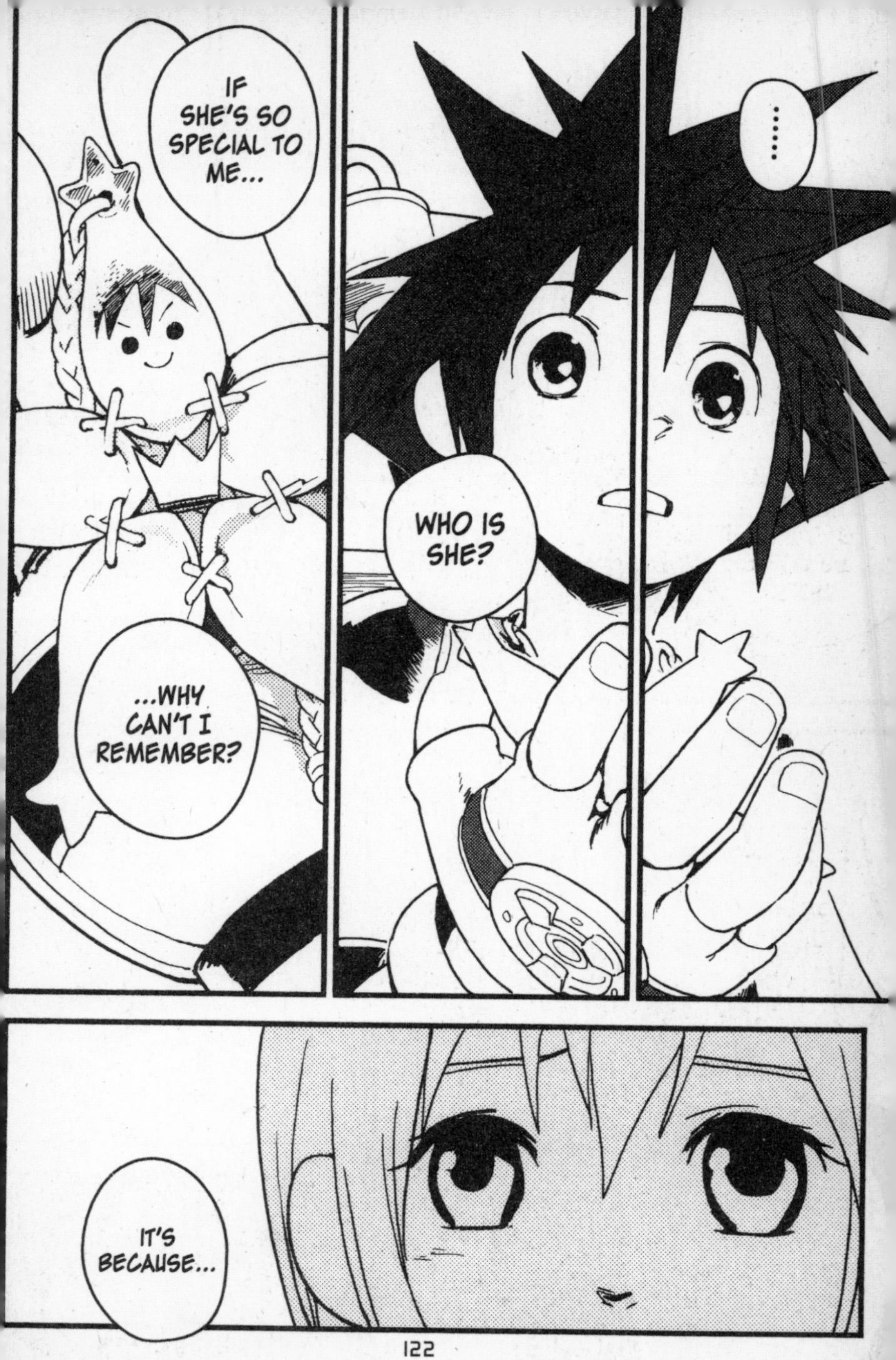
……
WHO IS SHE?
IF SHE'S SO SPECIAL TO ME...
...WHY CAN'T I REMEMBER?
IT'S BECAUSE...

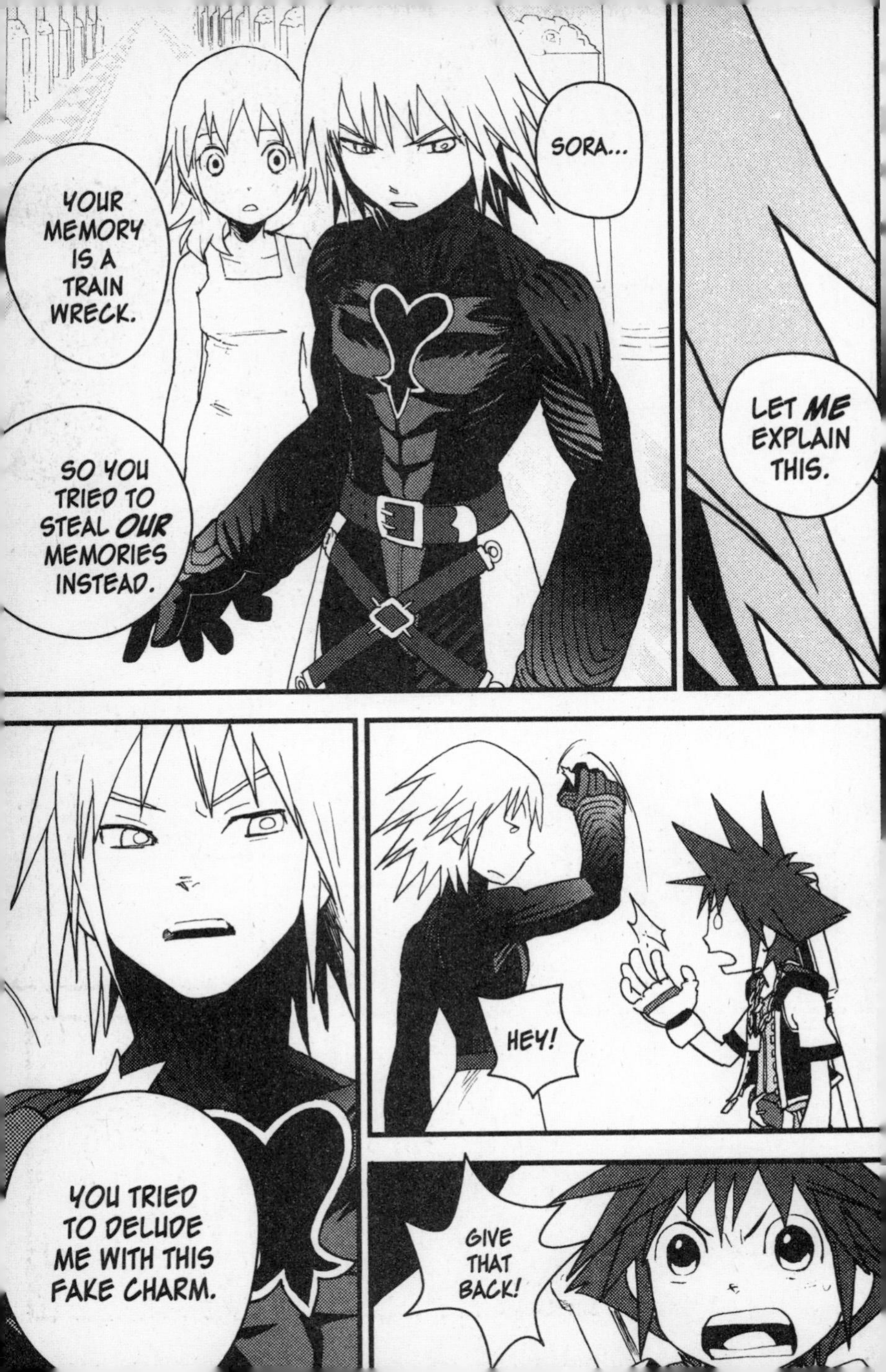
LET ME EXPLAIN THIS.
SORA...
YOUR MEMORY IS A TRAIN WRECK.
SO YOU TRIED TO STEAL OUR MEMORIES INSTEAD.
HEY!
GIVE THAT BACK!
YOU TRIED TO DELUDE ME WITH THIS FAKE CHARM.

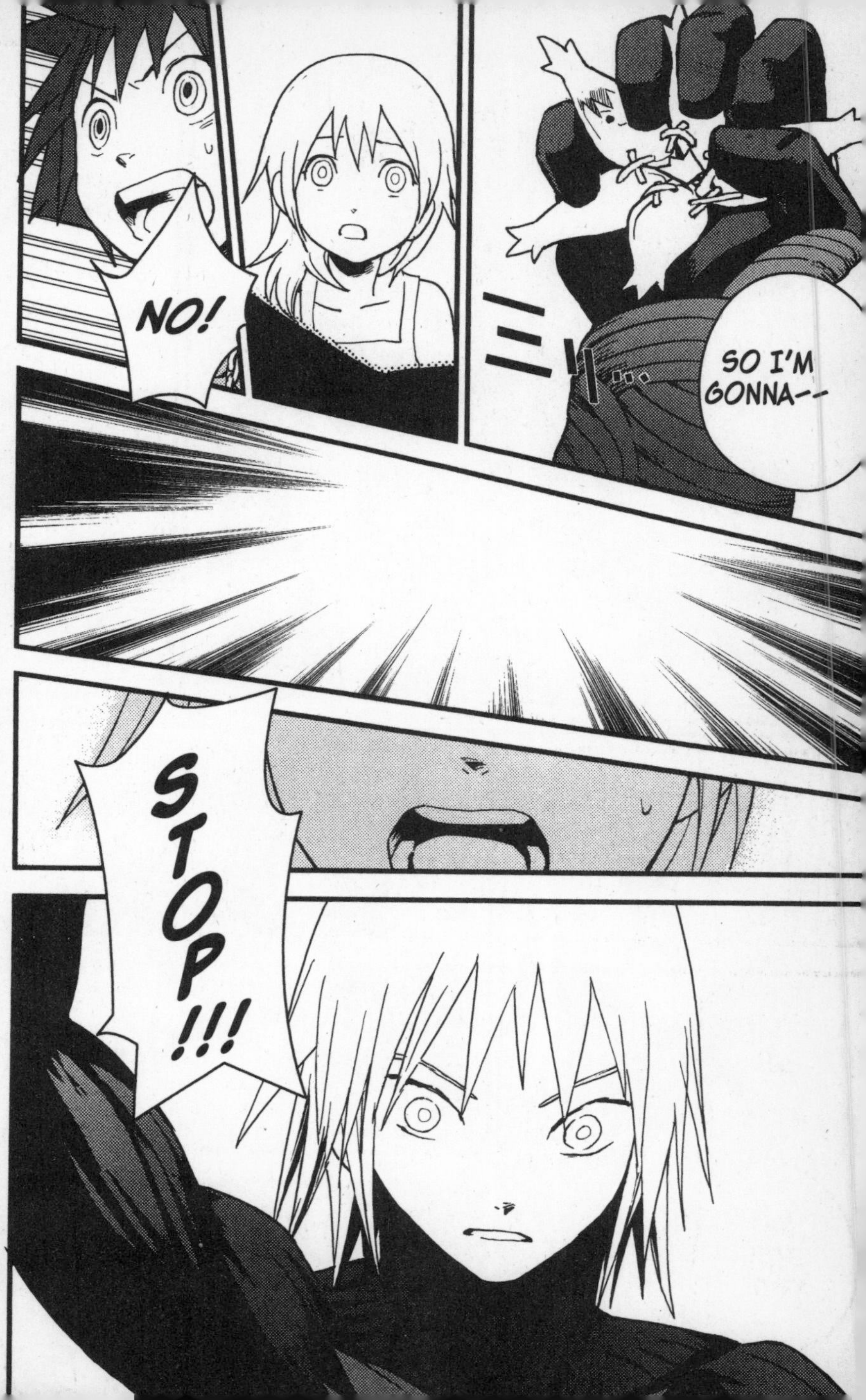
SO I'M GONNA--
NO!
STOP!!!

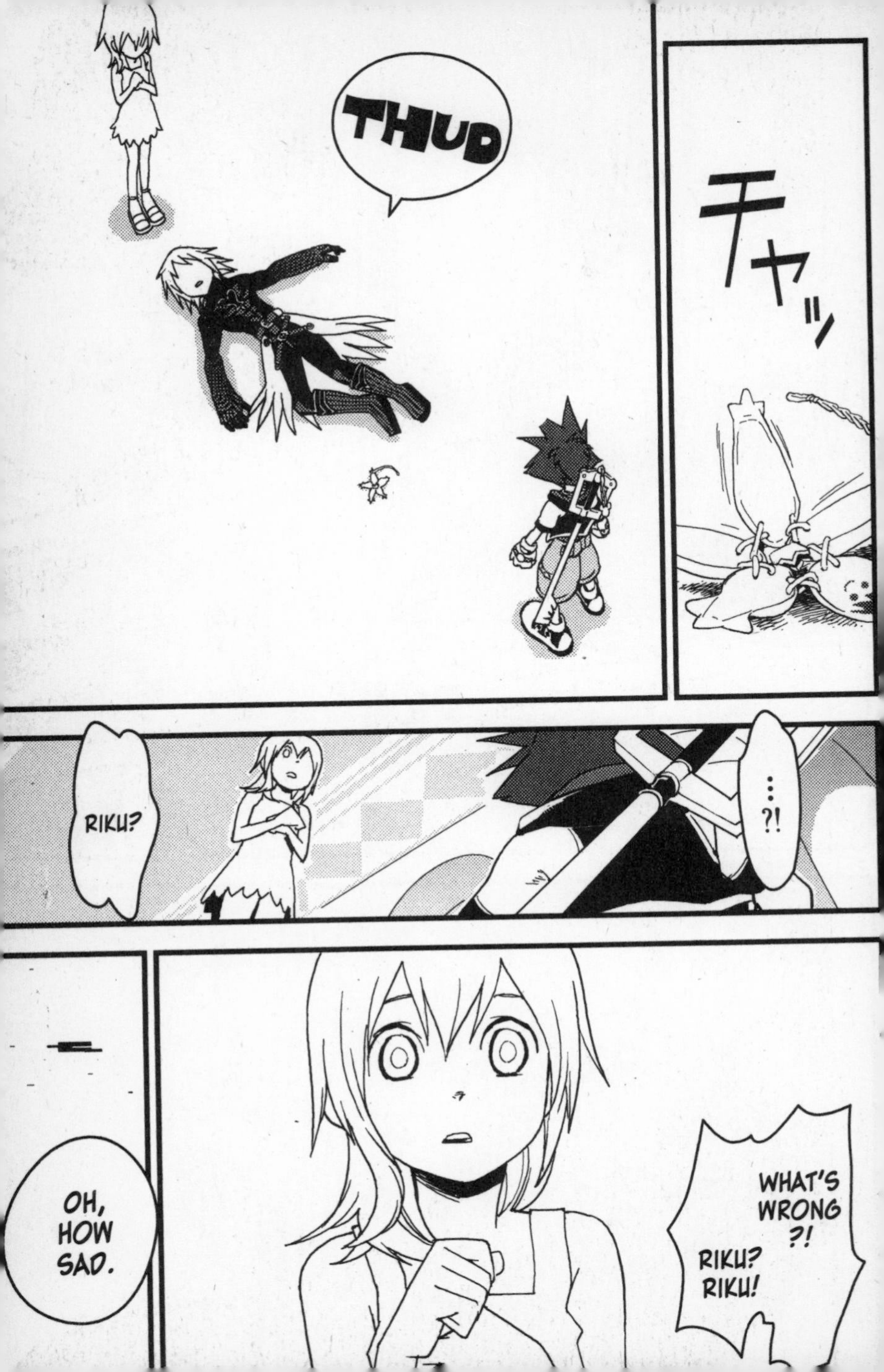
チャッ
THUD
...?!
RIKU?
WHAT'S WRONG?! RIKU? RIKU!
OH, HOW SAD.

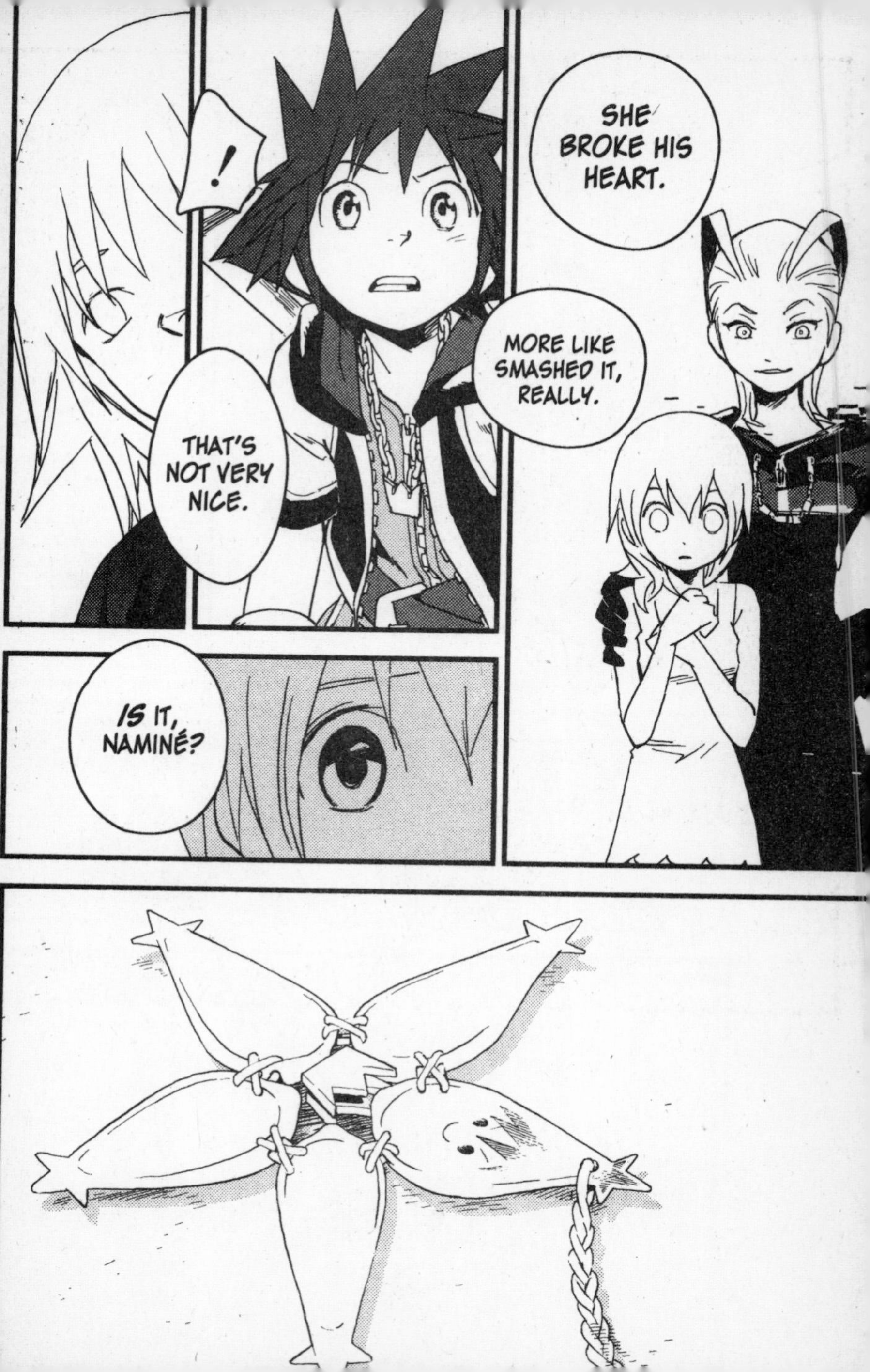
SHE BROKE HIS HEART.
!
MORE LIKE SMASHED IT, REALLY.
THAT'S NOT VERY NICE.
IS IT, NAMINÉ?

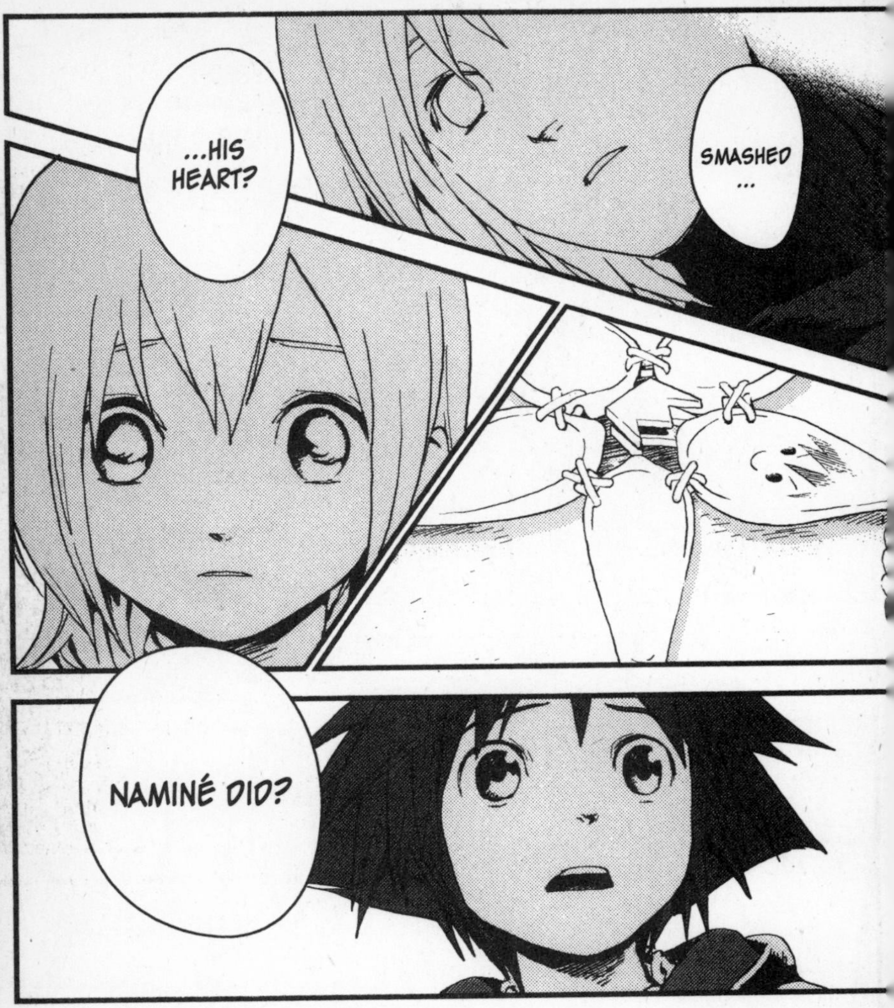
SMASHED ...
...HIS HEART?
NAMINÉ DID?

Card 11 SHOCK!!!

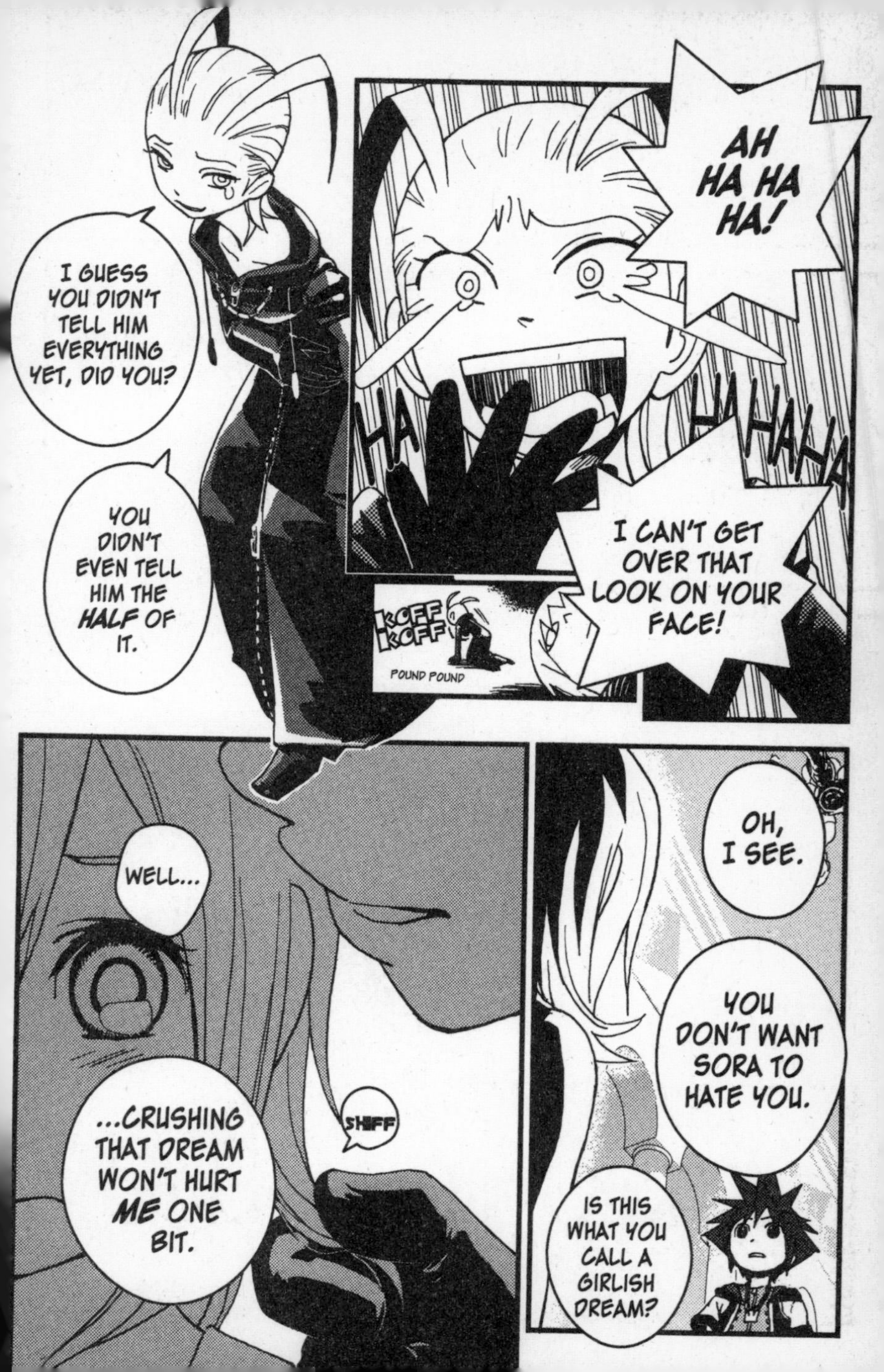
AH HA HA HA!
HA
HAHAHA
I CAN'T GET OVER THAT LOOK ON YOUR FACE!
KOFF KOFF
POUND POUND
I GUESS YOU DIDN'T TELL HIM EVERYTHING YET, DID YOU?
YOU DIDN'T EVEN TELL HIM THE *HALF* OF IT.
OH, I SEE.
YOU DON'T WANT SORA TO HATE YOU.
IS THIS WHAT YOU CALL A GIRLISH DREAM?
WELL...
SNIFF
...CRUSHING THAT DREAM WON'T HURT *ME* ONE BIT.

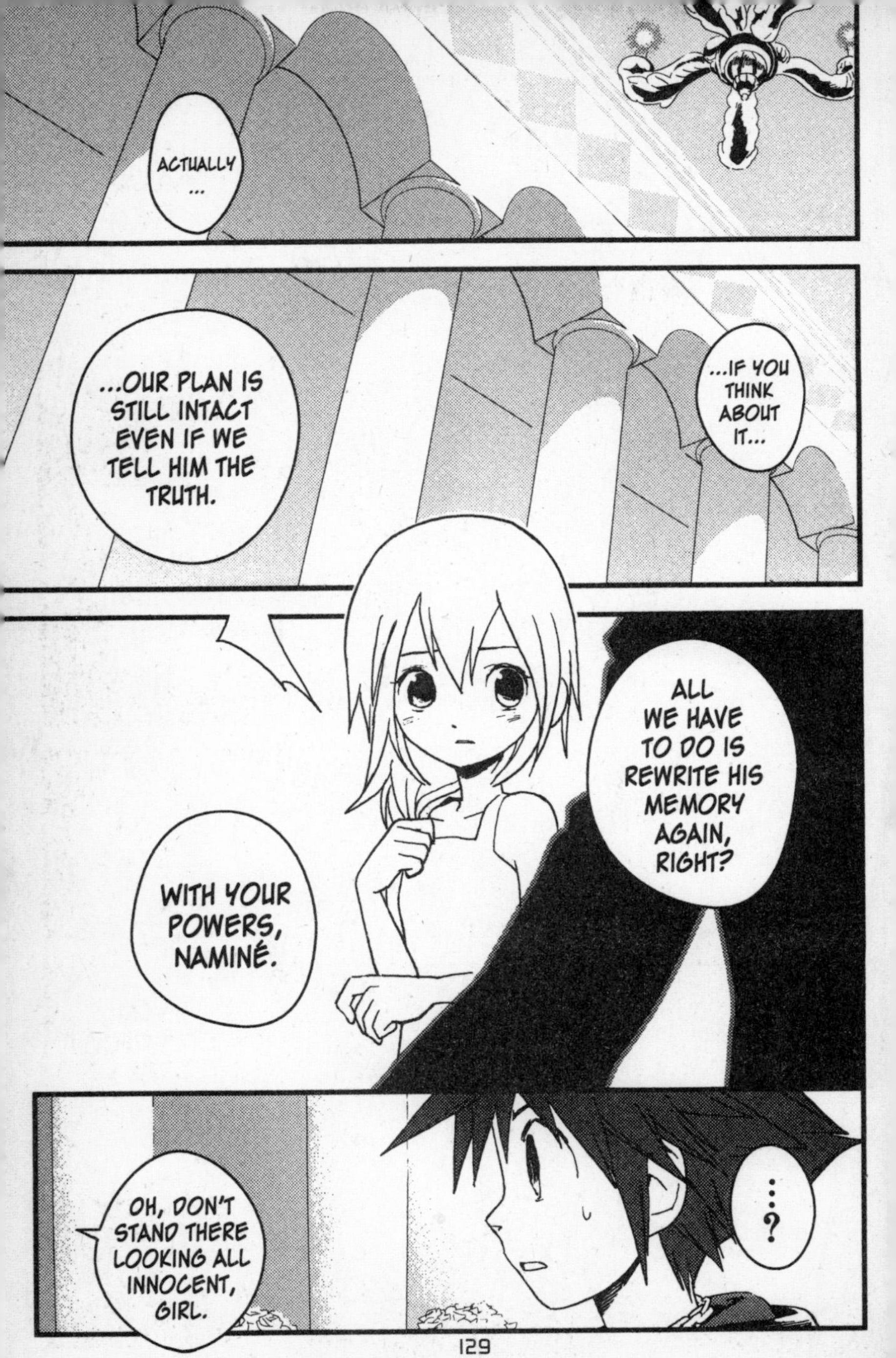
ACTUALLY...
...IF YOU THINK ABOUT IT...
...OUR PLAN IS STILL INTACT EVEN IF WE TELL HIM THE TRUTH.
ALL WE HAVE TO DO IS REWRITE HIS MEMORY AGAIN, RIGHT?
WITH YOUR POWERS, NAMINÉ.
...?
OH, DON'T STAND THERE LOOKING ALL INNOCENT, GIRL.

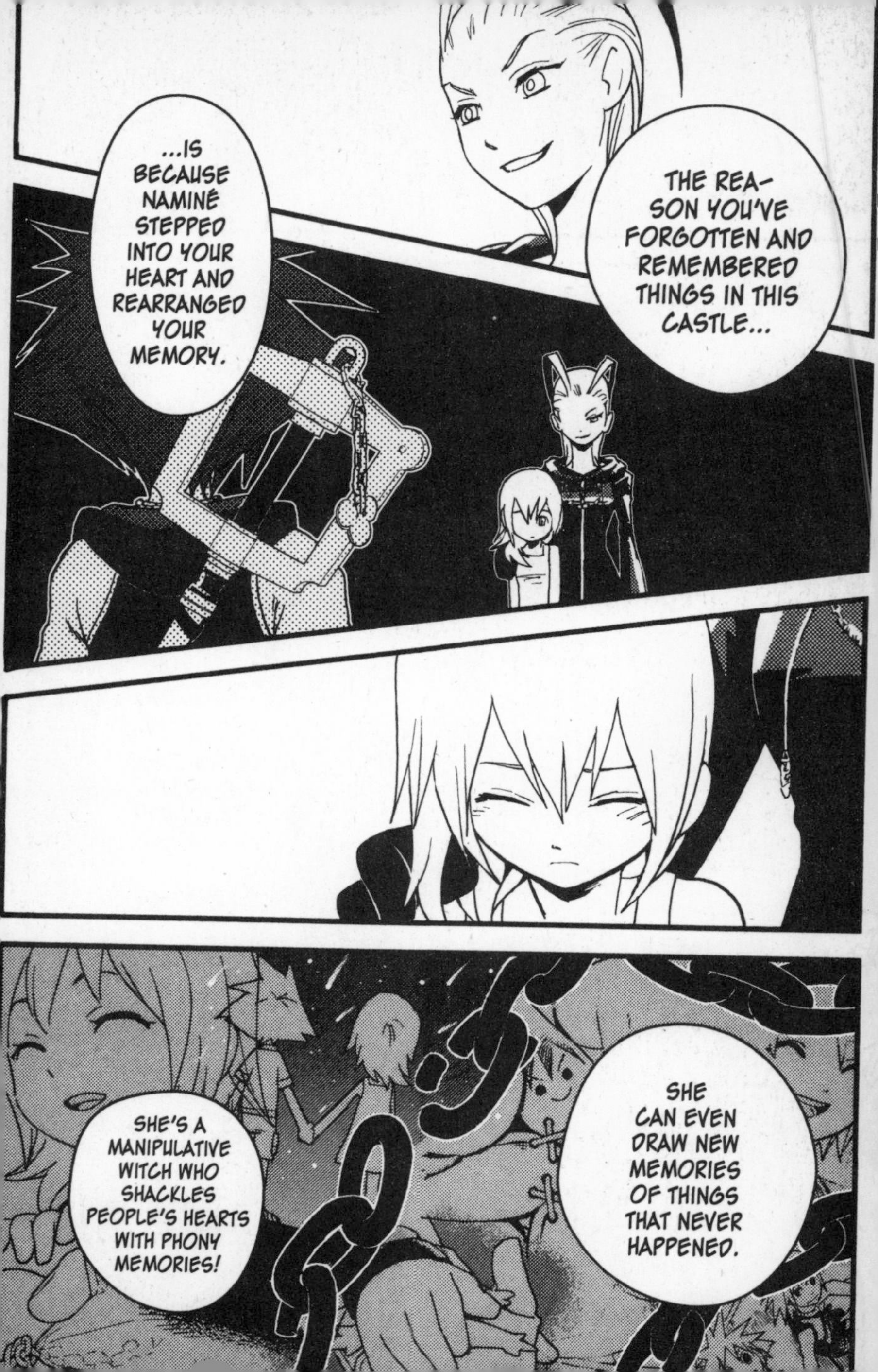
THE REA-SON YOU'VE FORGOTTEN AND REMEMBERED THINGS IN THIS CASTLE...
...IS BECAUSE NAMINÉ STEPPED INTO YOUR HEART AND REARRANGED YOUR MEMORY.
SHE CAN EVEN DRAW NEW MEMORIES OF THINGS THAT NEVER HAPPENED.
SHE'S A MANIPULATIVE WITCH WHO SHACKLES PEOPLE'S HEARTS WITH PHONY MEMORIES!

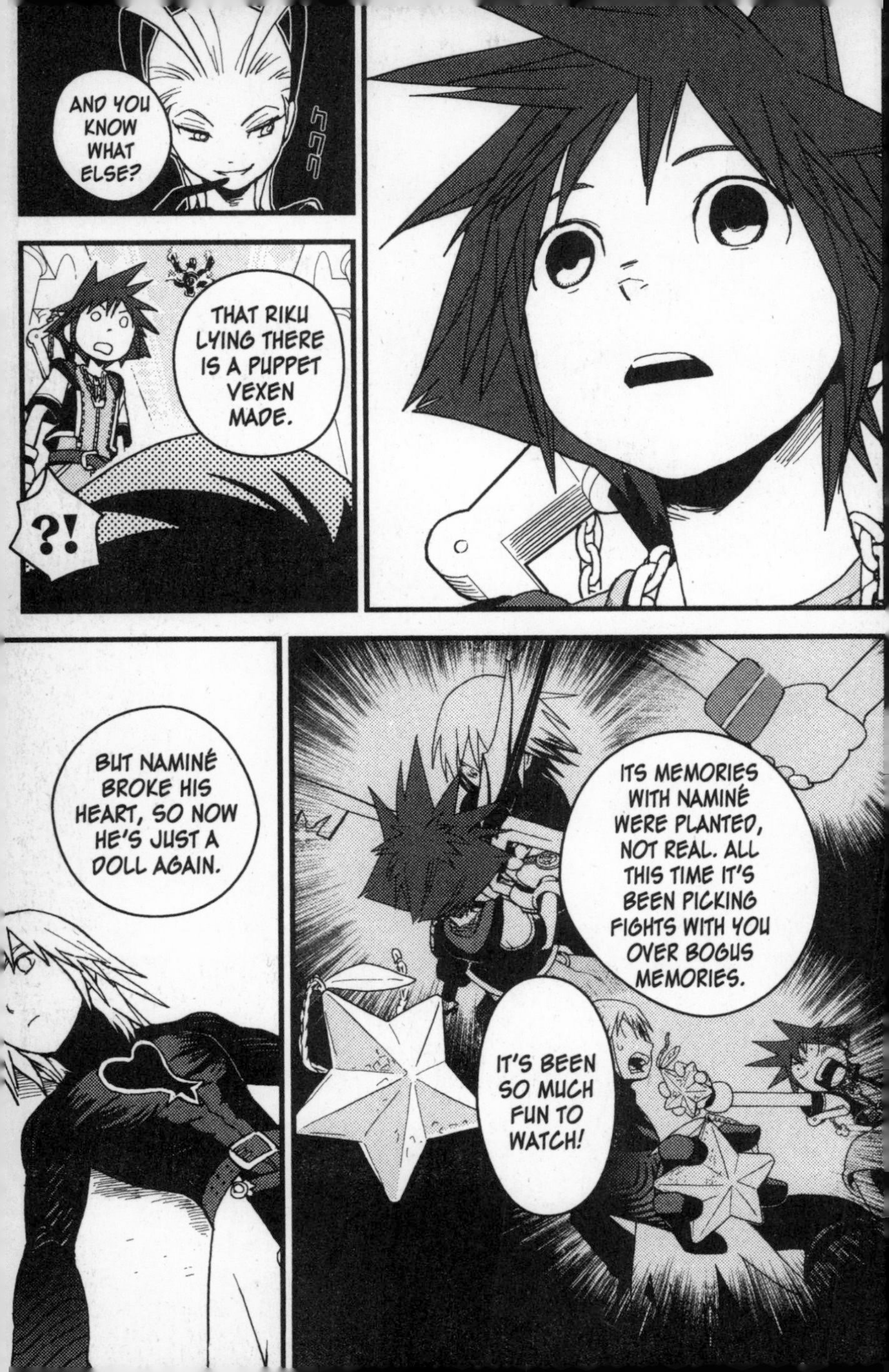
AND YOU KNOW WHAT ELSE?
THAT RIKU LYING THERE IS A PUPPET VEXEN MADE.
?!
ITS MEMORIES WITH NAMINÉ WERE PLANTED, NOT REAL. ALL THIS TIME IT'S BEEN PICKING FIGHTS WITH YOU OVER BOGUS MEMORIES.
IT'S BEEN SO MUCH FUN TO WATCH!
BUT NAMINÉ BROKE HIS HEART, SO NOW HE'S JUST A DOLL AGAIN.

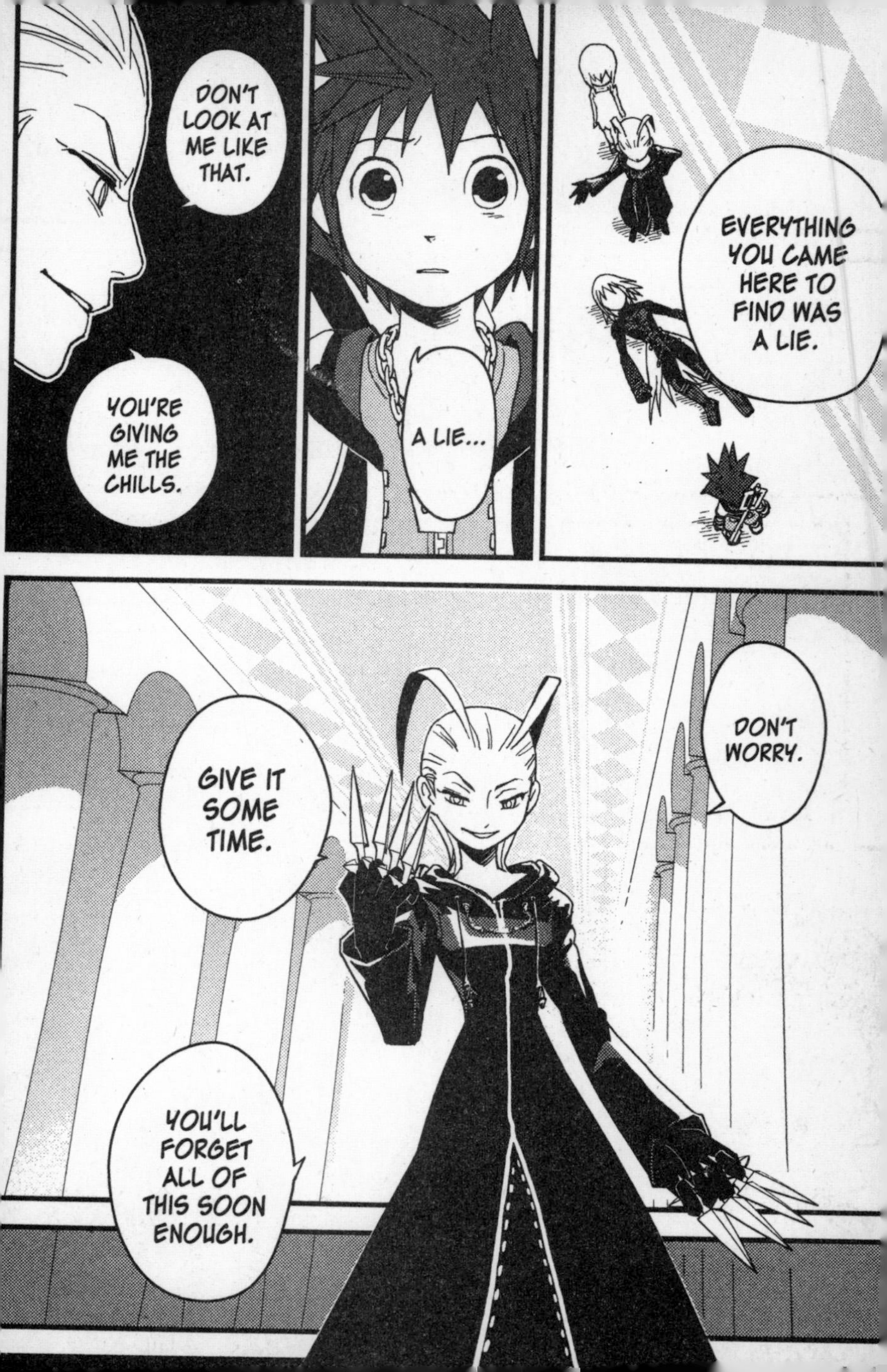
EVERYTHING YOU CAME HERE TO FIND WAS A LIE.
A LIE...
DON'T LOOK AT ME LIKE THAT.
YOU'RE GIVING ME THE CHILLS.
DON'T WORRY.
GIVE IT SOME TIME.
YOU'LL FORGET ALL OF THIS SOON ENOUGH.

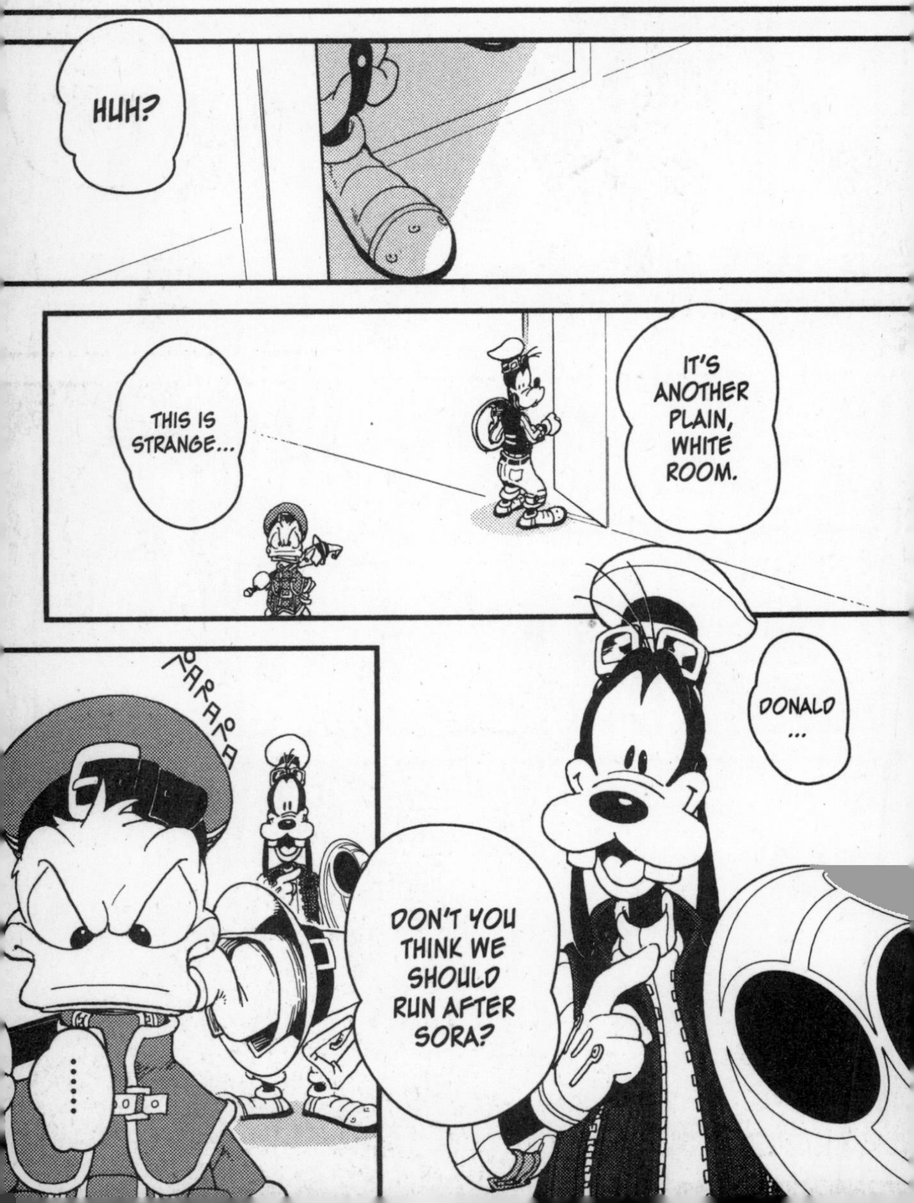
HUH?
IT'S ANOTHER PLAIN, WHITE ROOM.
THIS IS STRANGE...
DONALD ...
DON'T YOU THINK WE SHOULD RUN AFTER SORA?
......

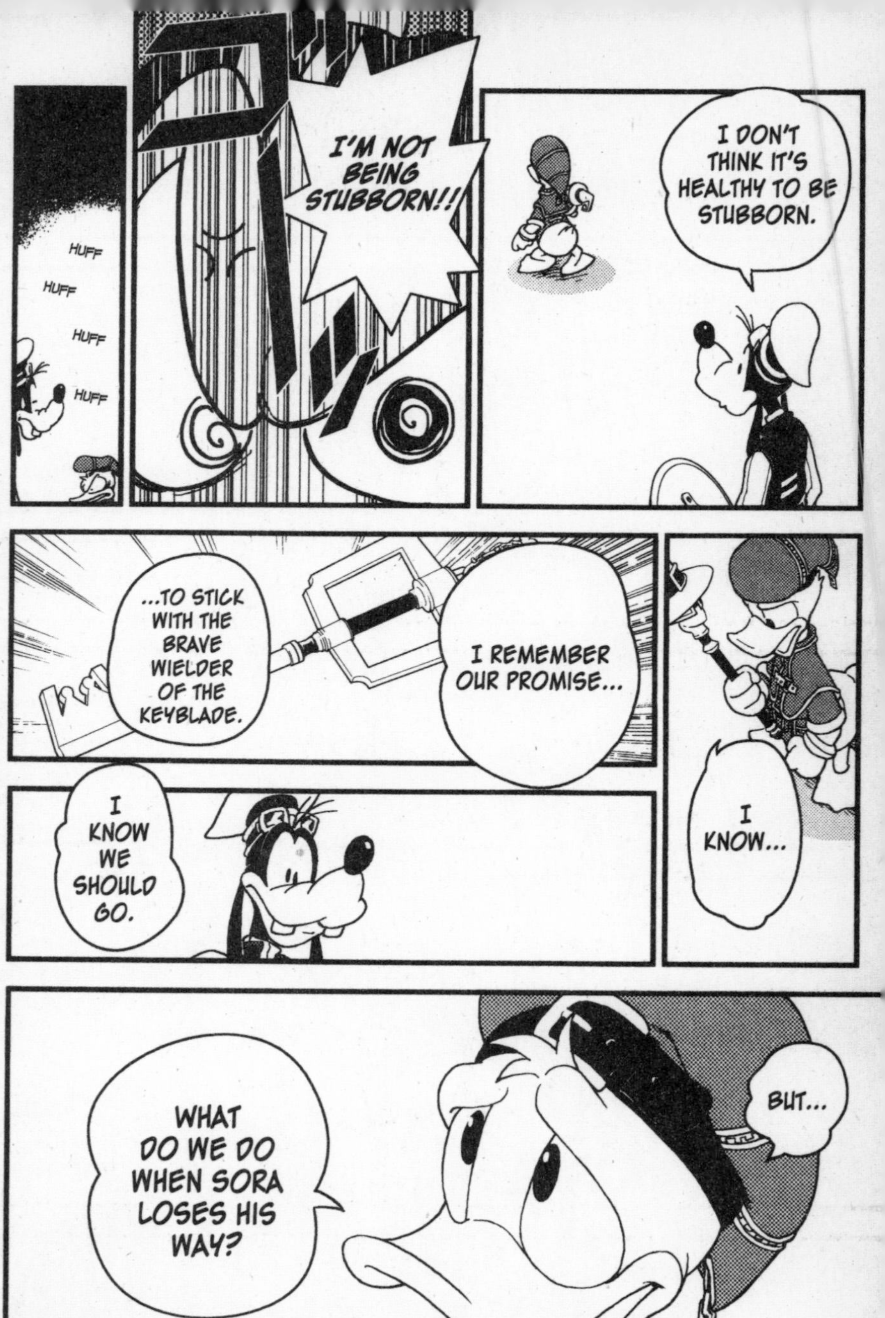
I DON'T THINK IT'S HEALTHY TO BE STUBBORN.
I'M NOT BEING STUBBORN!!
HUFF
HUFF
HUFF
HUFF
I KNOW...
I REMEMBER OUR PROMISE...
...TO STICK WITH THE BRAVE WIELDER OF THE KEYBLADE.
I KNOW WE SHOULD GO.
BUT...
WHAT DO WE DO WHEN SORA LOSES HIS WAY?

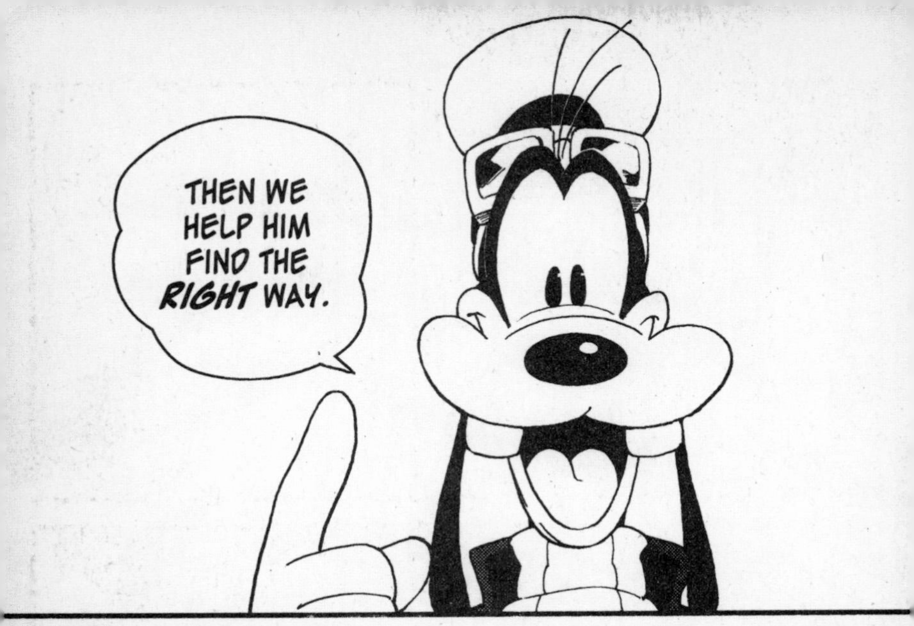
THEN WE HELP HIM FIND THE RIGHT WAY.

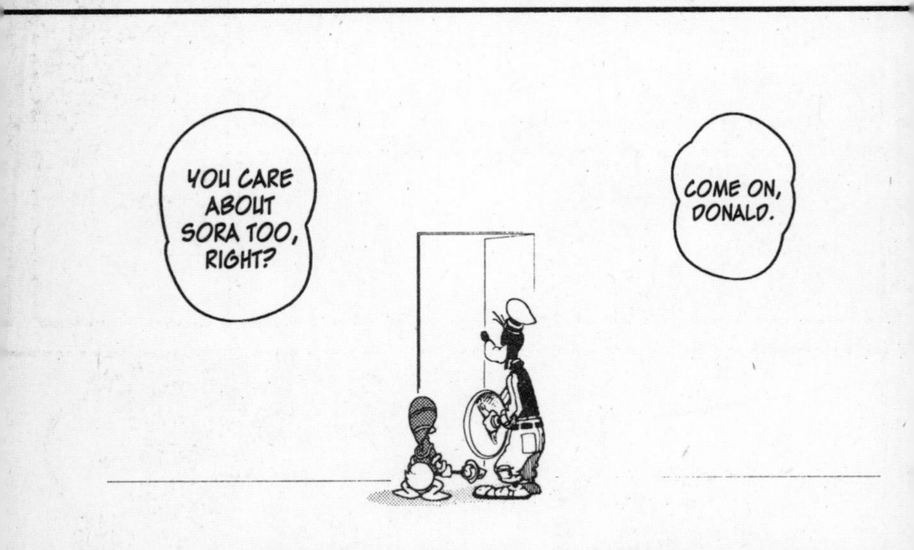
COME ON, DONALD.
YOU CARE ABOUT SORA TOO, RIGHT?

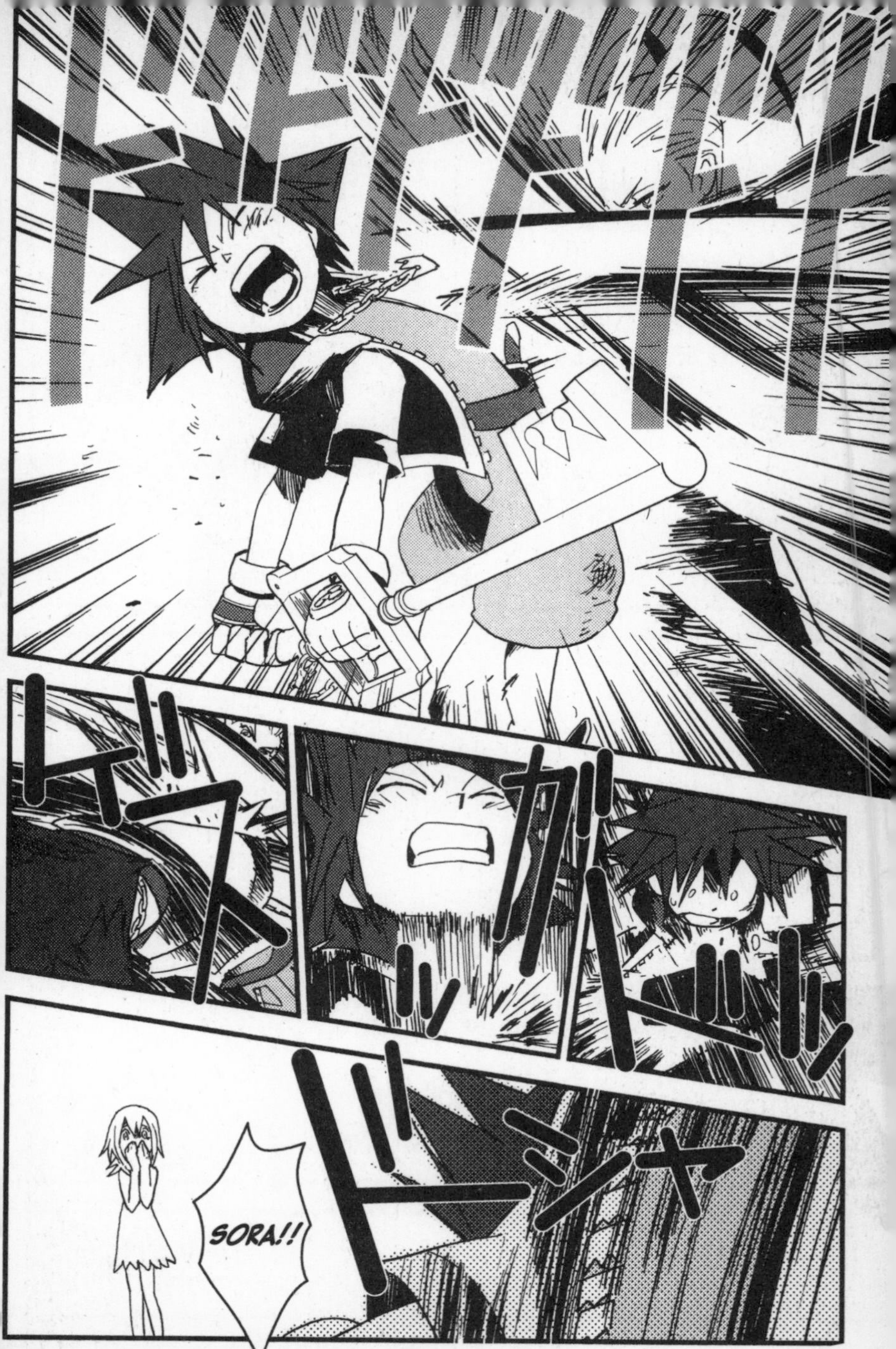
SORA!!

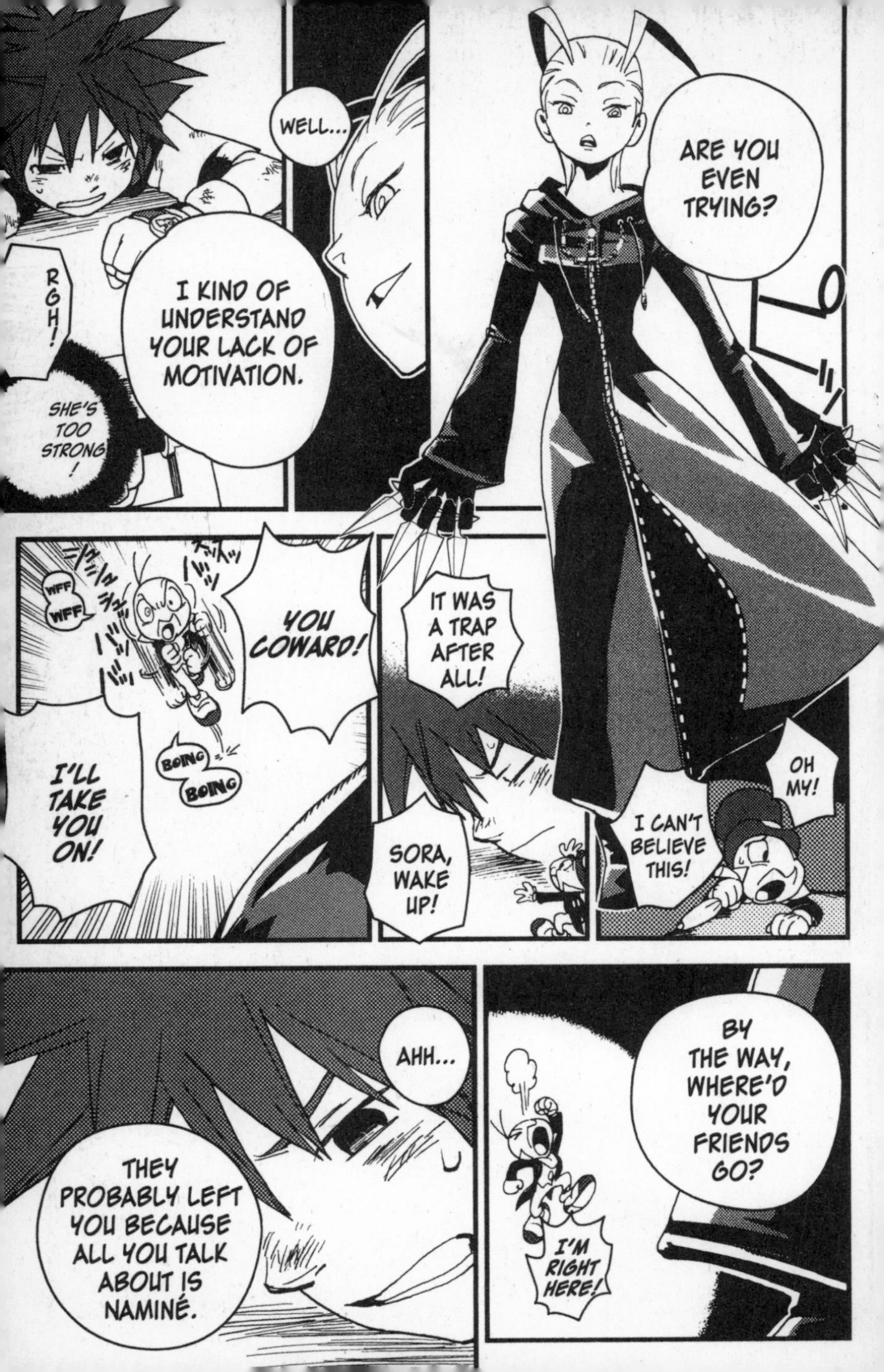
ARE YOU EVEN TRYING?
WELL...
I KIND OF UNDERSTAND YOUR LACK OF MOTIVATION.
RGH!
SHE'S TOO STRONG!
OH MY!
I CAN'T BELIEVE THIS!
IT WAS A TRAP AFTER ALL!
SORA, WAKE UP!
YOU COWARD!
WFF WFF
BOING BOING
I'LL TAKE YOU ON!
BY THE WAY, WHERE'D YOUR FRIENDS GO?
I'M RIGHT HERE!
AHH...
THEY PROBABLY LEFT YOU BECAUSE ALL YOU TALK ABOUT IS NAMINÉ.

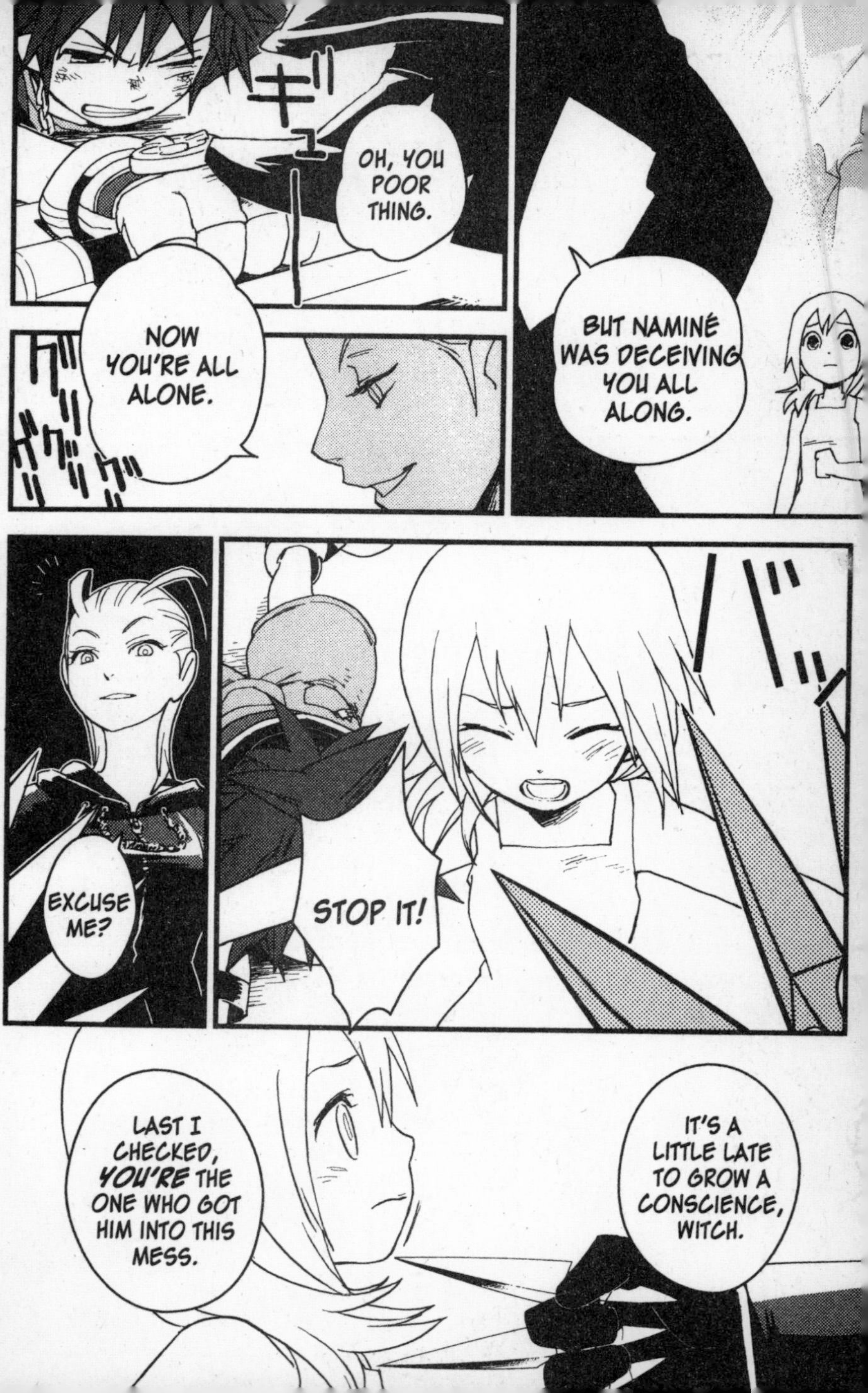
BUT NAMINÉ WAS DECEIVING YOU ALL ALONG.
OH, YOU POOR THING.
ギュ
NOW YOU'RE ALL ALONE.
バッ
STOP IT!
EXCUSE ME?
IT'S A LITTLE LATE TO GROW A CONSCIENCE, WITCH.
LAST I CHECKED, *YOU'RE* THE ONE WHO GOT HIM INTO THIS MESS.

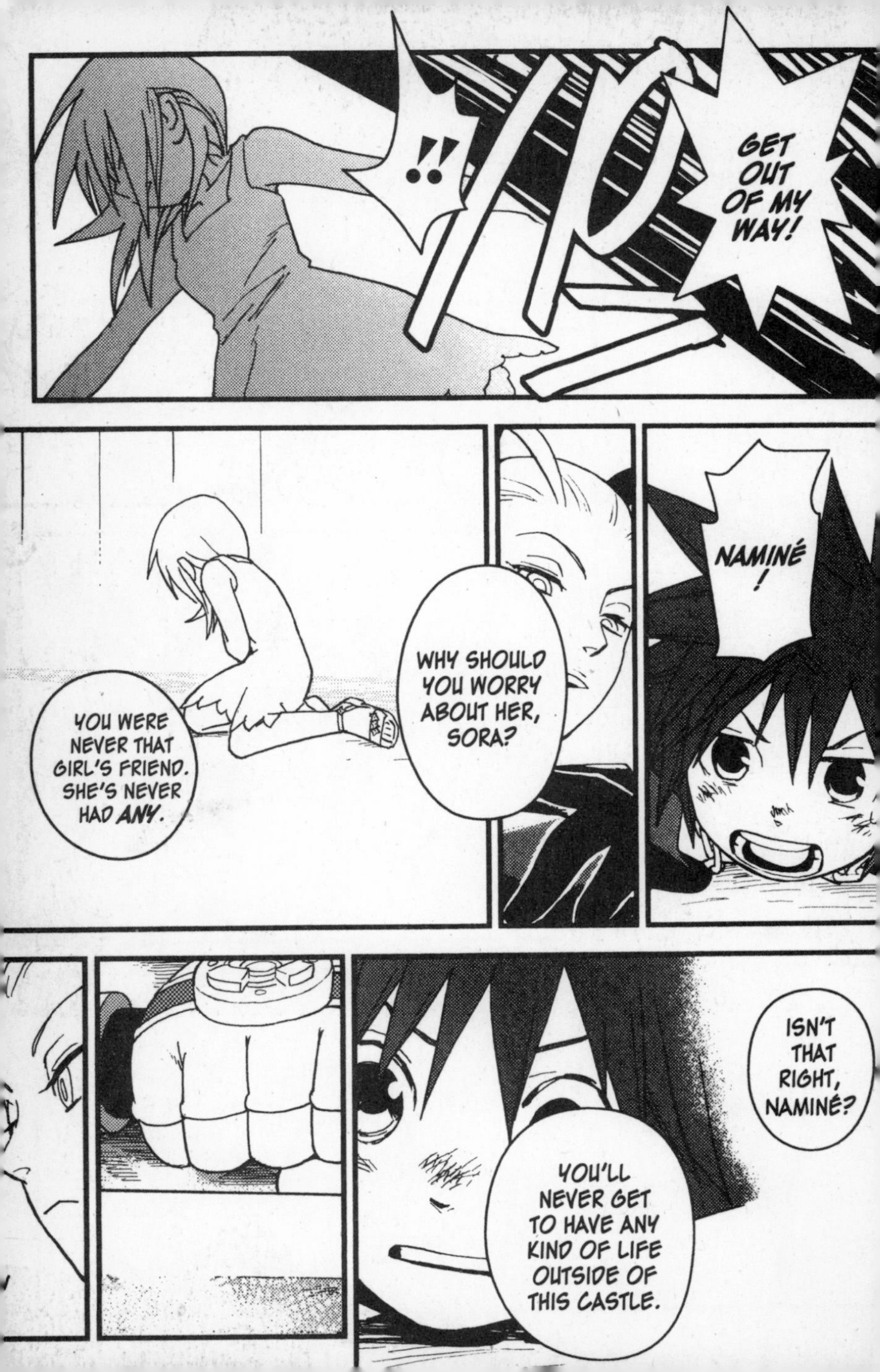
GET OUT OF MY WAY!
!!
NAMINÉ!
WHY SHOULD YOU WORRY ABOUT HER, SORA?
YOU WERE NEVER THAT GIRL'S FRIEND. SHE'S NEVER HAD *ANY*.
ISN'T THAT RIGHT, NAMINÉ?
YOU'LL NEVER GET TO HAVE ANY KIND OF LIFE OUTSIDE OF THIS CASTLE.

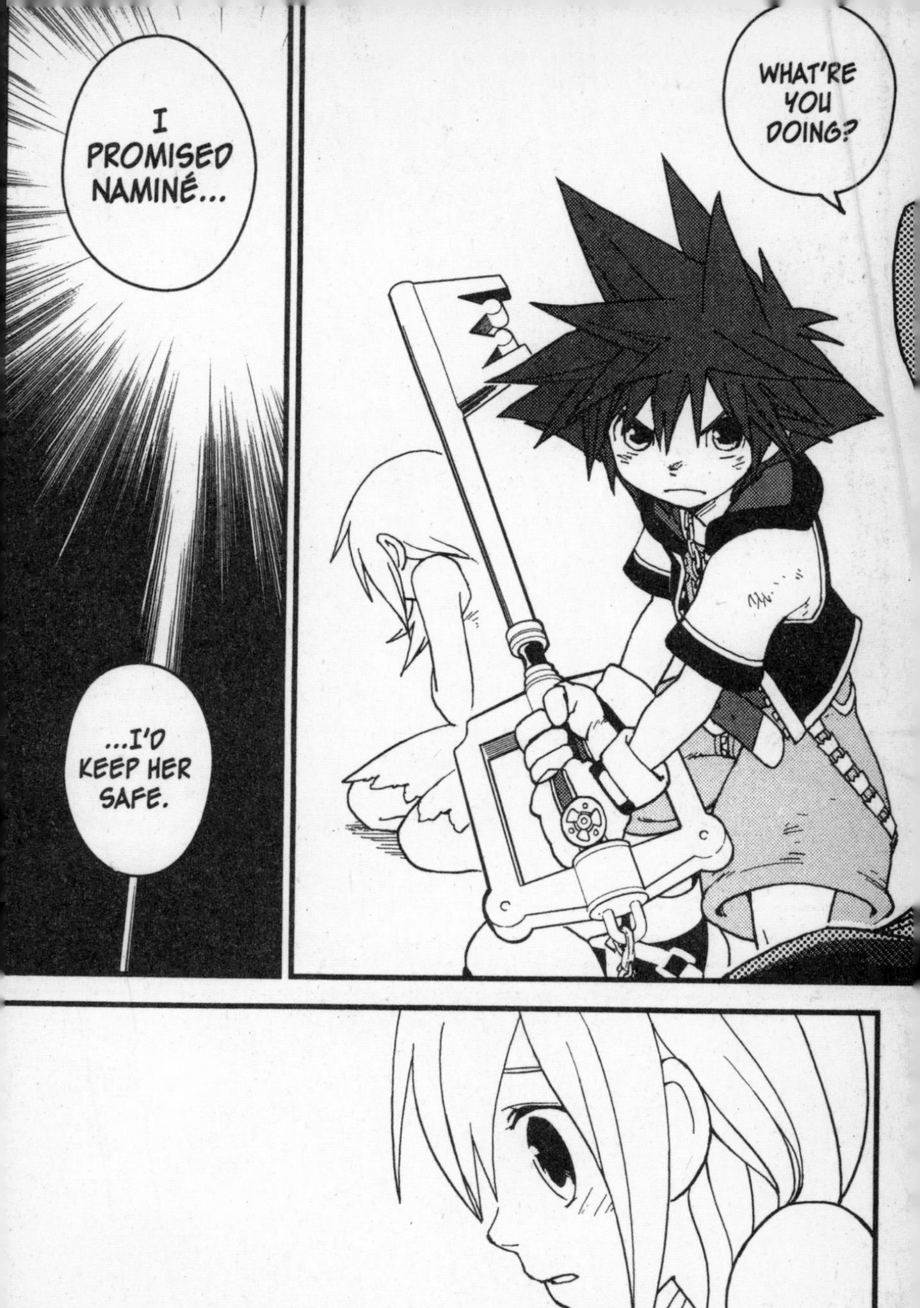
WHAT'RE YOU DOING?
I PROMISED NAMINÉ...
...I'D KEEP HER SAFE.

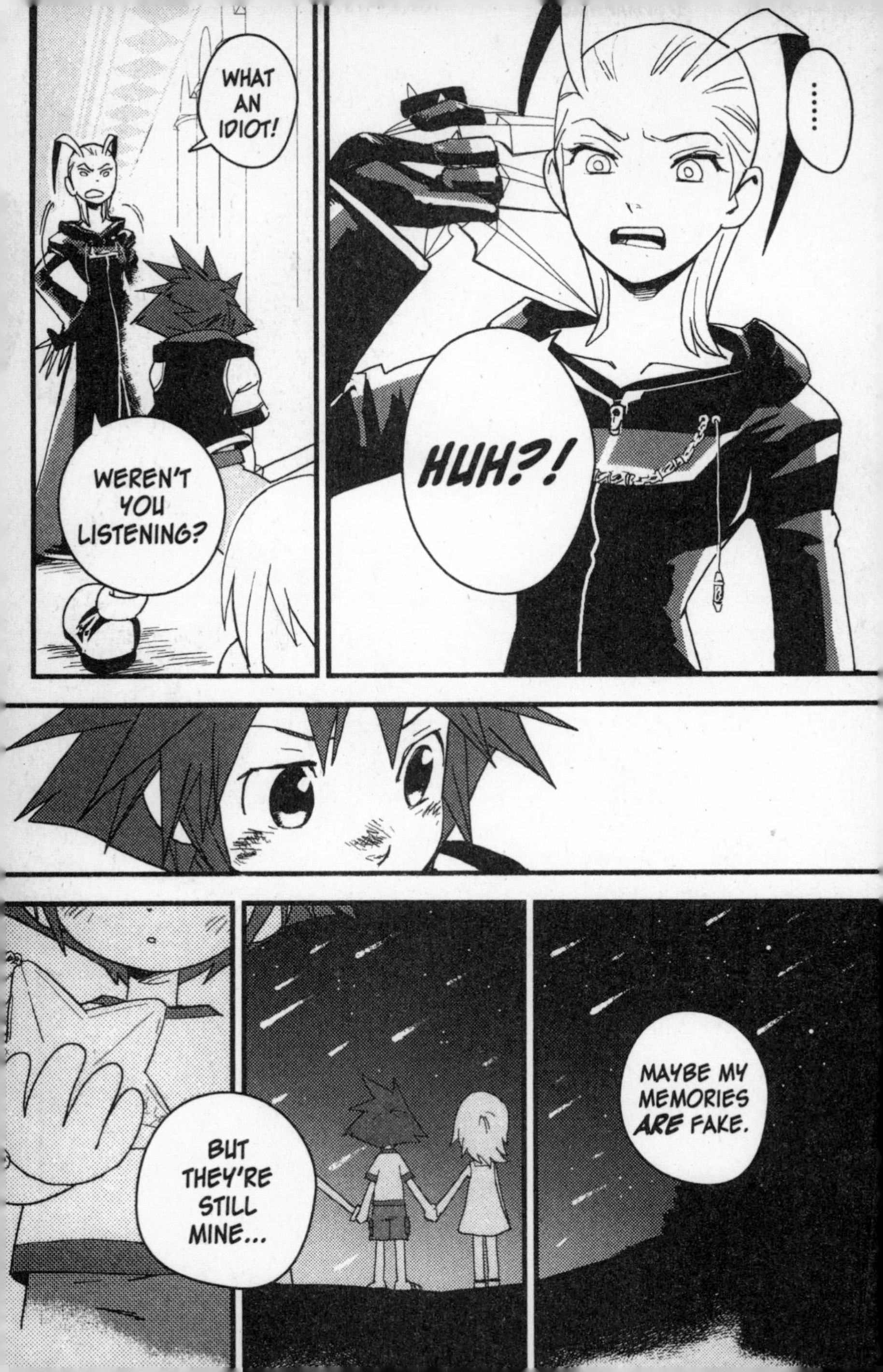

......
HUH?!
WHAT AN IDIOT!
WEREN'T YOU LISTENING?
MAYBE MY MEMORIES ARE FAKE.
BUT THEY'RE STILL MINE...

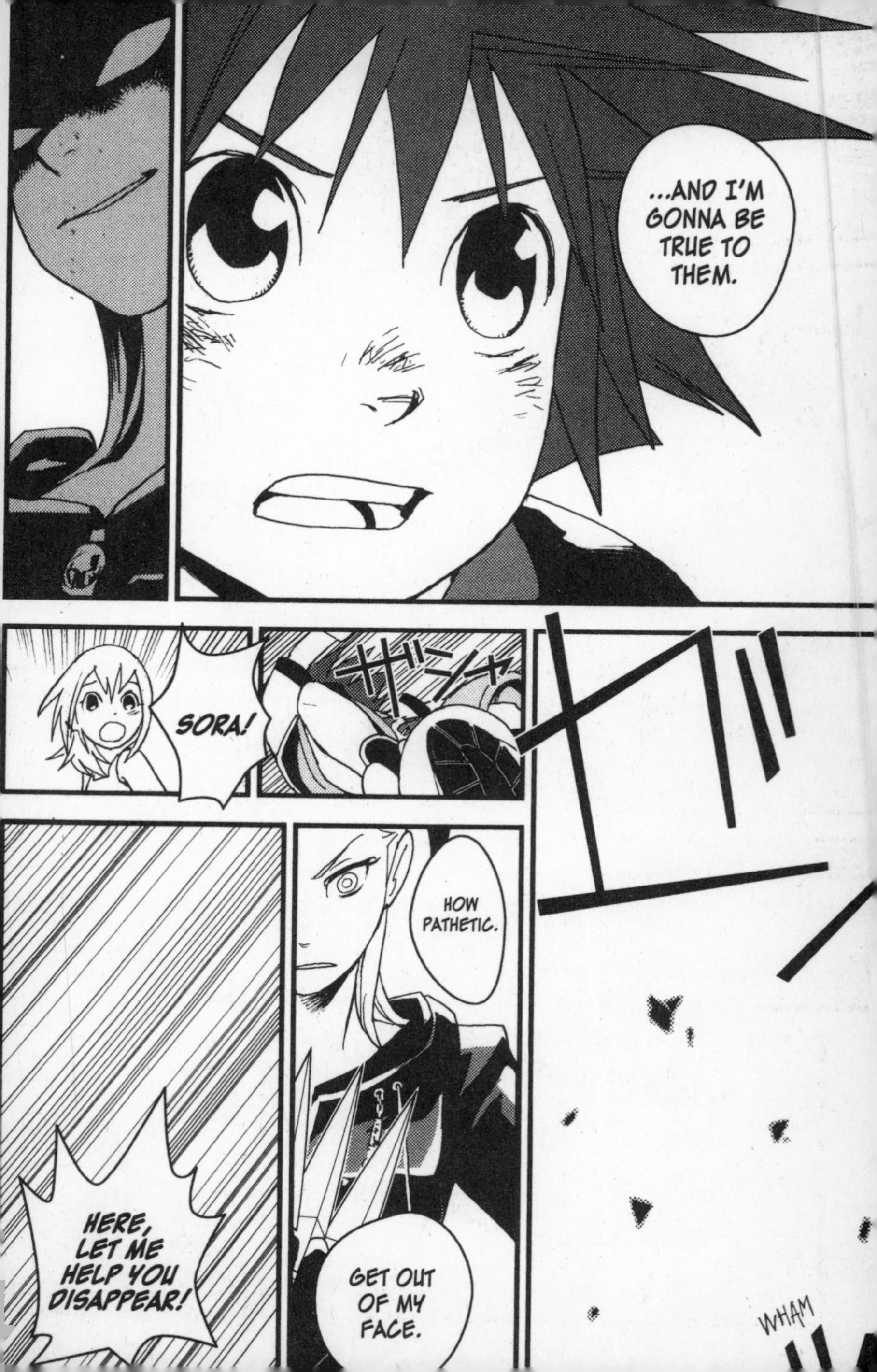
...AND I'M GONNA BE TRUE TO THEM.
WHAM
SORA!
HOW PATHETIC.
GET OUT OF MY FACE.
HERE, LET ME HELP YOU DISAPPEAR!

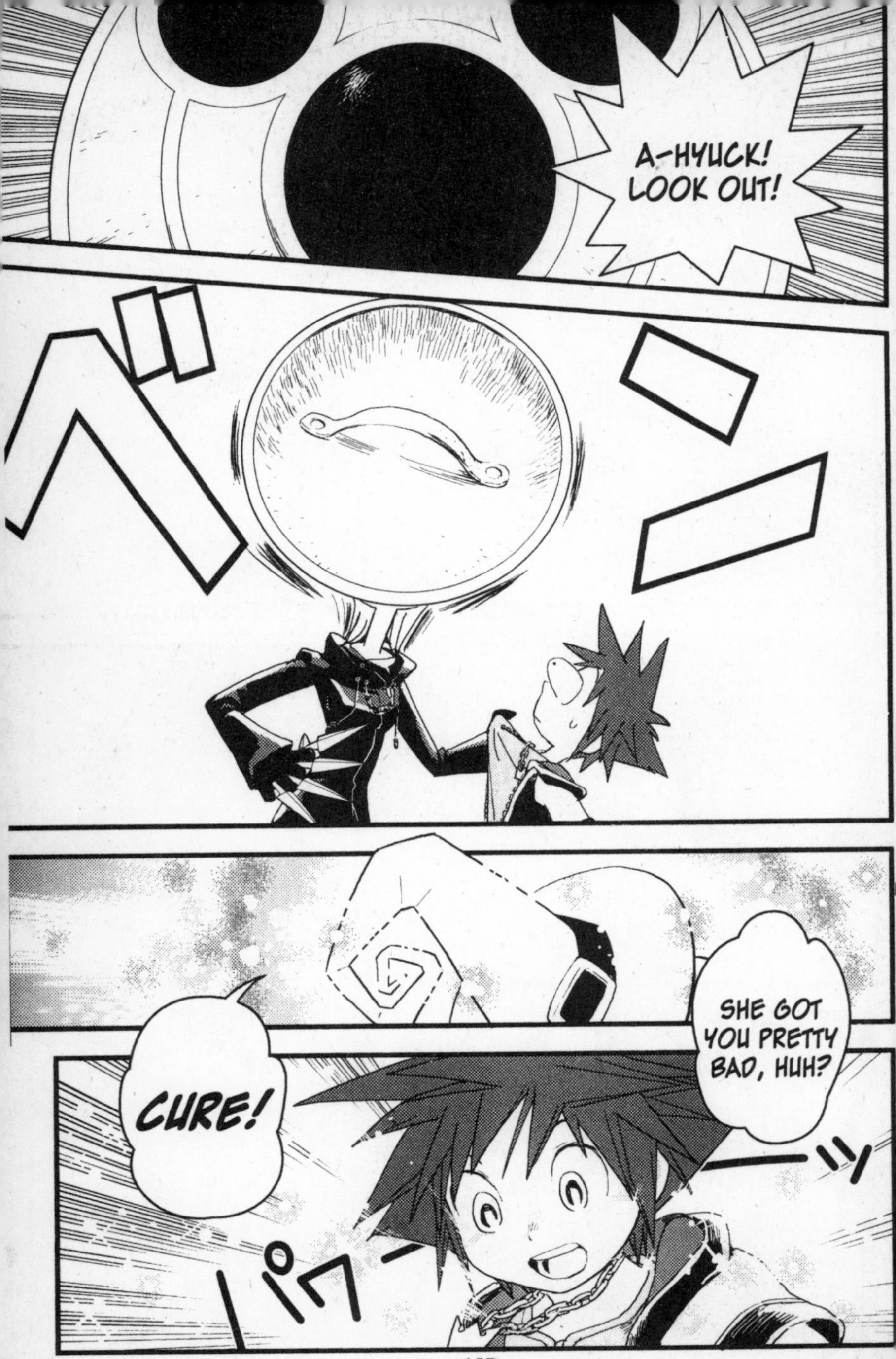
A-HYUCK! LOOK OUT!
SHE GOT YOU PRETTY BAD, HUH?
CURE!

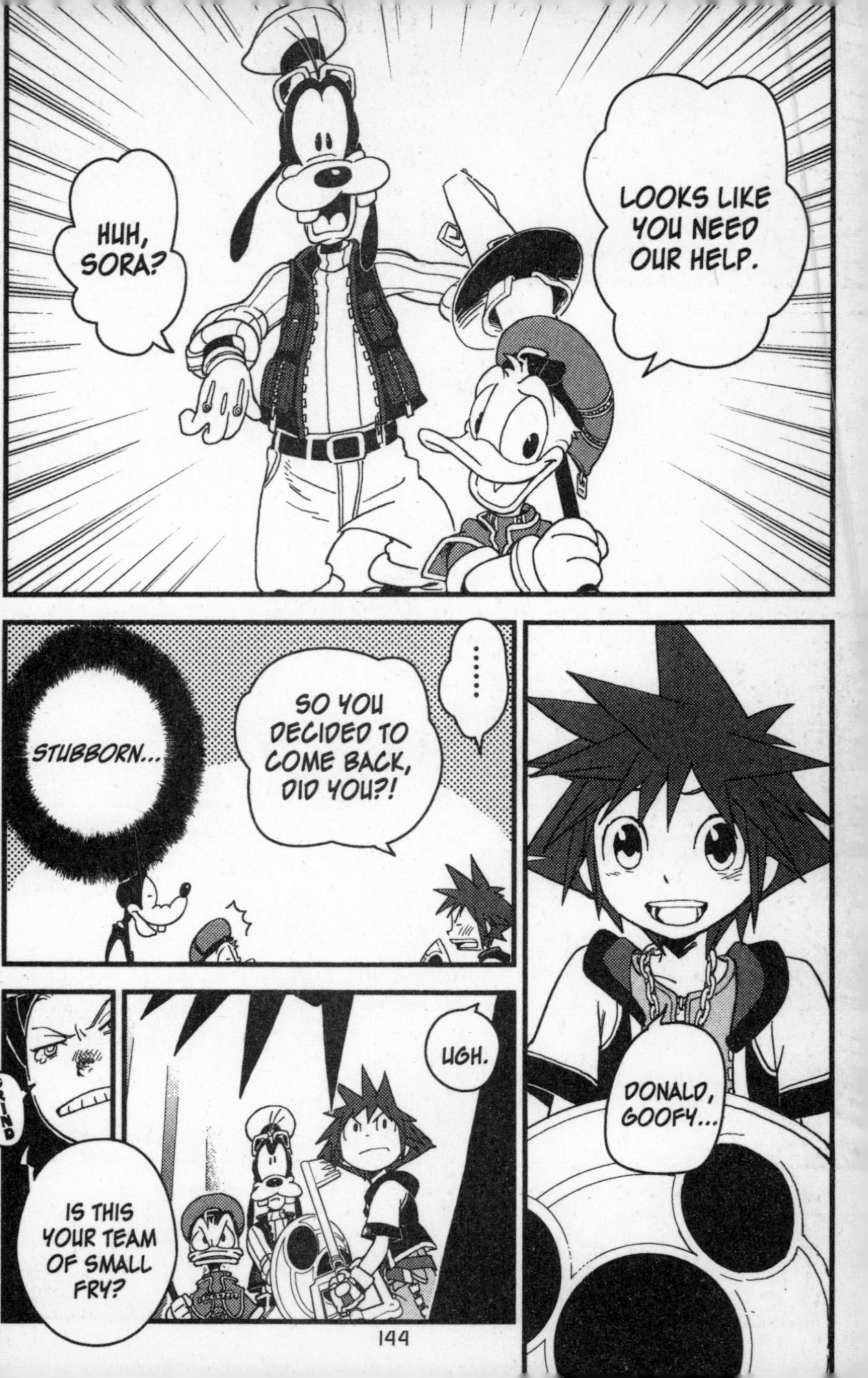
LOOKS LIKE YOU NEED OUR HELP.
HUH, SORA?
DONALD, GOOFY...
......
SO YOU DECIDED TO COME BACK, DID YOU?!
STUBBORN...
UGH.
GRIND
IS THIS YOUR TEAM OF SMALL FRY?

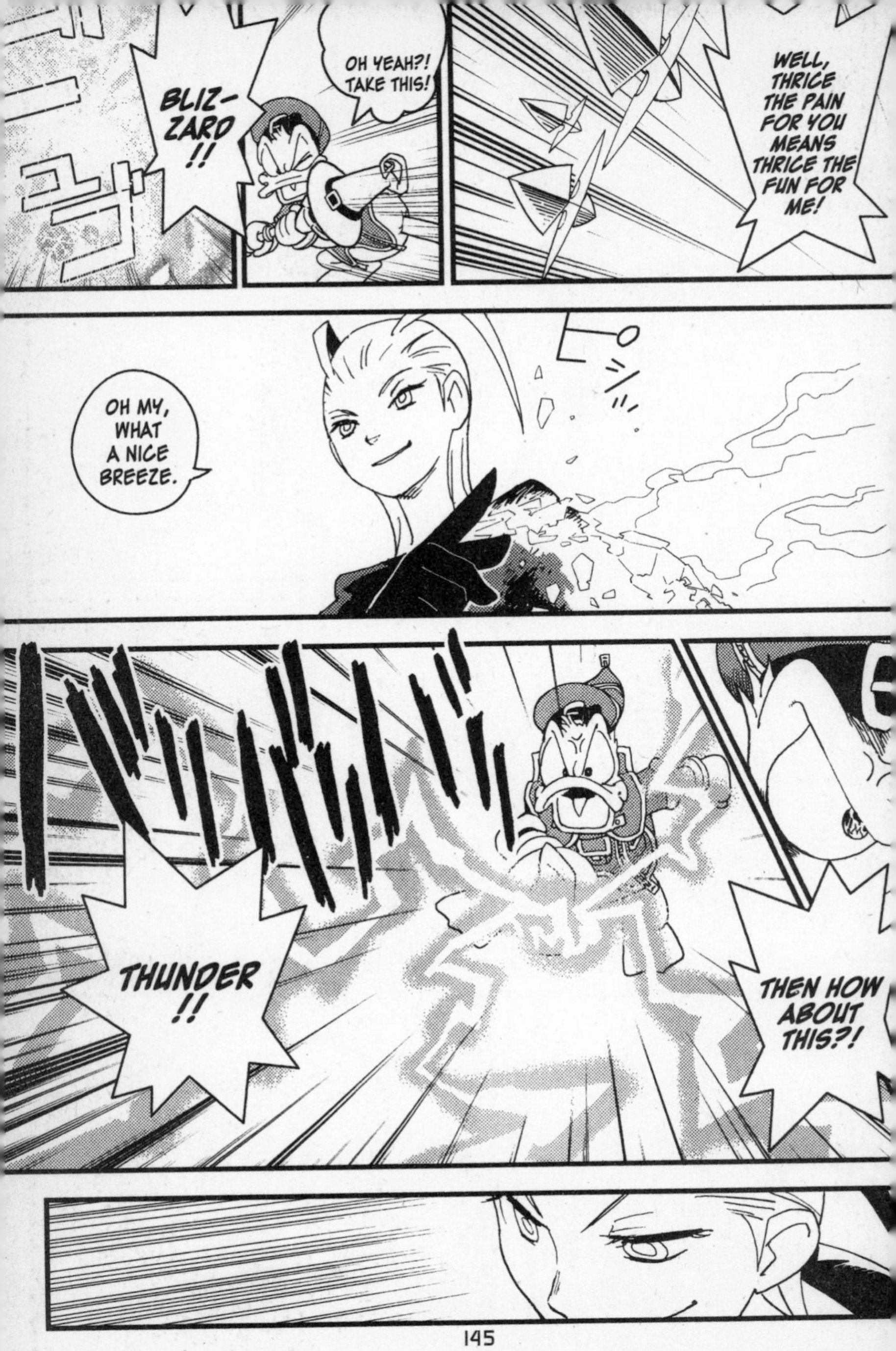
WELL, THRICE THE PAIN FOR YOU MEANS THRICE THE FUN FOR ME!
OH YEAH?! TAKE THIS!
BLIZ-ZARD !!
OH MY, WHAT A NICE BREEZE.
THEN HOW ABOUT THIS?!
THUNDER !!

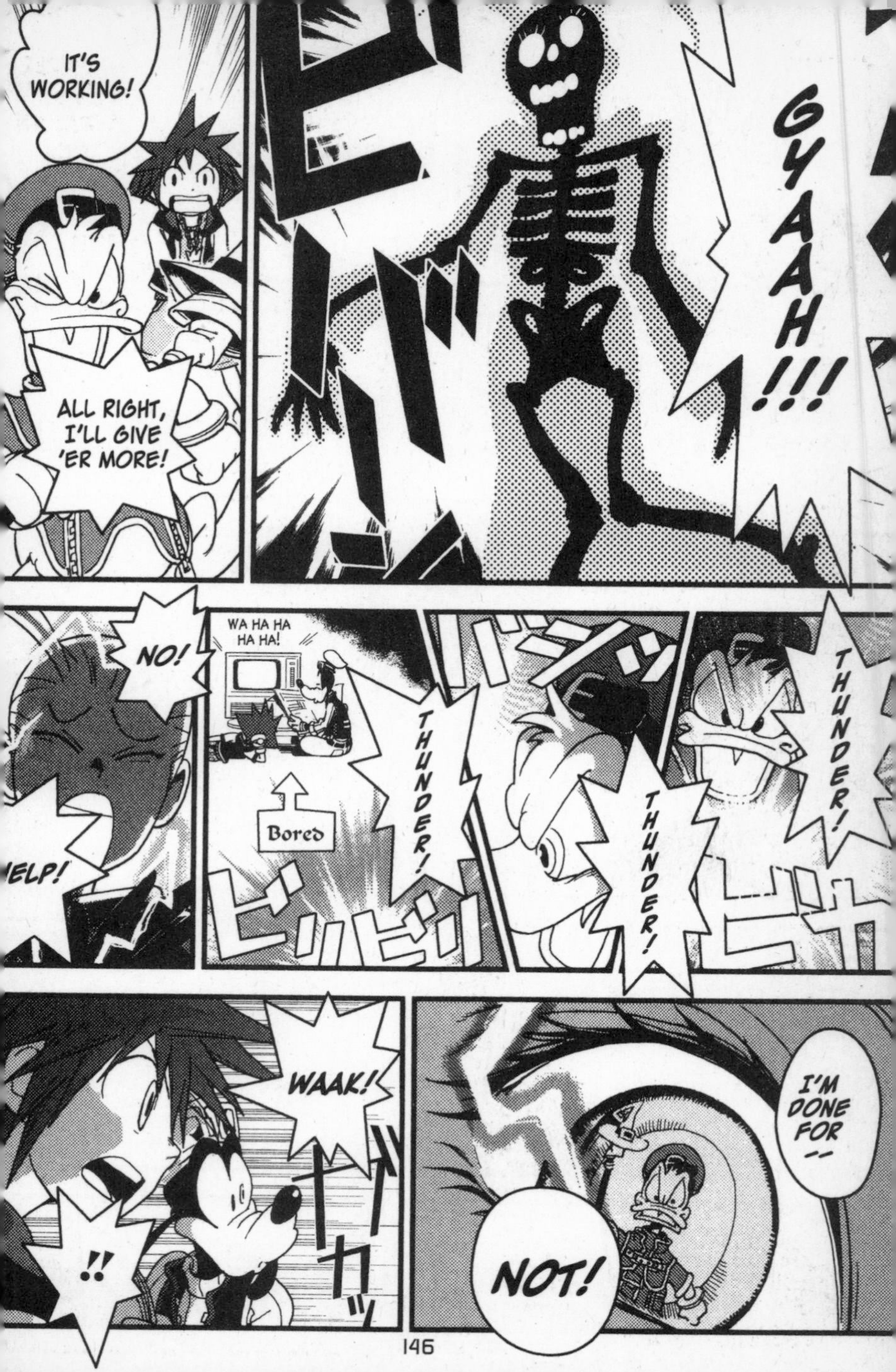
GYAAH!!!
IT'S WORKING!
ALL RIGHT, I'LL GIVE 'ER MORE!
THUNDER!
THUNDER!
WA HA HA HA HA!
THUNDER!
Bored
NO!
ELP!
I'M DONE FOR --
NOT!
WAAK!
!!

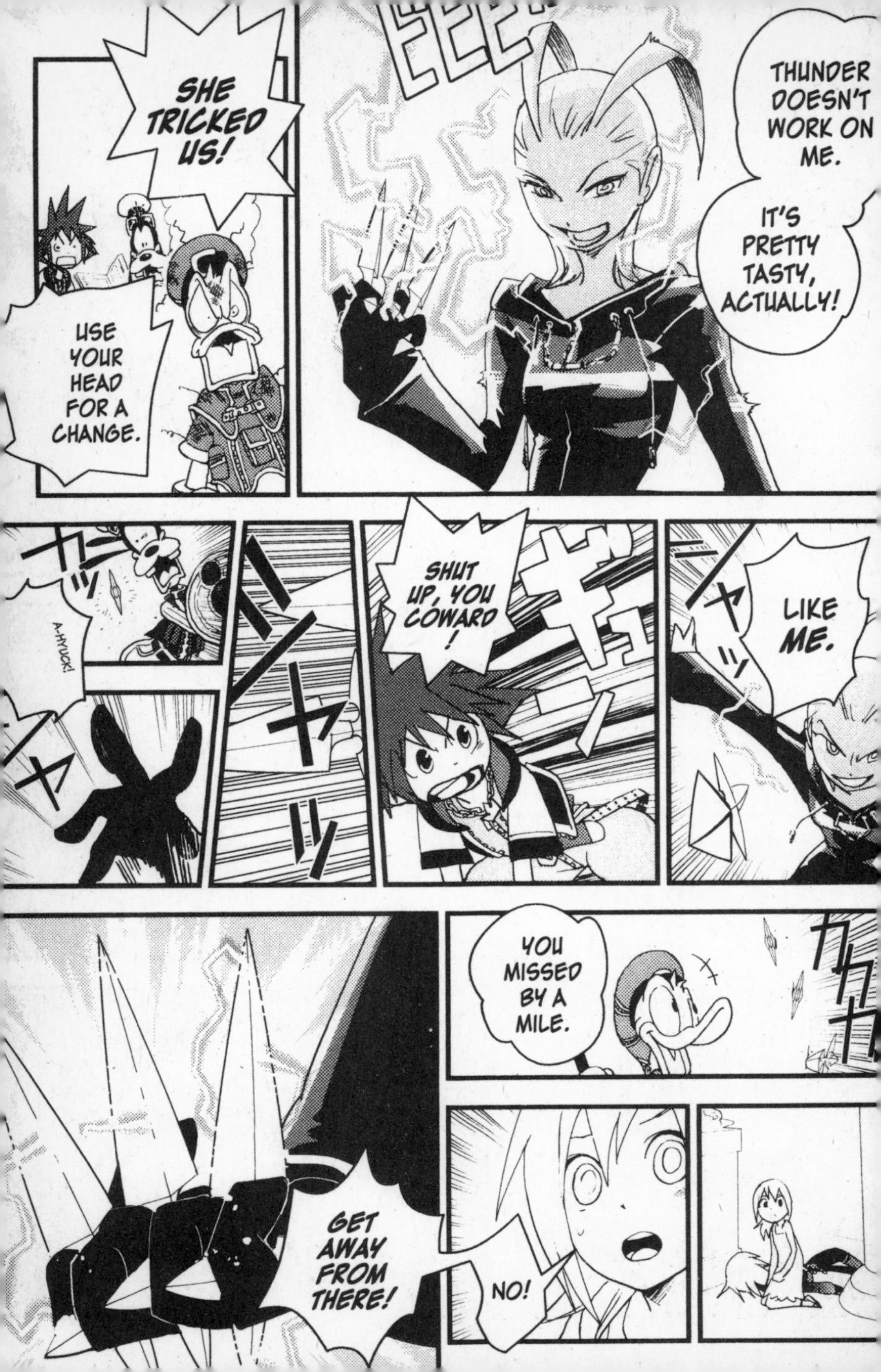
THUNDER DOESN'T WORK ON ME.
IT'S PRETTY TASTY, ACTUALLY!
SHE TRICKED US!
USE YOUR HEAD FOR A CHANGE.
LIKE ME.
SHUT UP, YOU COWARD!
A-HYUCK!
YOU MISSED BY A MILE.
NO!
GET AWAY FROM THERE!

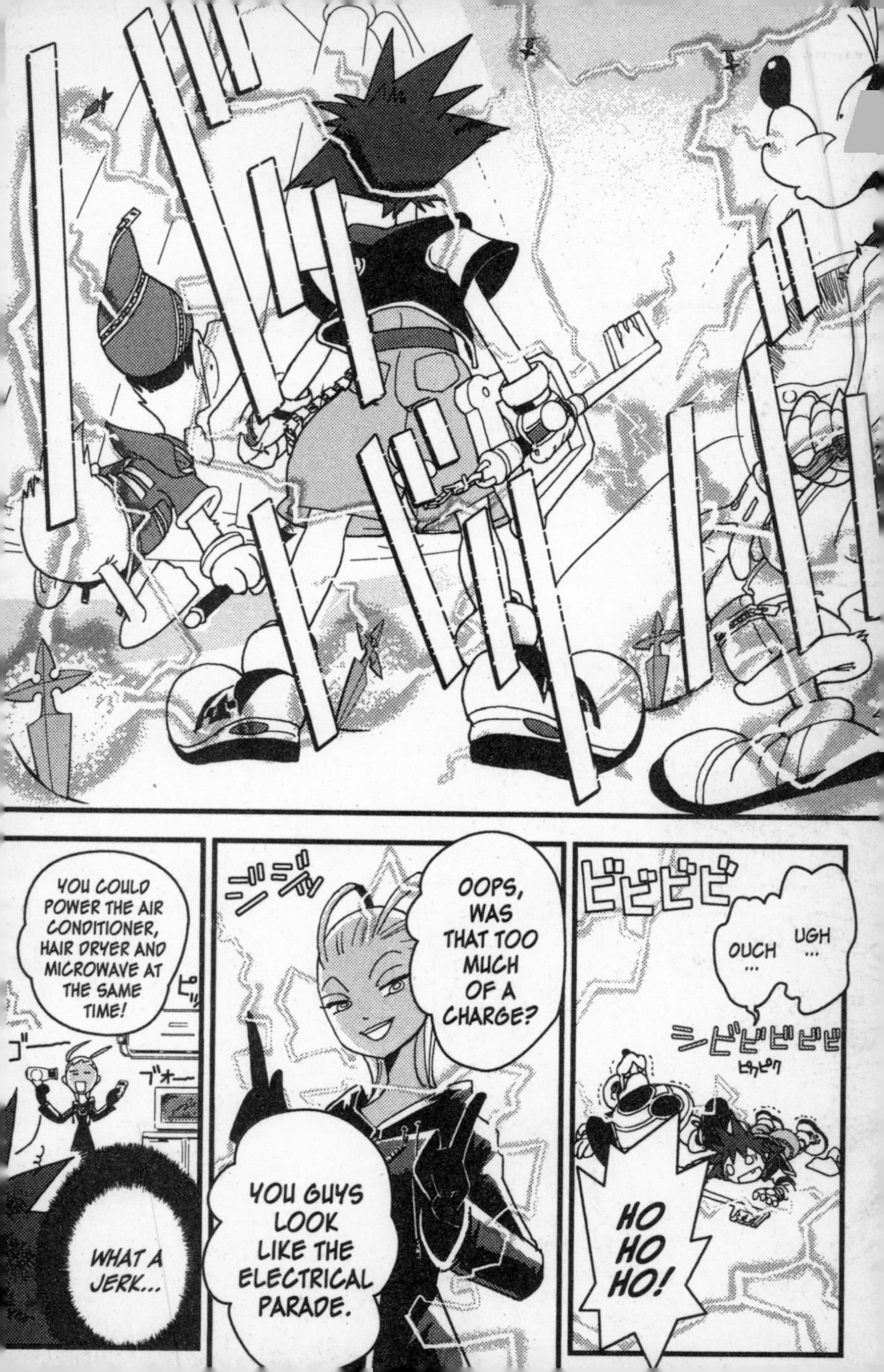

OUCH ... UGH ...
ビビビビ
ピクピク
HO HO HO!
OOPS, WAS THAT TOO MUCH OF A CHARGE?
YOU GUYS LOOK LIKE THE ELECTRICAL PARADE.
YOU COULD POWER THE AIR CONDITIONER, HAIR DRYER AND MICROWAVE AT THE SAME TIME!
ピッ
ゴー
ブオー
WHAT A JERK...

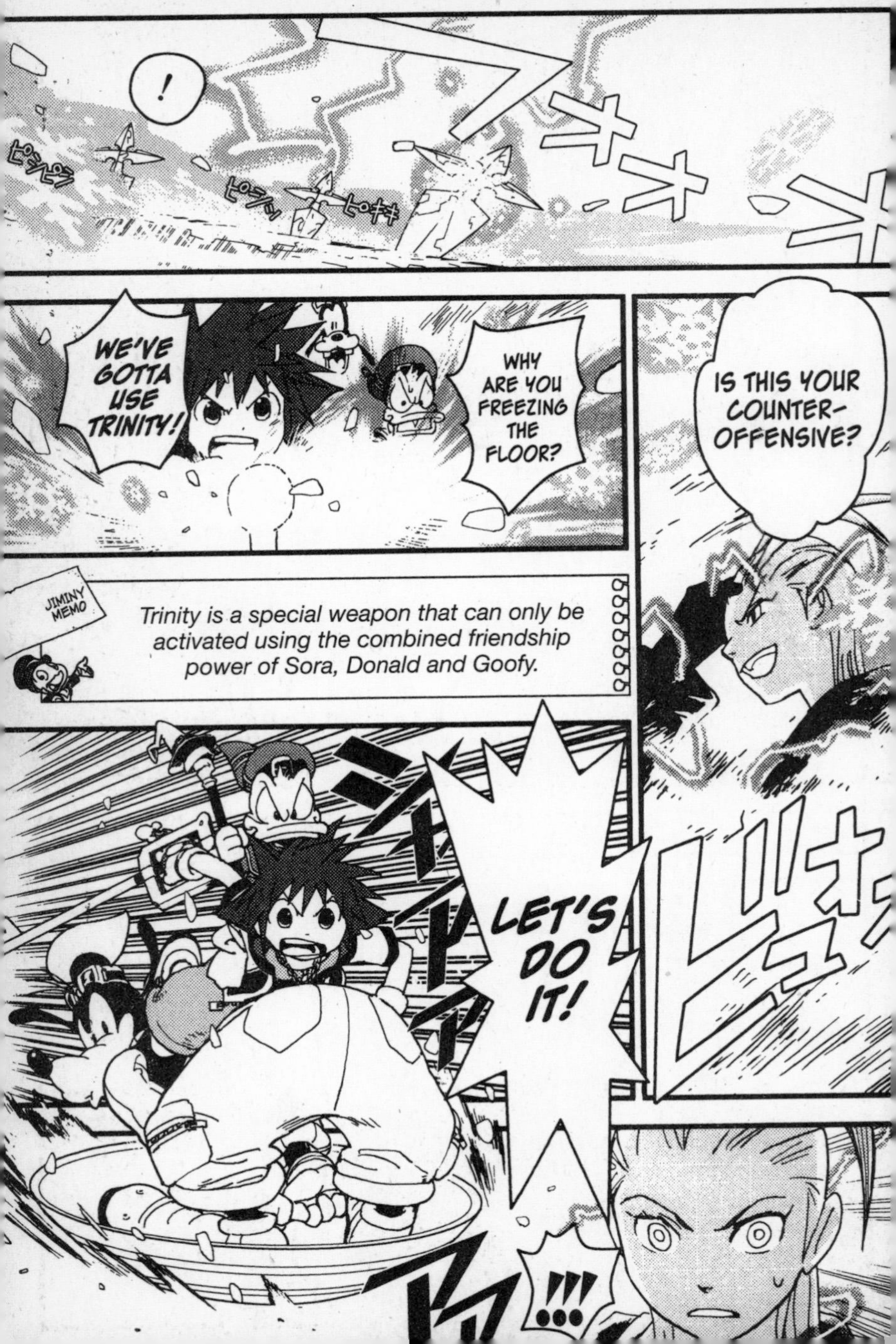
!
IS THIS YOUR COUNTER-OFFENSIVE?
WHY ARE YOU FREEZING THE FLOOR?
WE'VE GOTTA USE TRINITY!
JIMINY MEMO
Trinity is a special weapon that can only be activated using the combined friendship power of Sora, Donald and Goofy.
LET'S DO IT!
!!!

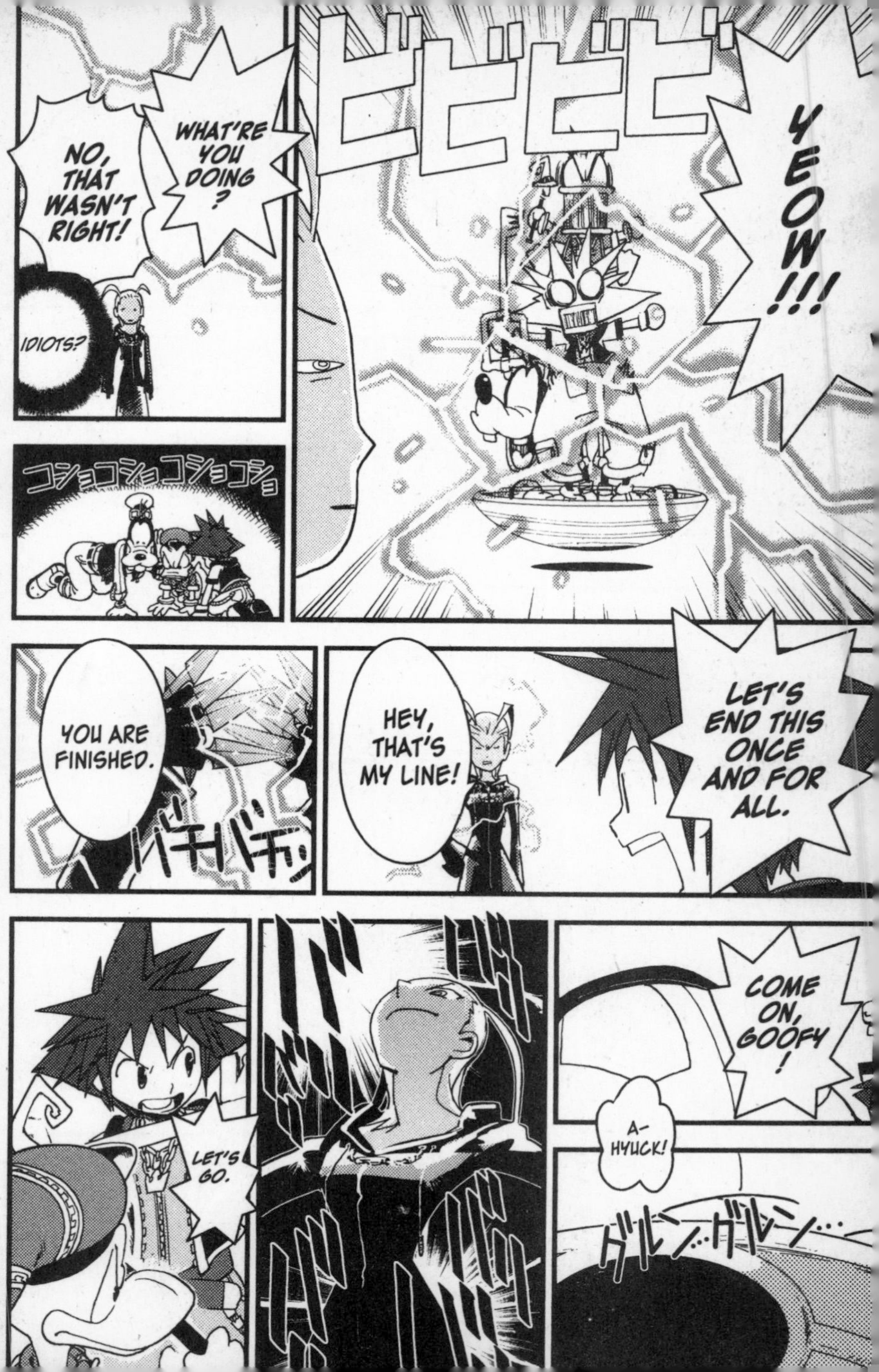
ビビビビ
YEOW!!!
WHAT'RE YOU DOING?
NO, THAT WASN'T RIGHT!
IDIOTS?
コショコショコショコショ
LET'S END THIS ONCE AND FOR ALL.
HEY, THAT'S MY LINE!
YOU ARE FINISHED.
バチバチッ
COME ON, GOOFY!
A-HYUCK!
グルン…グルン…
LET'S GO.

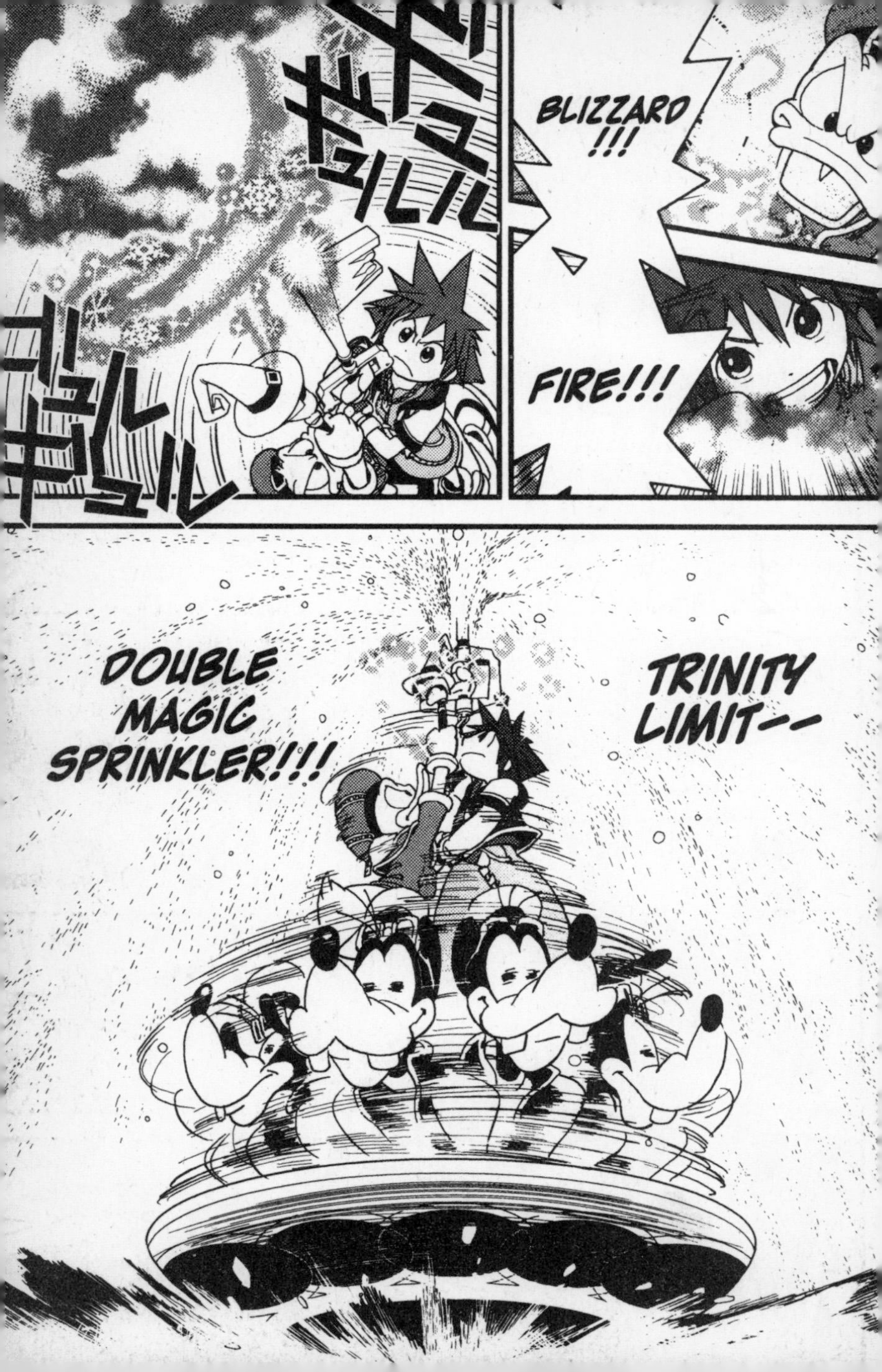
BLIZZARD
!!!
FIRE!!!
TRINITY
LIMIT--
DOUBLE
MAGIC
SPRINKLER!!!

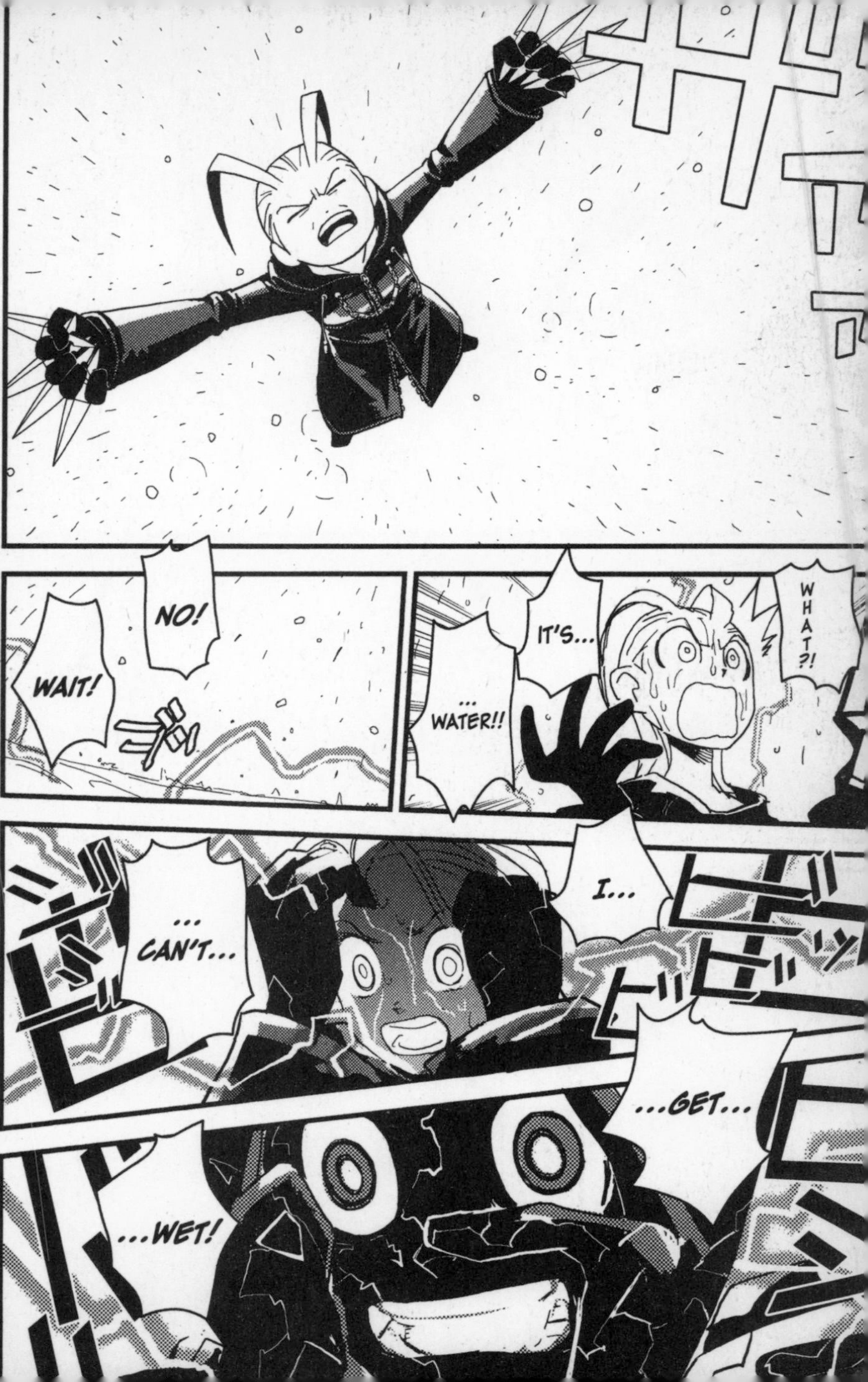
WHAT?!
IT'S...
...WATER!!
NO!
WAIT!
I...
...CAN'T...
...GET...
...WET!

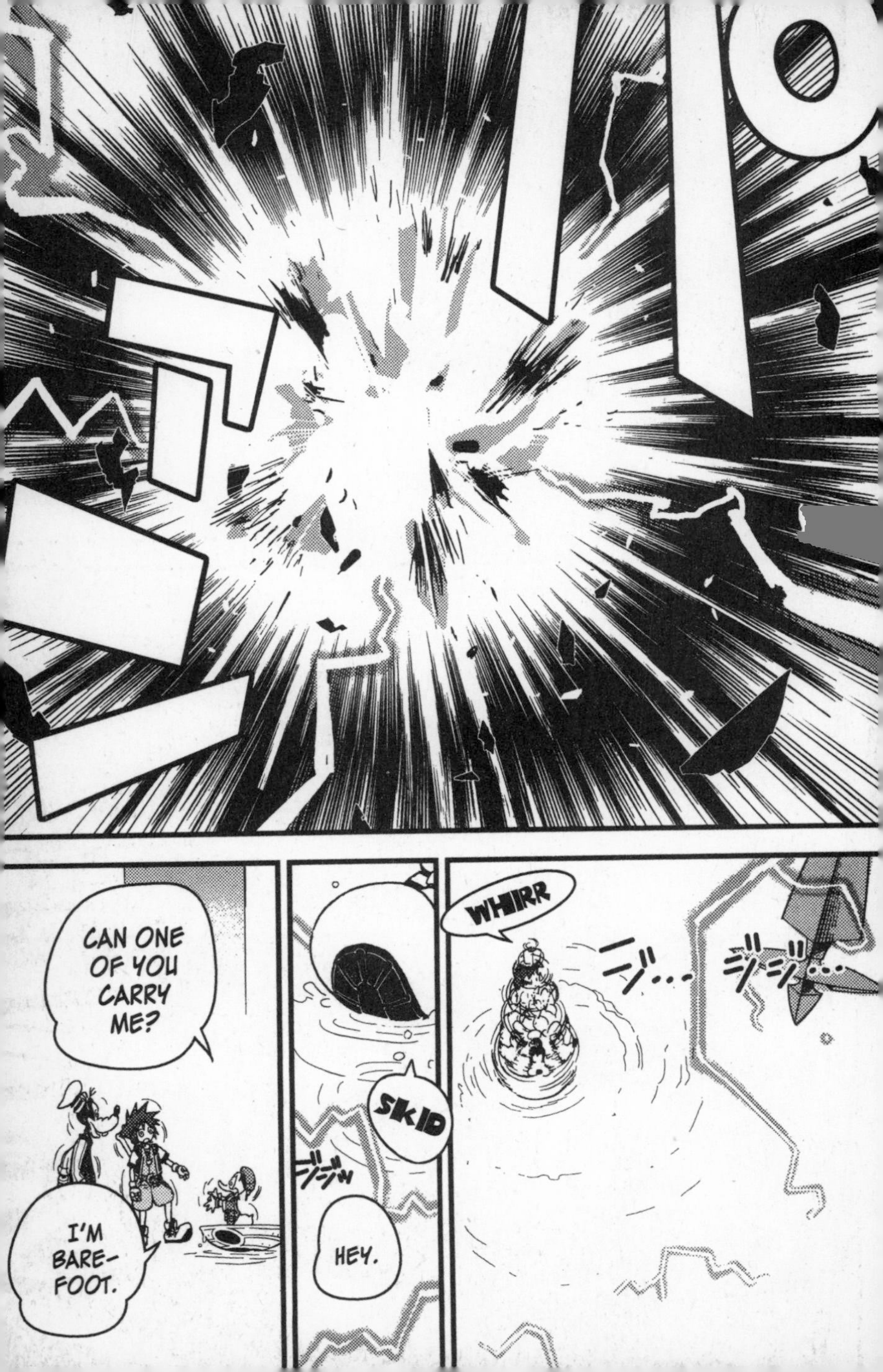
WHIRR
SKID
HEY.
CAN ONE OF YOU CARRY ME?
I'M BARE-FOOT.

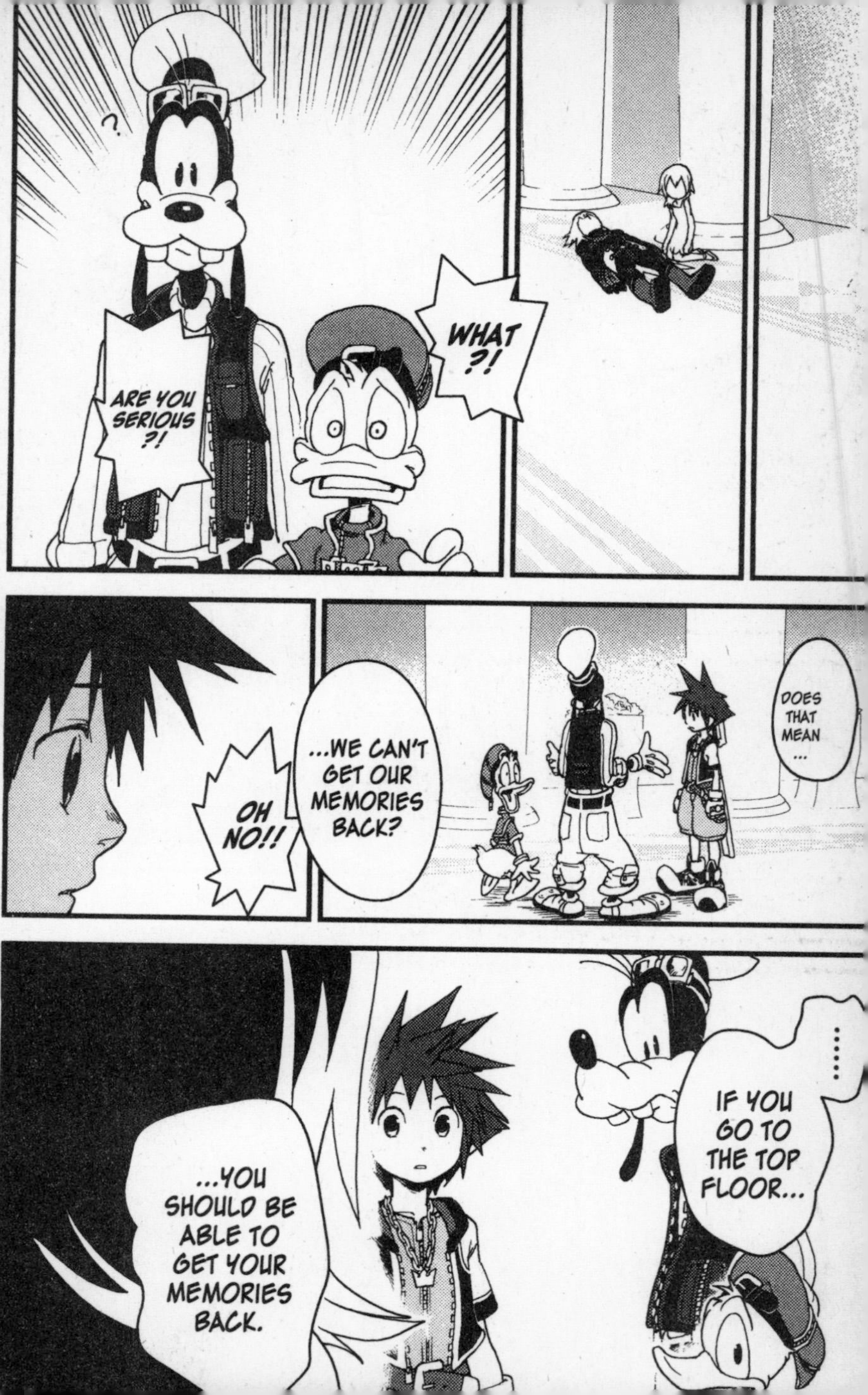
WHAT ?!
ARE YOU SERIOUS ?!
DOES THAT MEAN ...
...WE CAN'T GET OUR MEMORIES BACK?
OH NO!!
......
IF YOU GO TO THE TOP FLOOR...
...YOU SHOULD BE ABLE TO GET YOUR MEMORIES BACK.

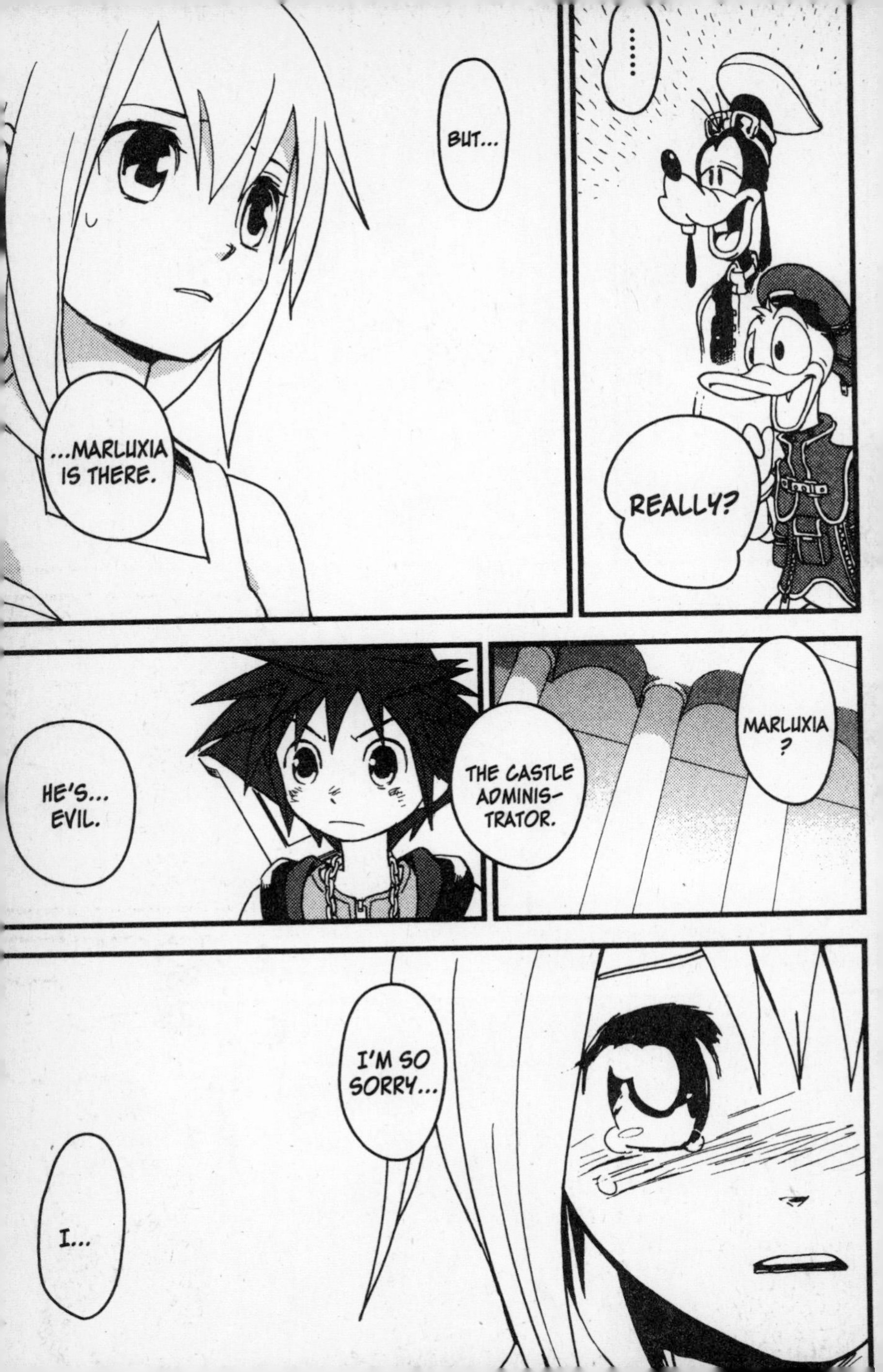
......
REALLY?
BUT...
...MARLUXIA IS THERE.
MARLUXIA ?
THE CASTLE ADMINIS-TRATOR.
HE'S... EVIL.
I'M SO SORRY...
I...

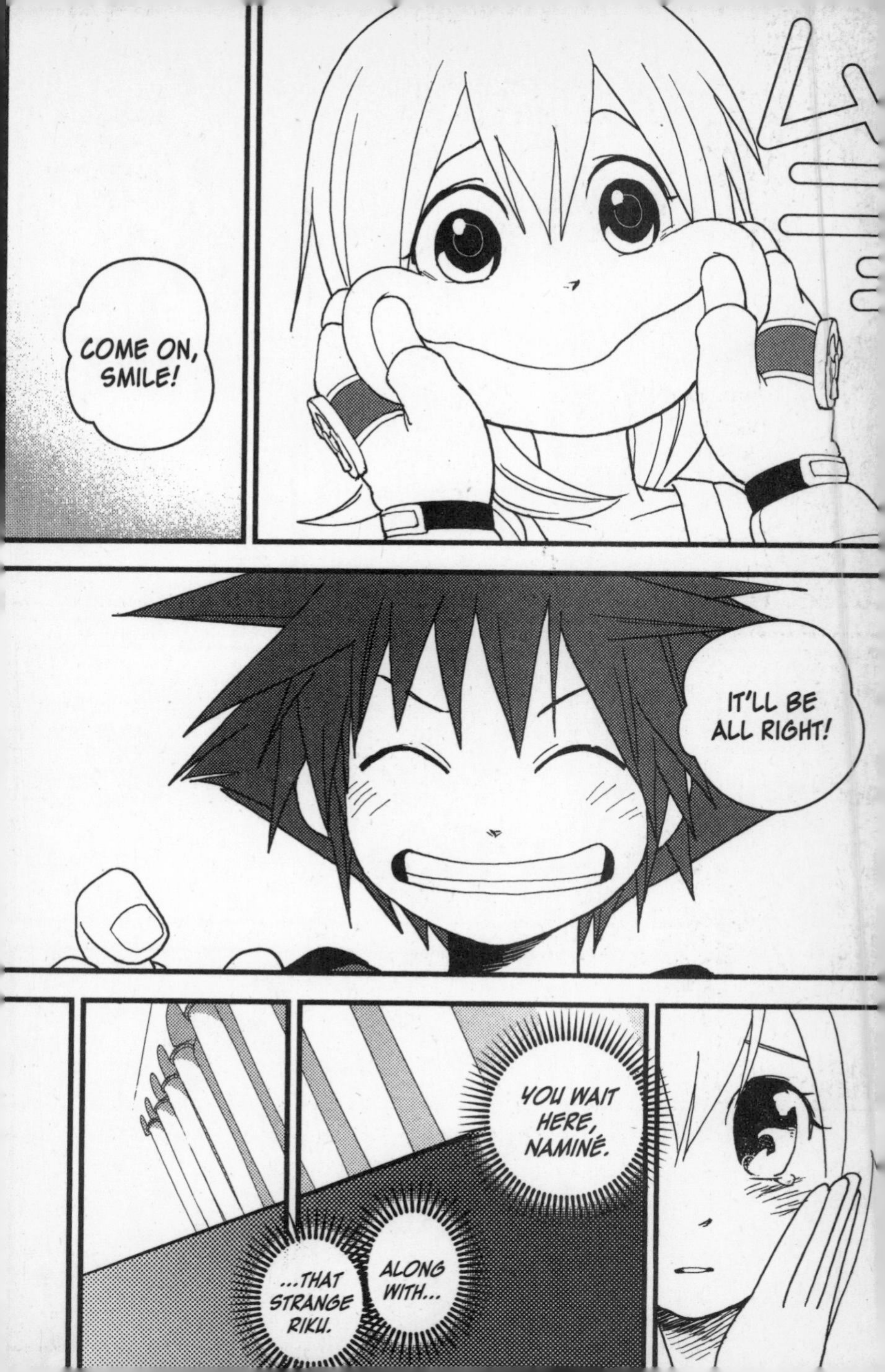
COME ON, SMILE!
IT'LL BE ALL RIGHT!
YOU WAIT HERE, NAMINÉ.
ALONG WITH...
...THAT STRANGE RIKU.

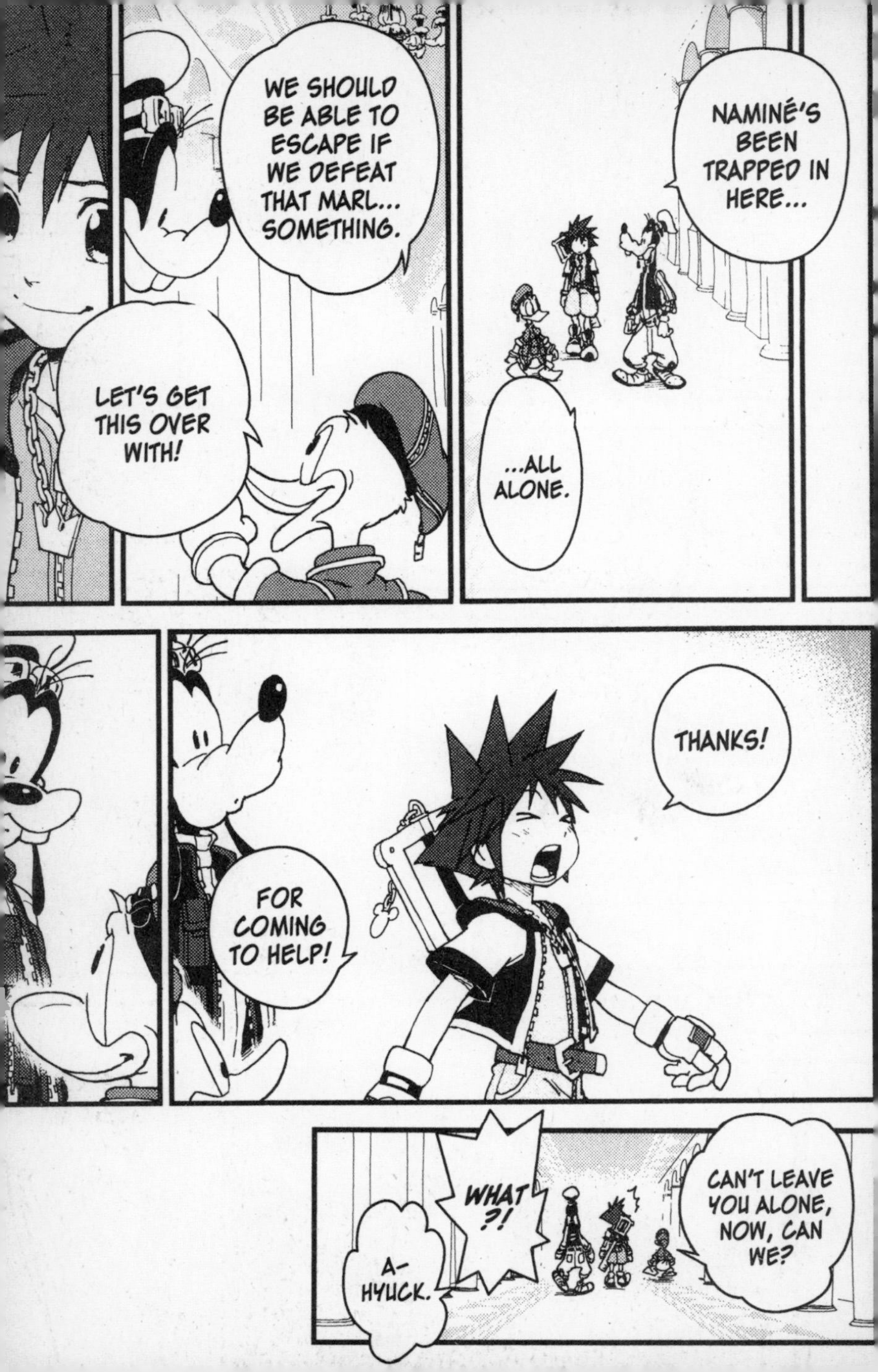
NAMINÉ'S BEEN TRAPPED IN HERE...
...ALL ALONE.
WE SHOULD BE ABLE TO ESCAPE IF WE DEFEAT THAT MARL... SOMETHING.
LET'S GET THIS OVER WITH!
THANKS!
FOR COMING TO HELP!
CAN'T LEAVE YOU ALONE, NOW, CAN WE?
WHAT?!
A-HYUCK.

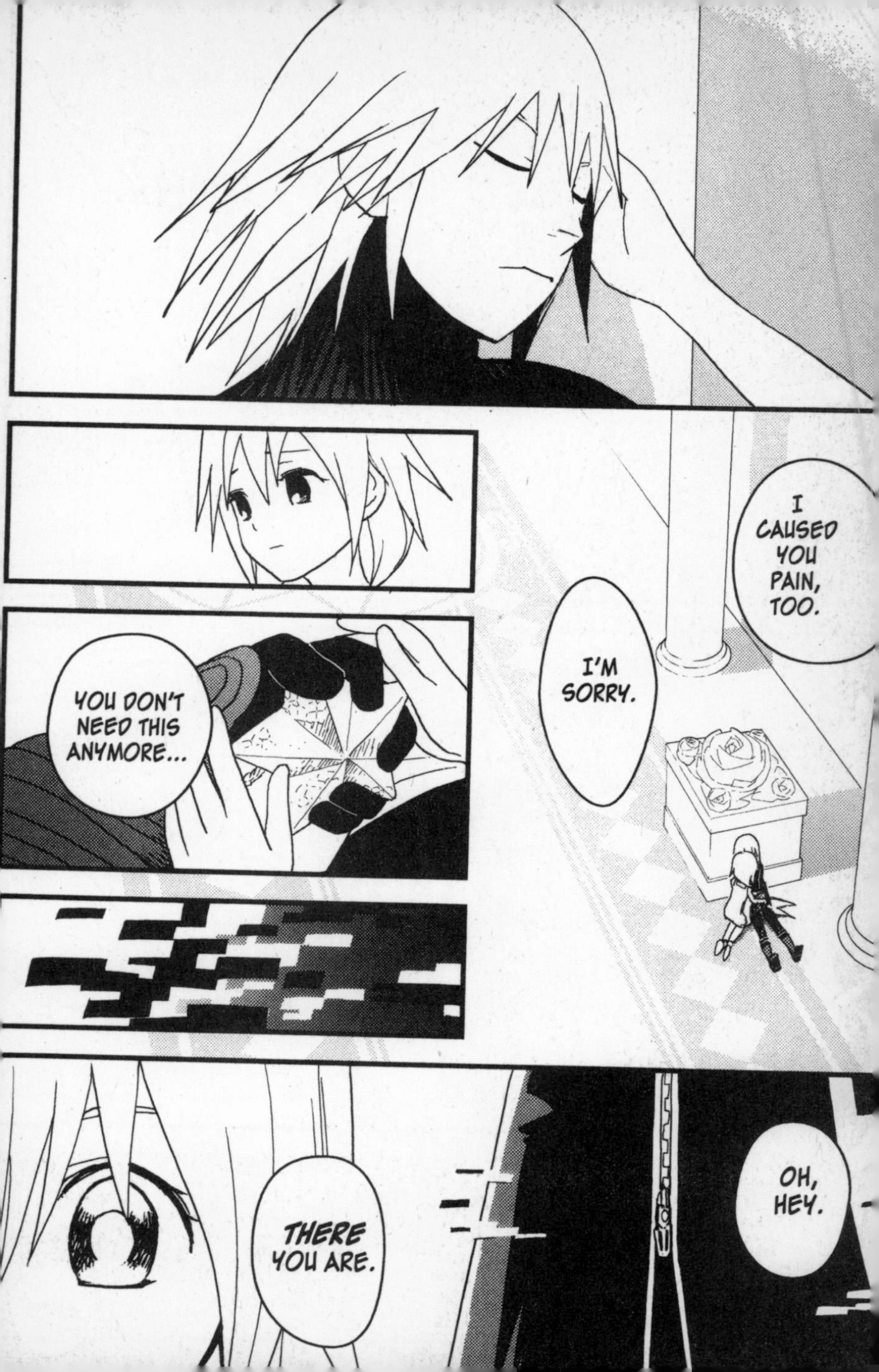
I CAUSED YOU PAIN, TOO.
I'M SORRY.
YOU DON'T NEED THIS ANYMORE...
OH, HEY.
THERE YOU ARE.

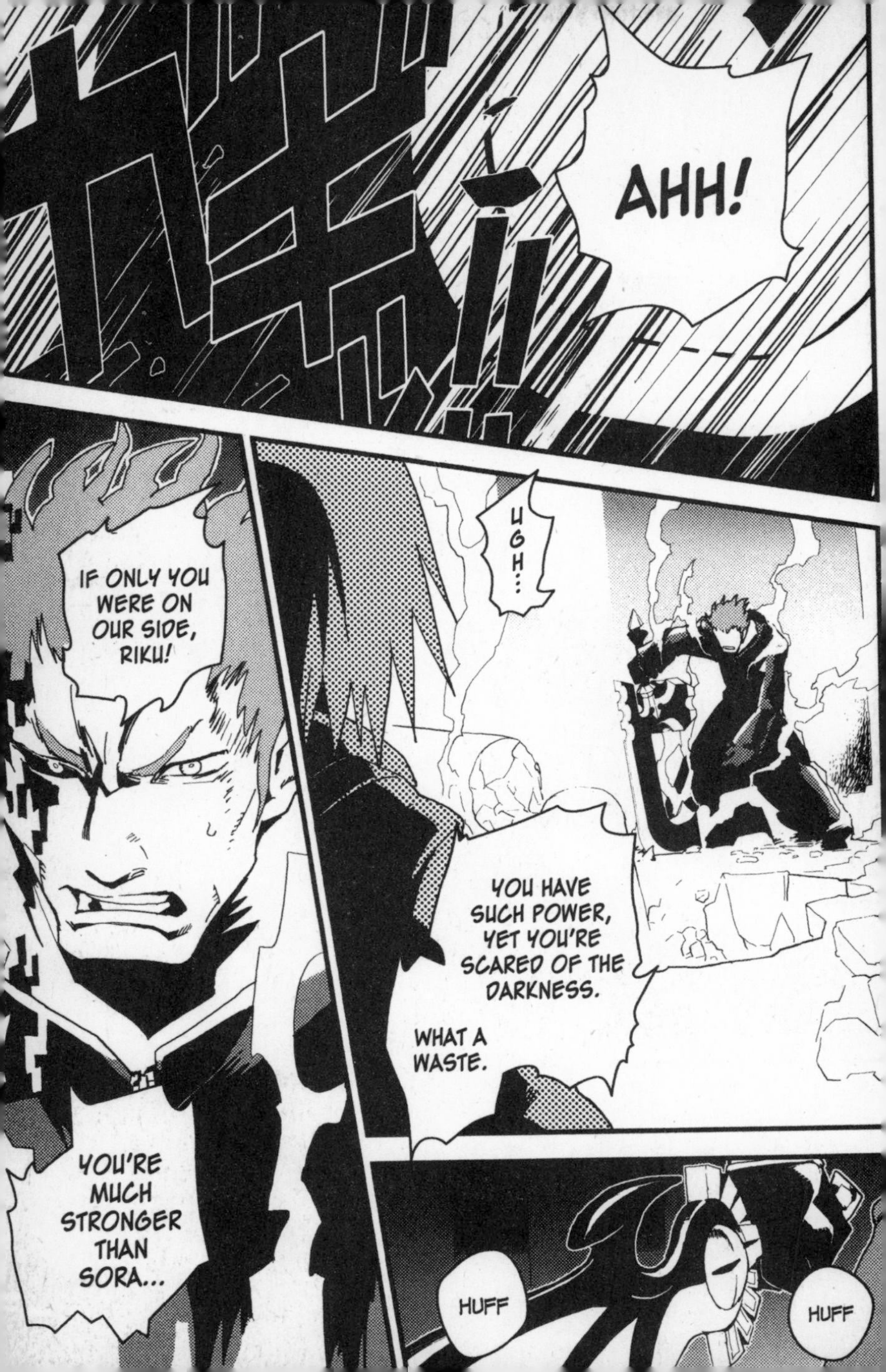
AHH!
UGH...
YOU HAVE SUCH POWER, YET YOU'RE SCARED OF THE DARKNESS.
WHAT A WASTE.
HUFF
HUFF
IF ONLY YOU WERE ON OUR SIDE, RIKU!
YOU'RE MUCH STRONGER THAN SORA...

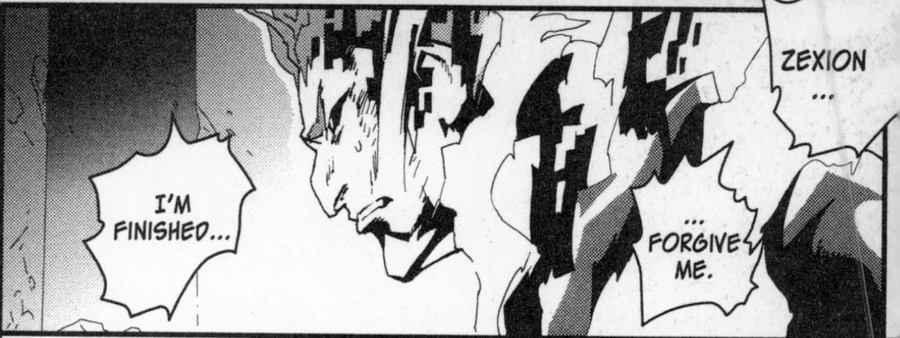
ZEXION ...
... FORGIVE ME.
I'M FINISHED...
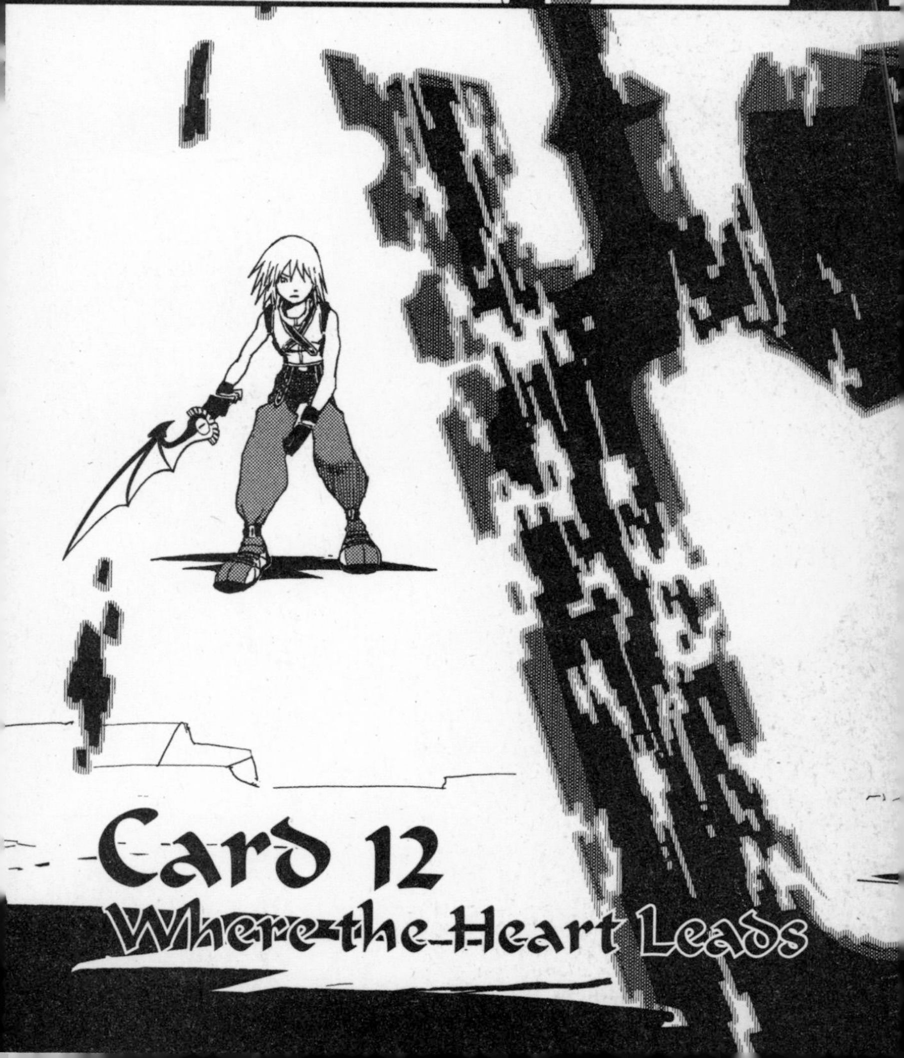
Card 12
Where the Heart Leads

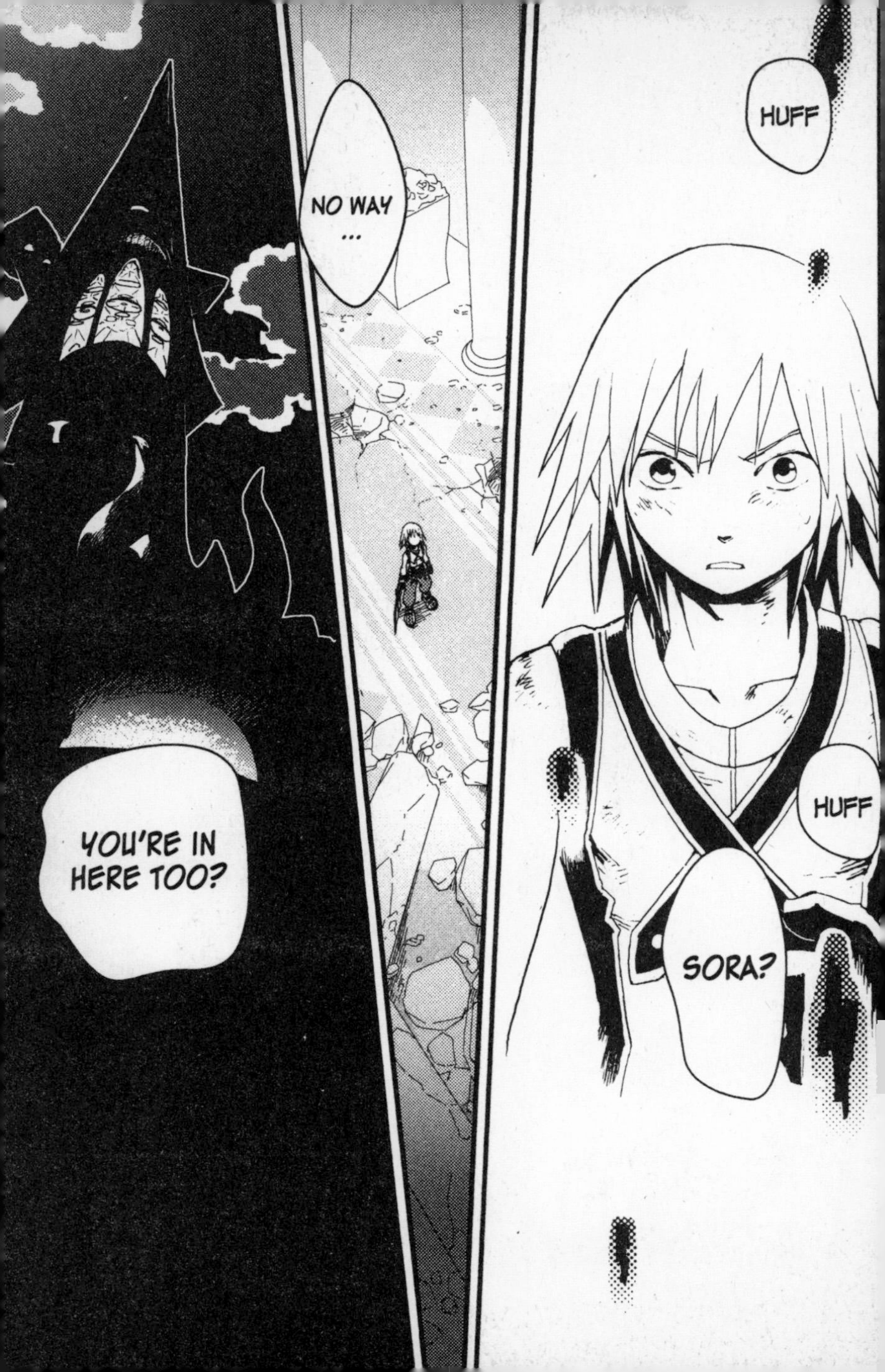
HUFF
HUFF
SORA?
NO WAY ...
YOU'RE IN HERE TOO?

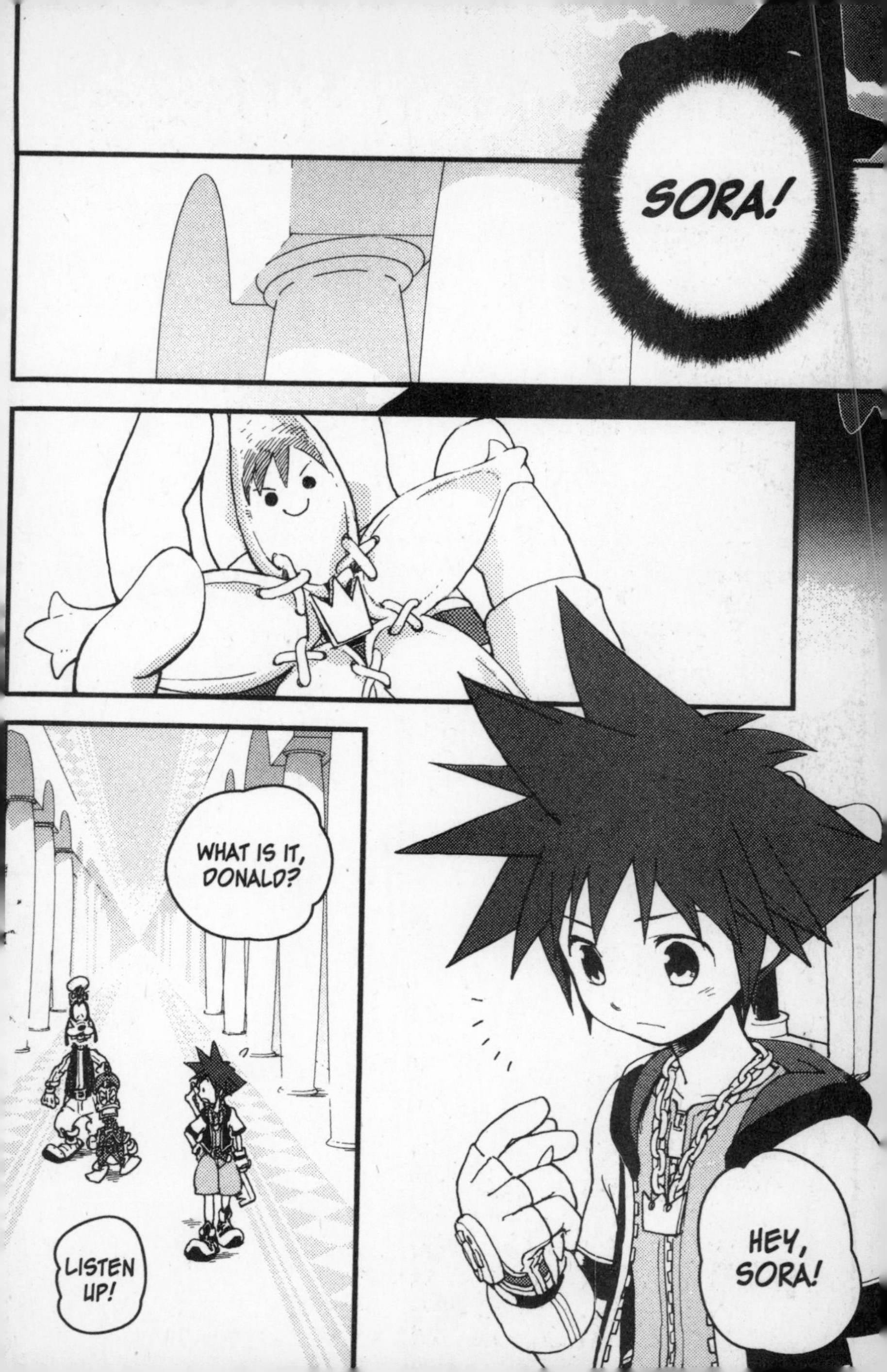
SORA!
HEY, SORA!
WHAT IS IT, DONALD?
LISTEN UP!

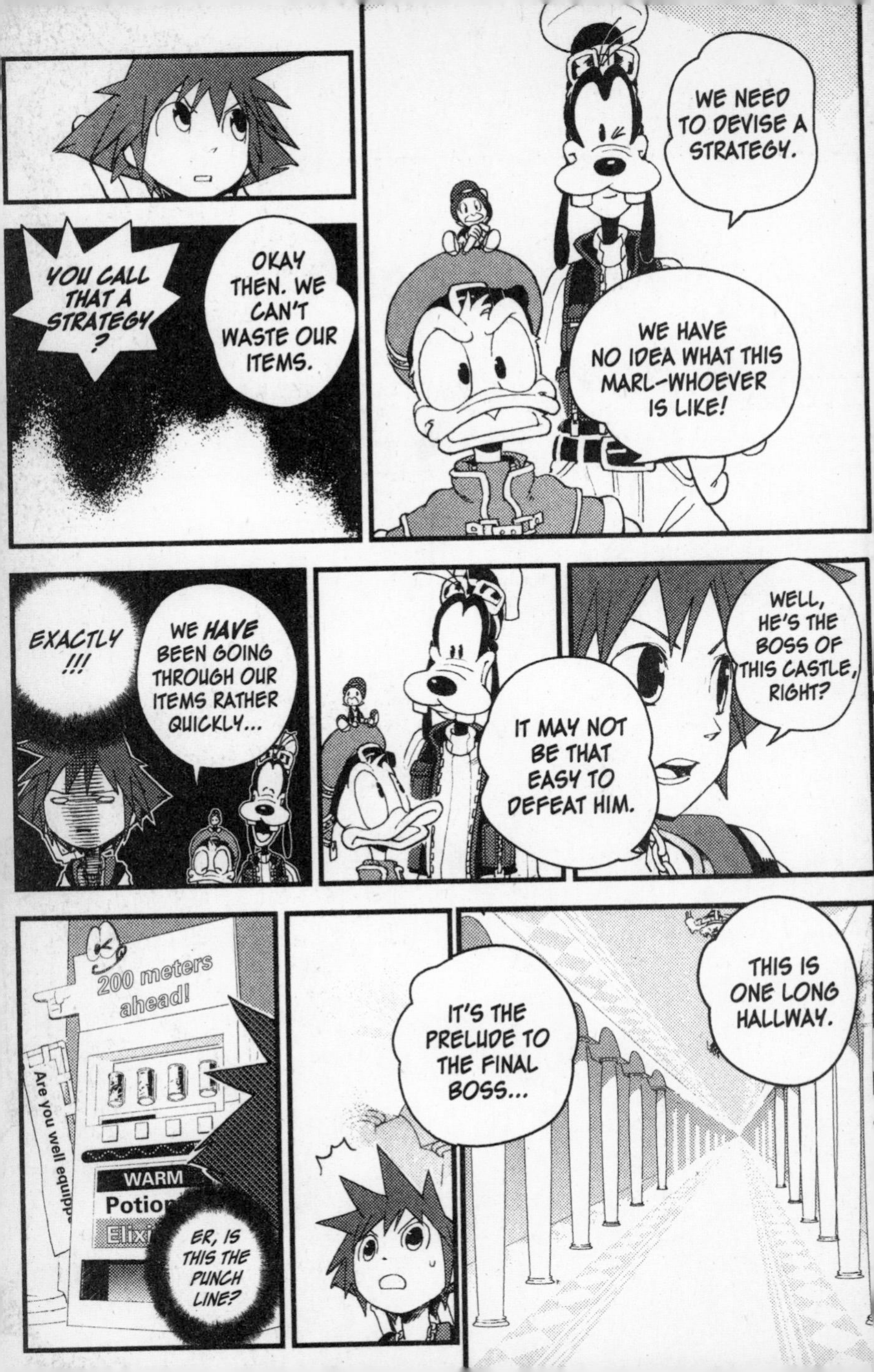
WE NEED TO DEVISE A STRATEGY.
WE HAVE NO IDEA WHAT THIS MARL-WHOEVER IS LIKE!
OKAY THEN. WE CAN'T WASTE OUR ITEMS.
YOU CALL THAT A STRATEGY?
WELL, HE'S THE BOSS OF THIS CASTLE, RIGHT?
IT MAY NOT BE THAT EASY TO DEFEAT HIM.
WE *HAVE* BEEN GOING THROUGH OUR ITEMS RATHER QUICKLY...
EXACTLY!!!
THIS IS ONE LONG HALLWAY.
IT'S THE PRELUDE TO THE FINAL BOSS...
200 meters ahead!
WARM
ER, IS THIS THE PUNCH LINE?

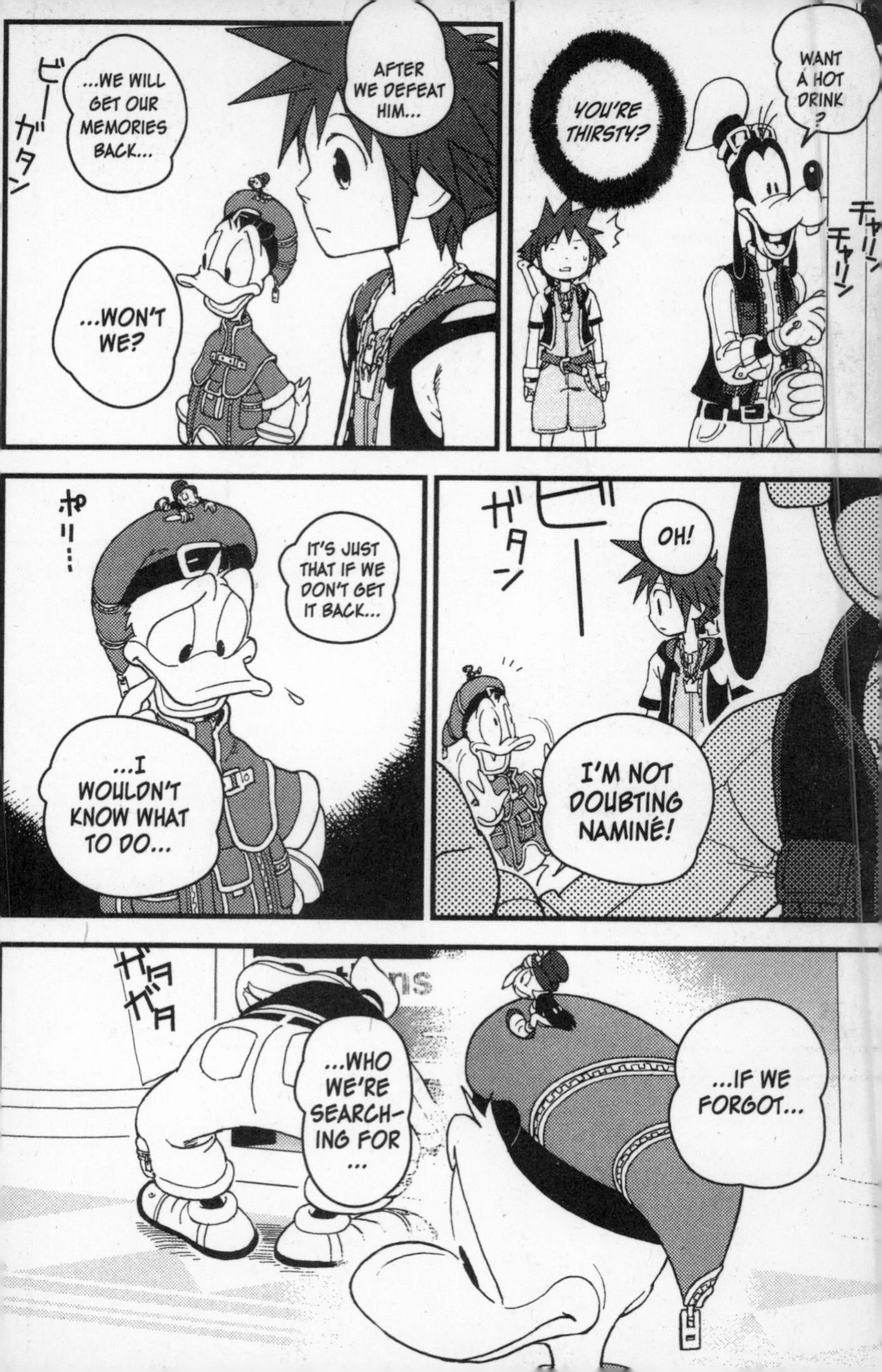

WANT A HOT DRINK?
YOU'RE THIRSTY?
チャリン
チャリン
AFTER WE DEFEAT HIM...
...WE WILL GET OUR MEMORIES BACK...
ビーガタン
...WON'T WE?
ビー
ガタン
OH!
I'M NOT DOUBTING NAMINÉ!
IT'S JUST THAT IF WE DON'T GET IT BACK...
ポリ…
...I WOULDN'T KNOW WHAT TO DO...
...IF WE FORGOT...
...WHO WE'RE SEARCHING FOR ...
ガタガタ

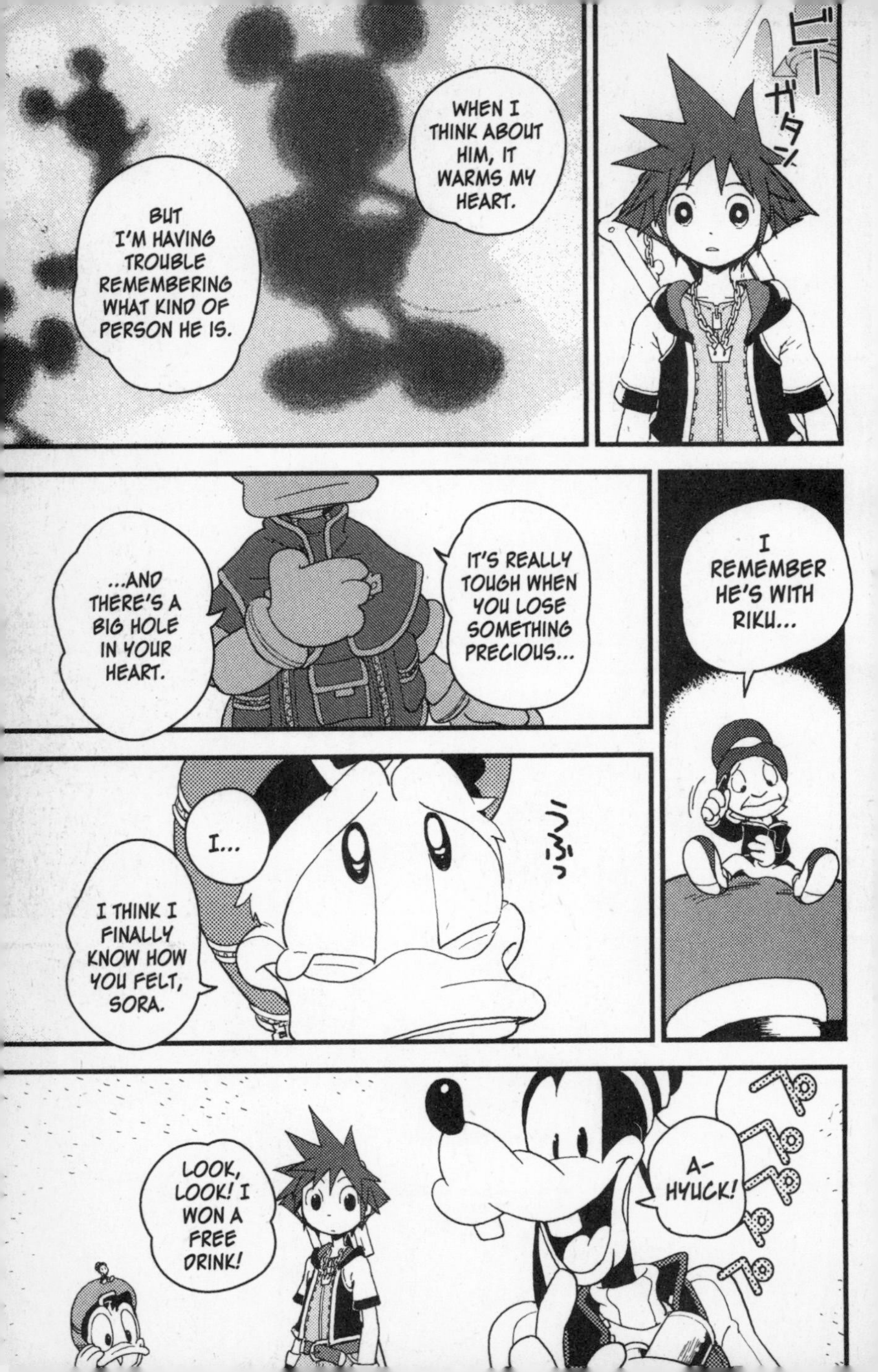
ビー
ガタン
WHEN I THINK ABOUT HIM, IT WARMS MY HEART.
BUT I'M HAVING TROUBLE REMEMBERING WHAT KIND OF PERSON HE IS.
I REMEMBER HE'S WITH RIKU...
IT'S REALLY TOUGH WHEN YOU LOSE SOMETHING PRECIOUS...
...AND THERE'S A BIG HOLE IN YOUR HEART.
I...
I THINK I FINALLY KNOW HOW YOU FELT, SORA.
A-HYUCK!
LOOK, LOOK! I WON A FREE DRINK!

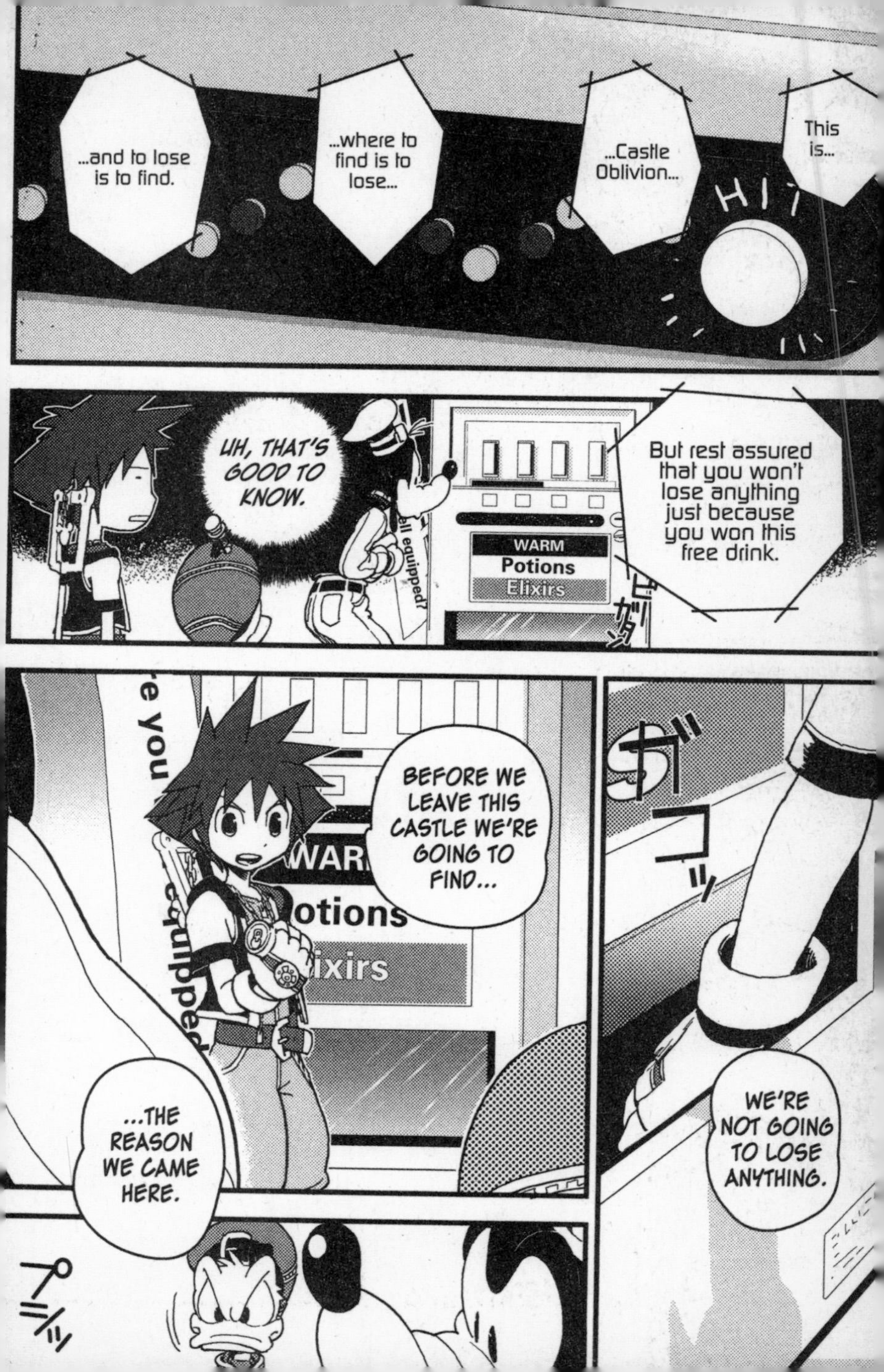
This is...
...Castle Oblivion...
...where to find is to lose...
...and to lose is to find.
HIT
But rest assured that you won't lose anything just because you won this free drink.
WARM
Potions
Elixirs
UH, THAT'S GOOD TO KNOW.
WE'RE NOT GOING TO LOSE ANYTHING.
BEFORE WE LEAVE THIS CASTLE WE'RE GOING TO FIND...
...THE REASON WE CAME HERE.

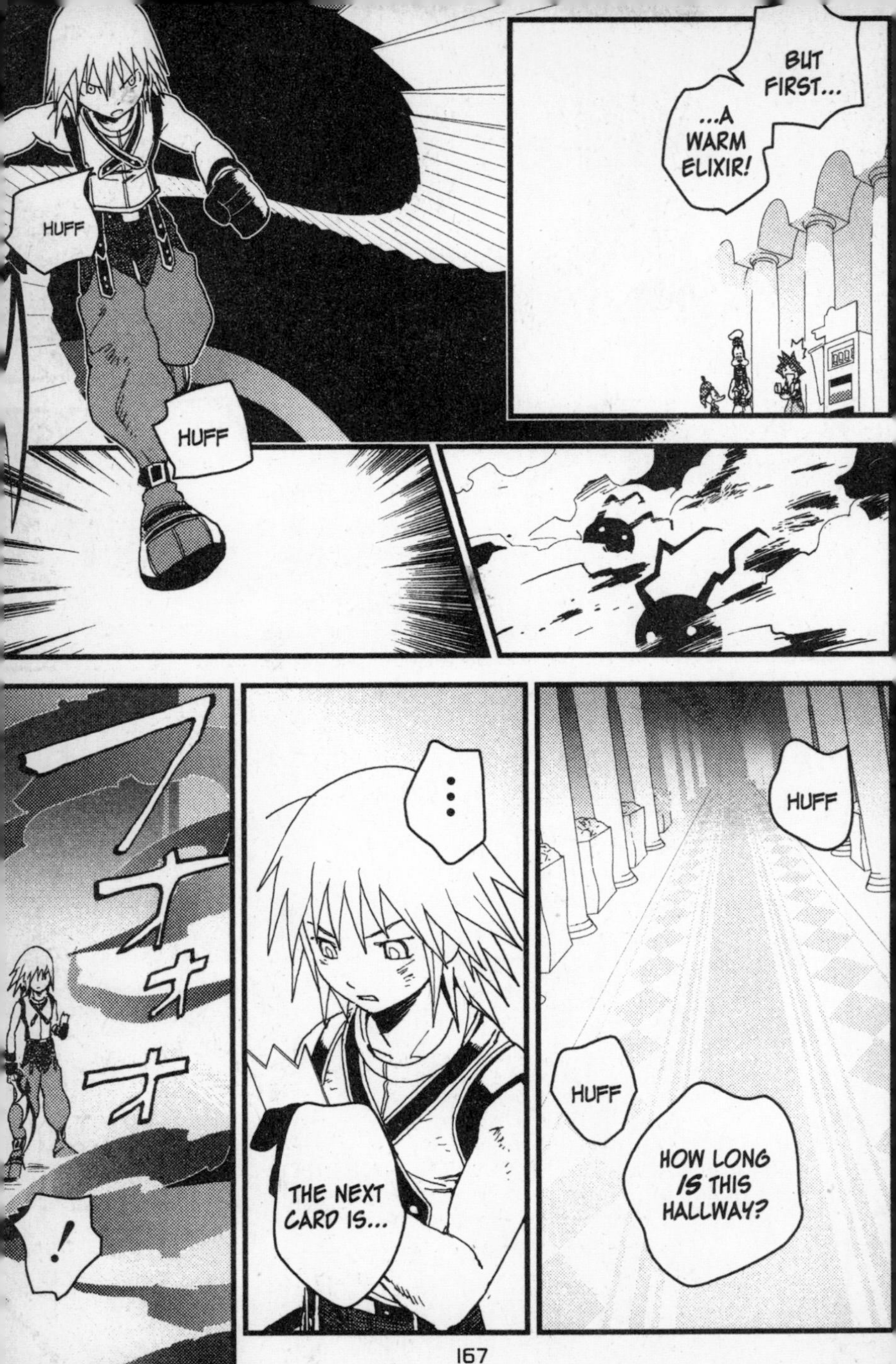

BUT FIRST...
...A WARM ELIXIR!
HUFF
HUFF
HUFF
HUFF
HOW LONG *IS* THIS HALLWAY?
...
THE NEXT CARD IS...
フォォォ
!

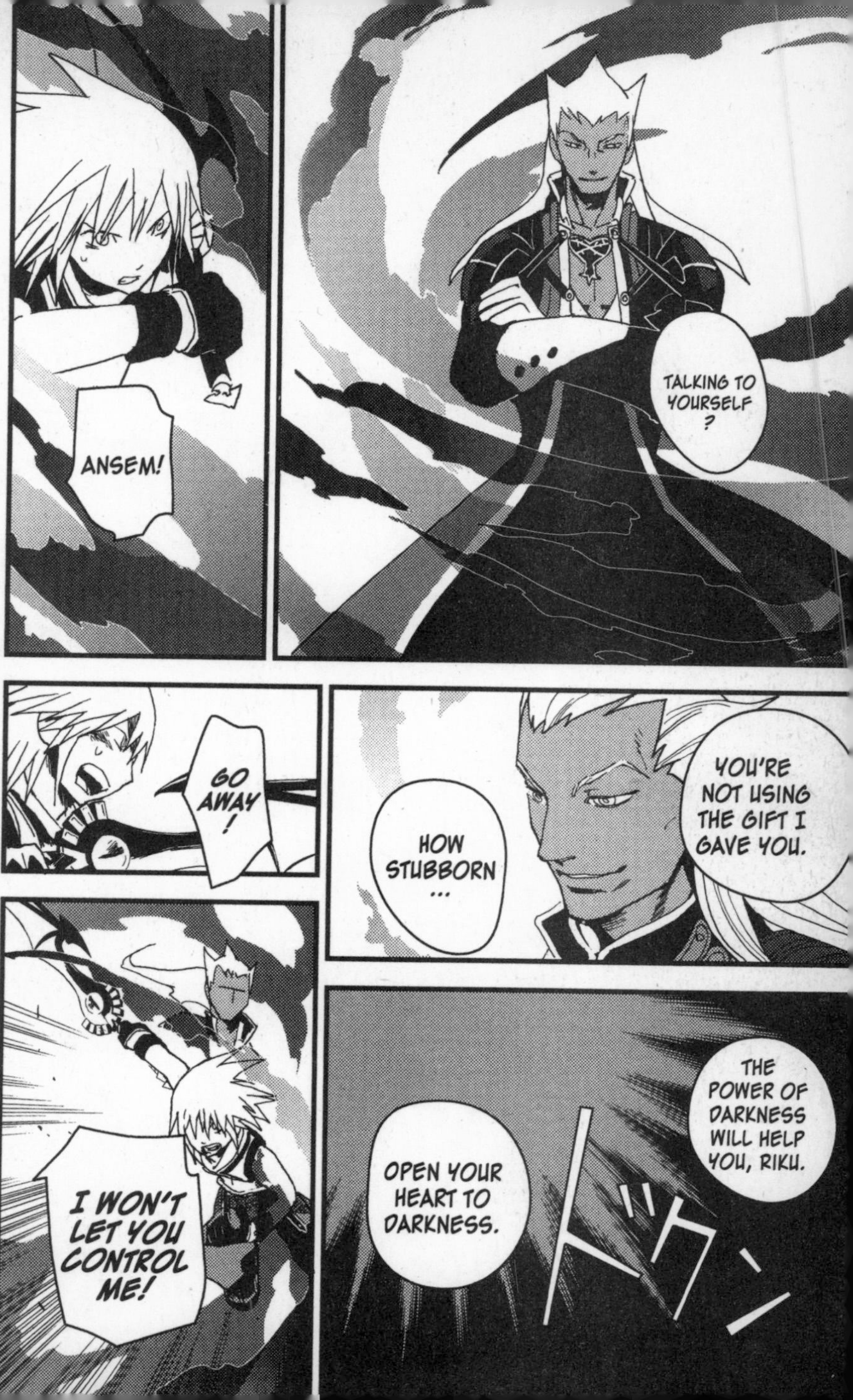
TALKING TO YOURSELF?
ANSEM!
YOU'RE NOT USING THE GIFT I GAVE YOU.
HOW STUBBORN...
GO AWAY!
THE POWER OF DARKNESS WILL HELP YOU, RIKU.
OPEN YOUR HEART TO DARKNESS.
ドクン
I WON'T LET YOU CONTROL ME!

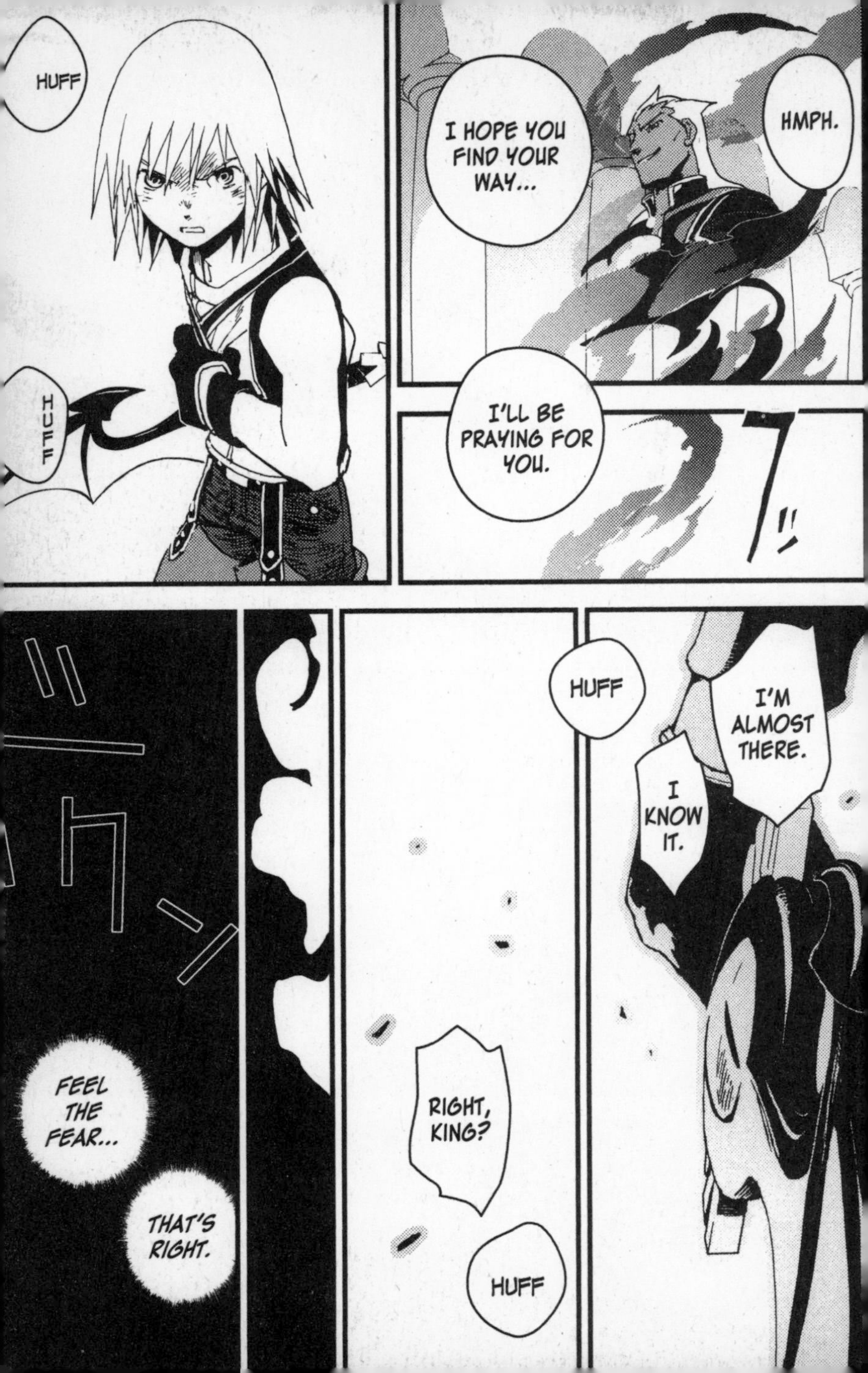
HMPH.
I HOPE YOU FIND YOUR WAY...
I'LL BE PRAYING FOR YOU.
HUFF
HUFF
HUFF
I'M ALMOST THERE.
I KNOW IT.
RIGHT, KING?
HUFF
FEEL THE FEAR...
THAT'S RIGHT.

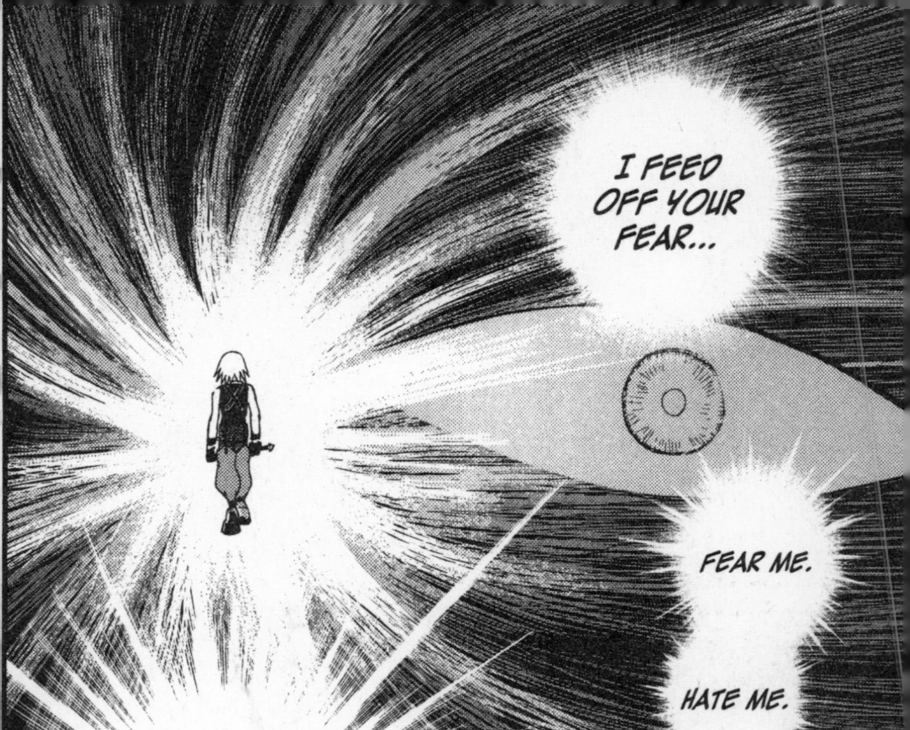
I FEED OFF YOUR FEAR...
FEAR ME.
HATE ME.
FIGHT ME.
STRONGER!
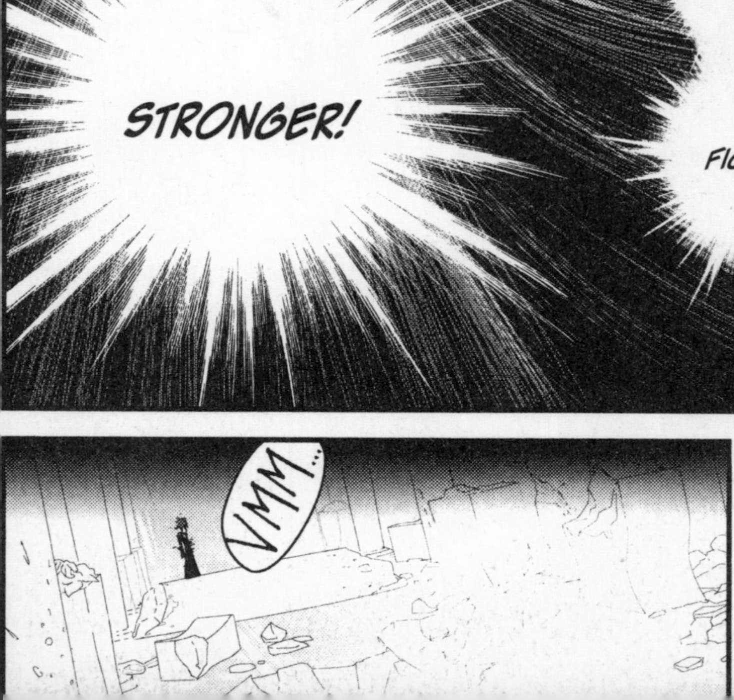
VMM...

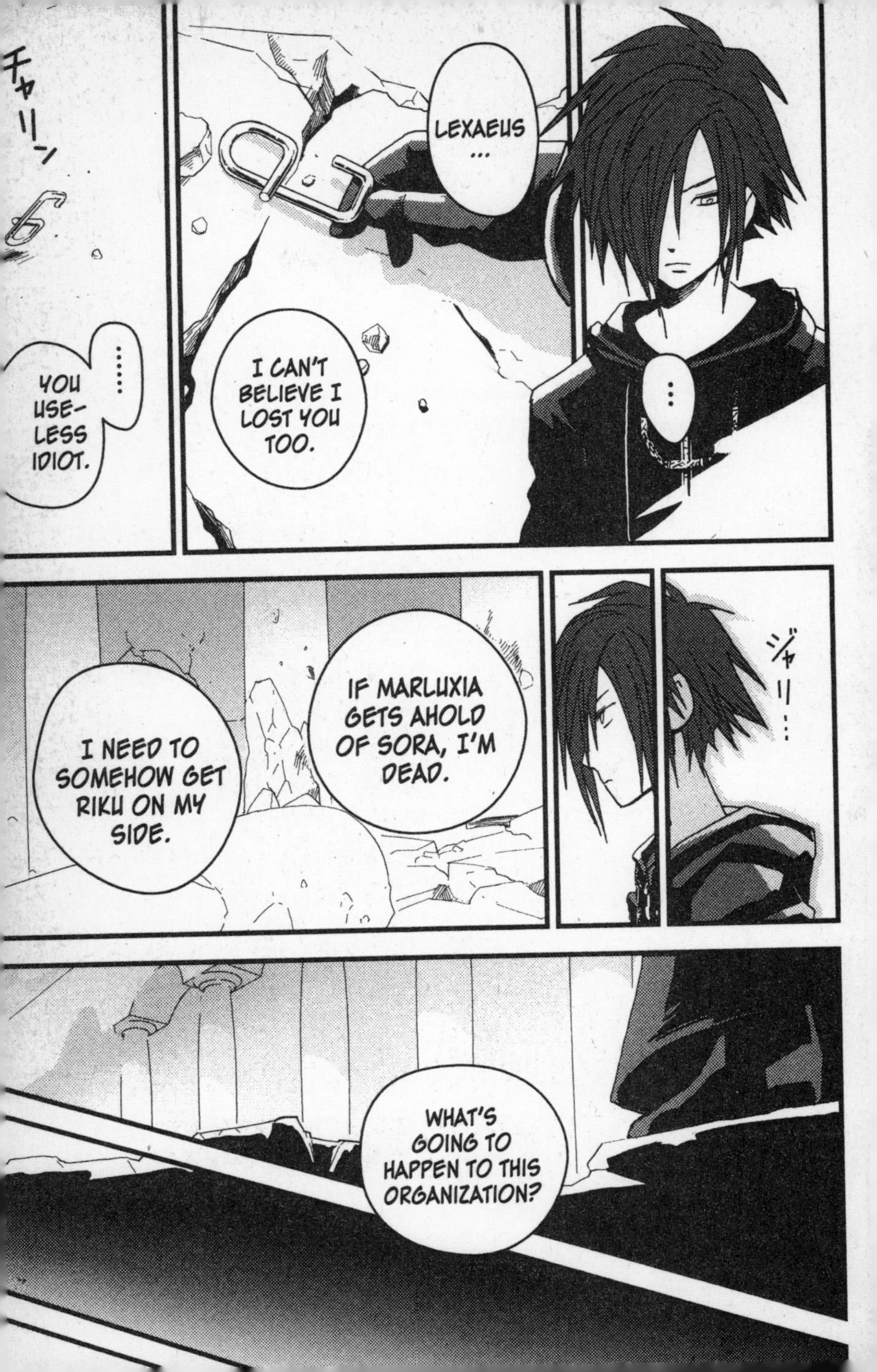
LEXAEUS ...
...
I CAN'T BELIEVE I LOST YOU TOO.
......
YOU USE-LESS IDIOT.
チャリーン
ジャリ…
IF MARLUXIA GETS AHOLD OF SORA, I'M DEAD.
I NEED TO SOMEHOW GET RIKU ON MY SIDE.
WHAT'S GOING TO HAPPEN TO THIS ORGANIZATION?

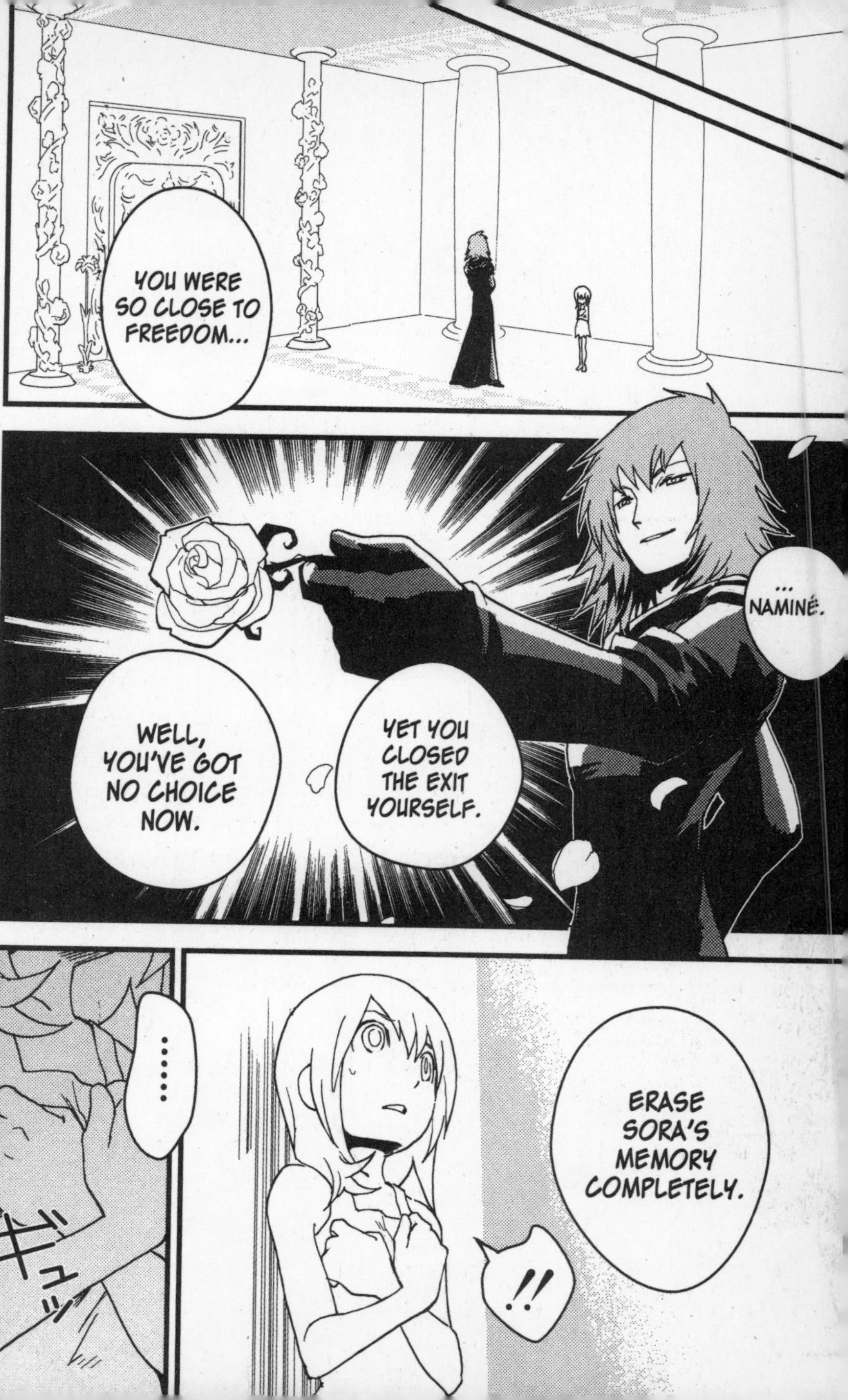
YOU WERE SO CLOSE TO FREEDOM...
...NAMINÉ.
YET YOU CLOSED THE EXIT YOURSELF.
WELL, YOU'VE GOT NO CHOICE NOW.
ERASE SORA'S MEMORY COMPLETELY.
!!
......
ギュッ

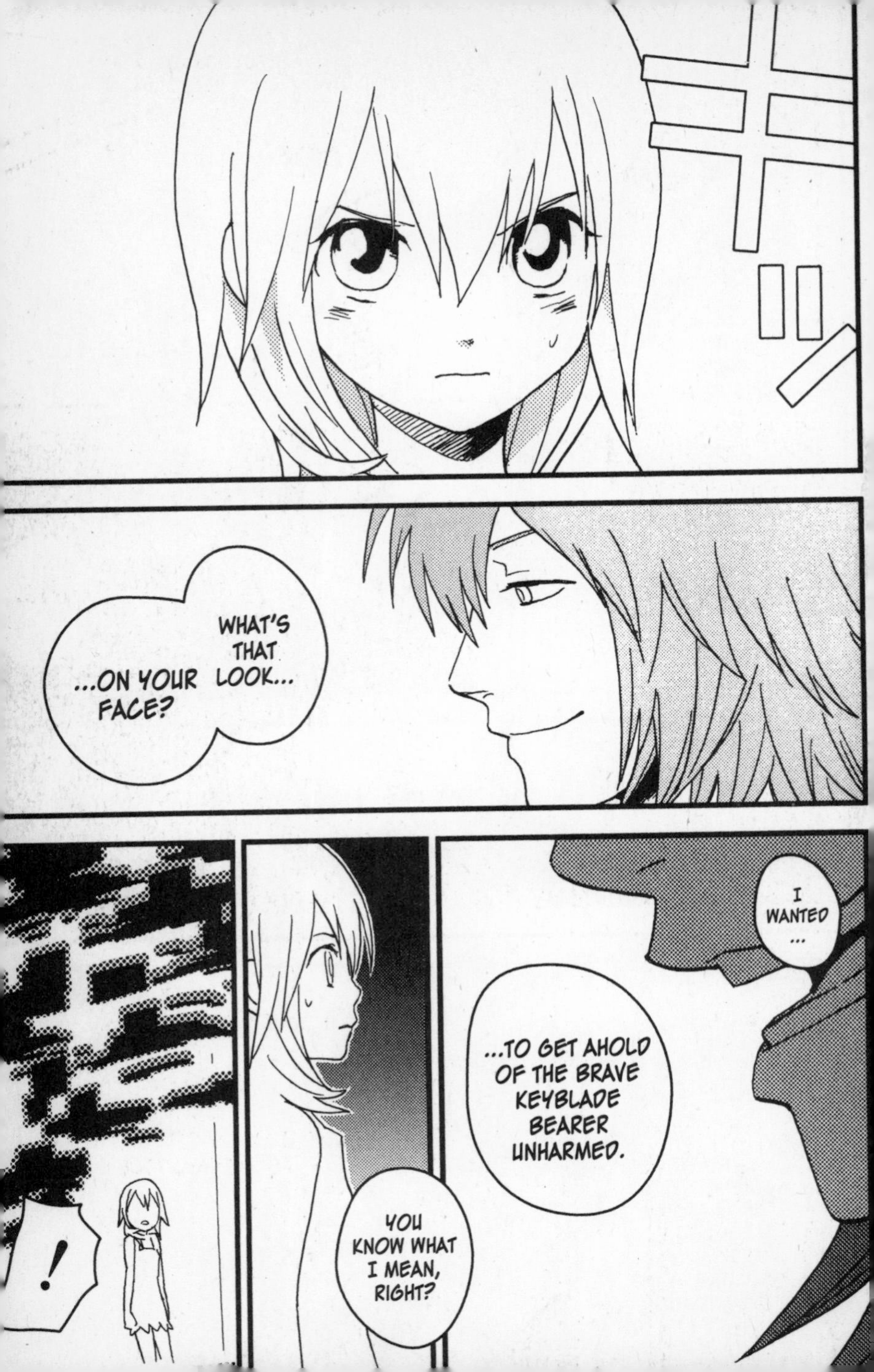
WHAT'S THAT LOOK...
...ON YOUR FACE?
I WANTED ...
...TO GET AHOLD OF THE BRAVE KEYBLADE BEARER UNHARMED.
YOU KNOW WHAT I MEAN, RIGHT?
!

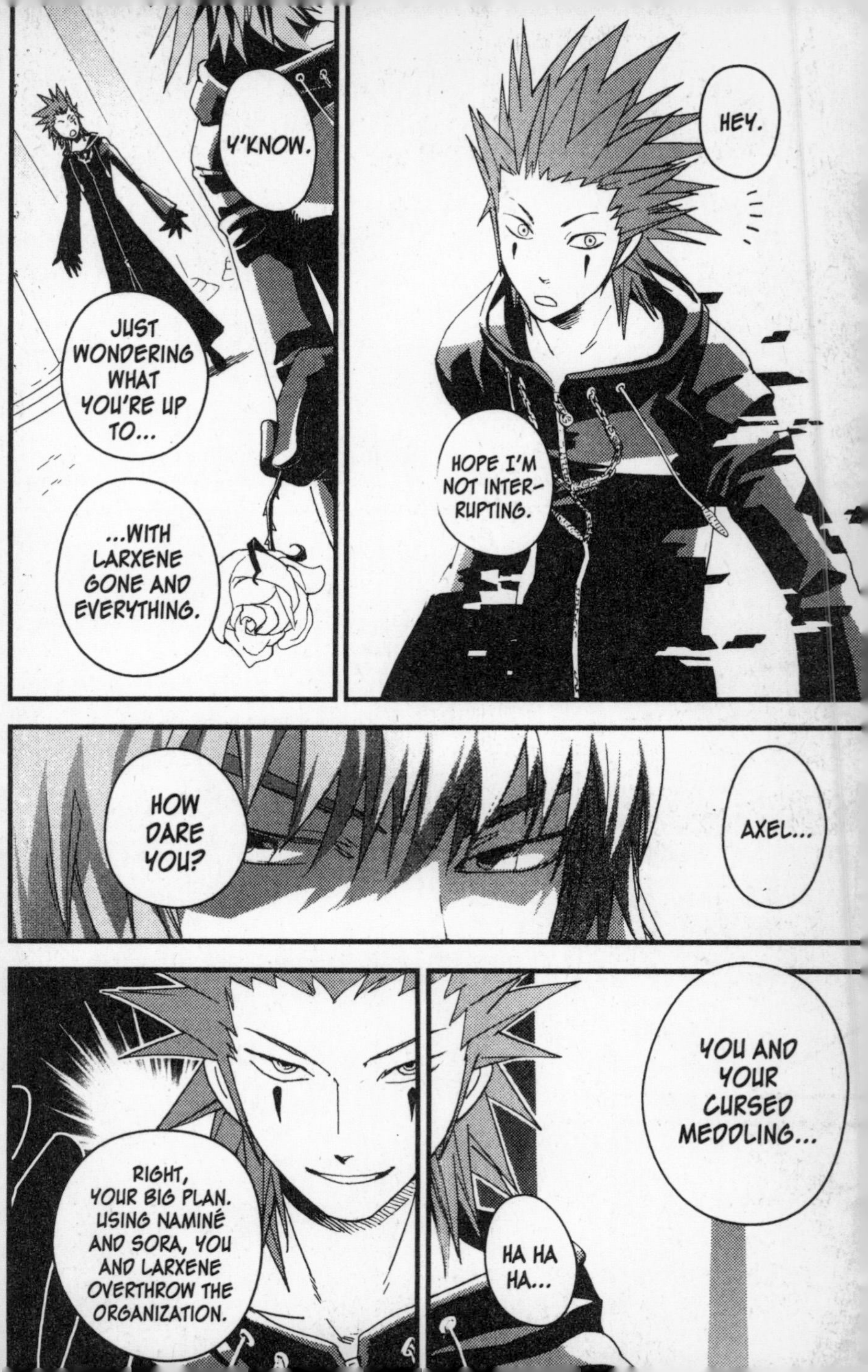
HEY.
HOPE I'M NOT INTER-RUPTING.
Y'KNOW.
JUST WONDERING WHAT YOU'RE UP TO...
...WITH LARXENE GONE AND EVERYTHING.
AXEL...
HOW DARE YOU?
YOU AND YOUR CURSED MEDDLING...
HA HA HA...
RIGHT, YOUR BIG PLAN. USING NAMINÉ AND SORA, YOU AND LARXENE OVERTHROW THE ORGANIZATION.

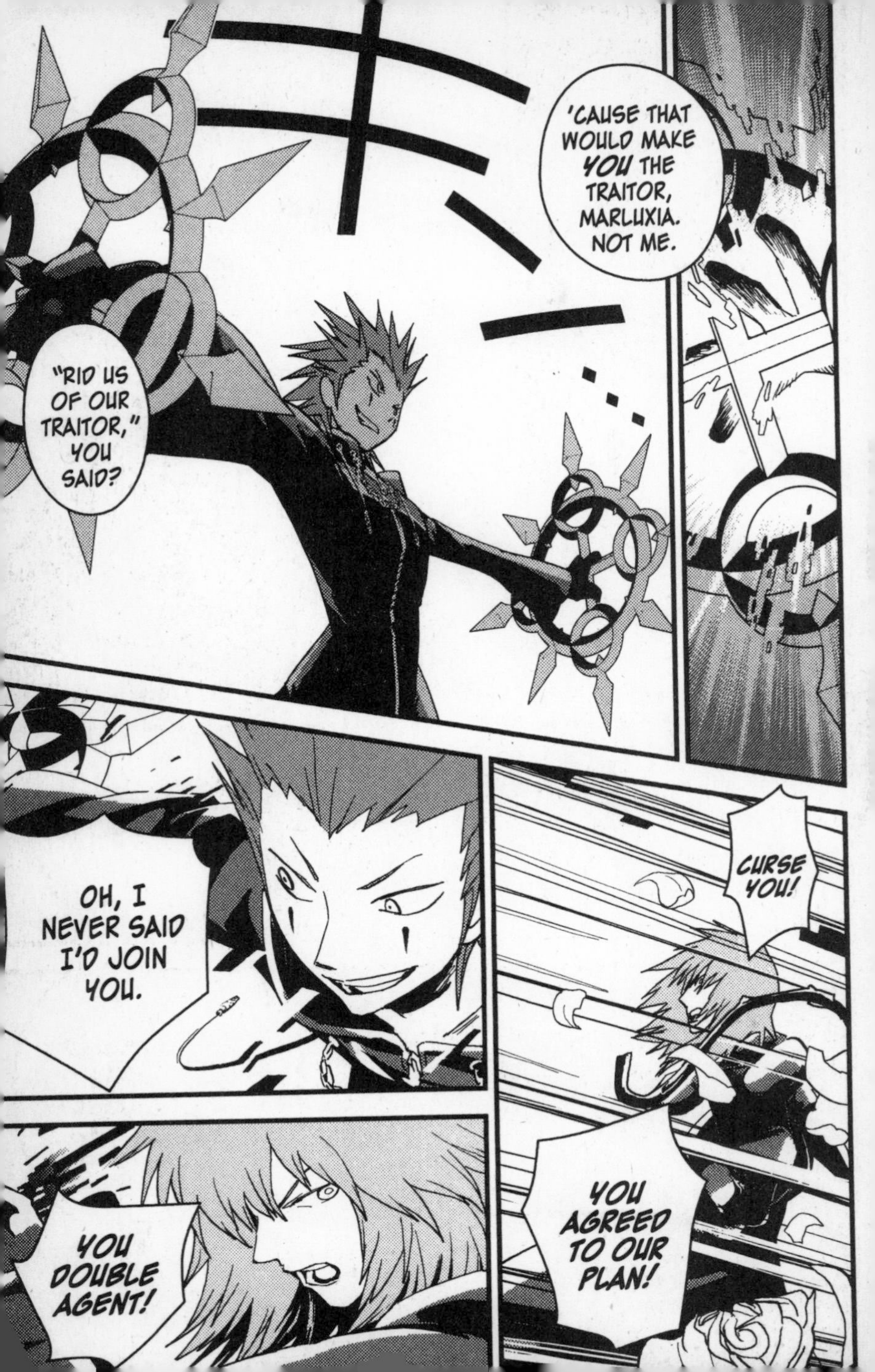
"RID US OF OUR TRAITOR," YOU SAID?
'CAUSE THAT WOULD MAKE *YOU* THE TRAITOR, MARLUXIA. NOT ME.
...
CURSE YOU!
YOU AGREED TO OUR PLAN!
OH, I NEVER SAID I'D JOIN YOU.
YOU DOUBLE AGENT!

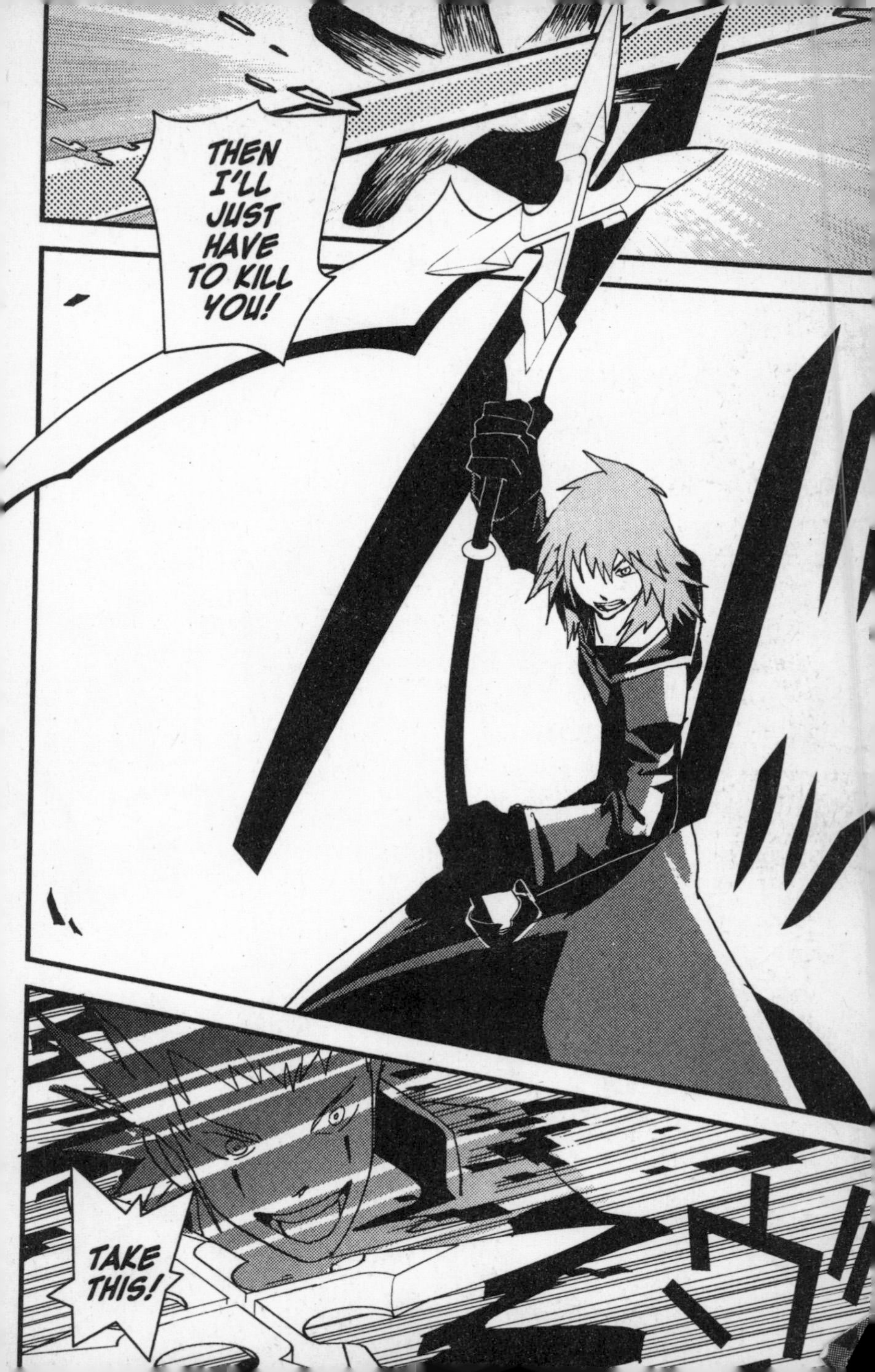
THEN I'LL JUST HAVE TO KILL YOU!
TAKE THIS!

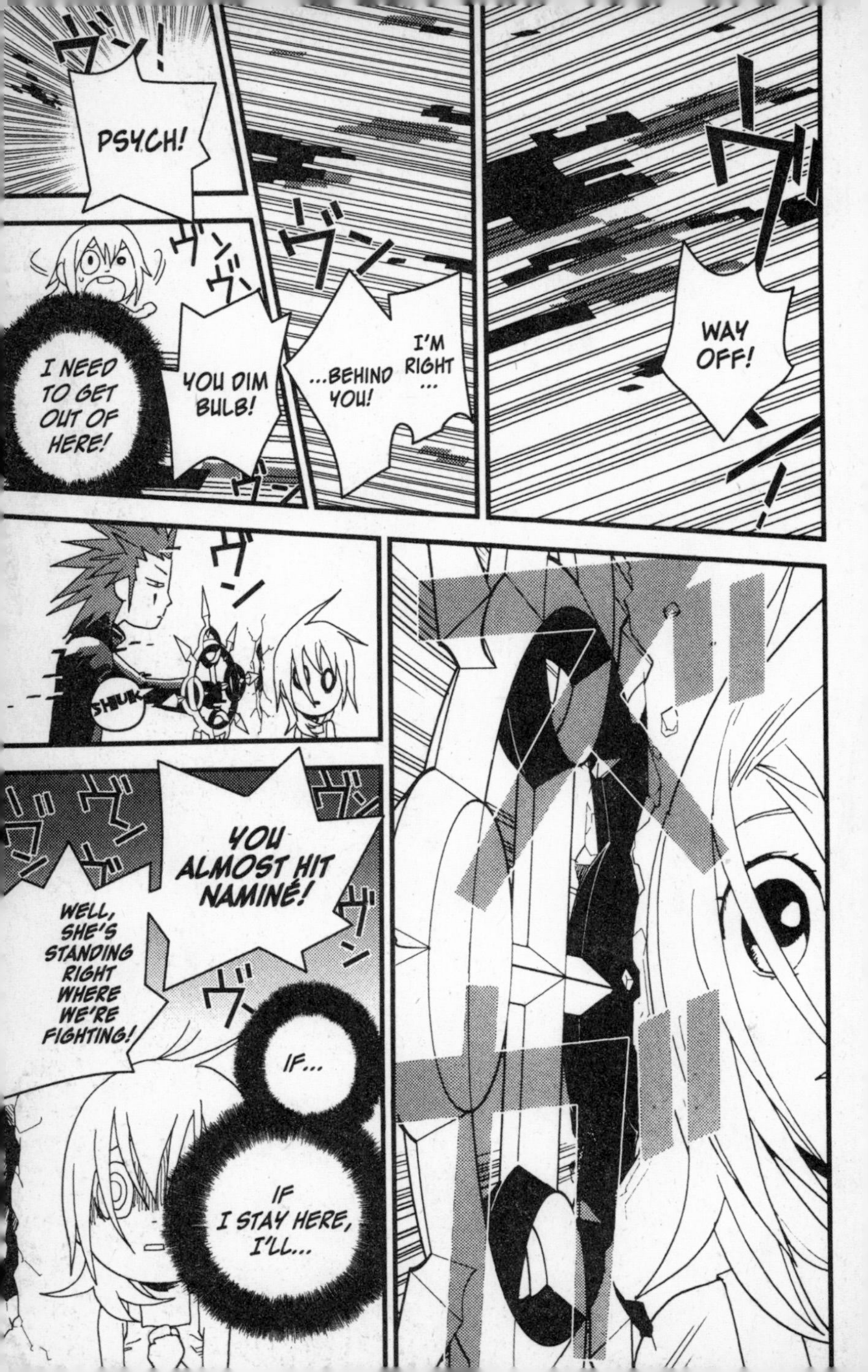
WAY OFF!
I'M RIGHT ...
...BEHIND YOU!
PSYCH!
YOU DIM BULB!
I NEED TO GET OUT OF HERE!
SHUK
YOU ALMOST HIT NAMINÉ!
WELL, SHE'S STANDING RIGHT WHERE WE'RE FIGHTING!
IF...
IF I STAY HERE, I'LL...

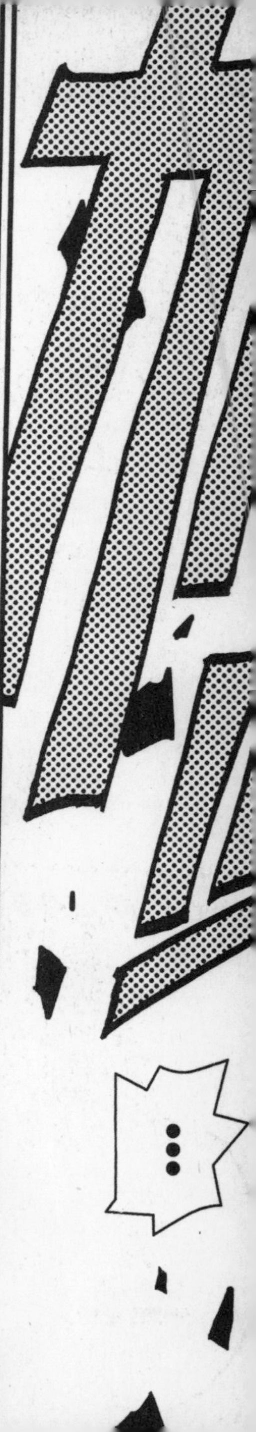
...
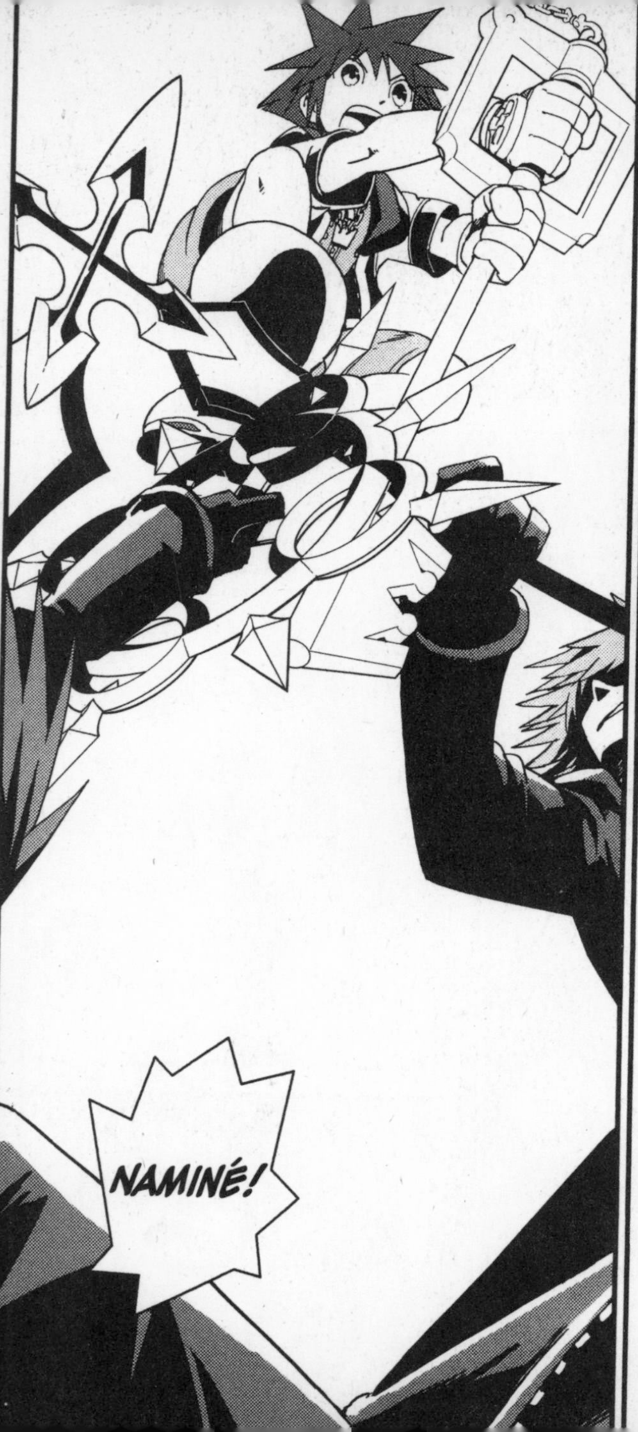
NAMINÉ!

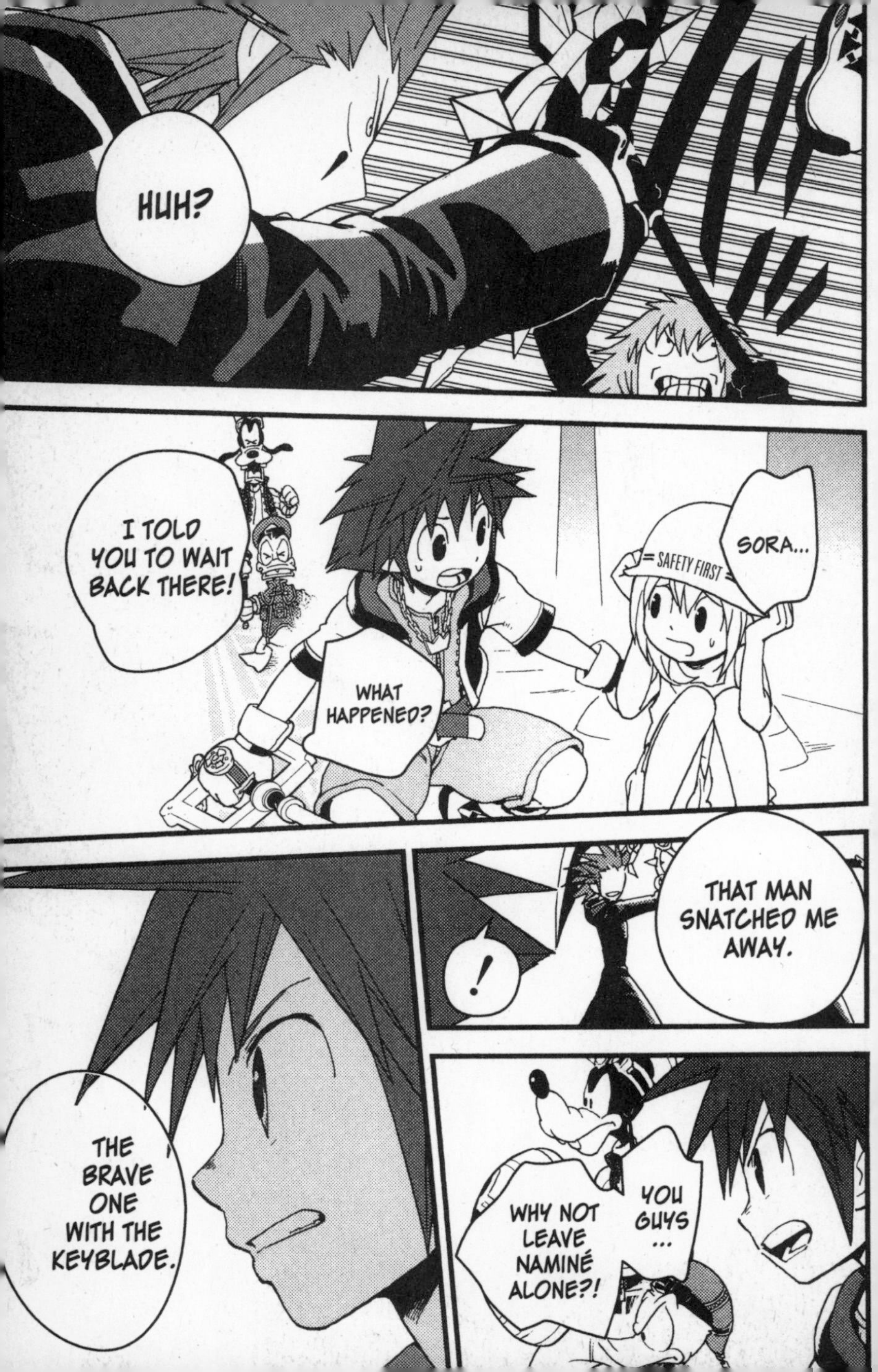
HUH?
SORA...
SAFETY FIRST
I TOLD YOU TO WAIT BACK THERE!
WHAT HAPPENED?
THAT MAN SNATCHED ME AWAY.
!
YOU GUYS ...
WHY NOT LEAVE NAMINÉ ALONE?!
THE BRAVE ONE WITH THE KEYBLADE.

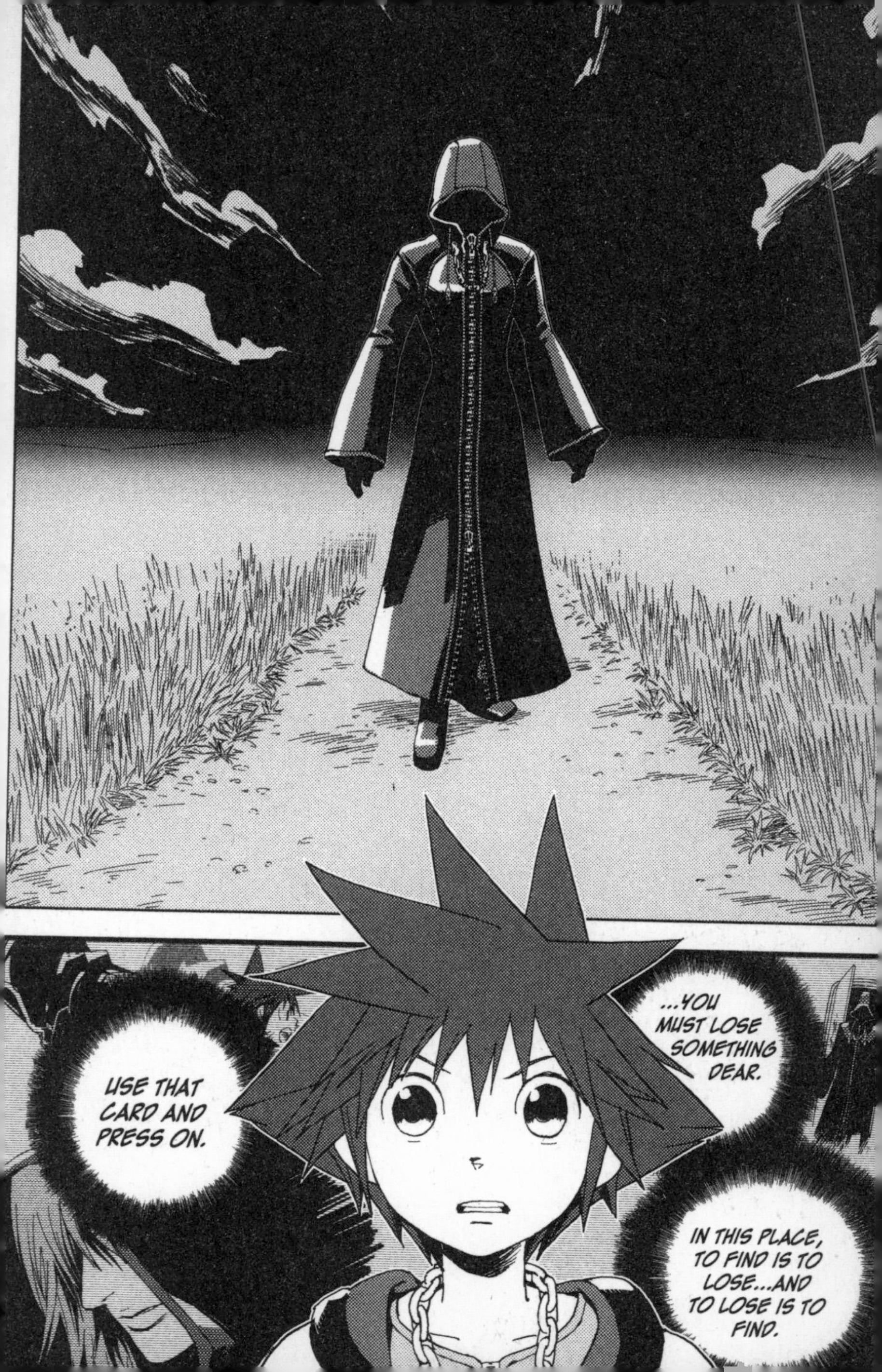
...YOU MUST LOSE SOMETHING DEAR.
USE THAT CARD AND PRESS ON.
IN THIS PLACE, TO FIND IS TO LOSE...AND TO LOSE IS TO FIND.

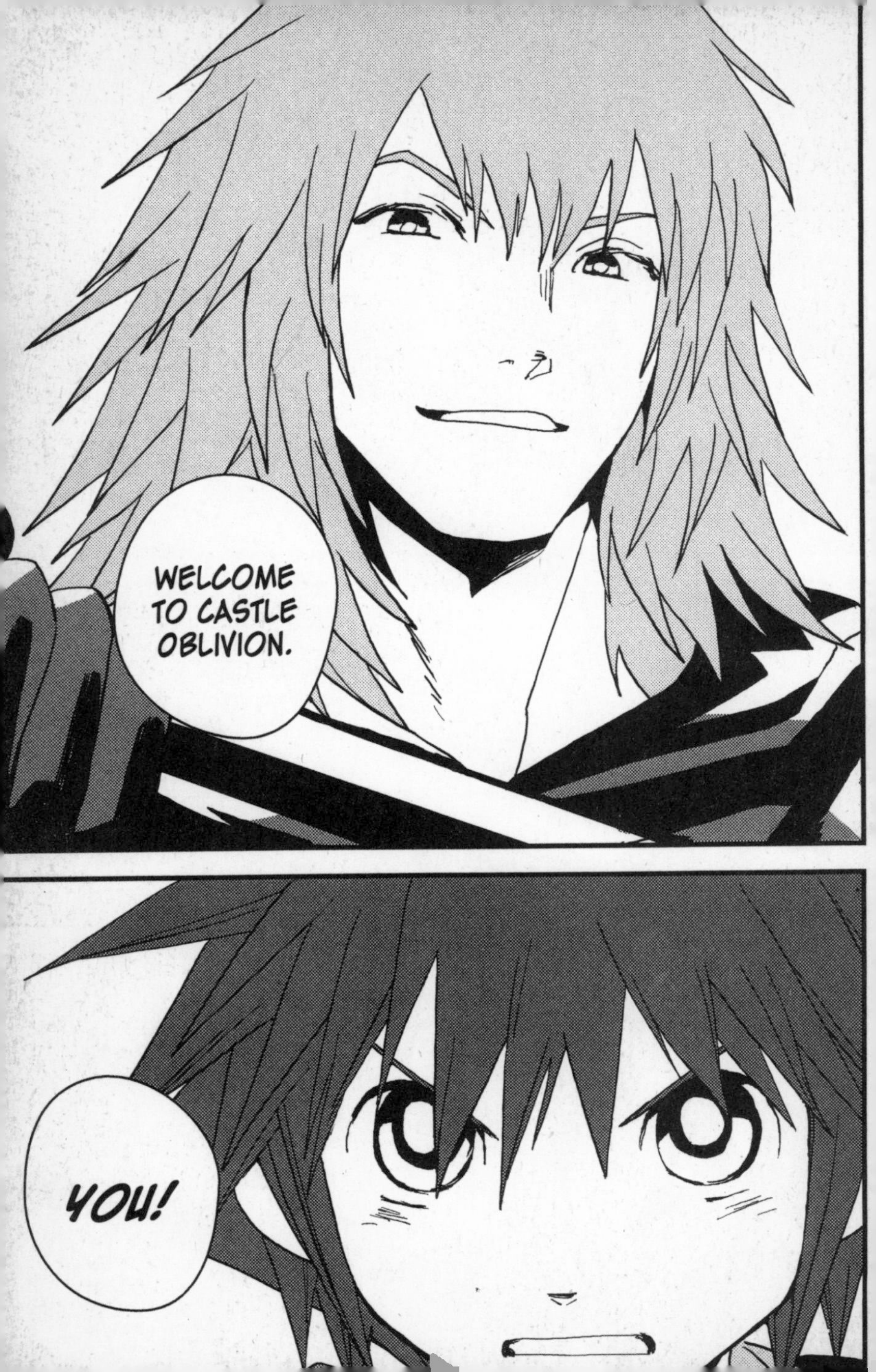
WELCOME TO CASTLE OBLIVION.
YOU!

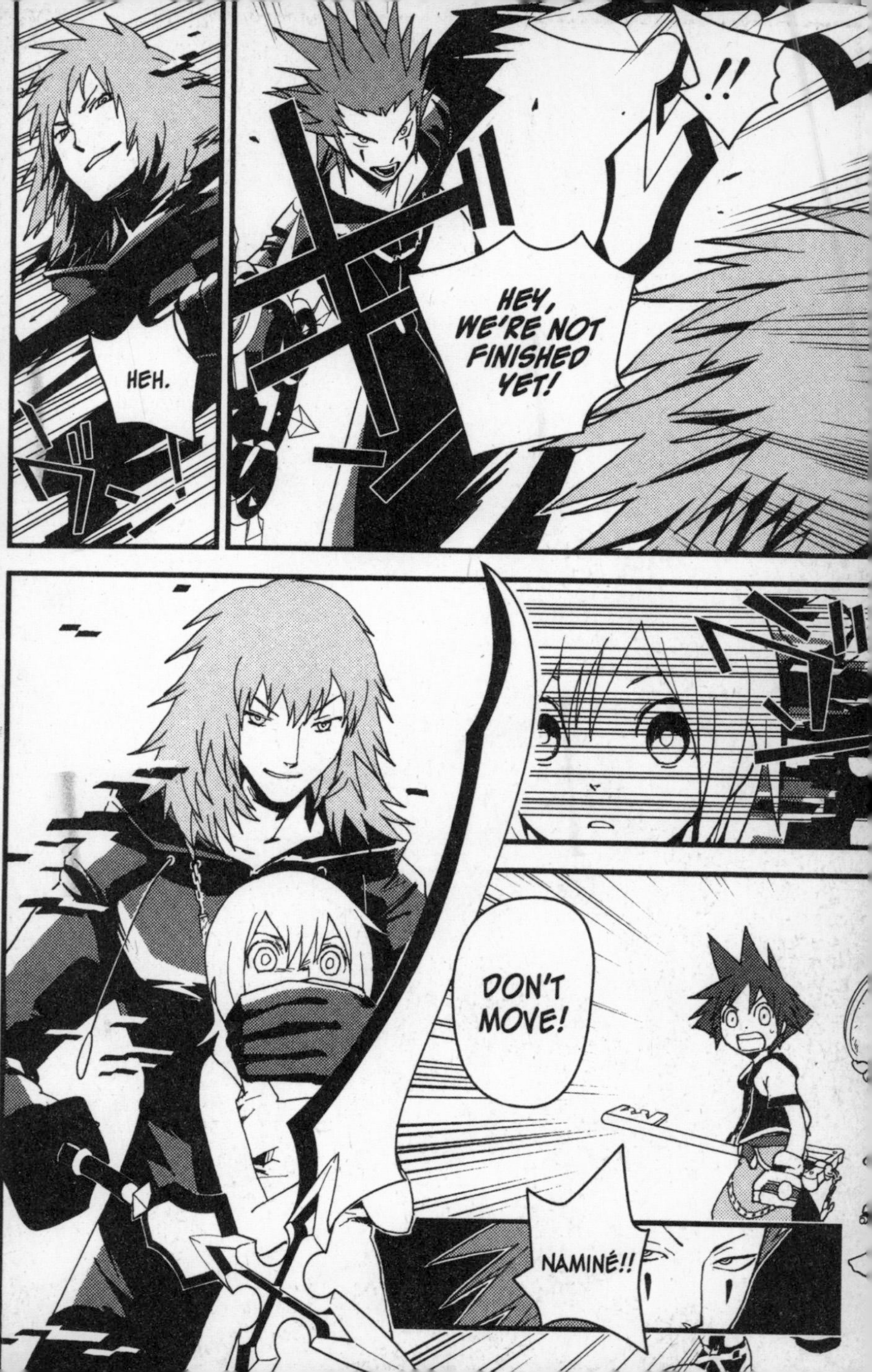
!!
HEY, WE'RE NOT FINISHED YET!
HEH.
DON'T MOVE!
NAMINÉ!!

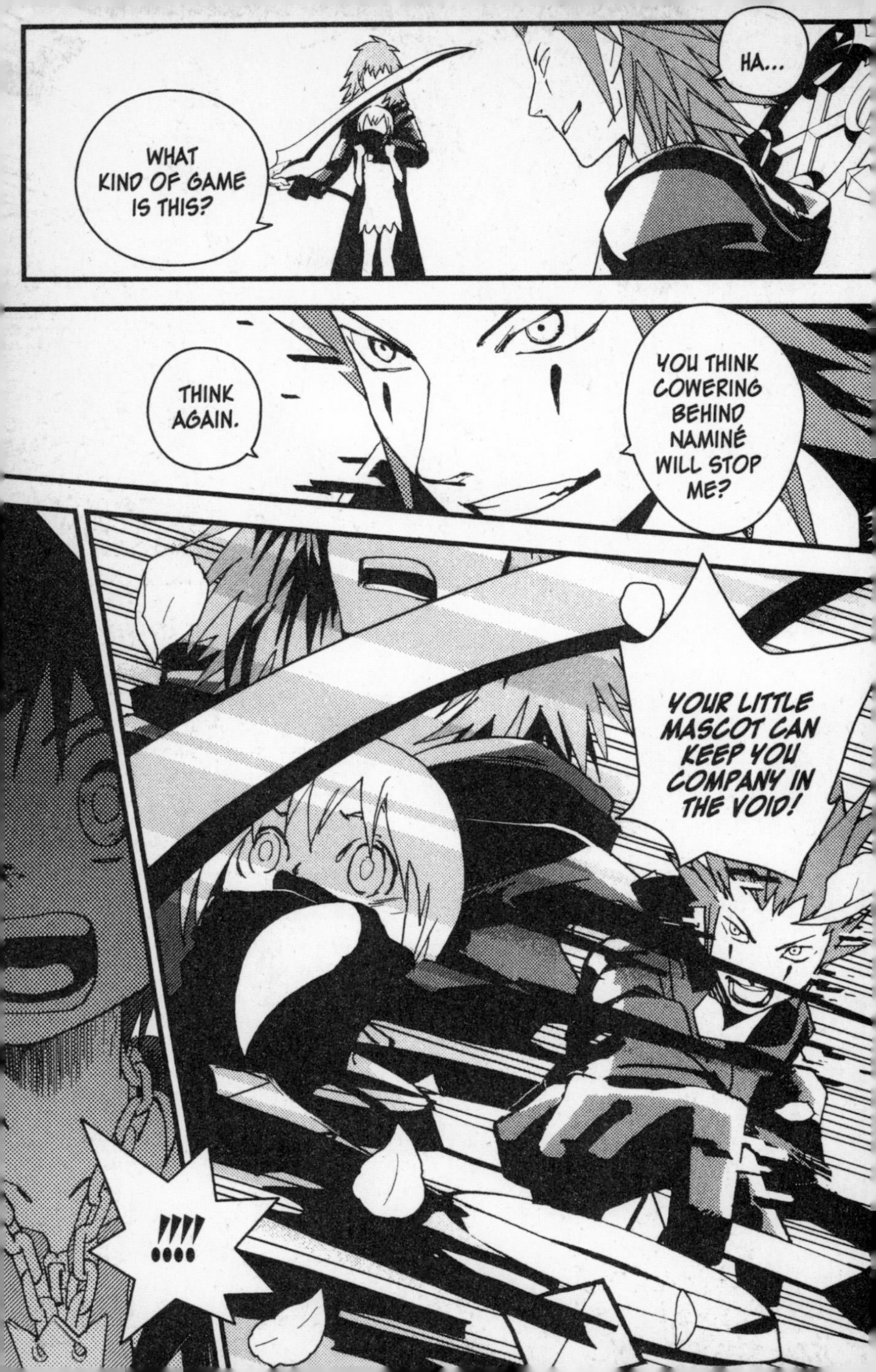
HA...
WHAT KIND OF GAME IS THIS?
YOU THINK COWERING BEHIND NAMINÉ WILL STOP ME?
THINK AGAIN.
YOUR LITTLE MASCOT CAN KEEP YOU COMPANY IN THE VOID!
!!!!

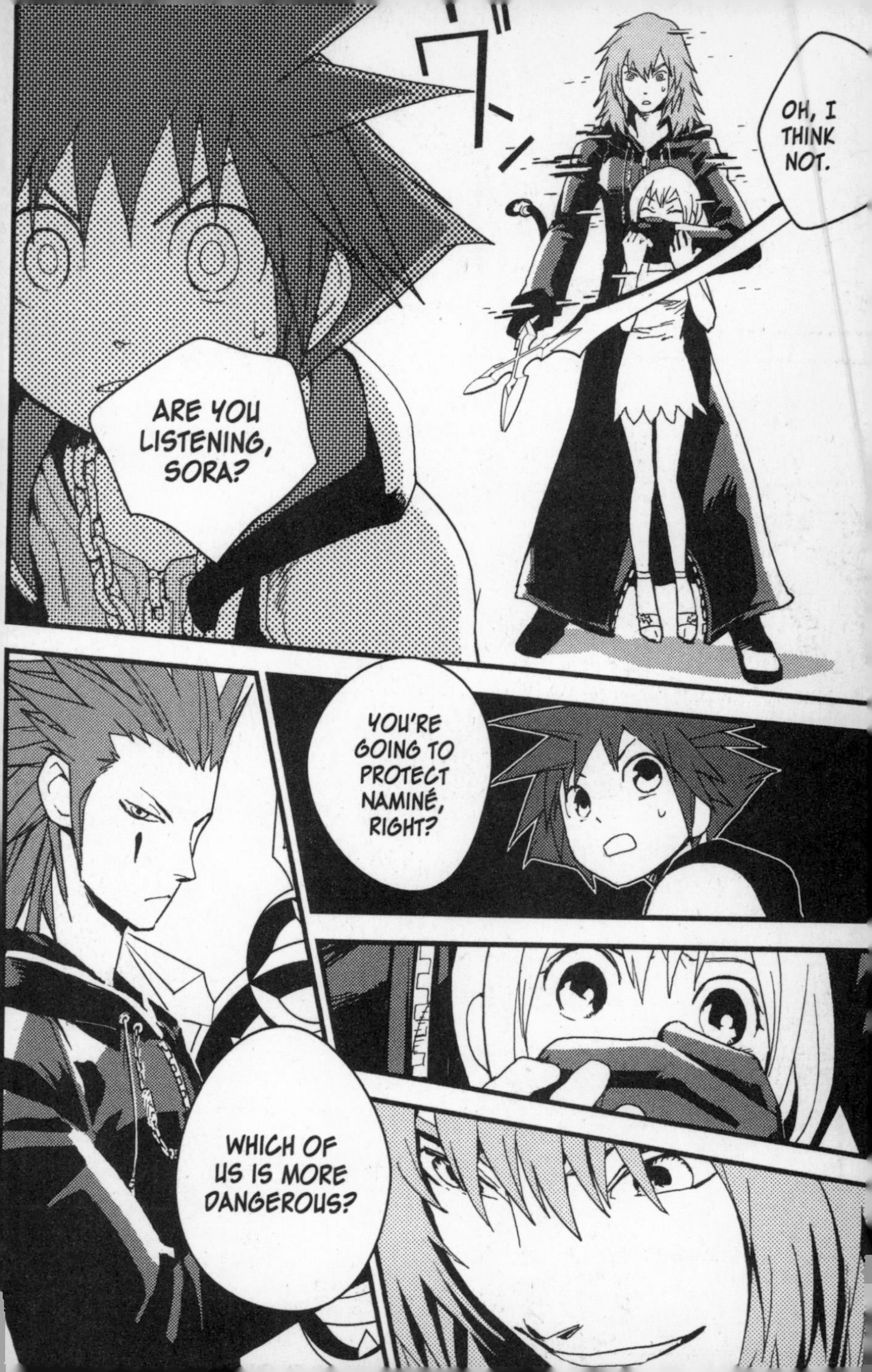
OH, I THINK NOT.
ARE YOU LISTENING, SORA?
YOU'RE GOING TO PROTECT NAMINÉ, RIGHT?
WHICH OF US IS MORE DANGEROUS?

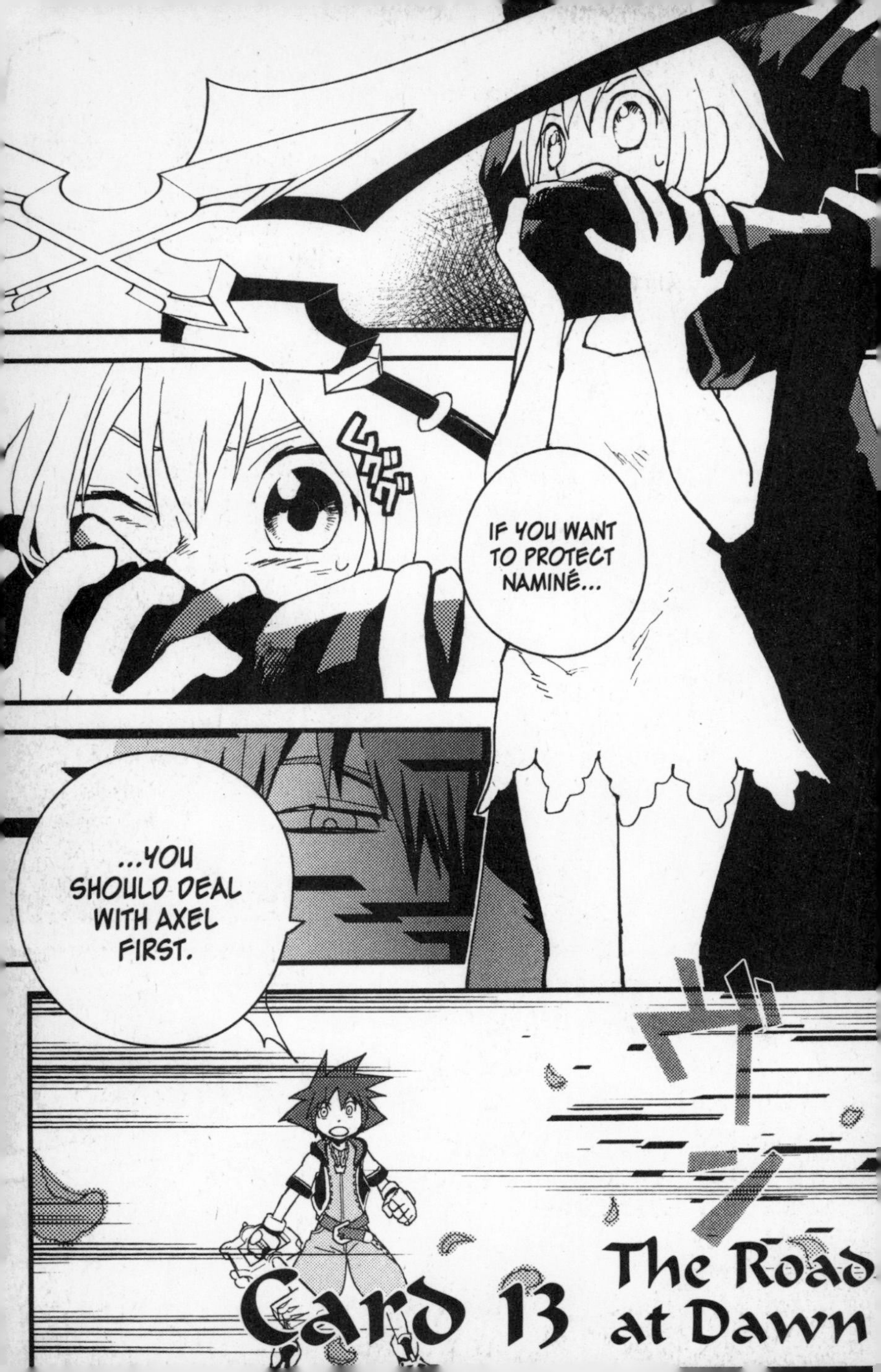
IF YOU WANT TO PROTECT NAMINÉ...
...YOU SHOULD DEAL WITH AXEL FIRST.
Card 13
The Road at Dawn

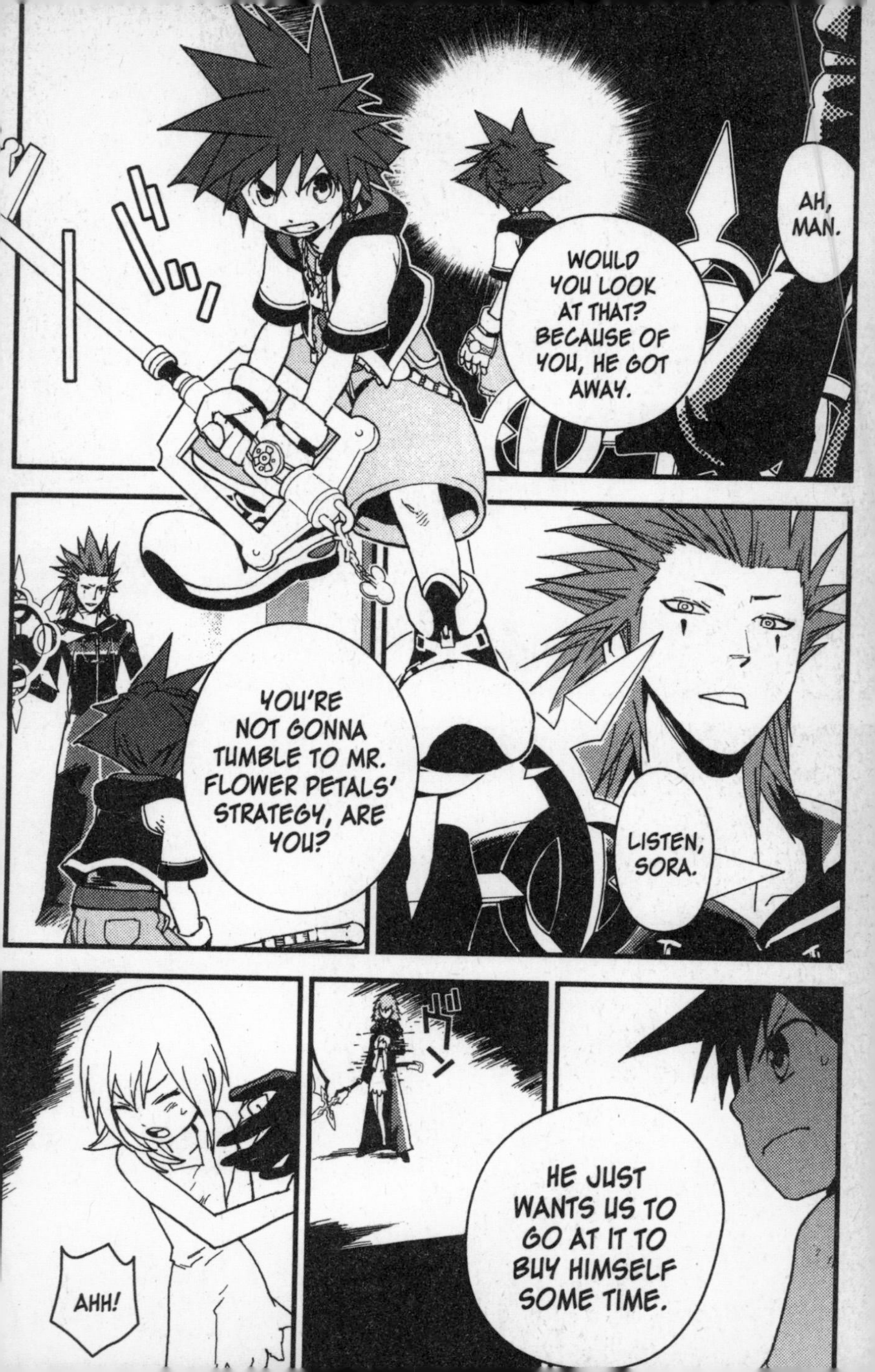
AH, MAN.
WOULD YOU LOOK AT THAT? BECAUSE OF YOU, HE GOT AWAY.
LISTEN, SORA.
YOU'RE NOT GONNA TUMBLE TO MR. FLOWER PETALS' STRATEGY, ARE YOU?
HE JUST WANTS US TO GO AT IT TO BUY HIMSELF SOME TIME.
AHH!

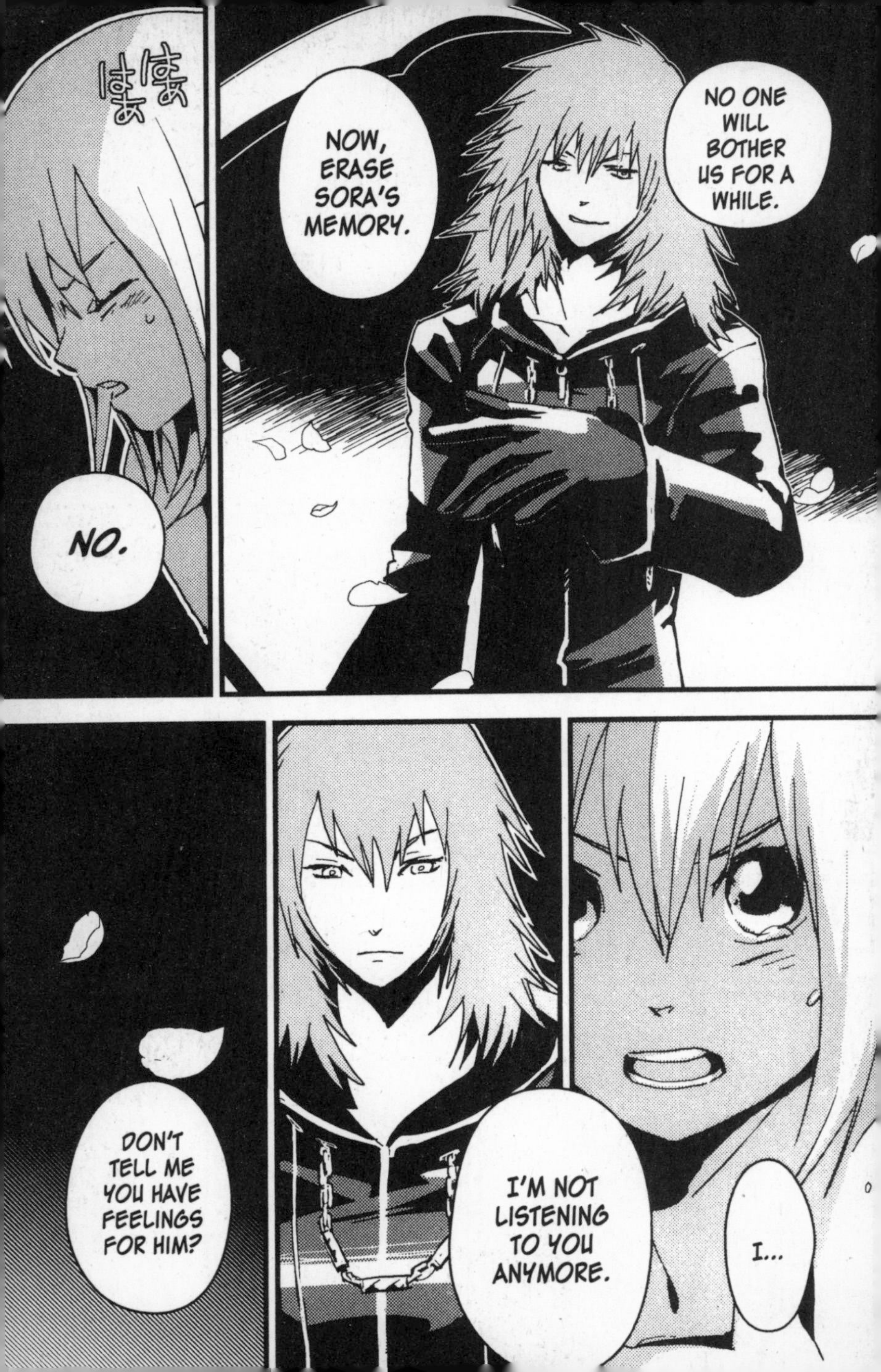
NO ONE WILL BOTHER US FOR A WHILE.
NOW, ERASE SORA'S MEMORY.
はぁはぁ
NO.
I...
I'M NOT LISTENING TO YOU ANYMORE.
DON'T TELL ME YOU HAVE FEELINGS FOR HIM?

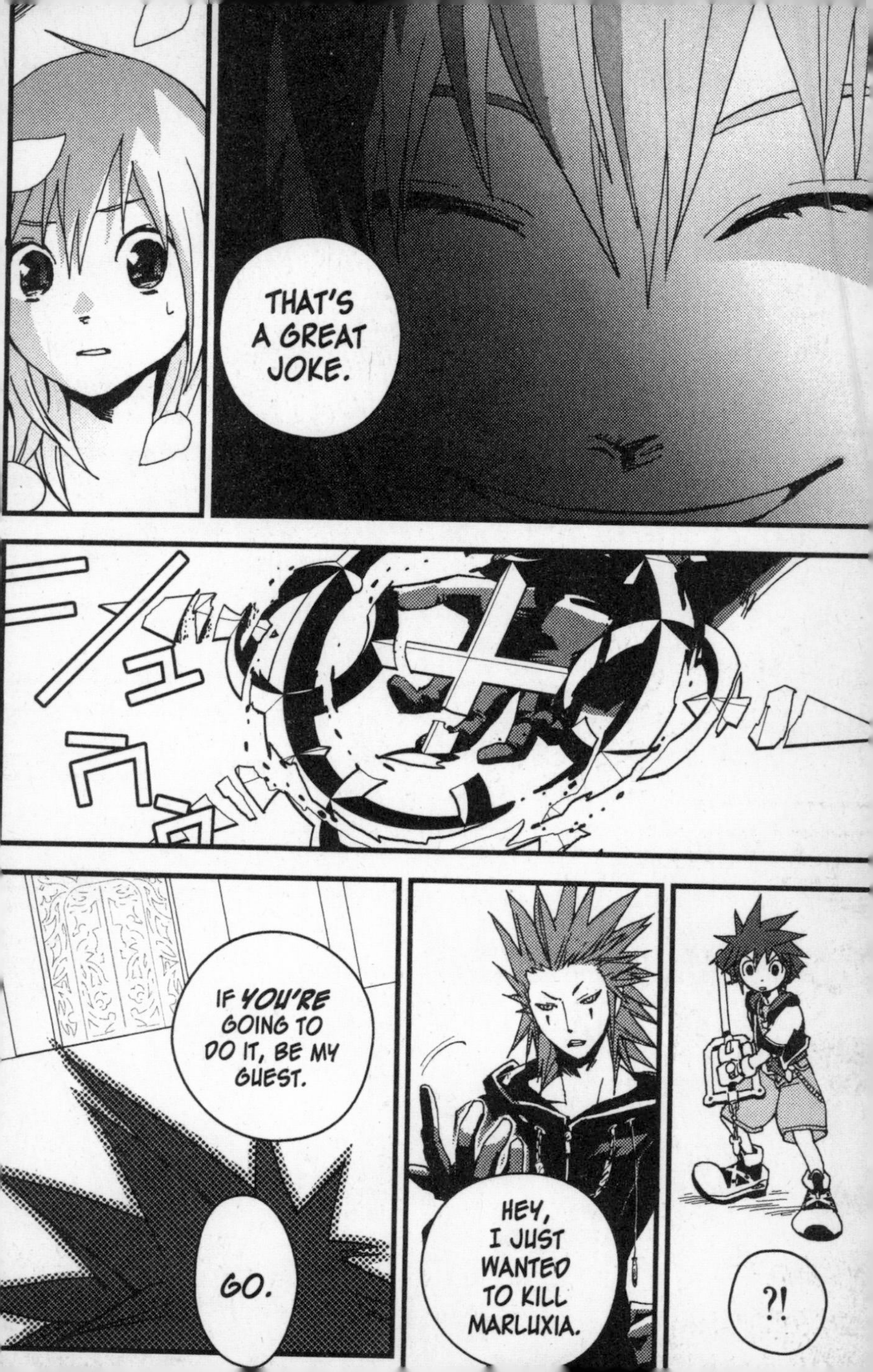
THAT'S A GREAT JOKE.
?!
HEY, I JUST WANTED TO KILL MARLUXIA.
IF YOU'RE GOING TO DO IT, BE MY GUEST.
GO.

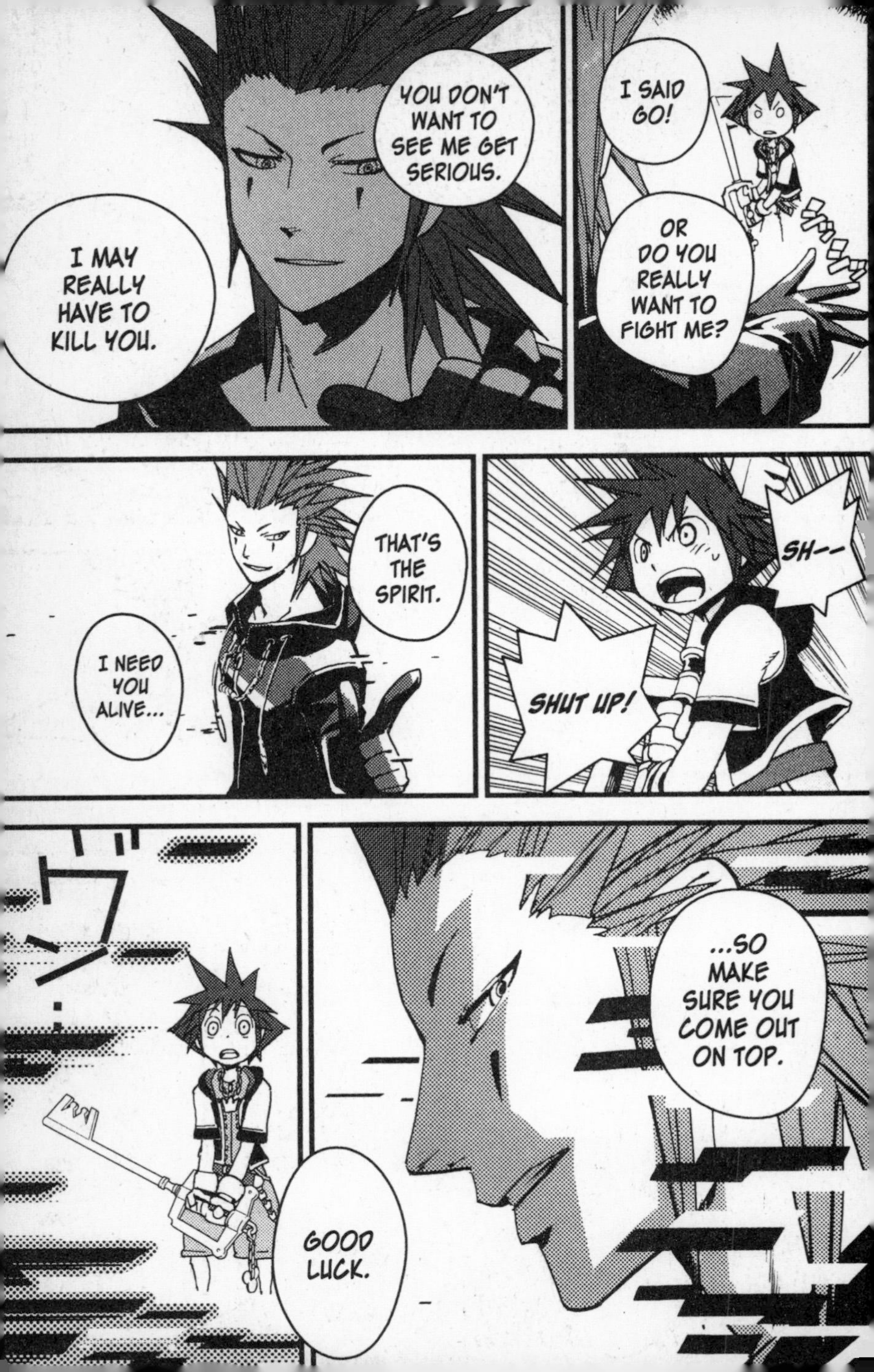
I SAID GO!
OR DO YOU REALLY WANT TO FIGHT ME?
YOU DON'T WANT TO SEE ME GET SERIOUS.
I MAY REALLY HAVE TO KILL YOU.
SH--
SHUT UP!
THAT'S THE SPIRIT.
I NEED YOU ALIVE...
...SO MAKE SURE YOU COME OUT ON TOP.
GOOD LUCK.

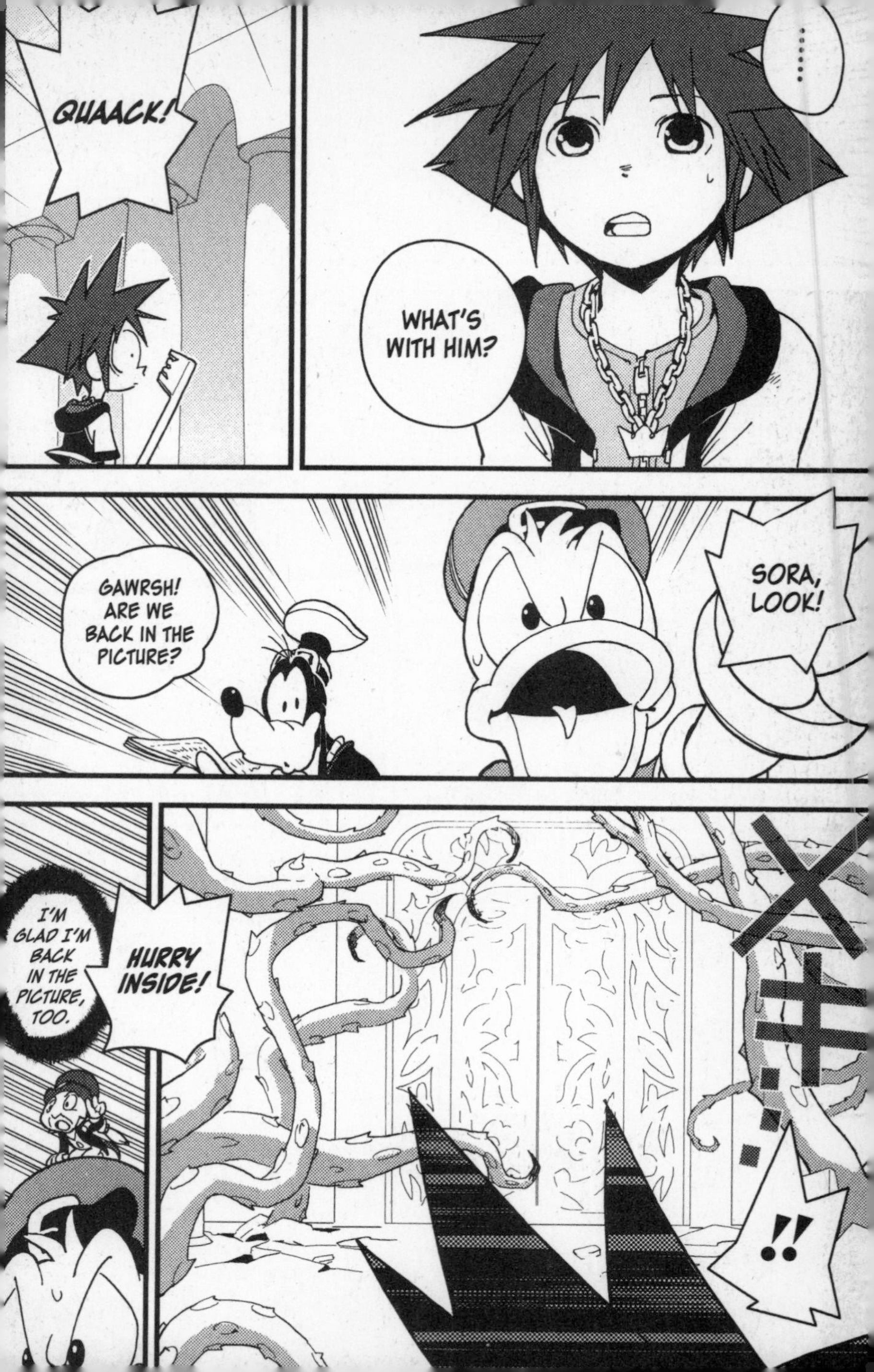
......
WHAT'S WITH HIM?
QUAACK!
SORA, LOOK!
GAWRSH! ARE WE BACK IN THE PICTURE?
!!
HURRY INSIDE!
I'M GLAD I'M BACK IN THE PICTURE, TOO.

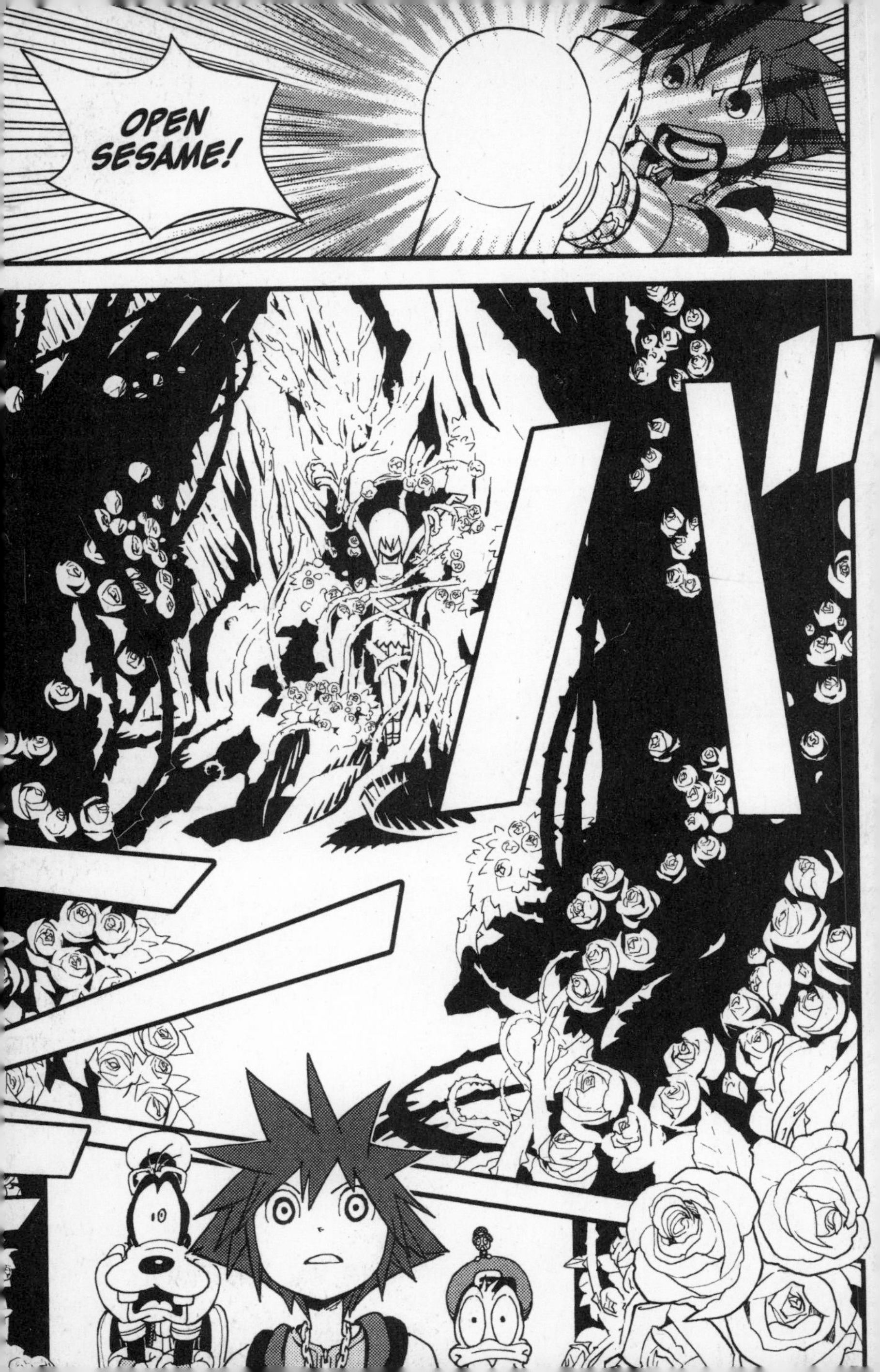
OPEN SESAME!

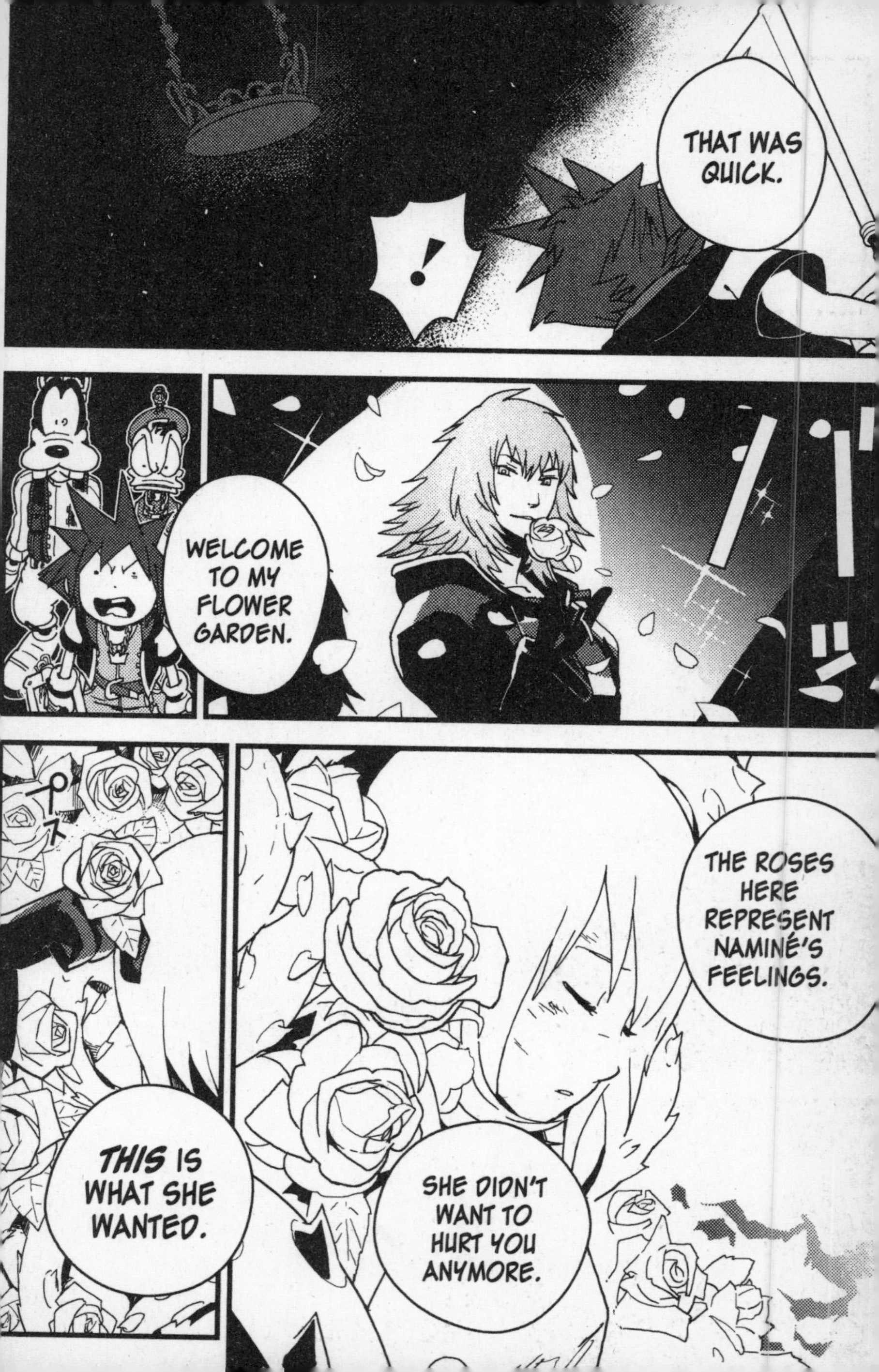
THAT WAS QUICK.
!
WELCOME TO MY FLOWER GARDEN.
THE ROSES HERE REPRESENT NAMINÉ'S FEELINGS.
SHE DIDN'T WANT TO HURT YOU ANYMORE.
THIS IS WHAT SHE WANTED.

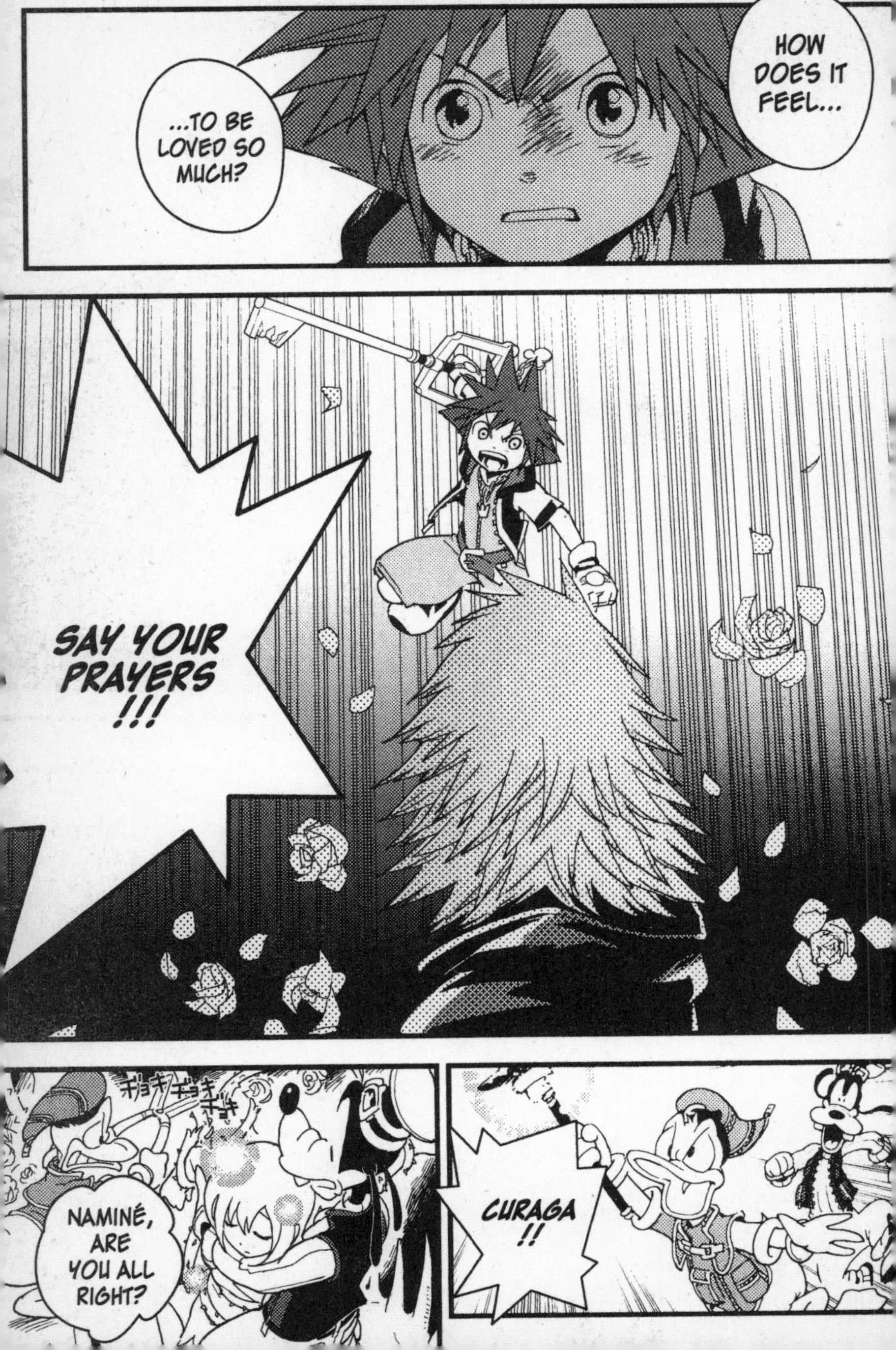
HOW DOES IT FEEL...
...TO BE LOVED SO MUCH?
SAY YOUR PRAYERS!!!
CURAGA!!
NAMINÉ, ARE YOU ALL RIGHT?

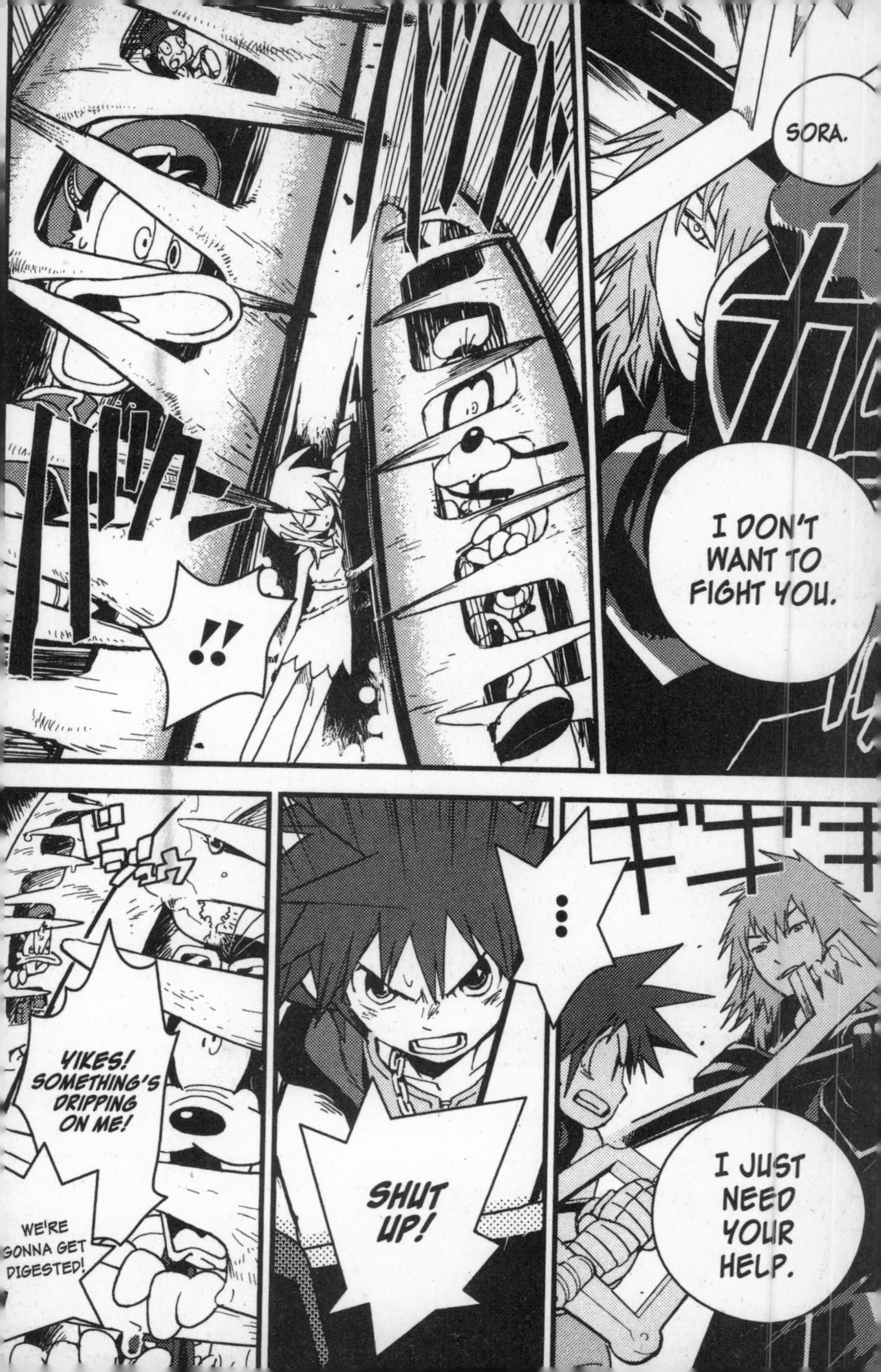
SORA.
I DON'T WANT TO FIGHT YOU.
!!
...
I JUST NEED YOUR HELP.
SHUT UP!
YIKES! SOMETHING'S DRIPPING ON ME!
WE'RE GONNA GET DIGESTED!

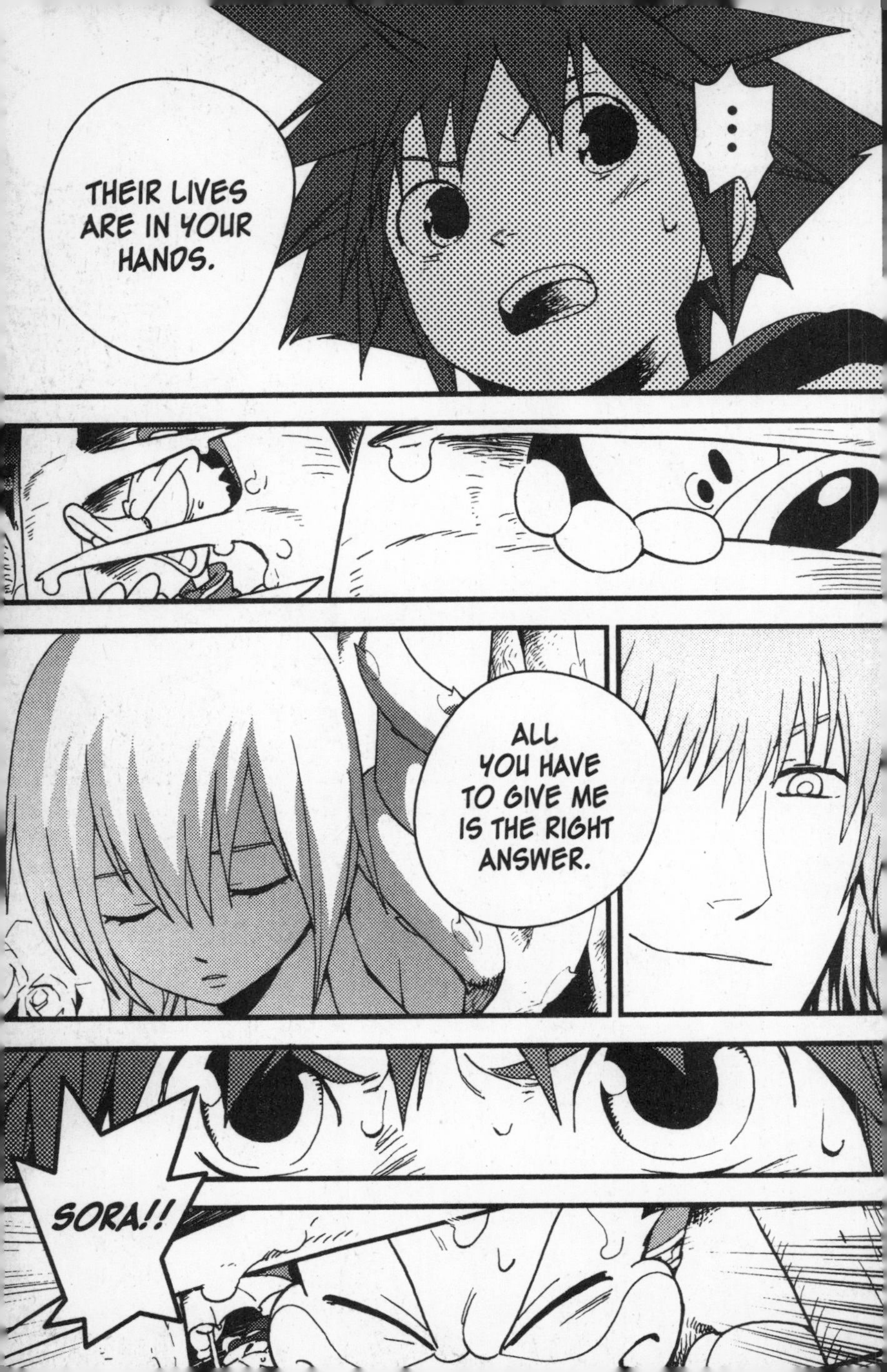
THEIR LIVES ARE IN YOUR HANDS.
...
ALL YOU HAVE TO GIVE ME IS THE RIGHT ANSWER.
SORA!!

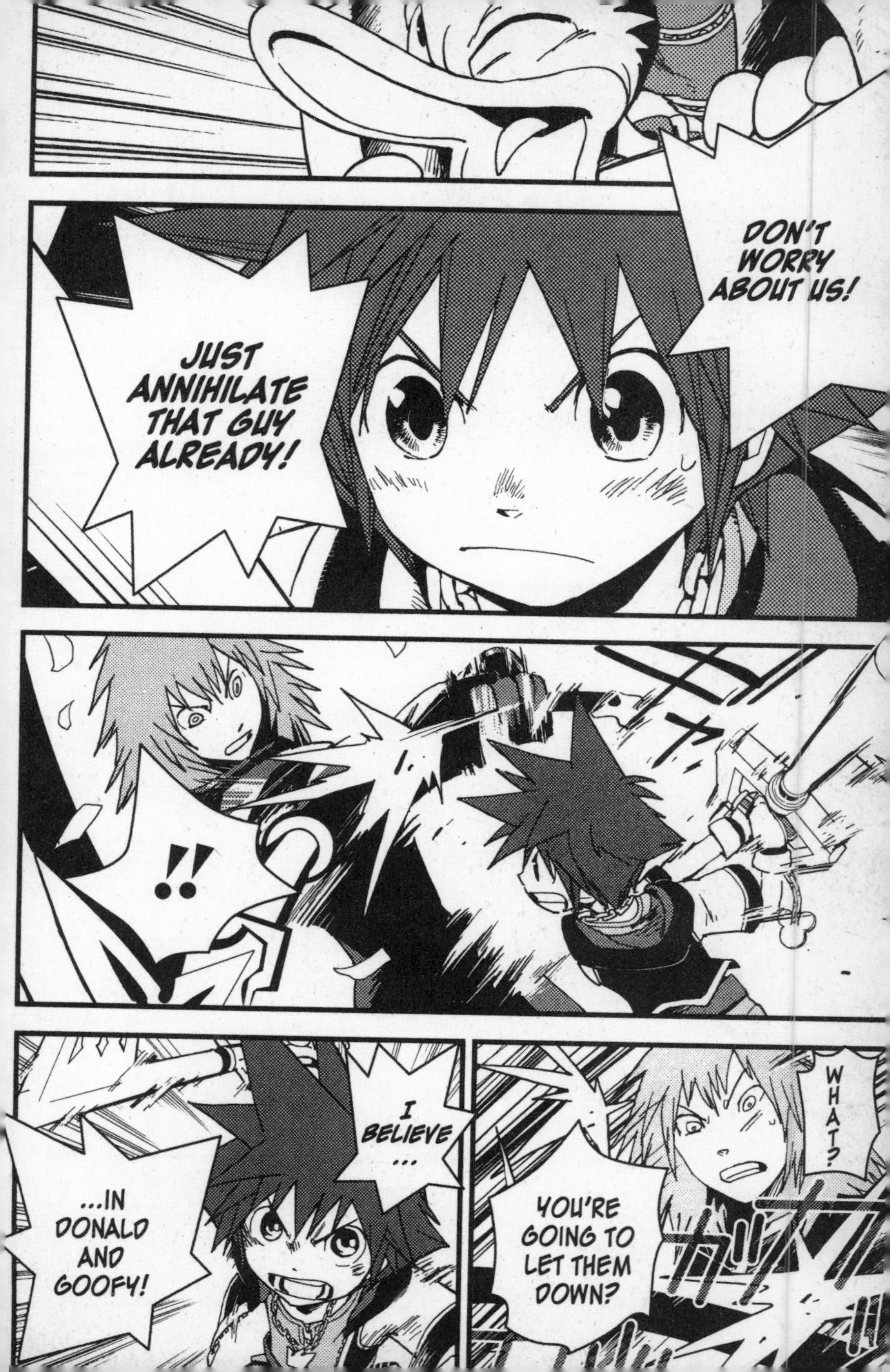
DON'T WORRY ABOUT US!
JUST ANNIHILATE THAT GUY ALREADY!
!!
WHAT?
YOU'RE GOING TO LET THEM DOWN?
I BELIEVE ...
...IN DONALD AND GOOFY!

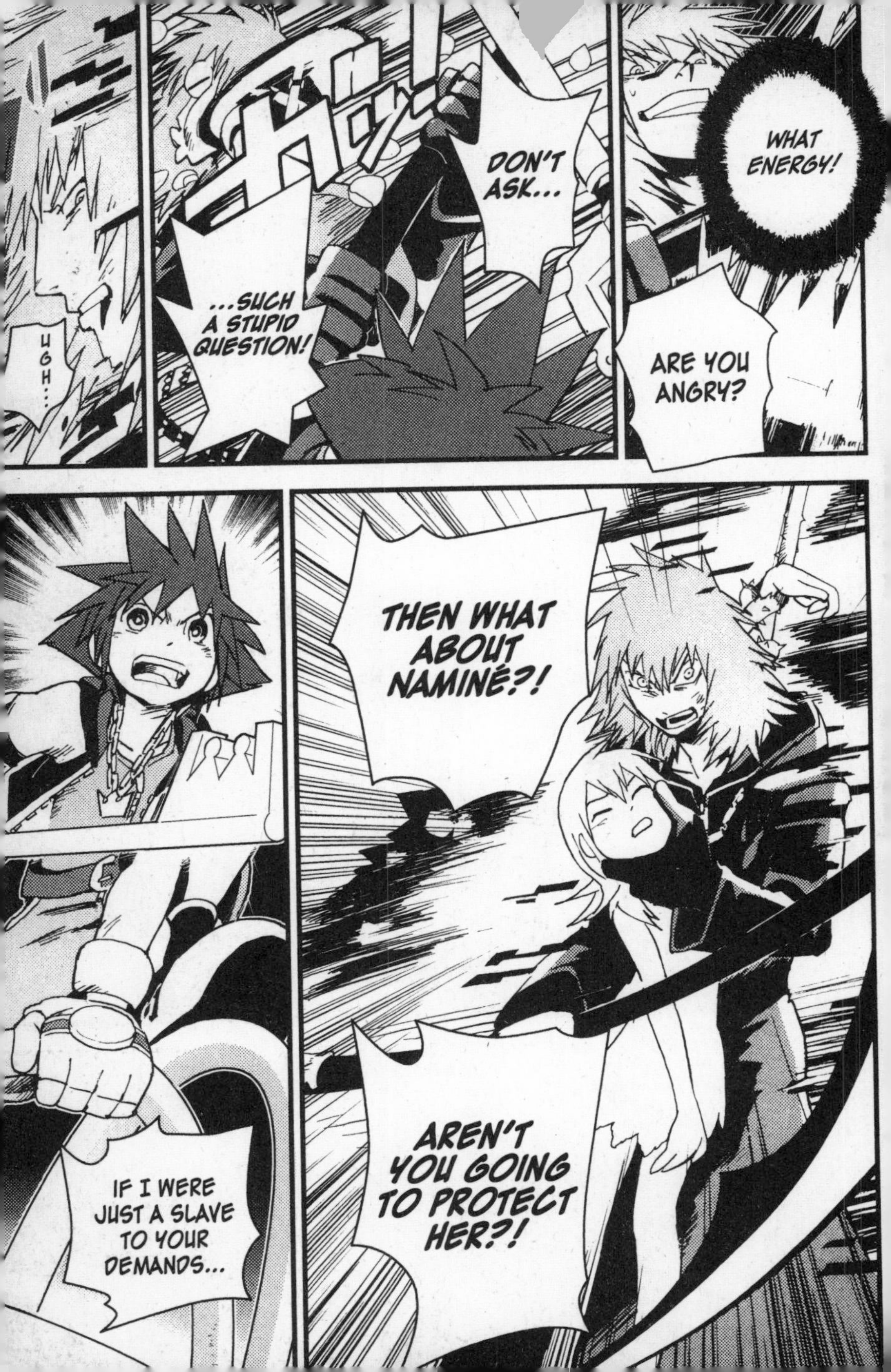
WHAT ENERGY!
ARE YOU ANGRY?
DON'T ASK...
...SUCH A STUPID QUESTION!
UGH...
THEN WHAT ABOUT NAMINÉ?!
AREN'T YOU GOING TO PROTECT HER?!
IF I WERE JUST A SLAVE TO YOUR DEMANDS...

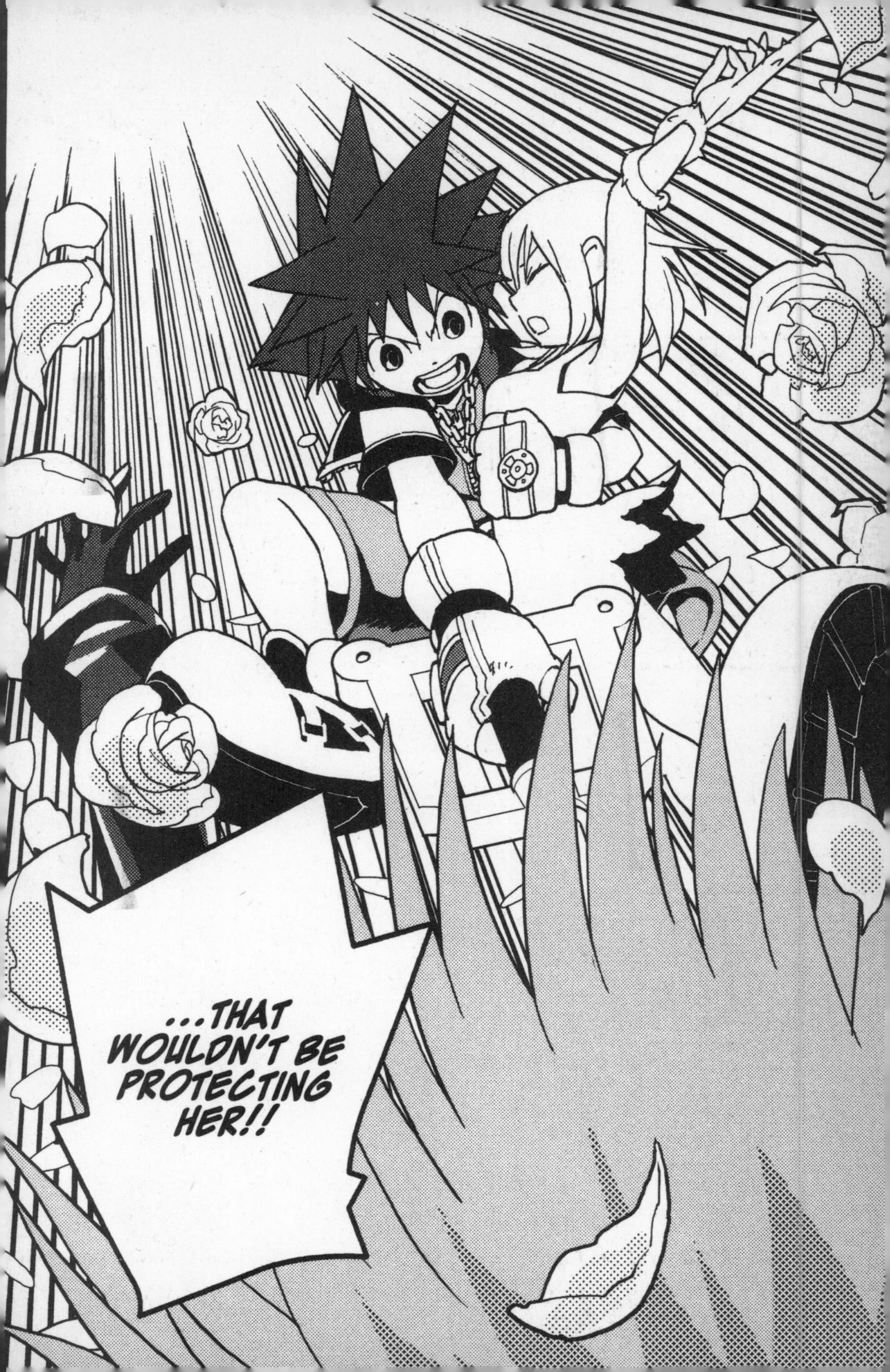
...THAT WOULDN'T BE PROTECTING HER!!

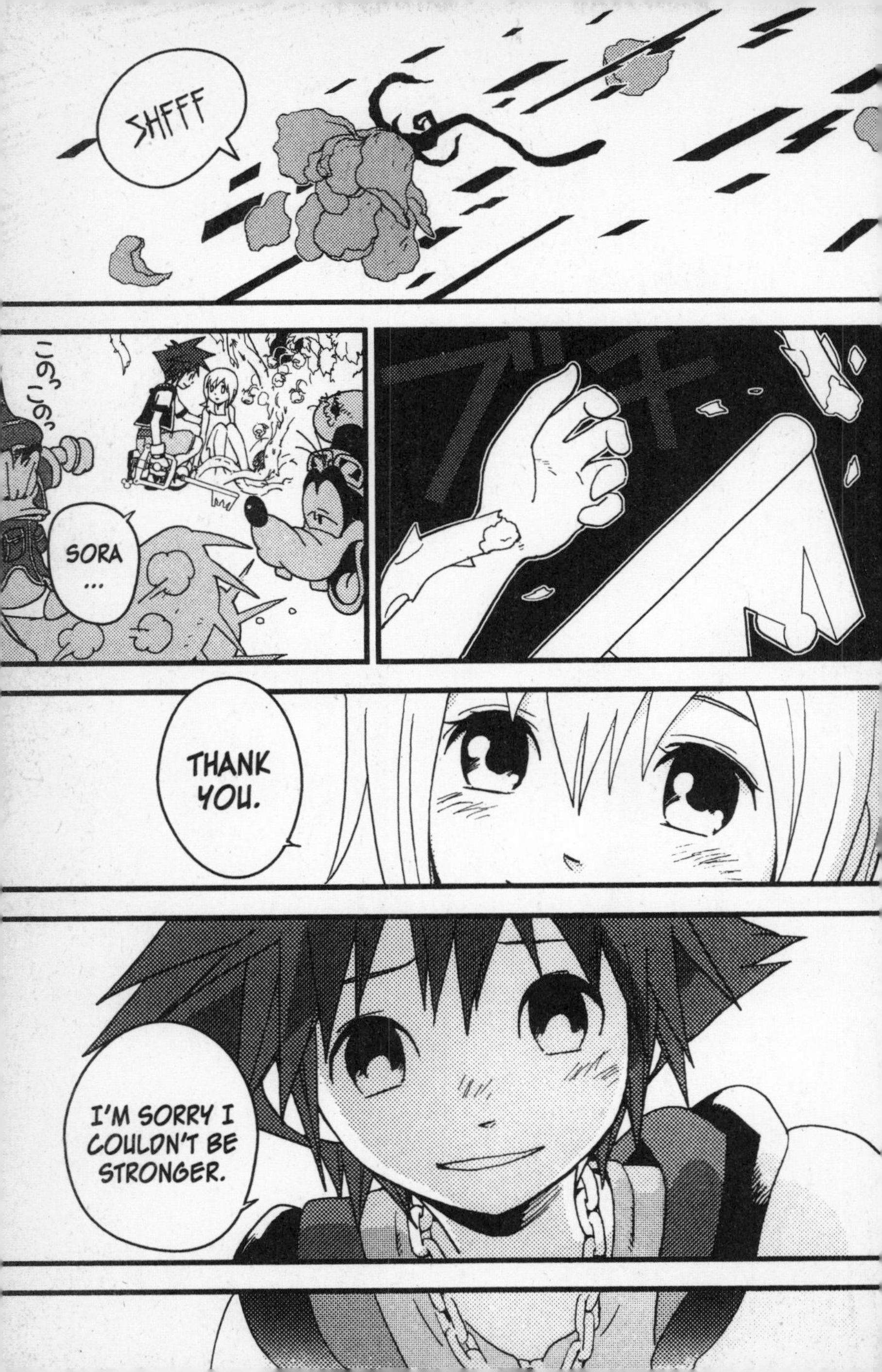
SHFFF
SORA ...
THANK YOU.
I'M SORRY I COULDN'T BE STRONGER.

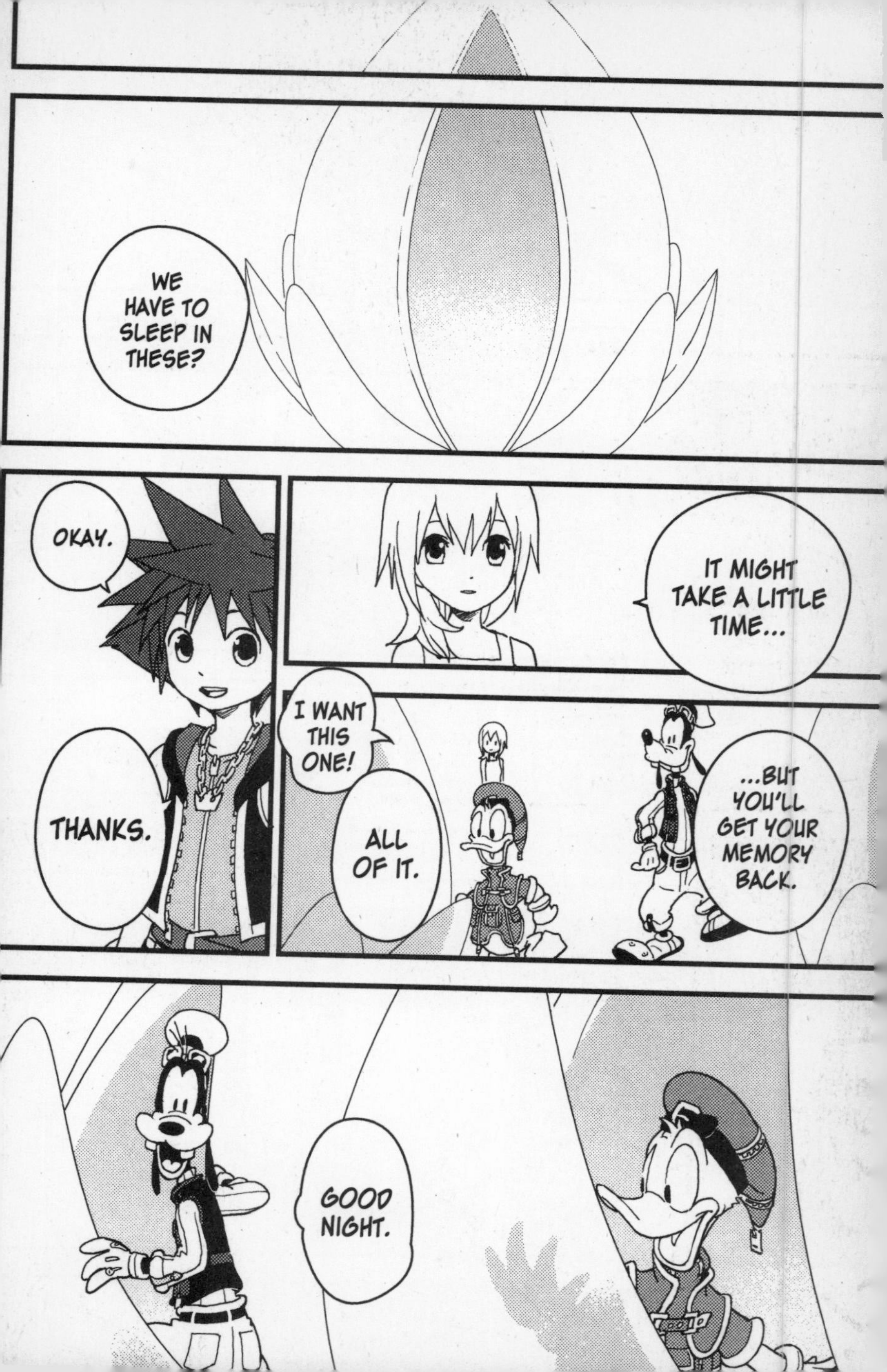
WE HAVE TO SLEEP IN THESE?
IT MIGHT TAKE A LITTLE TIME...
...BUT YOU'LL GET YOUR MEMORY BACK.
ALL OF IT.
I WANT THIS ONE!
OKAY.
THANKS.
GOOD NIGHT.

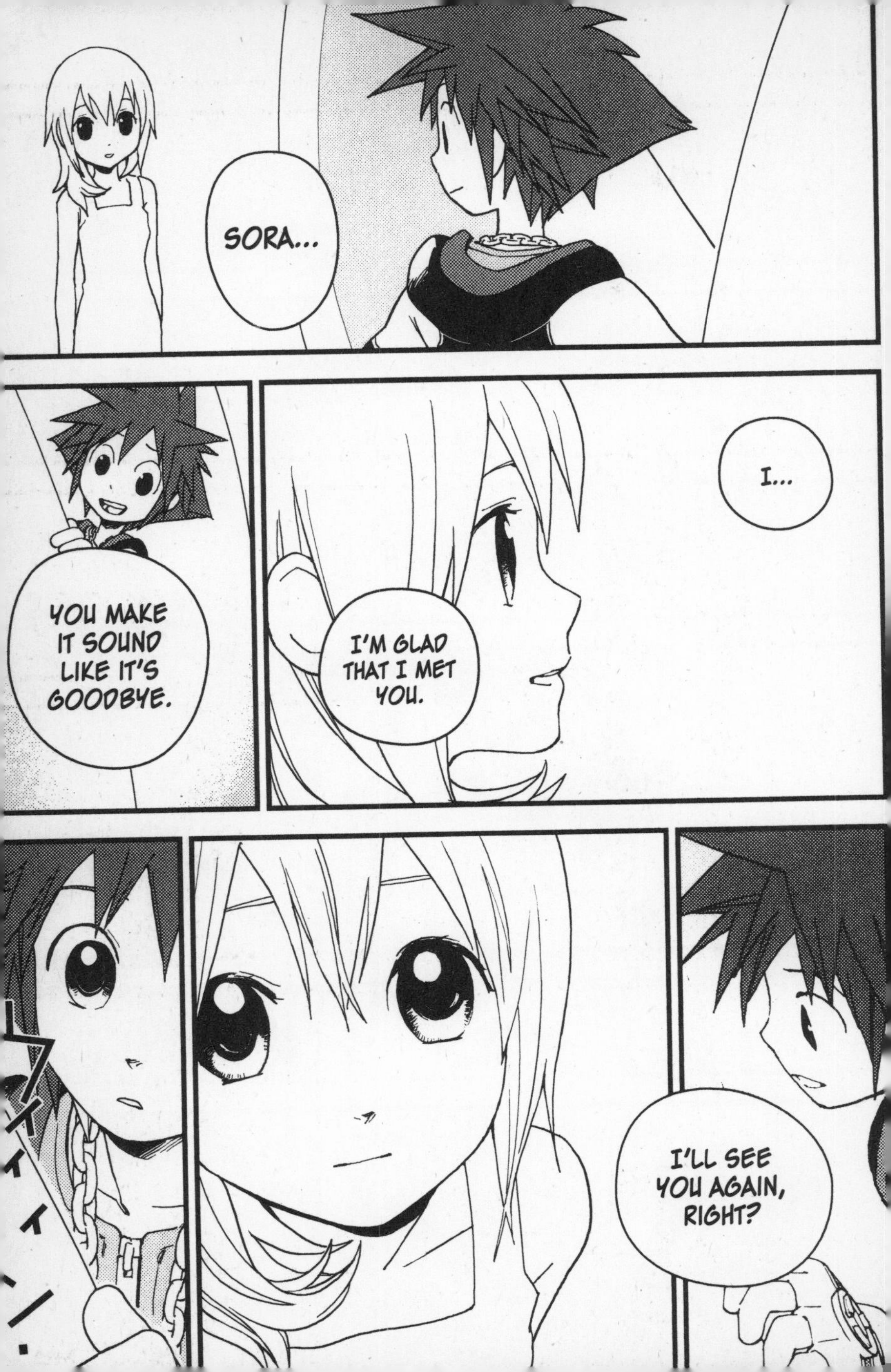
SORA...
I...
I'M GLAD THAT I MET YOU.
YOU MAKE IT SOUND LIKE IT'S GOODBYE.
I'LL SEE YOU AGAIN, RIGHT?

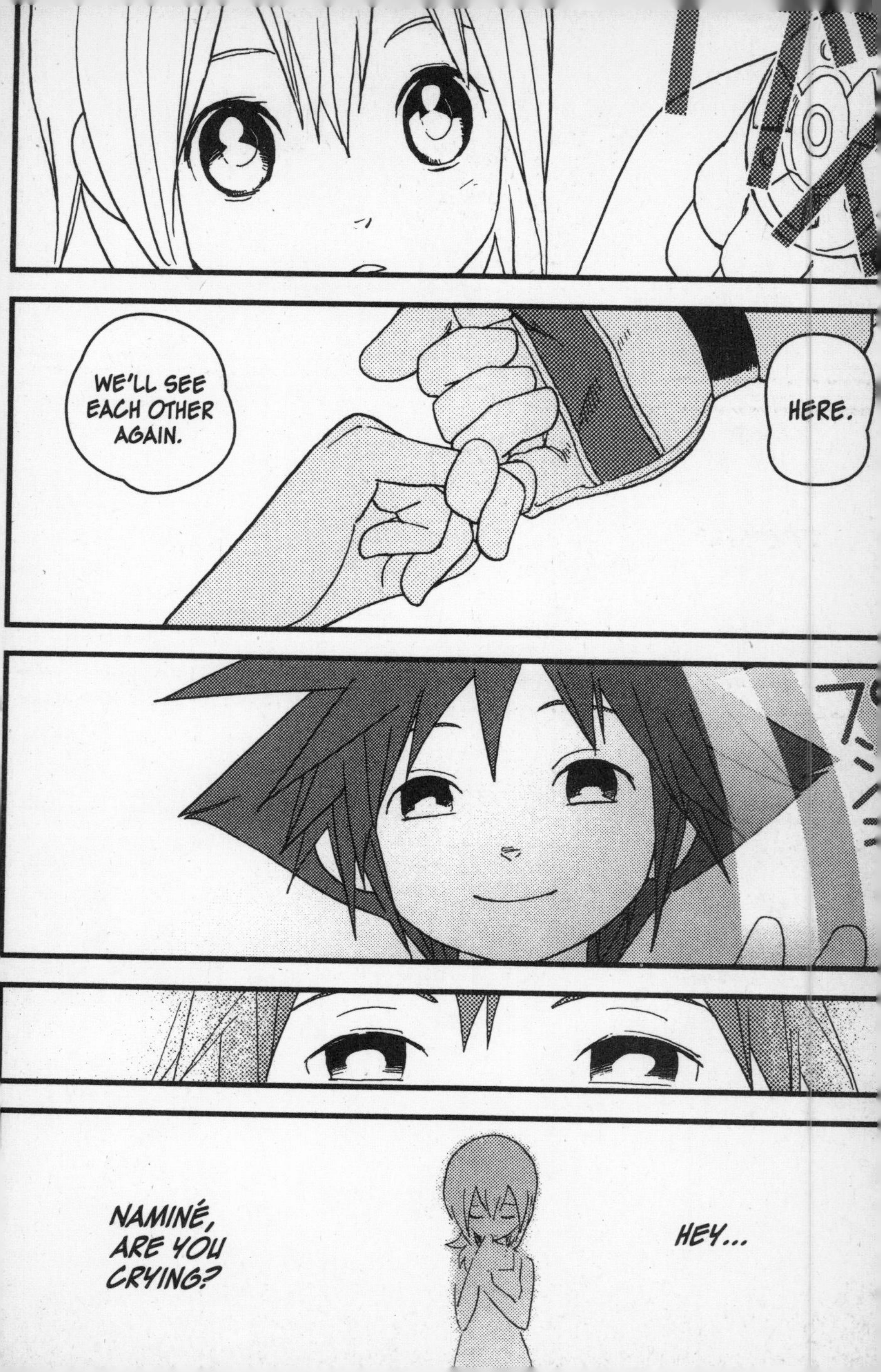
HERE.
WE'LL SEE EACH OTHER AGAIN.
HEY...
NAMINÉ, ARE YOU CRYING?

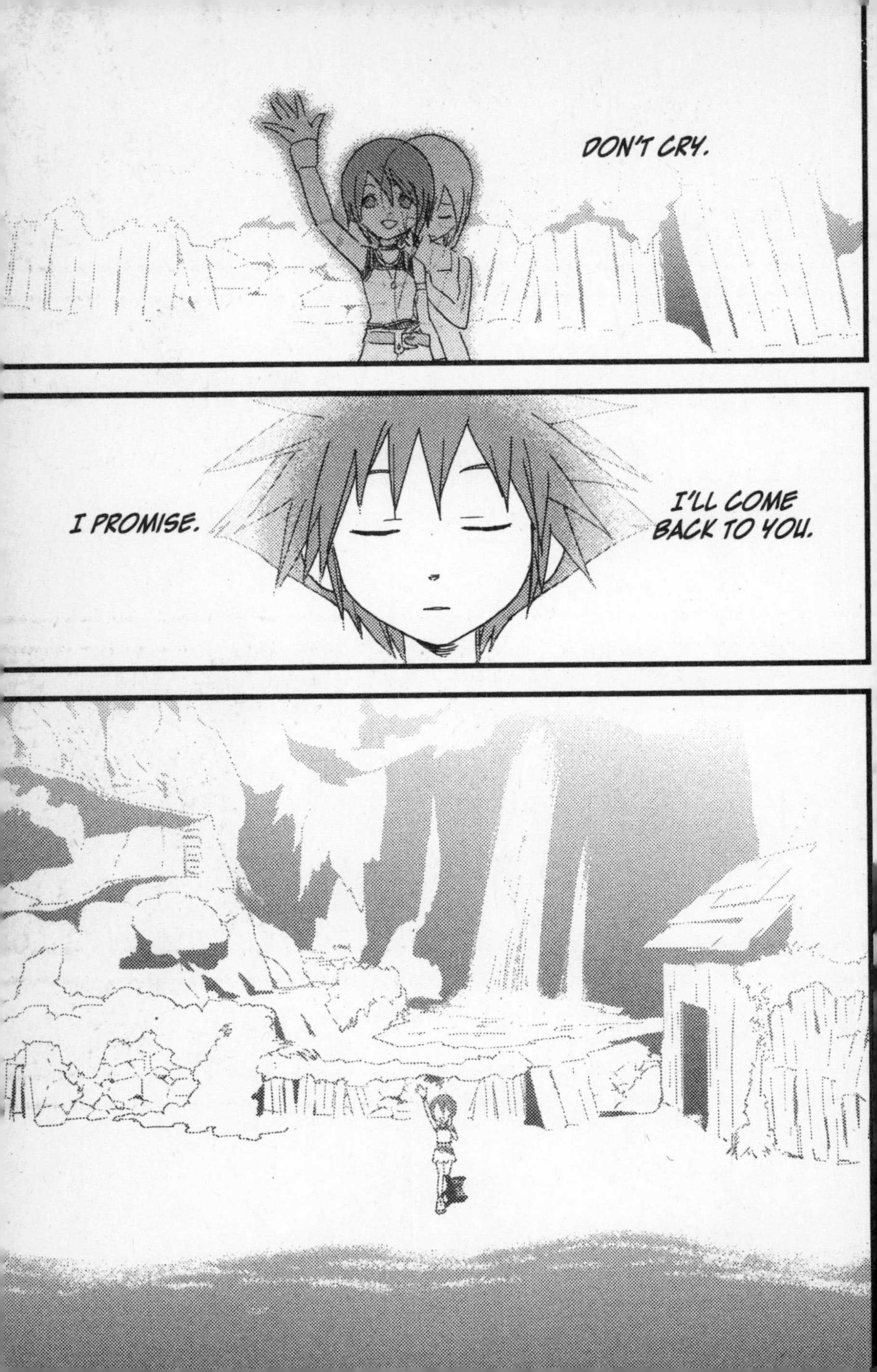
DON'T CRY.
I'LL COME BACK TO YOU.
I PROMISE.

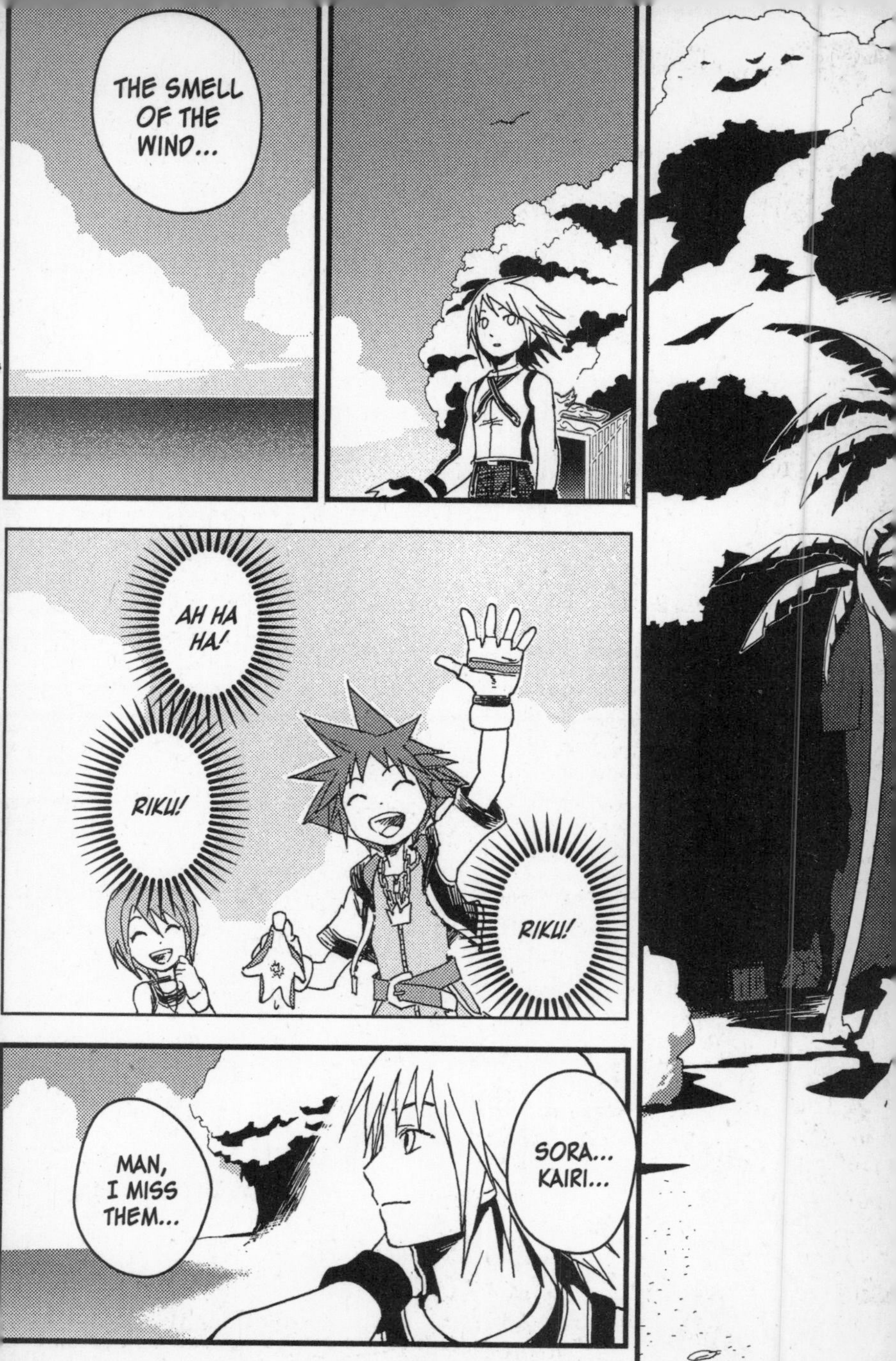
THE SMELL OF THE WIND...
AH HA HA!
RIKU!
RIKU!
SORA... KAIRI...
MAN, I MISS THEM...

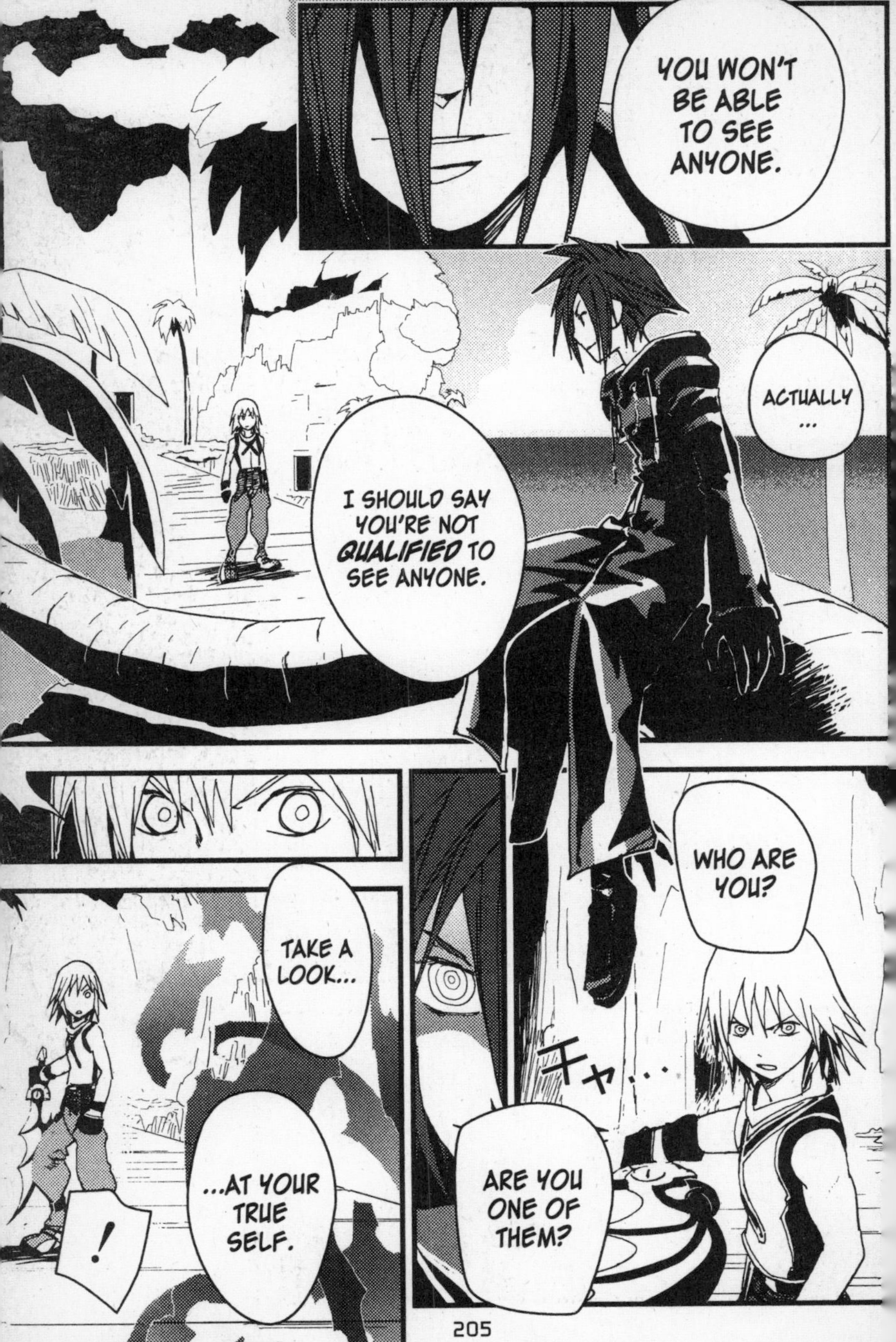
YOU WON'T BE ABLE TO SEE ANYONE.
ACTUALLY ...
I SHOULD SAY YOU'RE NOT QUALIFIED TO SEE ANYONE.
WHO ARE YOU?
チャ…
ARE YOU ONE OF THEM?
TAKE A LOOK...
...AT YOUR TRUE SELF.
!

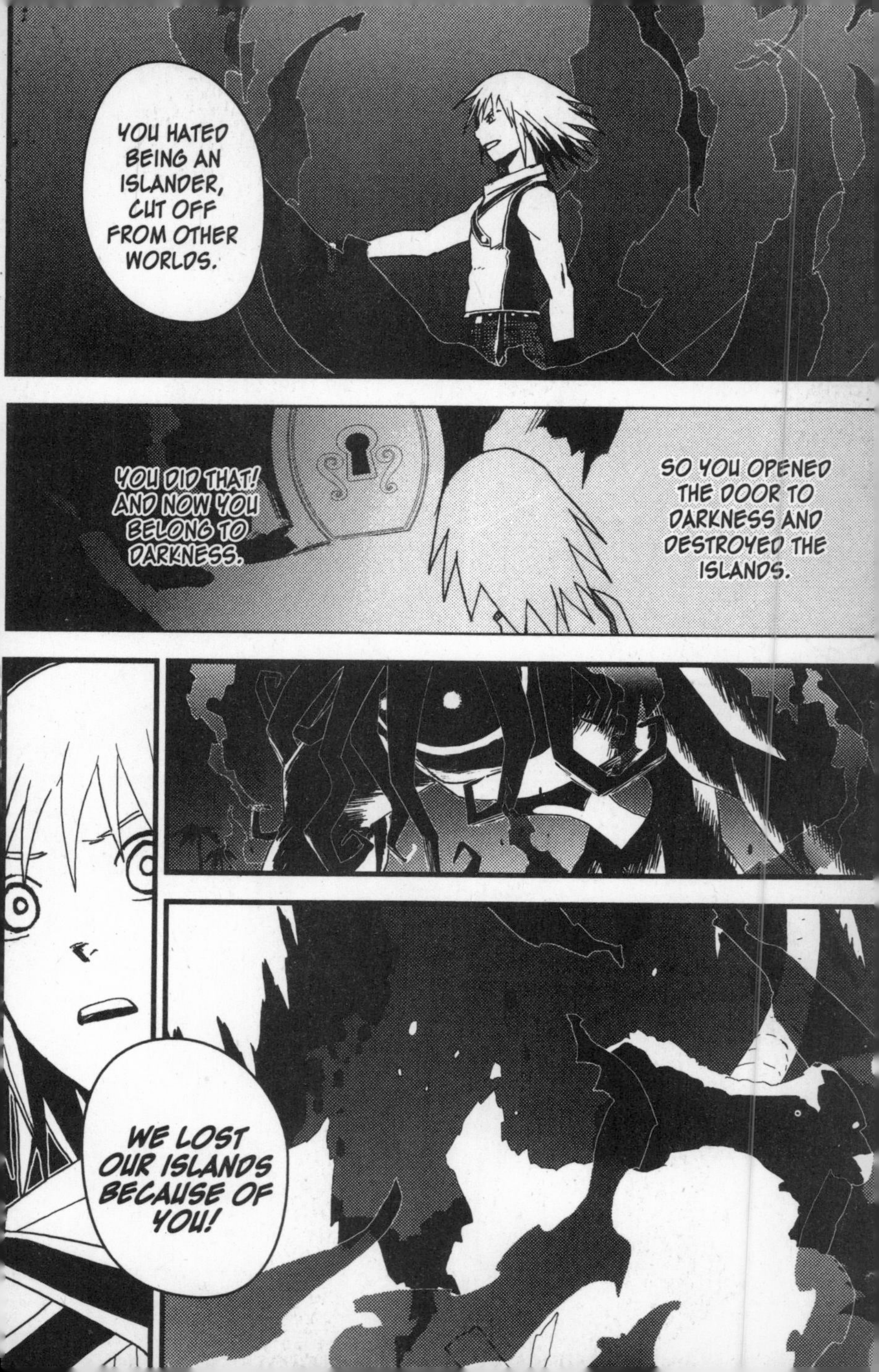
YOU HATED BEING AN ISLANDER, CUT OFF FROM OTHER WORLDS.
SO YOU OPENED THE DOOR TO DARKNESS AND DESTROYED THE ISLANDS.
YOU DID THAT! AND NOW YOU BELONG TO DARKNESS.
WE LOST OUR ISLANDS BECAUSE OF YOU!

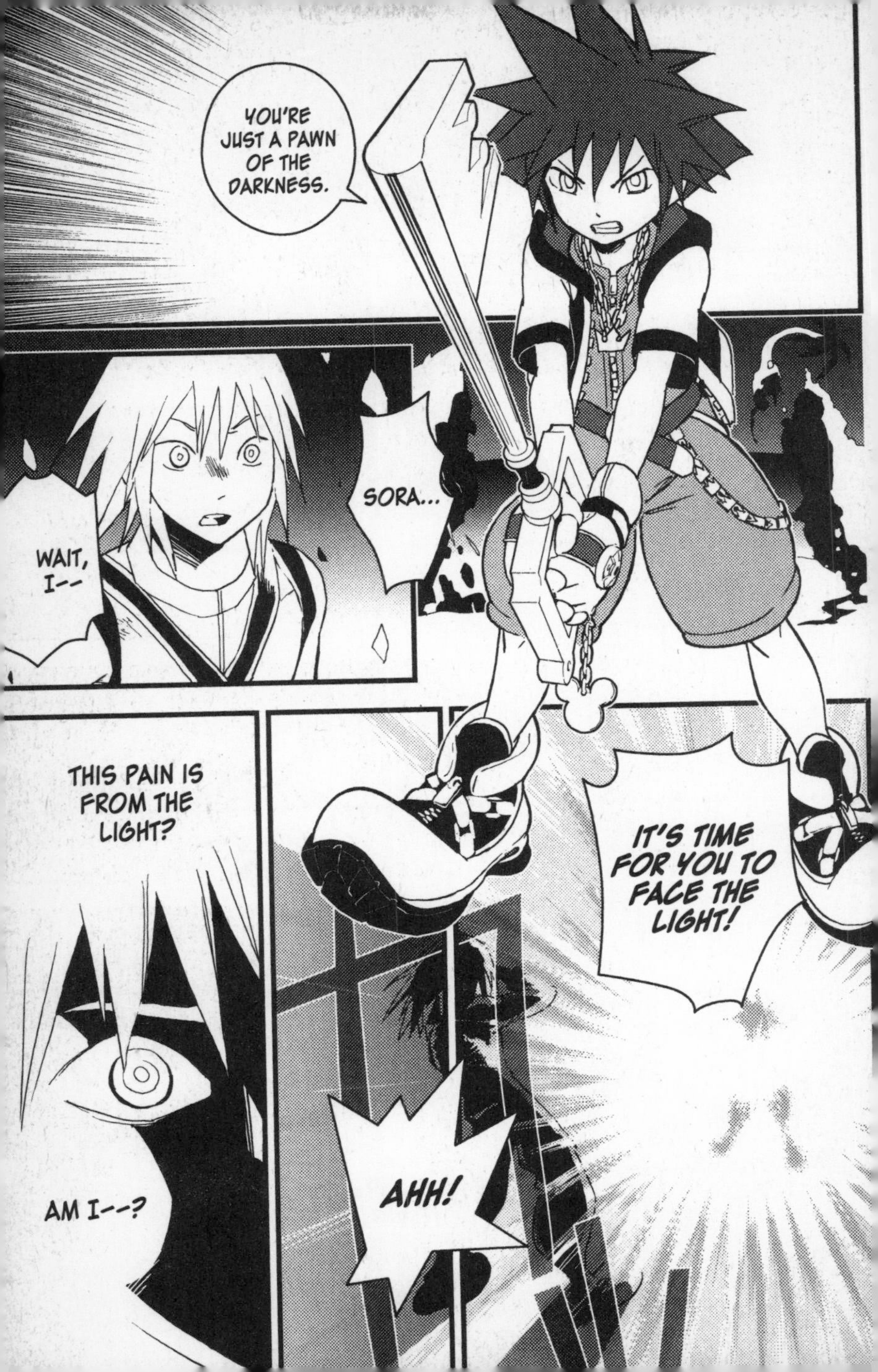
YOU'RE JUST A PAWN OF THE DARKNESS.
SORA...
WAIT, I--
IT'S TIME FOR YOU TO FACE THE LIGHT!
AHH!
THIS PAIN IS FROM THE LIGHT?
AM I--?

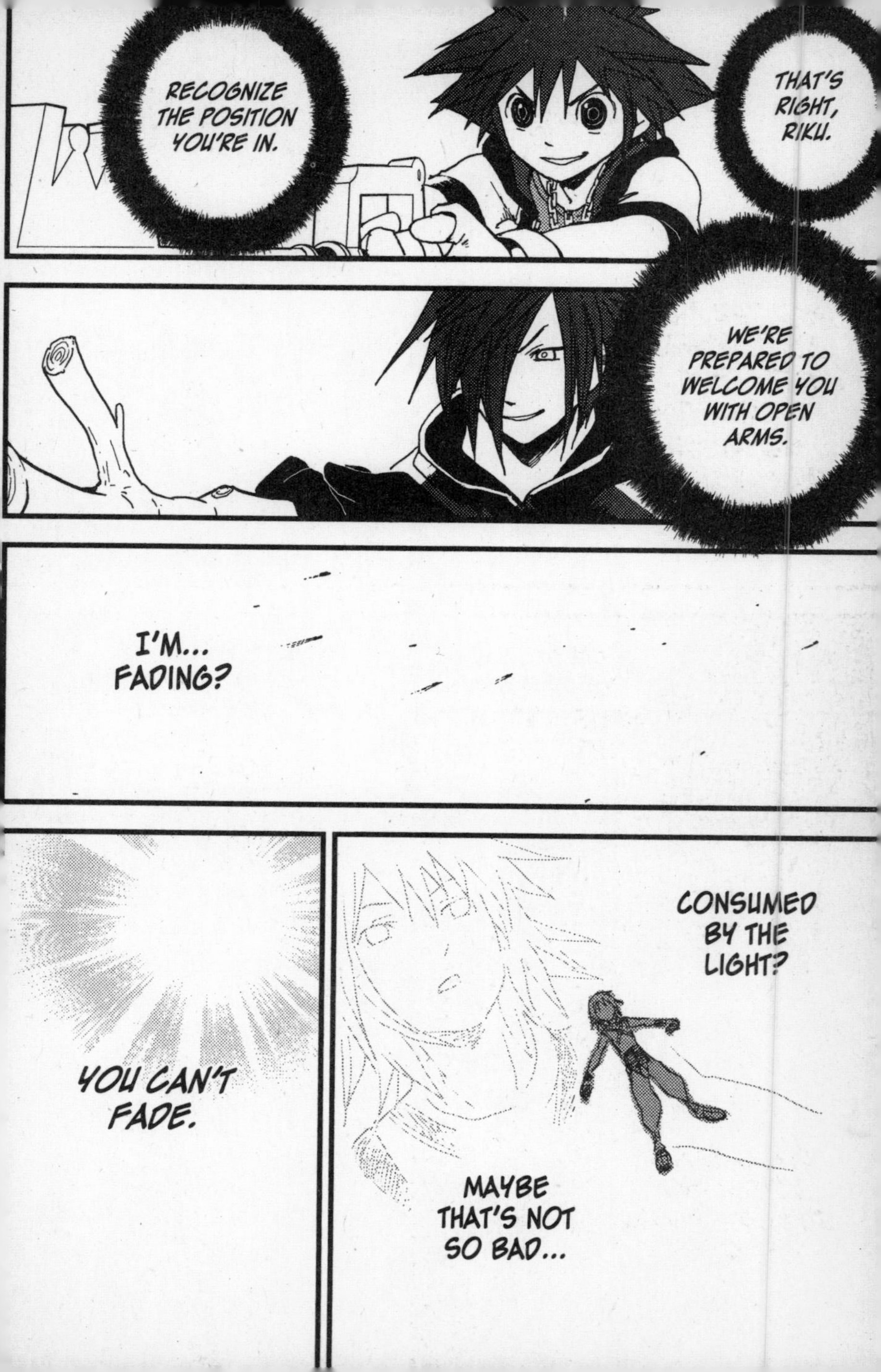
THAT'S RIGHT, RIKU.
RECOGNIZE THE POSITION YOU'RE IN.
WE'RE PREPARED TO WELCOME YOU WITH OPEN ARMS.
I'M... FADING?
CONSUMED BY THE LIGHT?
MAYBE THAT'S NOT SO BAD...
YOU CAN'T FADE.

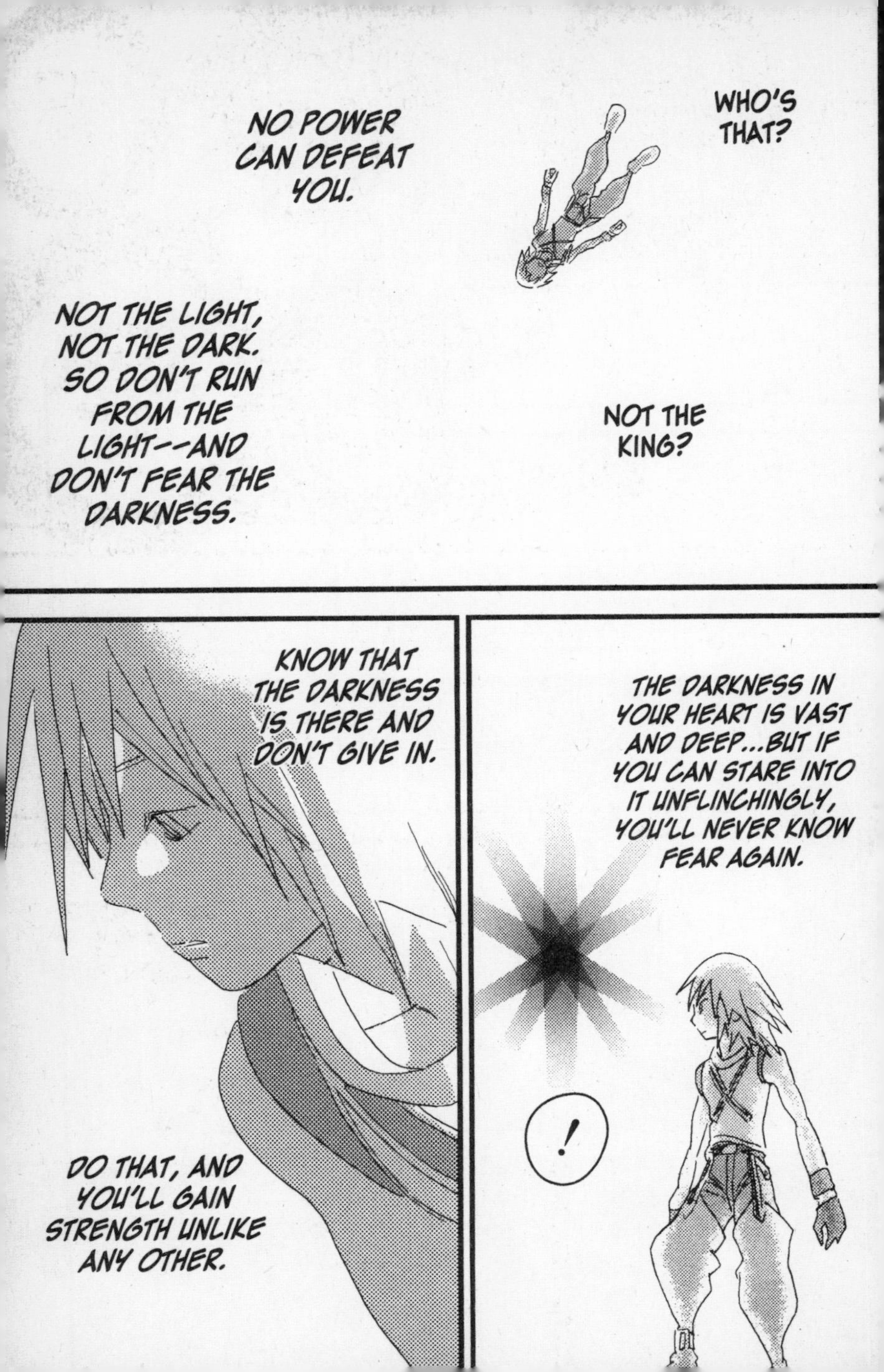
WHO'S THAT?
NO POWER CAN DEFEAT YOU.
NOT THE KING?
NOT THE LIGHT, NOT THE DARK. SO DON'T RUN FROM THE LIGHT--AND DON'T FEAR THE DARKNESS.
THE DARKNESS IN YOUR HEART IS VAST AND DEEP...BUT IF YOU CAN STARE INTO IT UNFLINCHINGLY, YOU'LL NEVER KNOW FEAR AGAIN.
!
KNOW THAT THE DARKNESS IS THERE AND DON'T GIVE IN.
DO THAT, AND YOU'LL GAIN STRENGTH UNLIKE ANY OTHER.

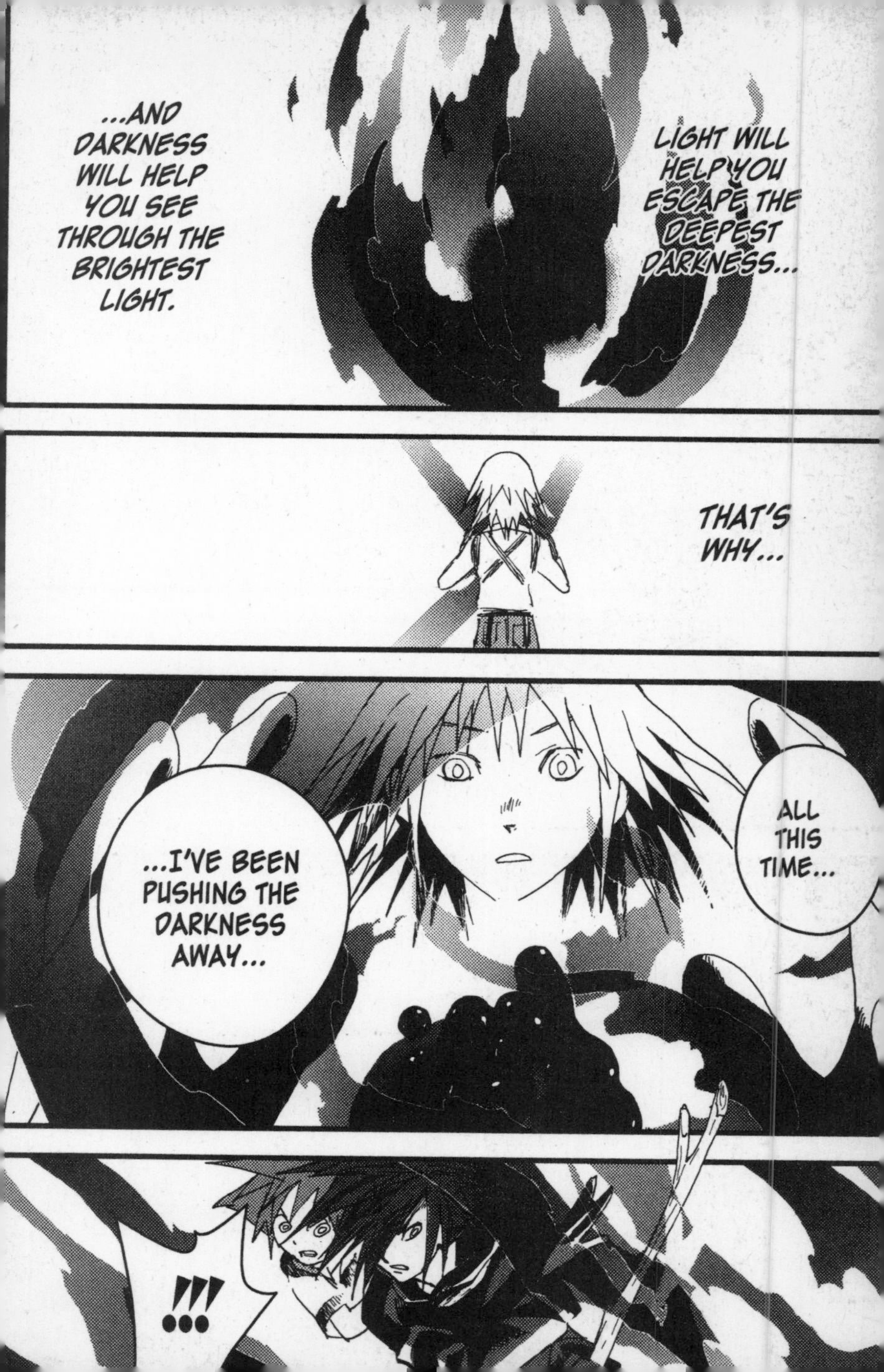
LIGHT WILL HELP YOU ESCAPE THE DEEPEST DARKNESS...
...AND DARKNESS WILL HELP YOU SEE THROUGH THE BRIGHTEST LIGHT.
THAT'S WHY...
ALL THIS TIME...
...I'VE BEEN PUSHING THE DARKNESS AWAY...
!!!
...

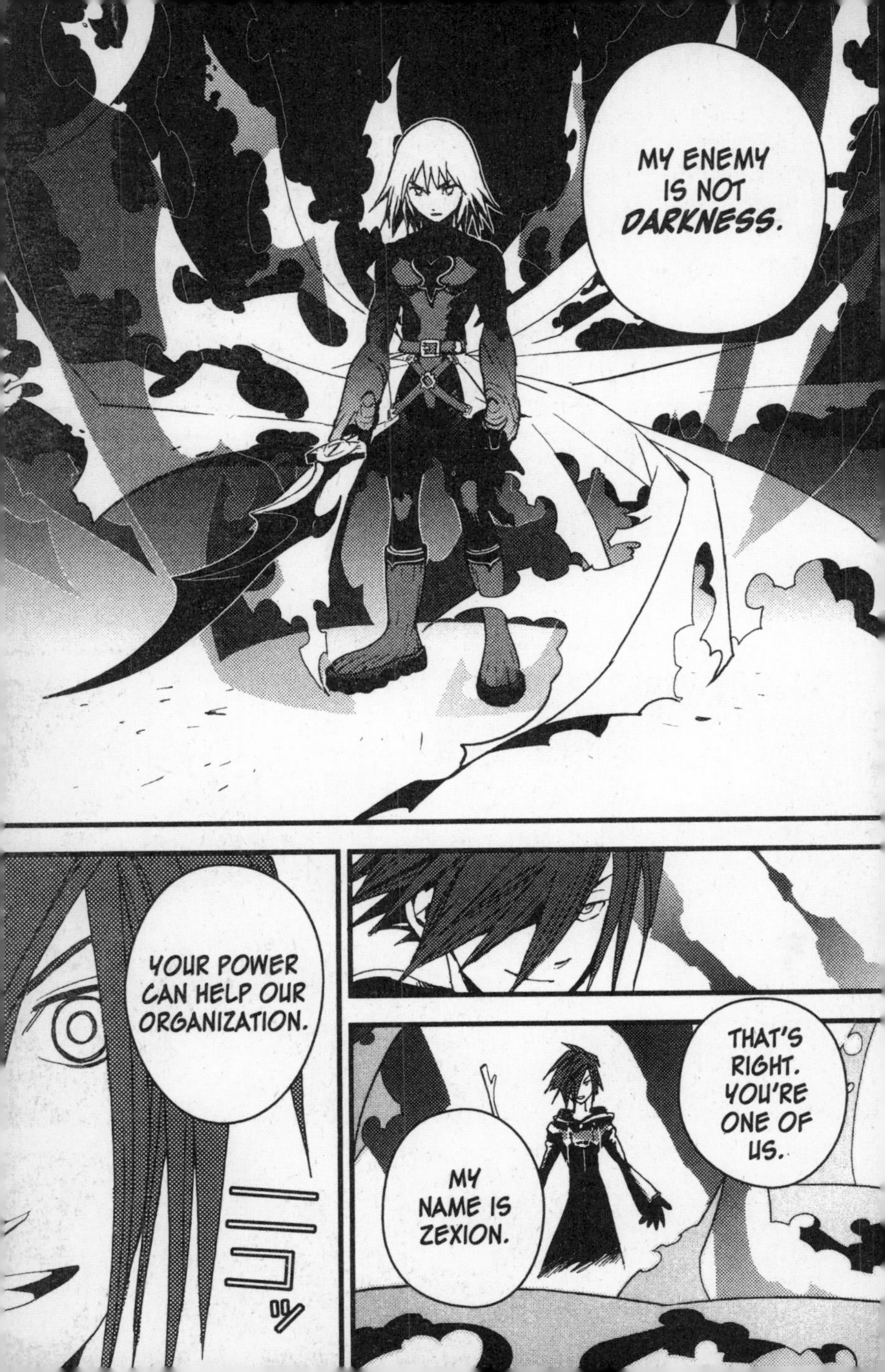
MY ENEMY IS NOT DARKNESS.
THAT'S RIGHT. YOU'RE ONE OF US.
MY NAME IS ZEXION.
YOUR POWER CAN HELP OUR ORGANIZATION.

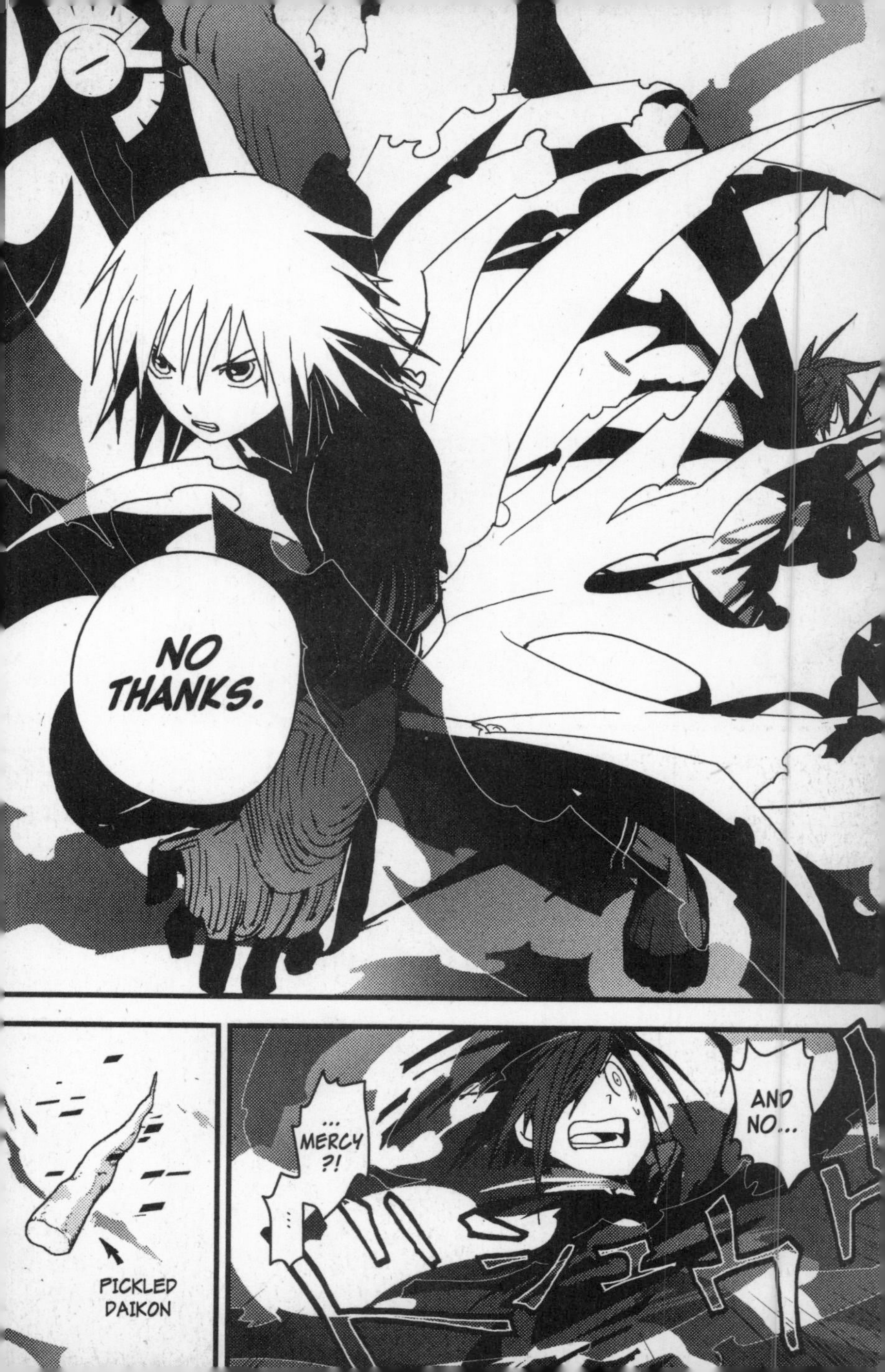
NO THANKS.
AND NO...
...MERCY?!
PICKLED DAIKON

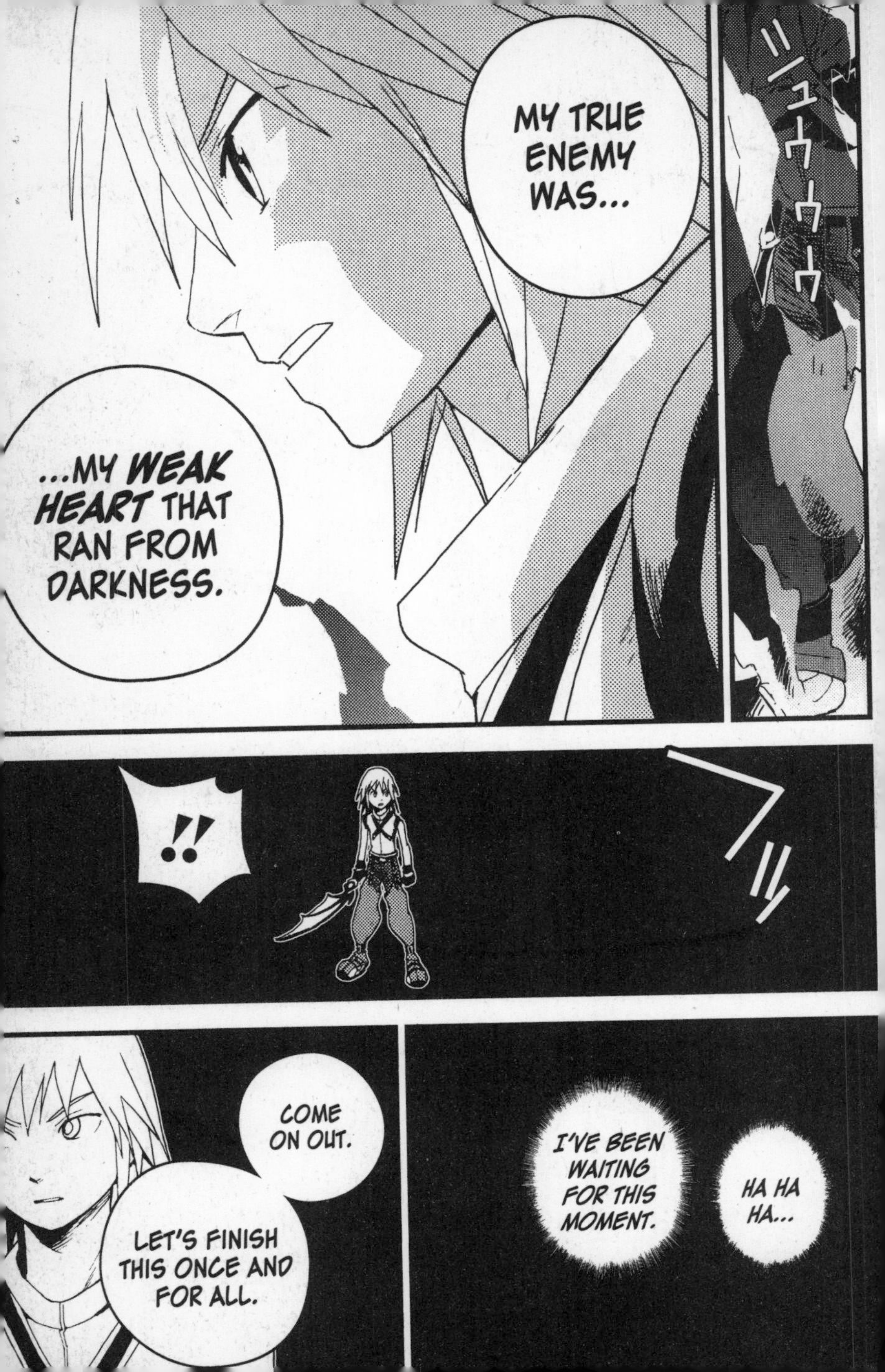
MY TRUE ENEMY WAS...
...MY WEAK HEART THAT RAN FROM DARKNESS.
!!
HA HA HA...
I'VE BEEN WAITING FOR THIS MOMENT.
COME ON OUT.
LET'S FINISH THIS ONCE AND FOR ALL.

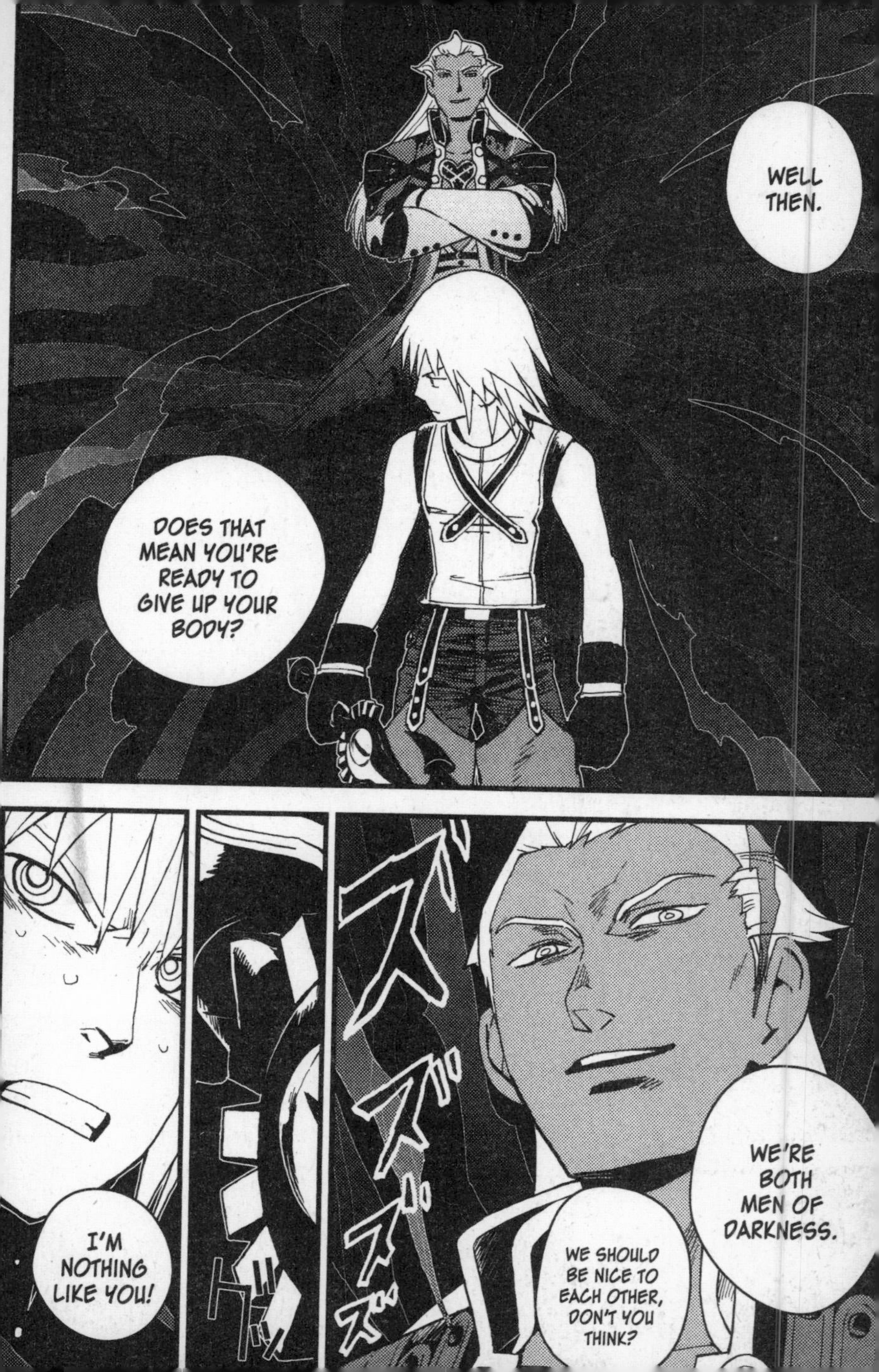
WELL THEN.
DOES THAT MEAN YOU'RE READY TO GIVE UP YOUR BODY?
WE'RE BOTH MEN OF DARKNESS.
WE SHOULD BE NICE TO EACH OTHER, DON'T YOU THINK?
I'M NOTHING LIKE YOU!

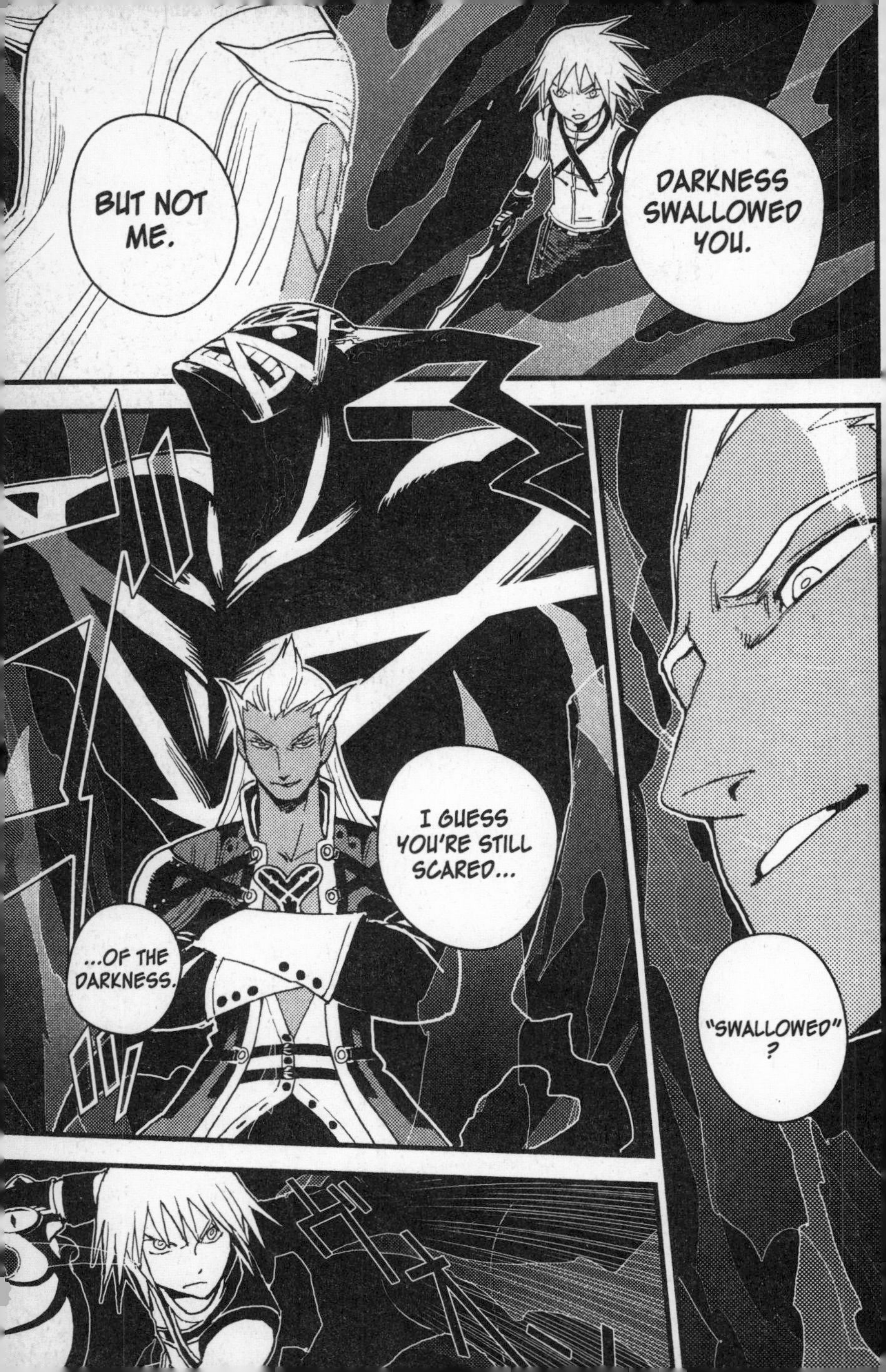
DARKNESS SWALLOWED YOU.
BUT NOT ME.
"SWALLOWED"?
I GUESS YOU'RE STILL SCARED...
...OF THE DARKNESS.

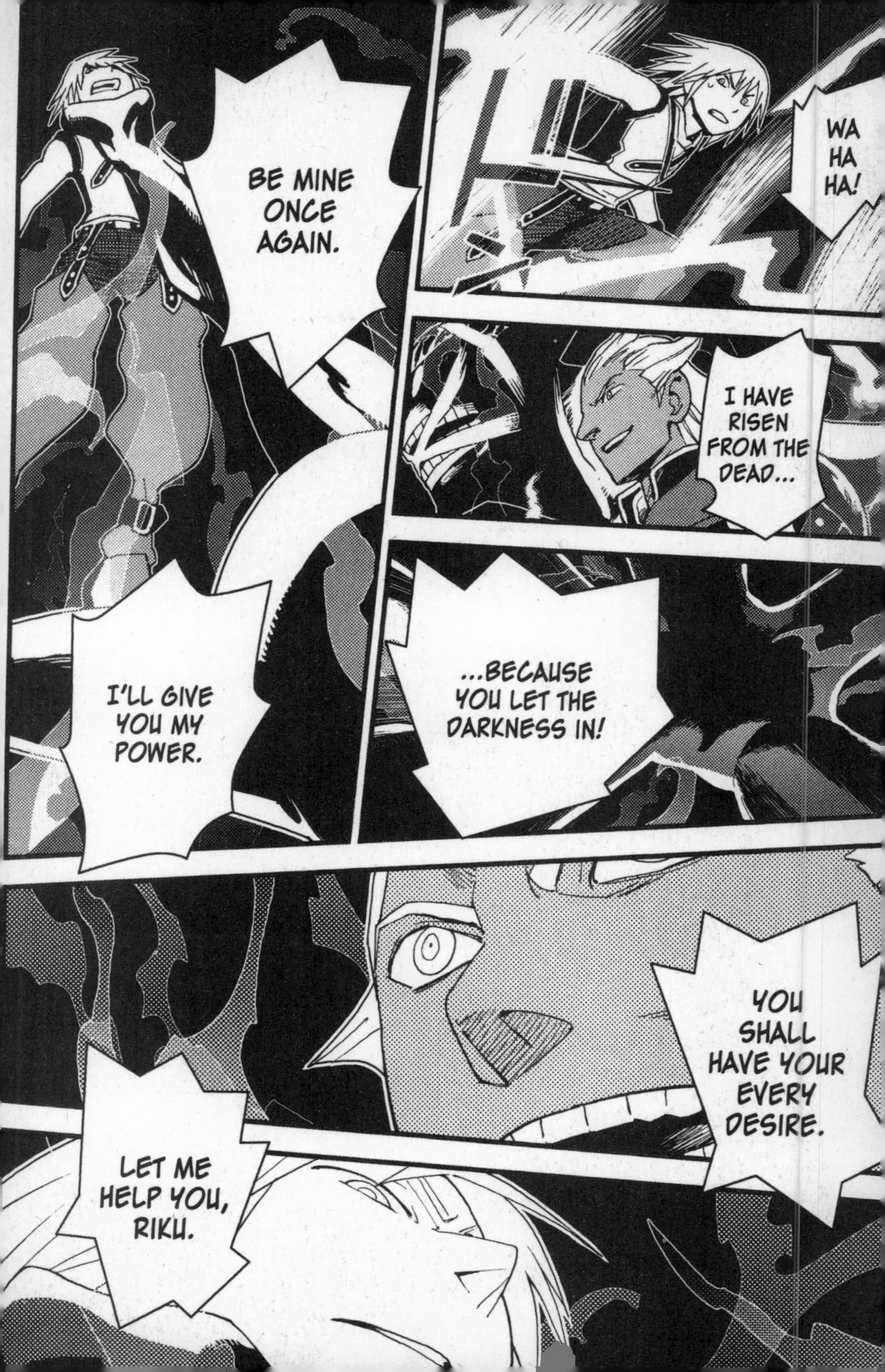
WA HA HA!
I HAVE RISEN FROM THE DEAD...
...BECAUSE YOU LET THE DARKNESS IN!
BE MINE ONCE AGAIN.
I'LL GIVE YOU MY POWER.
YOU SHALL HAVE YOUR EVERY DESIRE.
LET ME HELP YOU, RIKU.

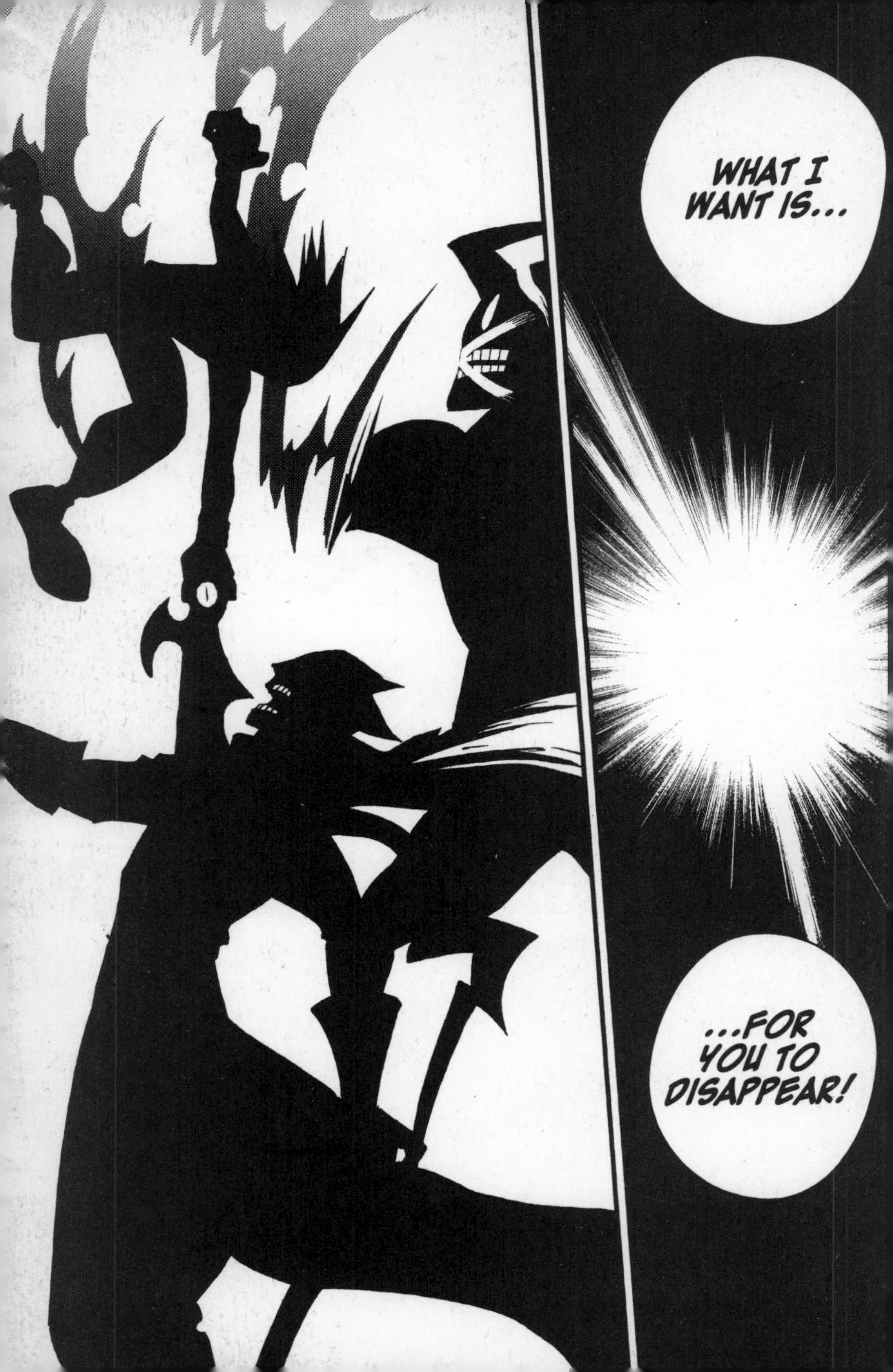
WHAT I WANT IS...
...FOR YOU TO DISAPPEAR!

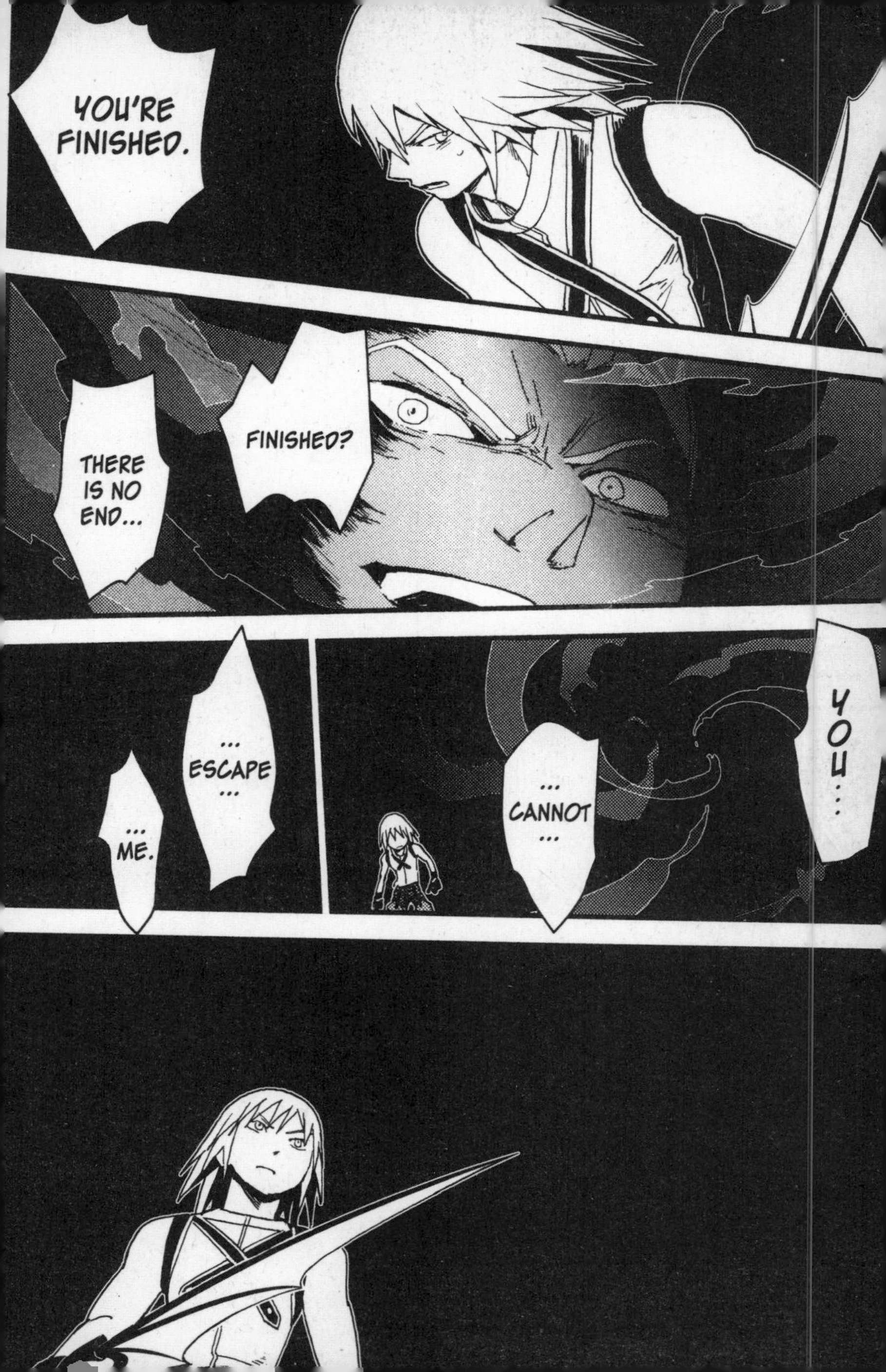
YOU'RE FINISHED.
FINISHED?
THERE IS NO END...
YOU...
...CANNOT...
...ESCAPE...
...ME.

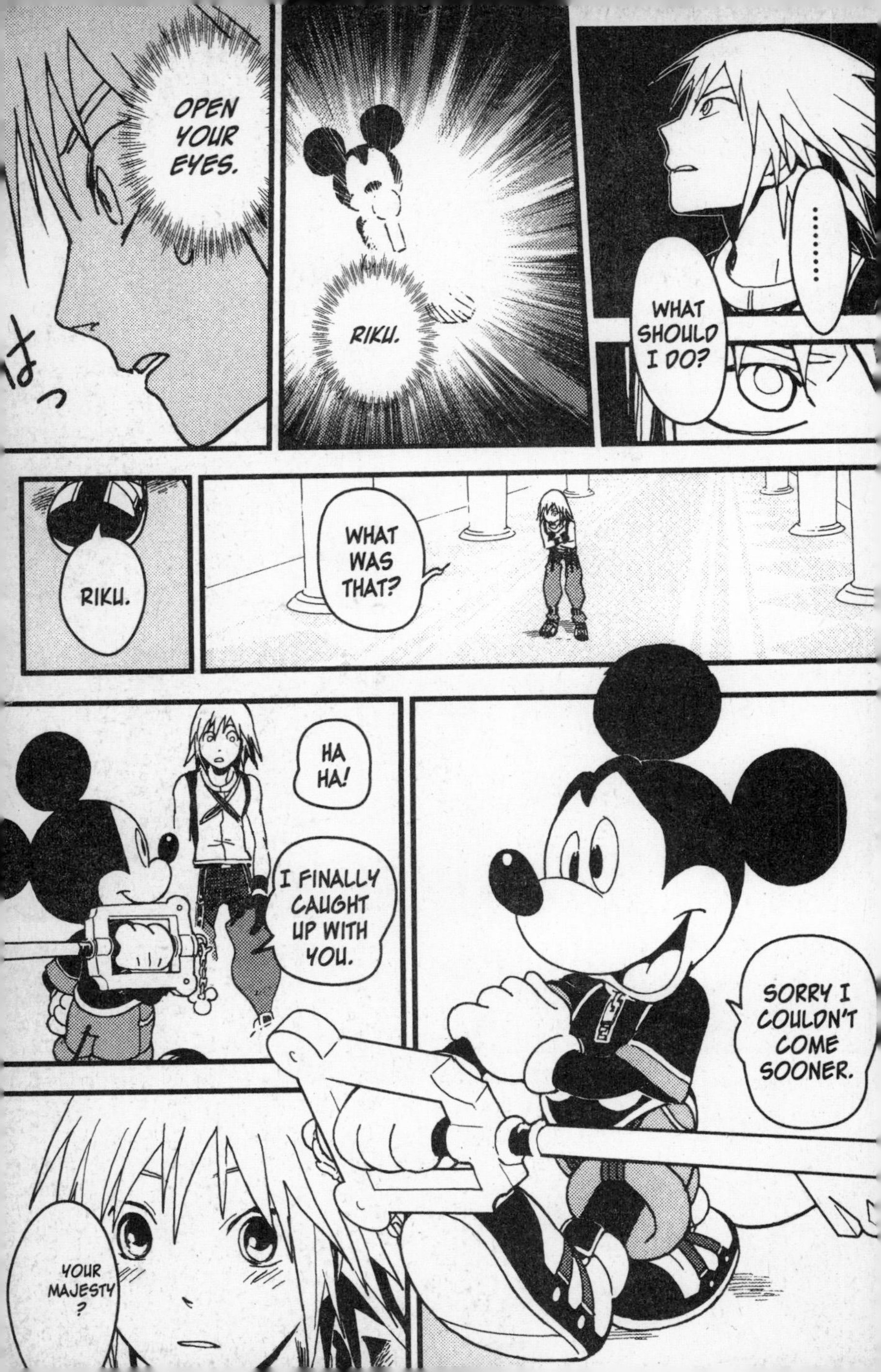
......
WHAT SHOULD I DO?
RIKU.
OPEN YOUR EYES.
はっ
WHAT WAS THAT?
RIKU.
SORRY I COULDN'T COME SOONER.
HA HA!
I FINALLY CAUGHT UP WITH YOU.
YOUR MAJESTY?

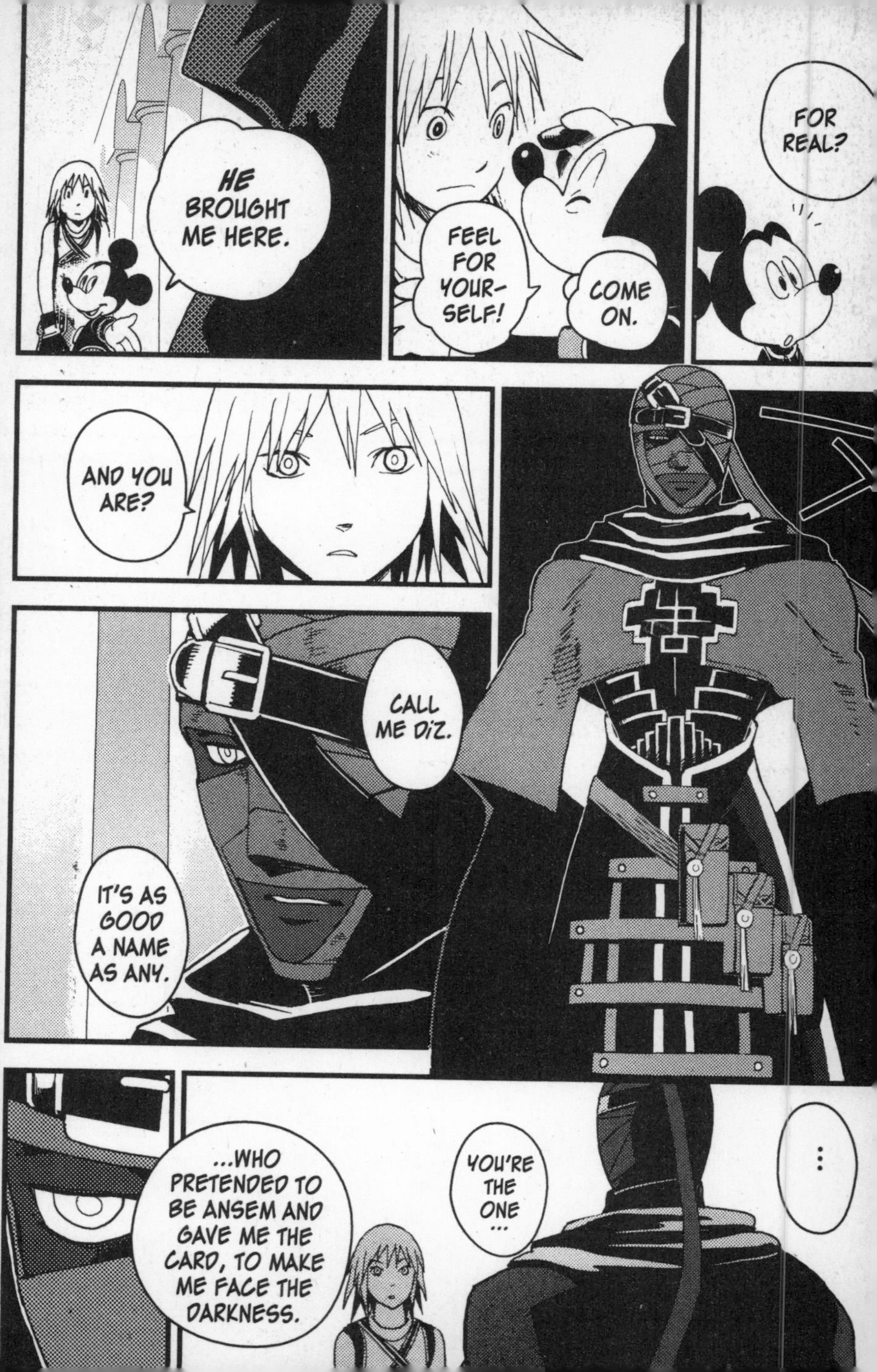
FOR REAL?
COME ON.
FEEL FOR YOURSELF!
HE BROUGHT ME HERE.
AND YOU ARE?
CALL ME DiZ.
IT'S AS GOOD A NAME AS ANY.
…
YOU'RE THE ONE …
...WHO PRETENDED TO BE ANSEM AND GAVE ME THE CARD, TO MAKE ME FACE THE DARKNESS.

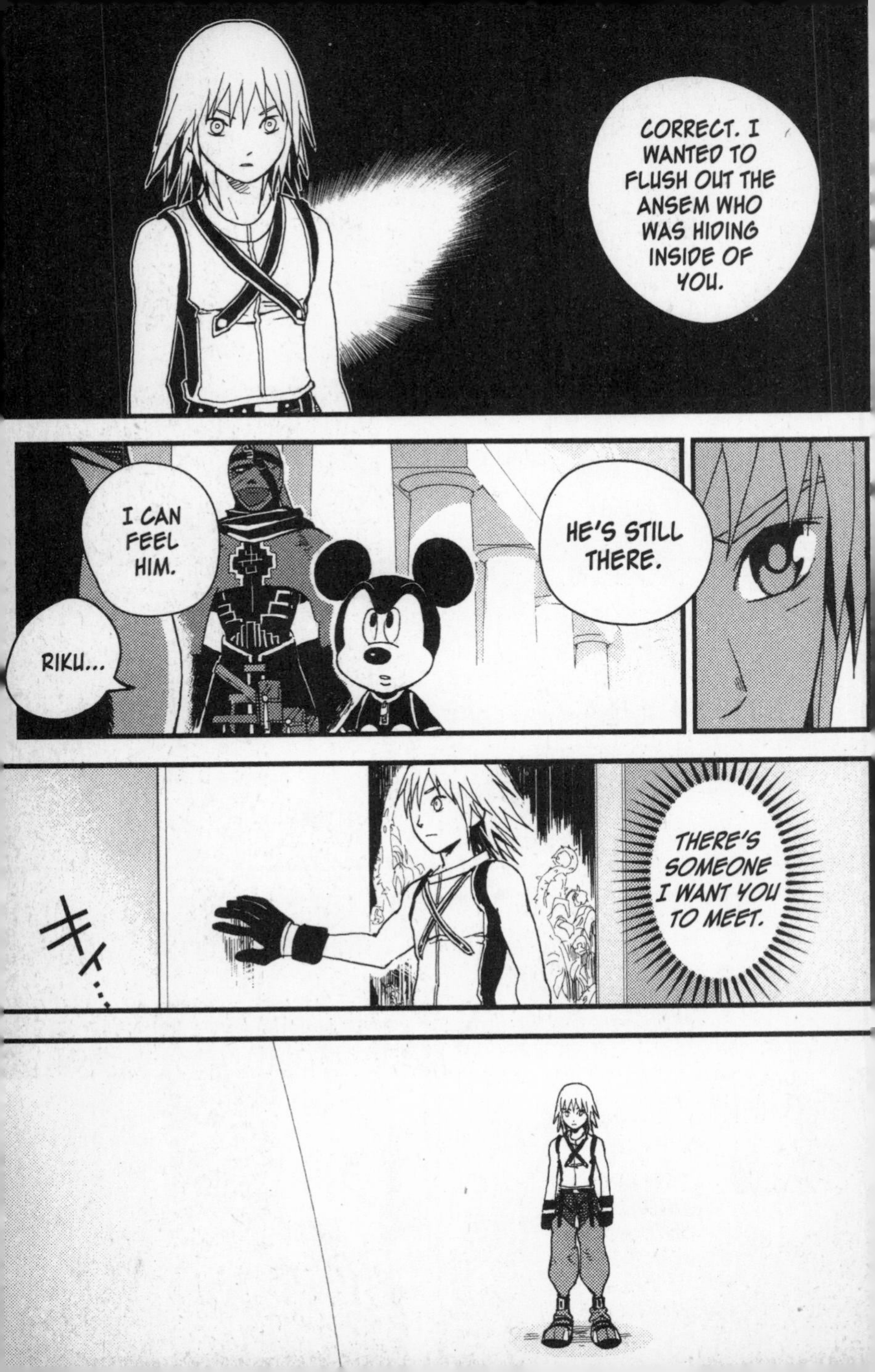
CORRECT. I WANTED TO FLUSH OUT THE ANSEM WHO WAS HIDING INSIDE OF YOU.
HE'S STILL THERE.
I CAN FEEL HIM.
RIKU...
THERE'S SOMEONE I WANT YOU TO MEET.
キト...

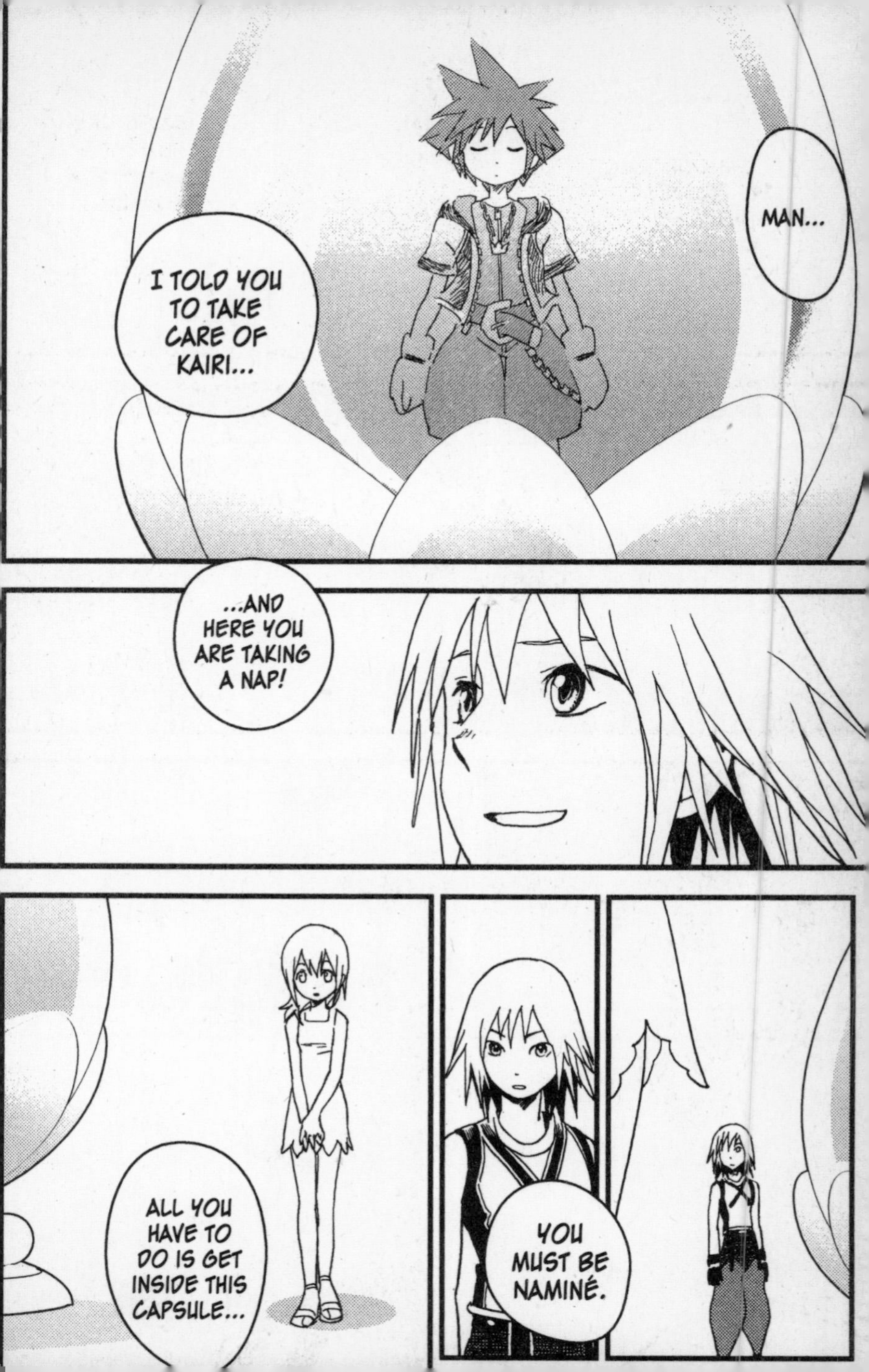
MAN...
I TOLD YOU TO TAKE CARE OF KAIRI...
...AND HERE YOU ARE TAKING A NAP!
YOU MUST BE NAMINÉ.
ALL YOU HAVE TO DO IS GET INSIDE THIS CAPSULE...

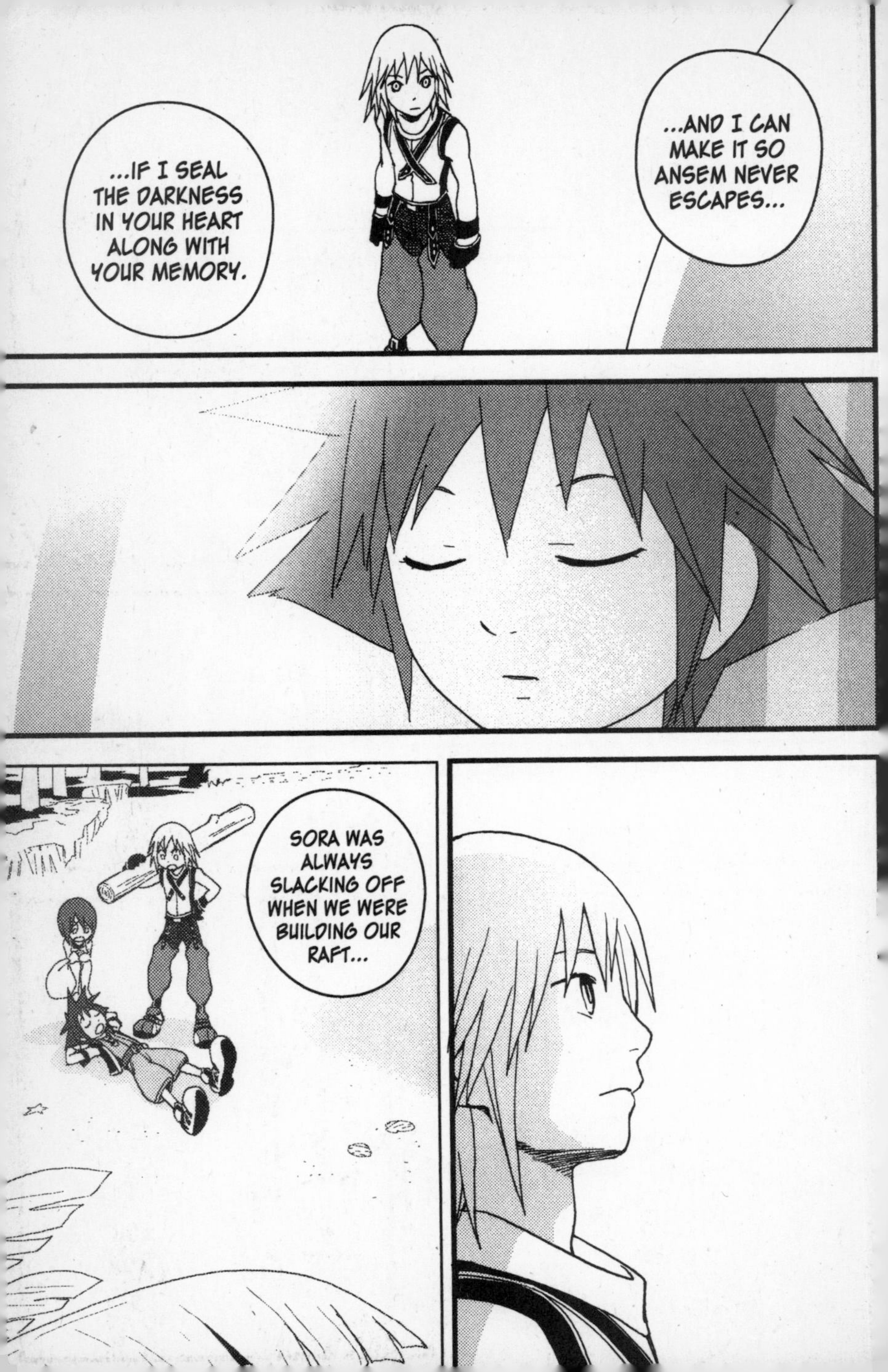
...AND I CAN MAKE IT SO ANSEM NEVER ESCAPES...
...IF I SEAL THE DARKNESS IN YOUR HEART ALONG WITH YOUR MEMORY.
SORA WAS ALWAYS SLACKING OFF WHEN WE WERE BUILDING OUR RAFT...

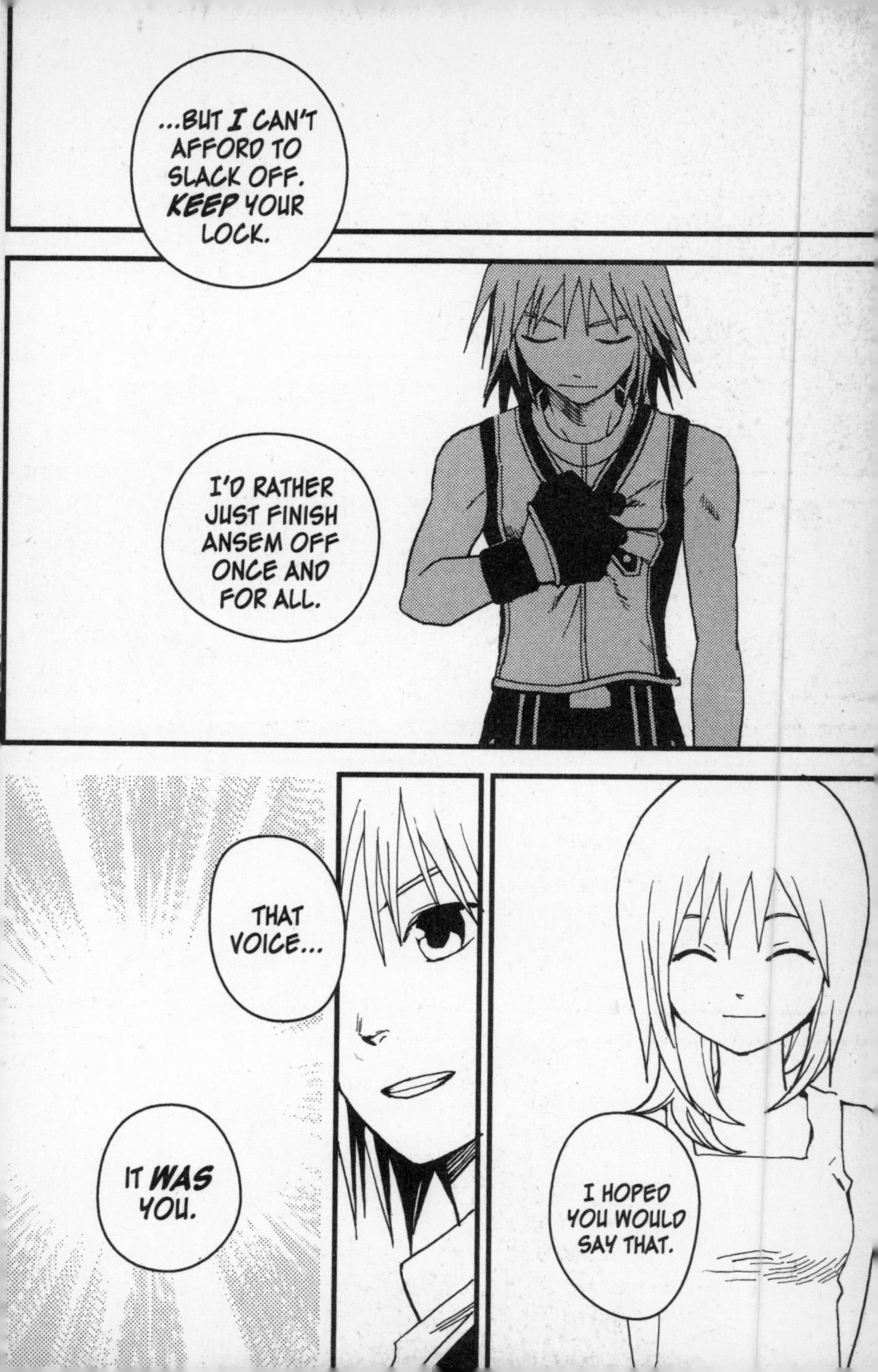
...BUT I CAN'T AFFORD TO SLACK OFF. KEEP YOUR LOCK.
I'D RATHER JUST FINISH ANSEM OFF ONCE AND FOR ALL.
I HOPED YOU WOULD SAY THAT.
THAT VOICE...
IT WAS YOU.

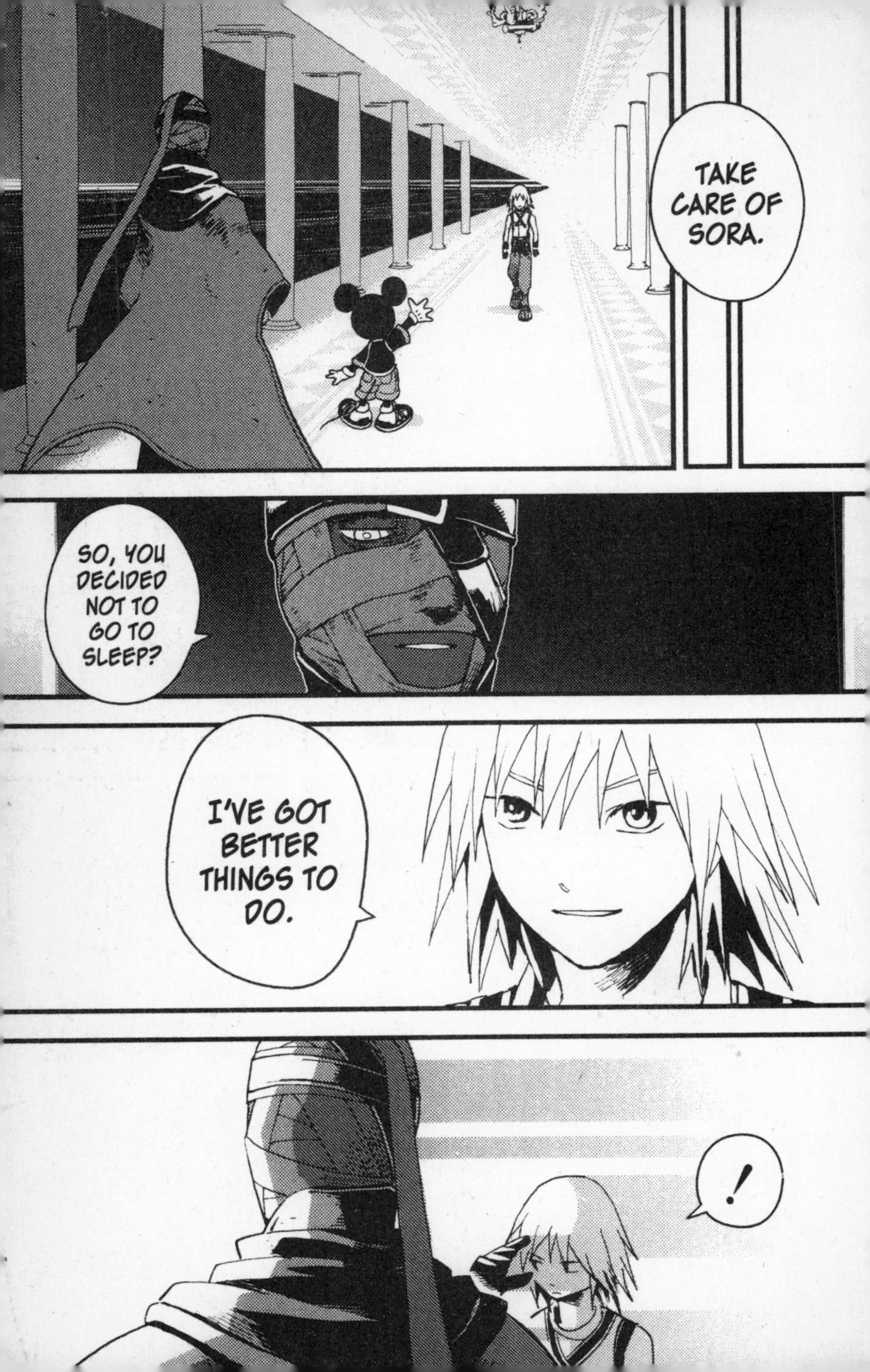
TAKE CARE OF SORA.
SO, YOU DECIDED NOT TO GO TO SLEEP?
I'VE GOT BETTER THINGS TO DO.
!

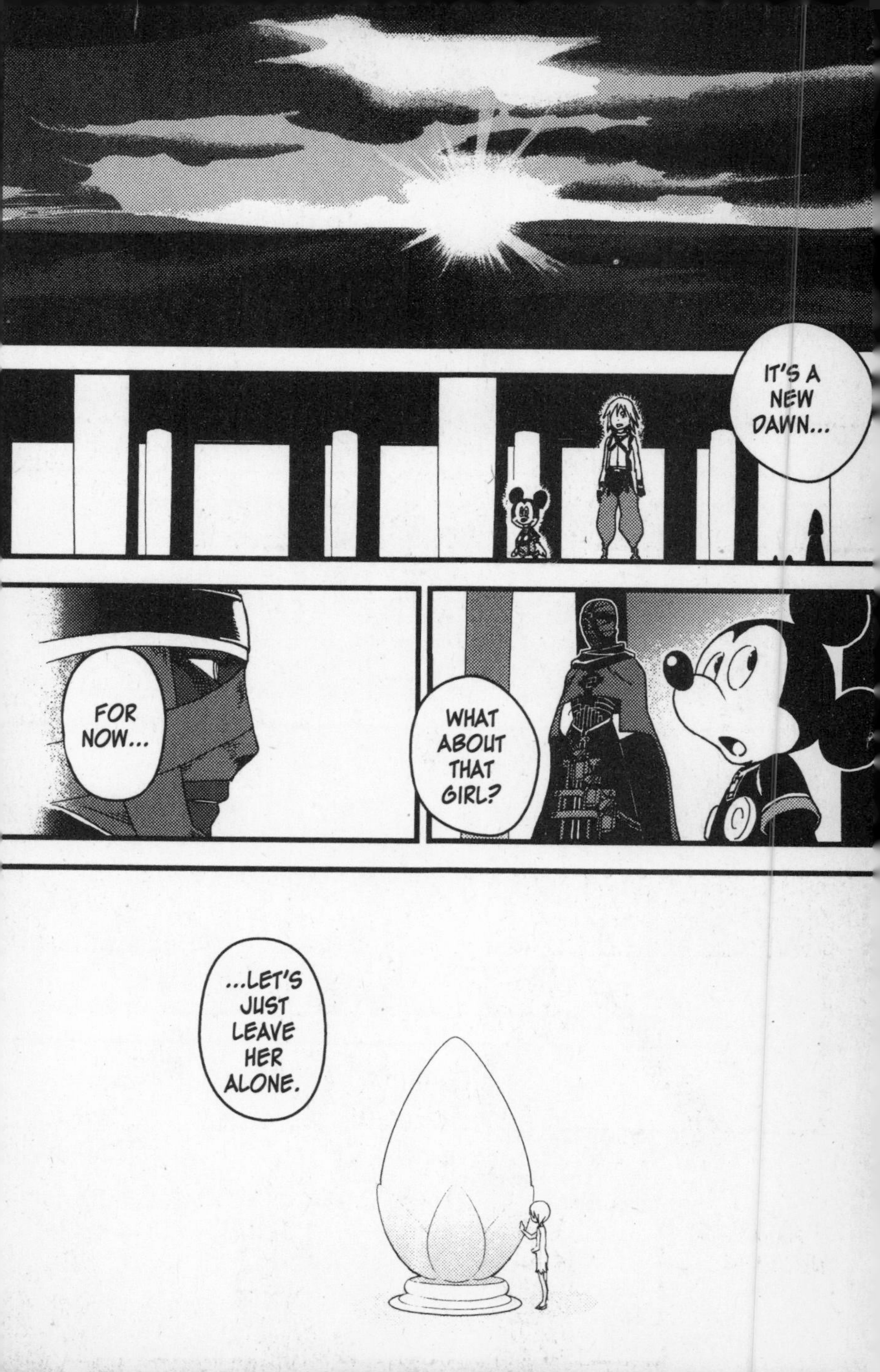
IT'S A NEW DAWN...
WHAT ABOUT THAT GIRL?
FOR NOW...
...LET'S JUST LEAVE HER ALONE.

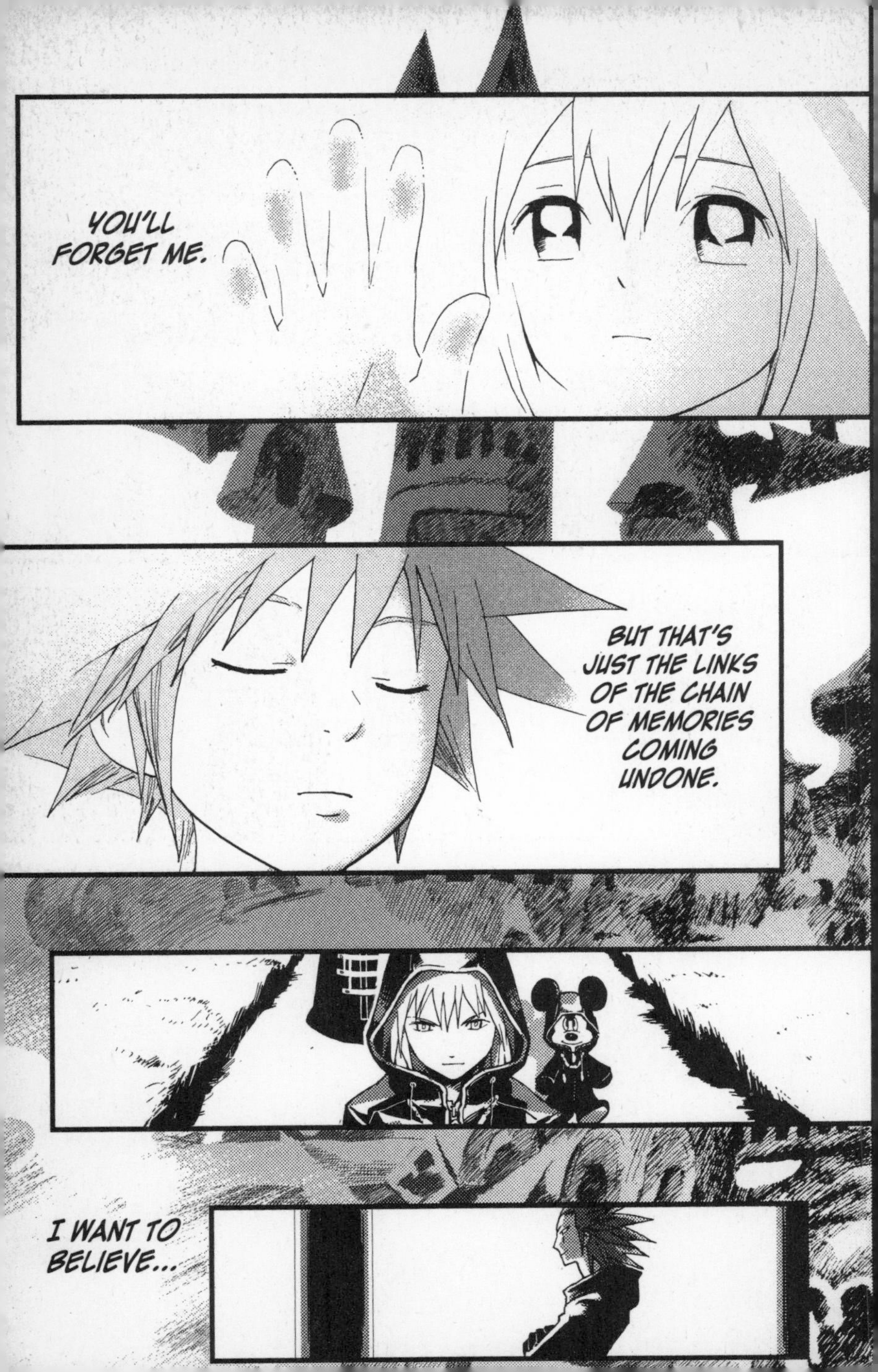
YOU'LL FORGET ME.
BUT THAT'S JUST THE LINKS OF THE CHAIN OF MEMORIES COMING UNDONE.
I WANT TO BELIEVE...

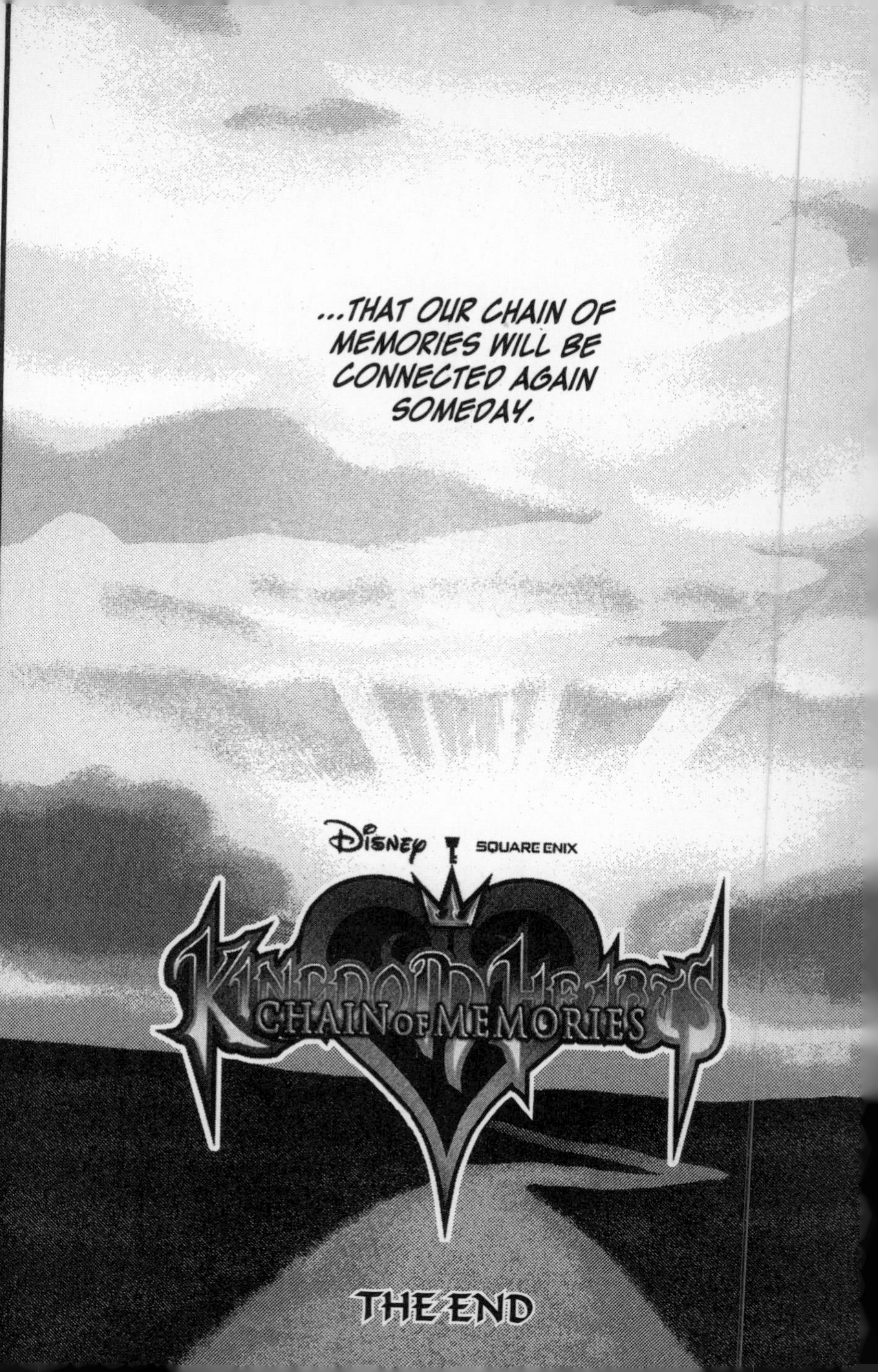
...THAT OUR CHAIN OF MEMORIES WILL BE CONNECTED AGAIN SOMEDAY.
Disney
SQUARE ENIX
KINGDOM HEARTS
CHAIN OF MEMORIES
THE END

Bonus Feature
Strange News of Riku–Strange Story of the Replica

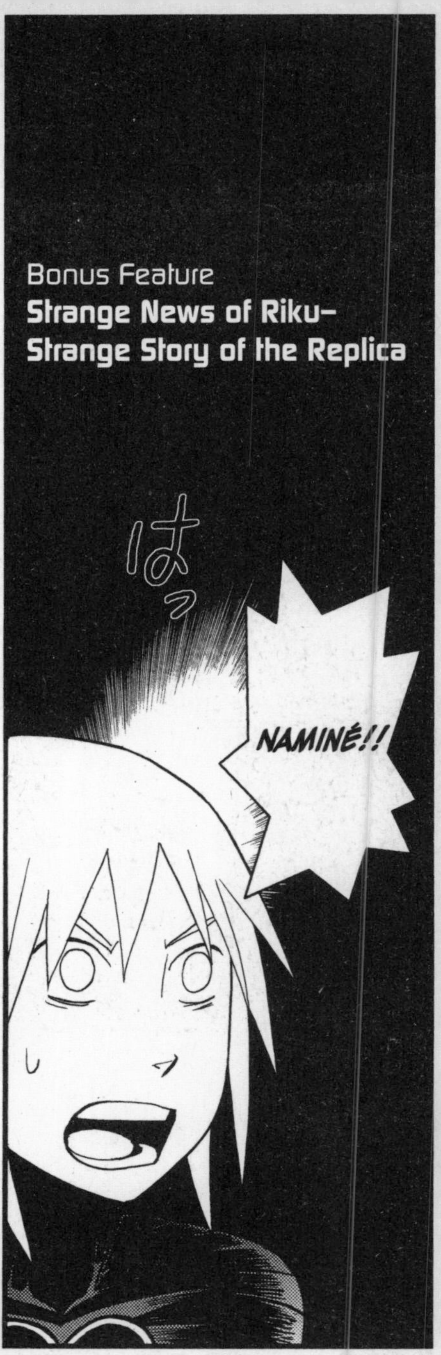
はっ
NAMINÉ!!

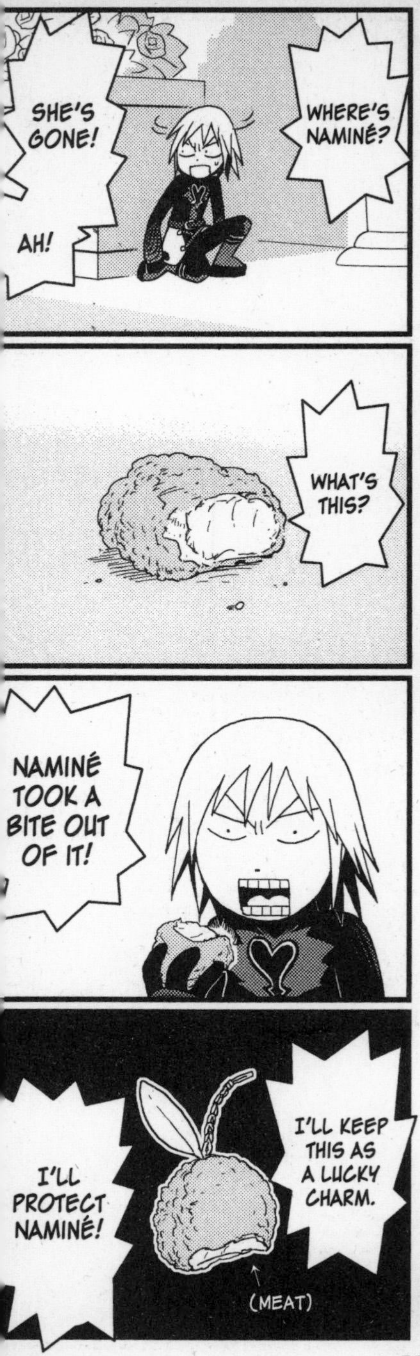
WHERE'S NAMINÉ?
SHE'S GONE!
AH!
WHAT'S THIS?
NAMINÉ TOOK A BITE OUT OF IT!
I'LL KEEP THIS AS A LUCKY CHARM.
I'LL PROTECT NAMINÉ!
(MEAT)

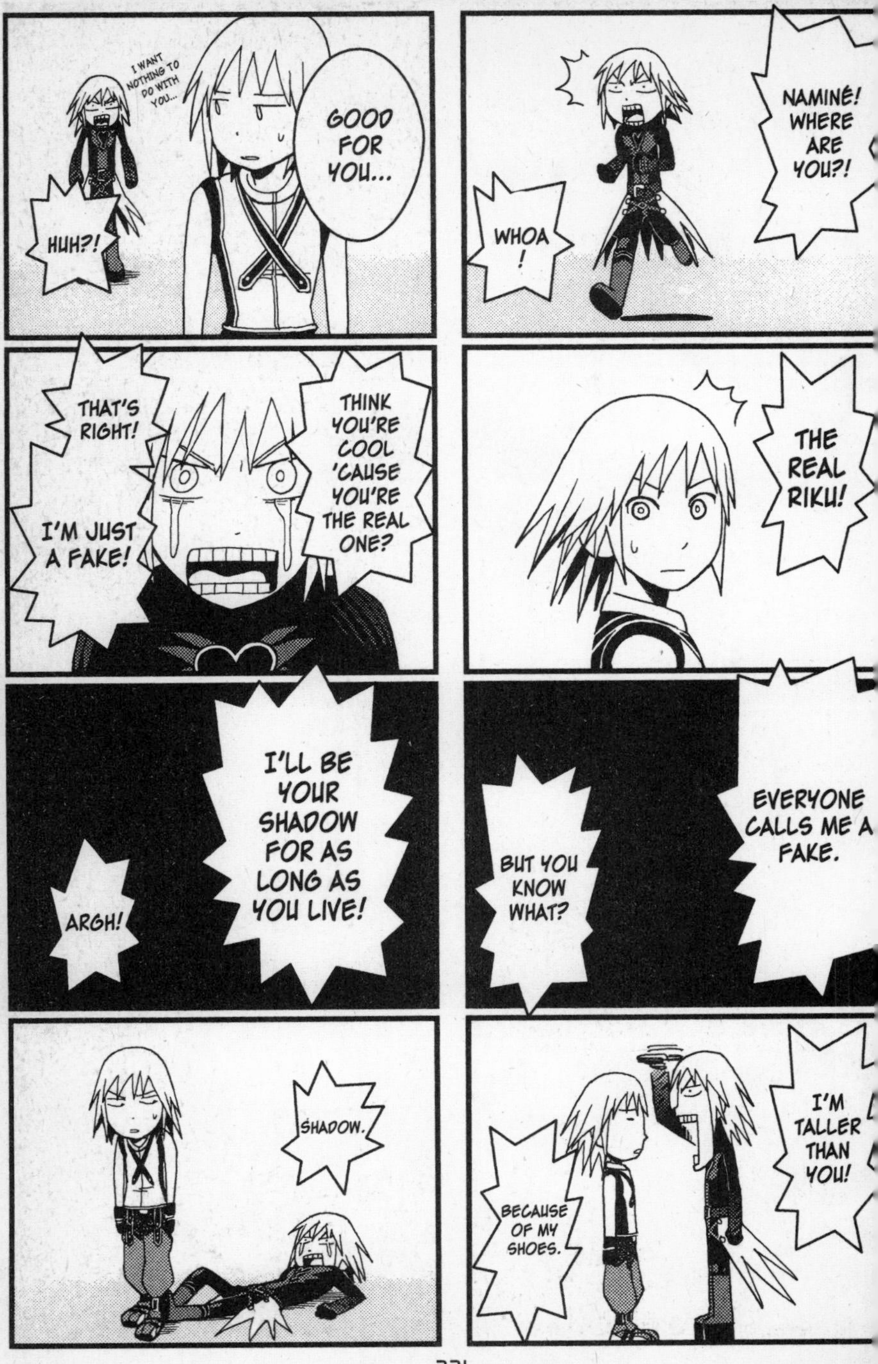
NAMINÉ! WHERE ARE YOU?!
WHOA!
I WANT NOTHING TO DO WITH YOU...
GOOD FOR YOU...
HUH?!
THE REAL RIKU!
THINK YOU'RE COOL 'CAUSE YOU'RE THE REAL ONE?
THAT'S RIGHT!
I'M JUST A FAKE!
EVERYONE CALLS ME A FAKE.
BUT YOU KNOW WHAT?
I'LL BE YOUR SHADOW FOR AS LONG AS YOU LIVE!
ARGH!
I'M TALLER THAN YOU!
BECAUSE OF MY SHOES.
SHADOW.

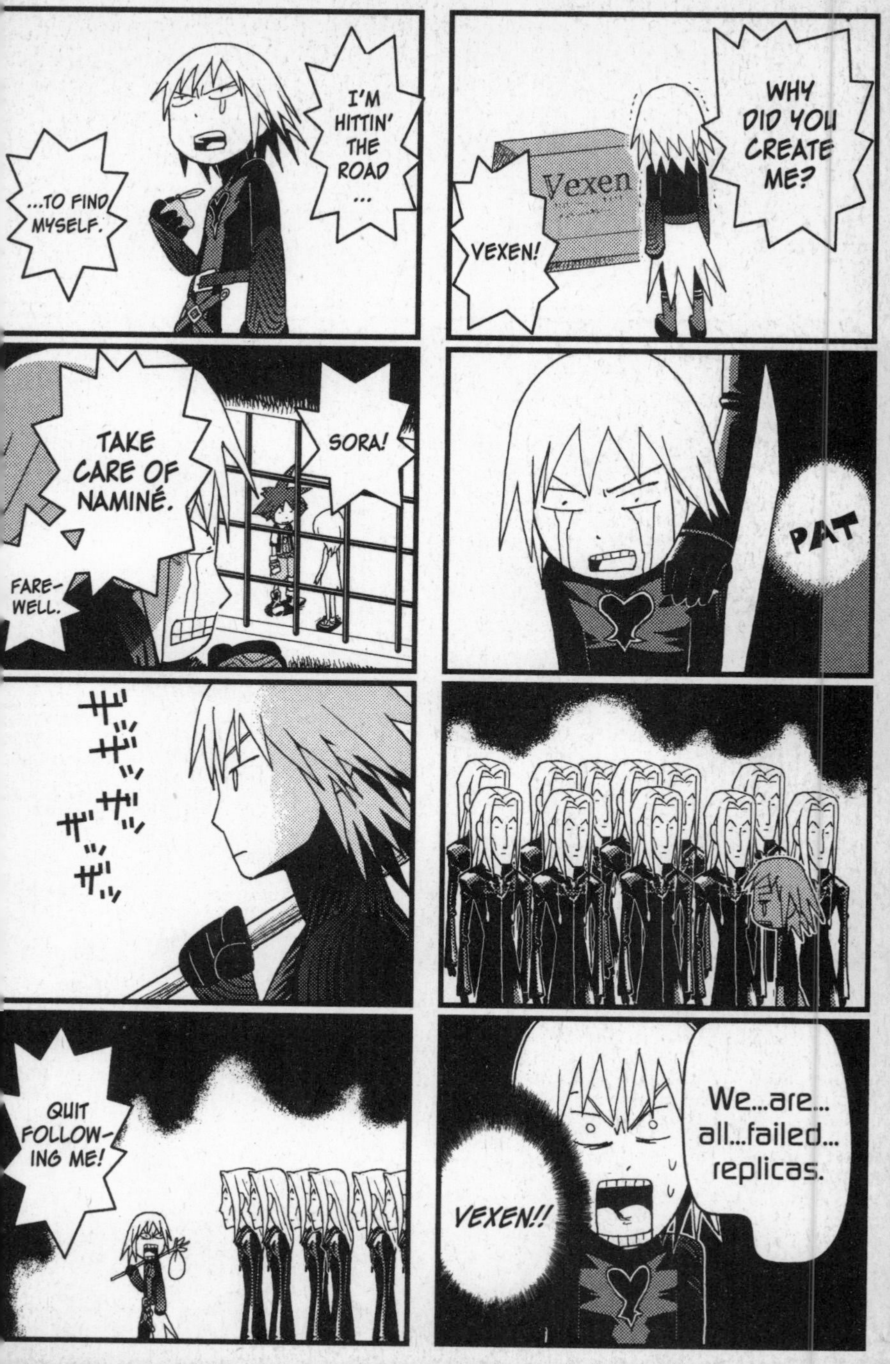
WHY DID YOU CREATE ME?
Vexen
VEXEN!
I'M HITTIN' THE ROAD ...
...TO FIND MYSELF.
PAT
SORA!
TAKE CARE OF NAMINÉ.
FARE-WELL.
ザッ ザッ ザッ ザッ ザッ ザッ
We...are... all...failed... replicas.
VEXEN!!
QUIT FOLLOW-ING ME!

DISNEY · SQUARE ENIX

KINGDOM HEARTS
CHAIN OF MEMORIES

As Sora slumbers we can only hope he
will regain the precious memories of his
friends. But at what cost? Will he in turn
forget all about his new friend, Naminé?
And what about Kairi? How long will she
wait for Sora's return?
Meanwhile, Riku remains awake in a
quest to help Sora regain his memory
and to defeat the darkness within himself
once and for all...

The adventure continues in the next
installment of the blockbuster series
KINGDOM HEARTS II
Coming Soon!!

Disney SQUARE ENIX

KINGDOM HEARTS CHAIN OF MEMORIES

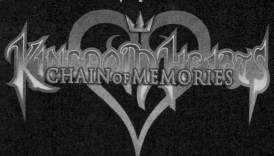

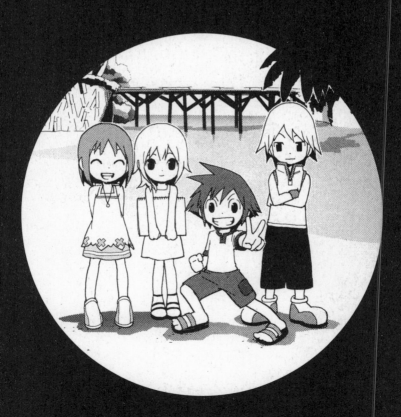

DISNEY SQUARE ENIX

KINGDOM HEARTS CHAIN OF MEMORIES

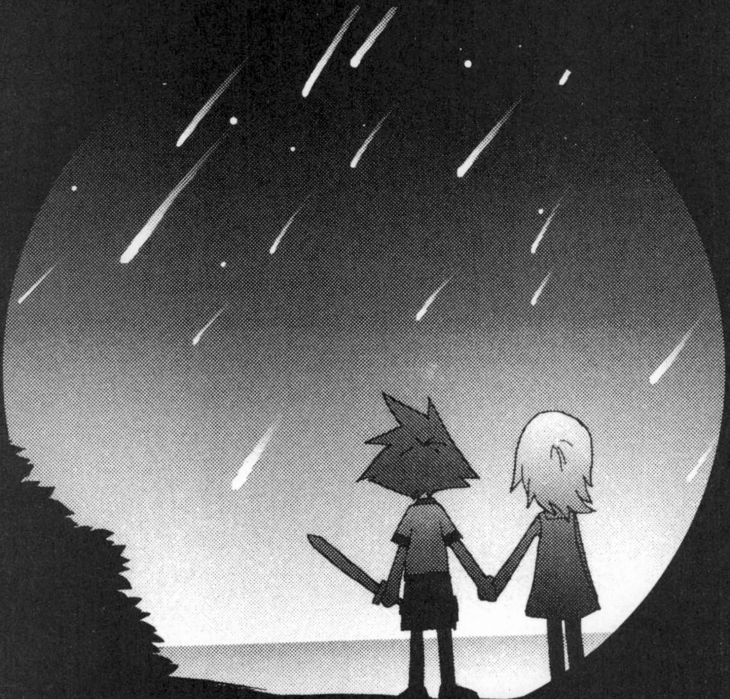

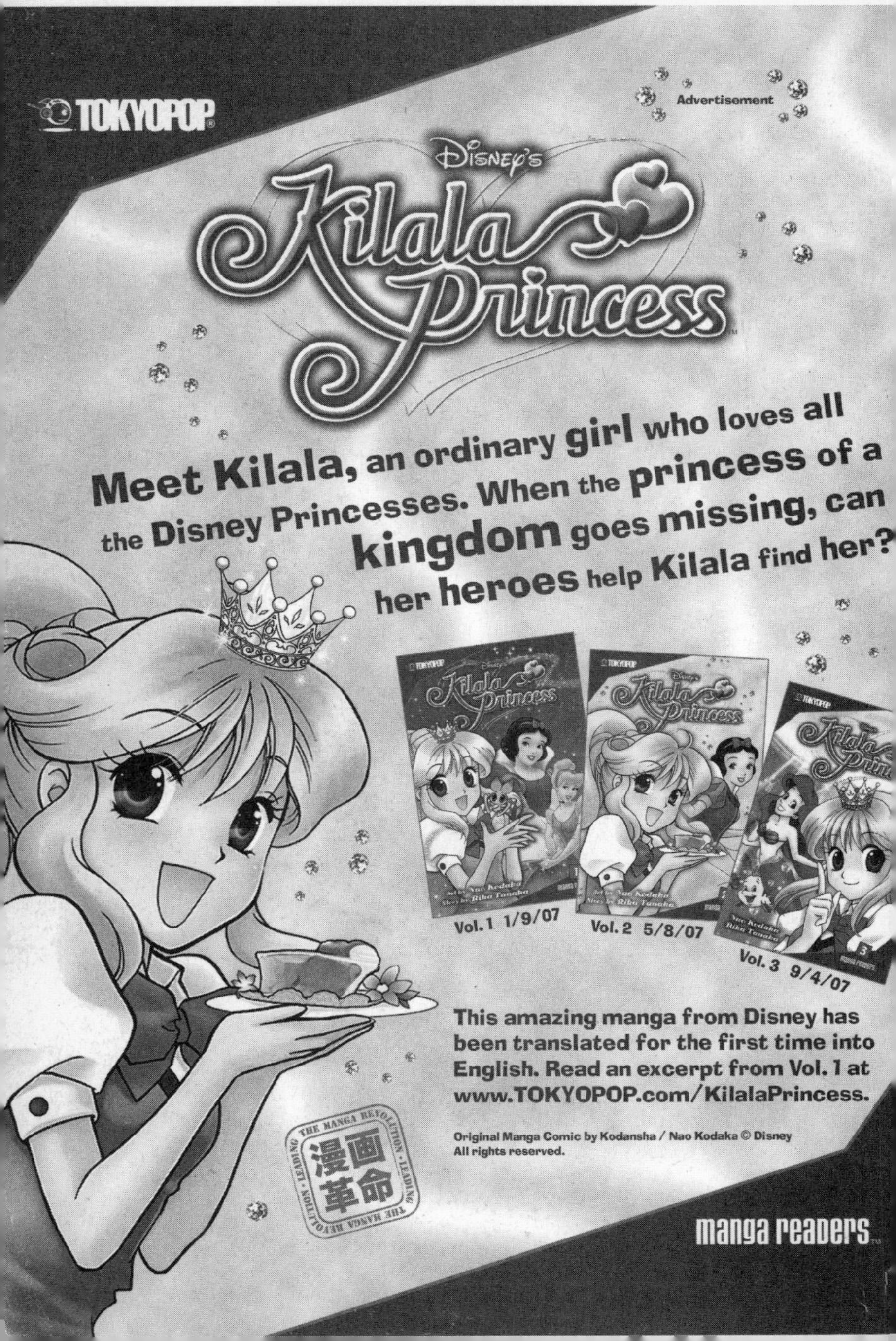

TOKYOPOP
Advertisement
Disney's
Kilala Princess
Meet Kilala, an ordinary girl who loves all the Disney Princesses. When the princess of a kingdom goes missing, can her heroes help Kilala find her?
Vol. 1 1/9/07
Vol. 2 5/8/07
Vol. 3 9/4/07
This amazing manga from Disney has been translated for the first time into English. Read an excerpt from Vol. 1 at www.TOKYOPOP.com/KilalaPrincess.
Original Manga Comic by Kodansha / Nao Kodaka © Disney
All rights reserved.
THE MANGA REVOLUTION · LEADING
漫画革命
manga readers

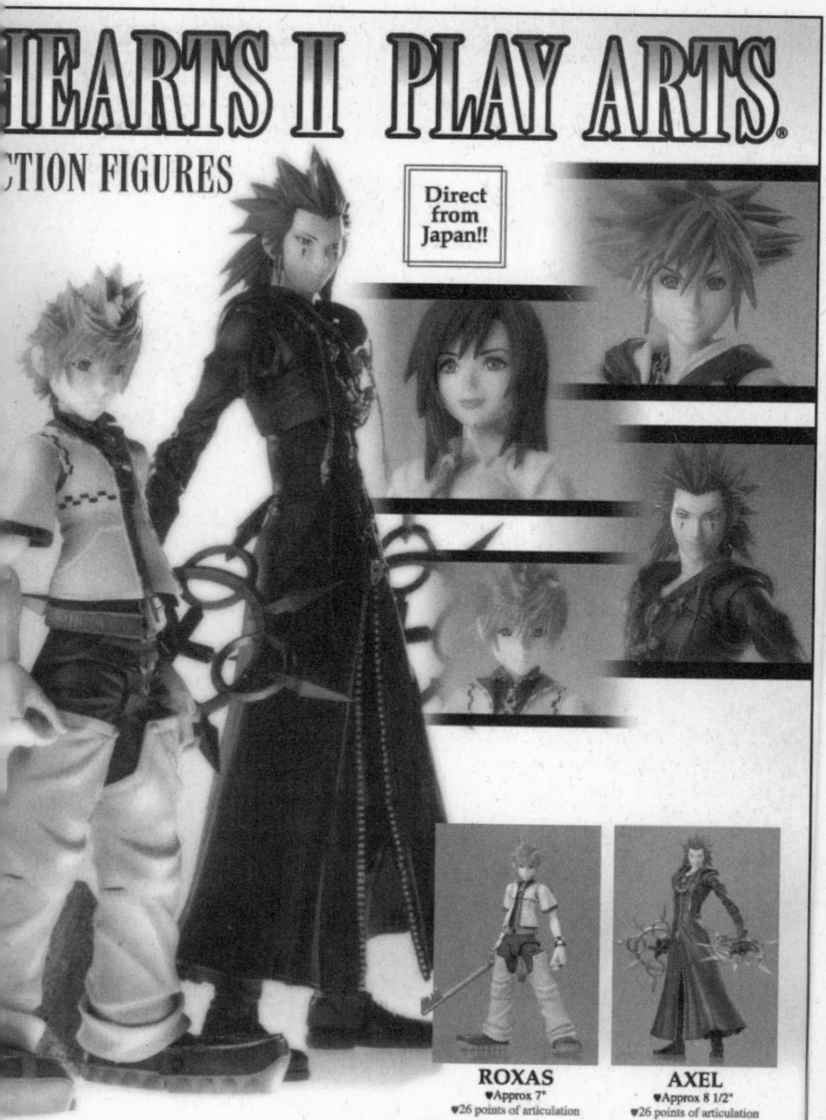
HEARTS II PLAY ARTS®
CTION FIGURES
Direct from Japan!!
ROXAS
♥Approx 7"
♥26 points of articulation
AXEL
♥Approx 8 1/2"
♥26 points of articulation
© Disney. SQUARE ENIX and the SQUARE ENIX logo are trademark of SQUARE ENIX Co.,Ltd.
SQUARE ENIX PRODUCTS
CRAFTSMANSHIP
OTOBUKIYA www.KotoUS.com
ORIGINAL PRODUCTS from SQUARE ENIX
http://www.square-enix.com/